Beauty

Beauty

A THEOLOGICAL ENGAGEMENT
WITH GREGORY OF NYSSA

Natalie Carnes

 CASCADE *Books* · Eugene, Oregon

BEAUTY
A Theological Engagement with Gregory of Nyssa

Cascade Books
An Imprint of Wipf and Stock Publishers
199 W. 8th Ave., Suite 3
Eugene, OR 97401

www.wipfandstock.com

ISBN 13: 978-1-62564-584-5

Cataloging-in-Publication data:

Carnes, Natalie Michelle.

Beauty : a theological engagement with Gregory of Nyssa / Natalie Carnes.

xvi + 272 p. ; 23 cm. —Includes bibliographical references and index.

ISBN 13: 978-1-62564-584-5

1. Aesthetics—Religious aspects—Christianity. 2. Gregory, of Nyssa, Saint, approximately 335–approximately 394. 3. Philosophical theology. I. Title.

BT55 .C38 2014

Manufactured in the U.S.A.

For Matthew

Contents

Acknowledgments

It is a happy task to count my blessings by numbering my debts, though the list here cannot exhaust them. This book began as a dissertation under the advisement of Stanley Hauerwas and with close attention from Paul Griffiths, each of whom read the manuscript multiple times and gifted me with their difficult questions. Warren Smith and Liz Clark patiently helped me navigate late antiquity, and Jeremy Begbie pressed me on questions of theological aesthetics and pneumatology. It is a better book for their support, suggestions, and puzzlements.

In 2009–10, I participated in a dissertation working group at the Franklin Humanities Institute. I am grateful for the feedback I received there, particularly from Ignacio Adriasola, Erica Fretwell, and Brian Goldstone. At least twice Brian introduced me to resources that became central to my argument and approach. Jonathan Tran likewise introduced me to material that has proven formative both for this book and for my development as a scholar, and I imagine my debt to him will only continue to multiply over the years. Sean Larsen and Ben Dillon offered questions and insights that improved two of these chapters directly and the rest indirectly. Crucial during the initial drafting of these chapters was the emotional and childcare support of Sarah Decker and Jessie Eubank as well as conversations with Pete Jordan, Andréa Taylor, Sheryl Overmyer, Greg Lee, T. J. Lang, Nathan Eubank, and Carole Baker.

Baylor has given me valuable institutional support in the form of summer sabbaticals for 2012 and 2013, supportive and interesting colleagues, and Bill Bellinger, who is unanimously regarded by the Baylor Religion Department as the world's greatest boss. I might also be lucky enough to have the world's greatest graduate assistant, as I am much indebted to David Cramer for his possibly obsessive attention to editorial detail. My thanks also to Mike Whitenton, who spent a summer editing a manuscript far from his own field.

I thank the people at Cascade Books, particularly Charlie Collier, for support, flexibility, and speed in seeing this project through. In the shrinking world of academic publishing, Cascade continues to take risks, benefiting all of us who work in theology.

Writing a book, of course, requires support beyond academia and its institutions. I have been fortunate to have an extended family that has helped by offering encouragement, mustering interest, and caring for children. I thank my parents Mike and Suzi, my parents-in-law Pam and Will, and my sisters and siblings-in-law: Rosalind, Victoria, Mathew, Kevin, Kiraz, Elizabeth, Joseph, and Kate.

My daughter Chora arrived at the beginning of my writing and Edith in the midst of revisions. They have contributed very little to this book, but their presence fills my life with beauty.

My daughters are gifts I receive together with my husband, Matthew, whose love funds my life. From countless conversations, read-throughs, and edits, to his care for our children, to his prioritization of my work above his own—Matthew has made this book possible. There is no way properly to thank him, so I can only give to him what he has already given to me. Matthew, this book is for you.

Introduction

Meditating on divine transcendence, Gregory of Nazianzus describes what it means to do theology by offering a picture of *ho aristos theologos*, the most excellent theologian. Such a theologian is not one who has discovered the whole of God's being, he tells us, but one who has assembled more of truth's shadow.[1] As elsewhere, Nazianzen here chastens would-be theologians, cautioning them about the treacheries of theologizing and directing them to epistemological modesty. Gregory of Nyssa also uses the imagery of light to name the fullness and poverty of theological knowing. Theology, for these friends, is done in the shadows. I take their image of the theologian as a shadow-dweller to display the character of my own work.

It is especially important to remember the shadowy character of theology in a project that purports to explore a name for God—for that is what I, like Gregory of Nyssa, take Beauty to be. In conversation with Gregory, I elaborate a vision of beauty in which it is characterized by fittingness and gratuity. I argue that we can articulate the beauty of an object by naming an aspect under which it is fitting, and in describing its fittingness with that aspect, we will find that it does not *just* fit; it fits exceedingly well. There is an excess to its fittingness that suggests the inability of the aspect to exhaust the object of beauty. This surplus of meaning that overflows the threshold of fittingness names the beautiful object's gratuity. There is thus a gratuity to its fittingness. Together fittingness and gratuity suggest beauty's dynamism.

The significance of understanding beauty with the categories of fittingness and gratuity is manifold, but one of the most important features

---

1. καὶ οὗτος ἄριστος ἡμῖν θεολόγος, οὐχ ὃς εὗρε τὸ πᾶν, οὐδὲ γὰρ δέχεται τὸ πᾶν ὁ δεσμός, ἀλλ' ὃς ἂν ἄλλου φαντασθῇ πλέον, καὶ πλεῖον ἐν ἑαυτῷ συναγάγῃ τὸ τῆς ἀληθείας ἴνδαλμα, ἢ ἀποσκίασμα, ἢ ὅ τι καὶ ὀνομάσομεν. Gregory of Nazianzus, "De filio," 170.

of these terms is their elasticity. They are under-determined categories. They raise questions such as: Fitting with what? Gratuitous for whom? I take this elasticity as significant for illuminating both how beauty can go wildly wrong—how it can comply with cruelty and justify oppression—and also how it can be recovered as a form of resistance to cruelty and oppression. If we are going to reclaim beauty as the latter, we must be open-eyed about its history as the former. How can we avoid thinking of the devastation wreaked by the Nazi quest for the master race? Or the thousand ships launched by Paris's desire to possess Helen? Or the swelling numbers and decreasing ages of women (and, increasingly, men) suffering with eating disorders? Or Toni Morrison's Pecola, consumed and dis-integrated with the desire for blue eyes? Beauty has been implicated in misogyny, racism, war, and genocide. Even more: It is part of the entertainment that distracts us from these weighty concerns. Let's not be sentimental about beauty. It has a past that calls for sackcloth and ashes.

Beauty is not alone in its devastating past. Truth, goodness, kindness, courage, justice, and peace also have terrible histories—histories that should not, however, surprise us. In a world where we crucified Love, how can we be surprised that we have also inflicted our sins on truth, goodness, and beauty? I remind us of our dark past, first, to underscore that we work in shadows and, second, to demonstrate the significance of fittingness and gratuity, which can help us describe claims to beauty both when we are perceptive and when we go wrong. For example: The context for the Nazi valuation of fittingness was the heterosexual, healthful Aryan body, and those bodies that did not fit under that rubric were eliminated. With the selections and exterminations entailed in realizing their image of a master race, the Nazis aspiring to perfect fittingness committed one of the most horrifying atrocities in a terror-ridden century, the gratuity of their ideal echoed in the gratuity of their violence. Fittingness and gratuity are thus one way to describe beauty's implication in the Holocaust.

What this Nazi description should make plain to us is that a beauty characterized by fittingness and gratuity is at best morally neutral. That is, it is at least susceptible to implication in evil, if not given to it. If beauty is going to resist oppression, we need to give content to fittingness and gratuity. It is one thing to say that what a person perceives as beautiful can be described in terms of fittingness and gratuity. It is another to ask how our own perceptions of fittingness and gratuity can resist falling under the thrall of a master race or skinniness or whiteness. One way we might frame the possibility for a beauty that resists is to turn to Marxists, for example, to explain actions, social structures, and objects in terms and contexts that will illuminate just how *un*fitting, how *un*beautiful they are. Education into a critical apparatus will (or can) change what we find beautiful. One result of discussing beauty in terms of fittingness and gratuity is that it leaves open the possibility for training into descriptions that will change our mind about a thing's beauty, that will shed light on the object as unbeautiful or beautiful. The elasticity of fittingness and gratuity leaves room for catechesis into alternate descriptions of beauty, perhaps even a beauty that resists violence. Yet such resistance, in these cases, does not come from beauty itself. Beauty remains a capacious signifier that facilitates resistance energized by other sources.

Gregory of Nyssa claims more for beauty. He invokes a beauty that itself resists oppression, particularly the oppression of social structures that accommodate us to poverty, hunger, and suffering. Resistance comes both from the invisibility of Beauty and from its visibility on the face of the poor, as the image of God, and in eschatological glory. The way Gregory locates the beauty in which beautiful objects, actions, and people participate positions beauty to challenge assimilation to cruelty and sloth.

But this raises the question of how we access beauty as a form of resistance. How do we become a people who perceive the beauty Gregory describes, and not Nazis spellbound by the image of a master race? It turns out that training into perceiving Gregory's beauty is a lifelong process that engages every sense of our body and spirit, that requires cultivating relationships of love with our neighbor, and that includes our membership in a community named the church.

What I have been tracing here are the lines of argument in my three constructive chapters, which move from fittingness and gratuity to poverty to subjectivity. There is another, more explicitly theological, layer of argument driving these explorations. In chapter 2, I explore the significance of beauty as fittingness and gratuity by reframing fittingness and gratuity with Gregory's doctrine of God, particularly in the non-contrastive transcendence Gregory claims *creatio ex nihilo* entails. Because Beauty is a name for God, fittingness and gratuity disclose something of who God is, but what we know of God also requires a radicalization of fittingness and gratuity. That is, the internal relation of Beauty's fittingness and gratuity is in one way like a ladder: the gratuity of beauty's fittingness with one aspect impels ascent to another aspect. At different points, Gregory himself uses the ladder to describe both ascent to Beauty and ascent to God.

Still, the ladder image is not definitive of Beauty or God. Ultimately the relation between fittingness and gratuity cannot be like the relation of the rungs of a ladder to the sides, for, as Gregory claims, no created thing can claim to be fitting for God. As Gregory elaborates the significance of *creatio ex nihilo*, he suggests a relationship between fittingness and gratuity that is like the relationship between the radical transcendence and the utter immanence of God—the one elaborates the other.

In the third chapter, I turn from the doctrine of God to the more specific subject of Christology to consider beauty and poverty in light of the one who emptied himself of glory to take on the form of a bondservant. By framing the chapter with the concern that beauty is bourgeois, I address a critique that has kept beauty in academic exile for much of the twentieth century. Yet beauty's home, I argue, is not the sanitized spaces of bourgeois living. While modernity's articulation of beauty, like strands of its philosophy, has often deflected the difficulties of reality like horror and ugliness, Gregory's beauty, like his theological language, is formed in the difficulties of reality. It is a beauty that, while not reducible to ugliness or horror, cannot be found apart from them.

The fourth chapter, in which I explore how one accesses the beauty Gregory describes, takes us to pneumatology to complete the Trinitarian exploration of beauty. To ask how we become the kind of people who can perceive beauty rightly is inevitably, for Gregory, to ask how the Holy Spirit makes us the kind of people who can see beauty rightly. Here I develop lines of thought from Gregory on the self as wounded by love and consider the significance of such woundedness for perceiving beauty. As I do, I make plain that as bourgeois social spaces are not beauty's home, neither is bourgeois training the right way to draw near to beauty. This move is enabled by how Gregory locates the organ of beauty's perception: not, like so many modern accounts, in the imagination, which suggests training as exposure to the right literature and art, but in the entire anthropology of the human. Such perception is perfected for Gregory in the spiritual senses, which extend the capacity of the physical senses to perceive beauty and which are trained through attentive love to the neighbor and the afflicted and through the liturgy of the church.

Readers familiar with Gregory will note how little I work out of his theological treatises and polemics. *Against Eunomius, On the Making of the Human, On the Soul and the Resurrection, The Catechetical Oration,* and *On Not Three Gods* all make little to no appearance in what follows, even though they are rich and important texts. This is partly because I focus on those texts I find most generative of conversation about beauty. But this is also because I am interested in Gregory's texts that do not immediately present themselves to modern eyes as texts for theological study. These are the texts, by and large, in which systematic theologians have been slower to show interest. Gregory's hagiography of his sister, his first rhetorical exercise, his scriptural commentaries, his homilies—these are the texts on which I primarily work, trying as I do to attend to the literary conditions of theological writing and the theological commitments of Gregory's literariness. It seems fitting that the literary and the theological be joined in this way in a work that purports to explore beauty. For through these arguments, I hope to make clear not just the way theological descriptions give us a compelling vision of beauty, but also the way considerations of beauty should be central to generating theological descriptions.

If this last point sounds familiar, it is because rendering the significance of beauty to theologizing was also the project of Hans Urs von Balthasar and has influenced many theologians since. I am indebted to Balthasar in more ways than one. He not only thought about beauty, but exposited Gregory of Nyssa in his book *Presence and Thought* (*Présence et pensée*, 1942). In the preface to that book, Balthasar explains his retrieval of Gregory in terms that describe my own relationship to Gregory more than seventy years later. He writes:

> There is never a historical situation that is absolutely similar to any of the ones that preceded it in time. Thus there is no historical situation that can furnish us with its own solutions as a kind of master key capable of resolving all the problems that plague us today.[2]

Historical difference, while a cautionary tale for historians, can be generative for theologians. I look to Gregory, not out of nostalgia for a time past, but for a partner in diagnosing and moving beyond the problems currently

---

2. Balthasar, *Presence and Thought,* 10. I cannot resist quoting the several beautiful sentences immediately preceding, in which Balthasar elaborates his point through an extended analogy between artistic making and theological writing: "This return [of the theologian to the past] will be beneficial, but only on one condition: that he understand well that history, far from dispensing us from creative effort, imposes it on us. Our artists, and in particular our architects, all acknowledge this. A Greek temple, a Romanesque church, a Gothic cathedral all merit our admiration, because they are witnesses to a beauty and truth that are incarnate in time. But to reproduce them now in our present day would constitute an anachronism, all the more appalling to the extent the copies were more minutely exact. The intent to revive them, to adapt them to the needs of time, would be even worse. Such an effort could only beget horrors. All attempts at 'adaptation' to current tastes are doomed to the same fate. In neo-Greek style, the column of antiquity loses its original qualities of simplicity and becomes an intolerable imitation. And the same may be said of Saint Thomas: 'A great and estimable doctor, renowned, authoritative, canonized, and very much dead and buried' (Péguy). We should not imagine that there are other estimable figures who in our eyes are better capable of withstanding such treatment! We have turned our gaze on a more distant past, but we have not done so in the belief that, in order to give life to a languishing system of thought, it would suffice to exhume the 'Greek Fathers' and adapt them for better or worse to the needs of the modern soul. We are not ingenuous enough to prefer a 'neopatristic' theology to a 'neoscholastic' theology!" (10).

plaguing us. Such a constructive project, while not purposed toward histori-cal reconstruction, is improved by historical accuracy. Attending to the his-torical conditions of Gregory can tell us more about who this partner is and give us richer ways to interpret his texts; learning more about what beauty has signified and the work it has done in modernity can help us understand the limits and possibilities for it in contemporary conversations. Before any constructive work, then, we will begin with some historicizing, which takes us to chapter 1.

1

On Gregory of Nyssa and Beauty

GENEALOGICAL THREADS

Before a performance, the stage must be set. And to set the stage for this theological performance is to introduce its two main characters, first Gregory of Nyssa and then beauty, by telling a story about each character. Story one begins in the twilight of antiquity, as light grays around rhetorically gifted and beauty-loving bishop Gregory of Nyssa (c. 335–394). The second story opens as the starry medieval night breaks into the dawn of modernity. The new day glares on beauty, whose grandeur fades in the bright Enlightenment.[1] It fades as beauty suffers transformations that by late modernity have feminized beauty, marginalized her, and left her vilified as market promiscuous. She is exiled from her once-central location in theological thought and scholarly work.

This chapter recounts the stories of these characters to stage a performance in which Gregory wanders through the set of modernity, asking after, seeking, and finding beauty, to rehabilitate her as and for theology. The rehabilitation, however, cannot just be beauty's; the theological terms on which beauty's exile were approved must themselves recover. For to reclaim the theological significance of beauty is to suggest both that a full

---

1. In claiming that beauty fades in the Enlightenment, I do not mean to suggest that there was less beauty in the world at that time or that people produced fewer beautiful objects or even that people invoked and reflected on beauty less. I mean instead to draw attention to beauty's status in philosophy and theology and its invocation in academia. Even as many treatises and essays treat beauty in the eighteenth century and into the nineteenth, beauty, as I will argue, begins to lose its status in the philosophical world. This loss of status, moreover, precipitates beauty's later academic exile and twentieth-century valuations of ugliness.

and flourishing conception of beauty requires theological description and also that a full and flourishing theology does not marginalize beauty as a peripheral concern. So if one description of the performance might be tiresomely gendered—an active male character restoring a passive, feminized one—another account yields a fresher take: A feminized character redeems a rather male-dominated discipline. For, if beauty has become a woman for moderns, she names God for Gregory, and as a name for God, she rightly disciplines, guides, and proliferates theological work.

The present chapter prepares for this performance of double-restoration of beauty and theology by evoking the disparate worlds of the main characters. I begin with Gregory of Nyssa and reflect on his life by tracing themes especially significant for the constructive chapters: family and friendship, rhetoric, training, and death. I conclude the story of Gregory with a brief turn to the history of reception that yielded the narratives we tell and texts we have of Gregory today. From there I move on to beauty and attend to several voices accounting for how beauty came to be discussed (and not discussed) in the modern world. Of particular interest in these accounts are changes in its status and presence in North Atlantic academic conversation—changes that are not unrelated to the social and intellectual history of modernity. I end the chapter by noting recent theological performances on beauty—work I consider to be itself quite beautiful, and which gives me a loose model for how I will proceed. Gregory, then, need not pioneer beauty's reclamation, but only join a growing chorus of theologians sounding the centrality of beauty to theology.[2]

Story One: Gregory of Annisa, Caesarea, and Nyssa

Gregory lived in one of the most contentious centuries in Christian history. The church was evolving from persecuted to persecutor, and the ones whom it persecuted were its own. Gregory's story is woven into these power struggles of church and empire. He was himself one of the persecuted: Under the influence of the Eunomians,[3] Emperor Valens permitted his exile. Yet he

2. This chorus includes such theologians as Hans Urs von Balthasar, Jeremy Begbie, Paul Evdokimov, Alejandro García-Rivera, Richard Harries, Jacques Maritain, Francesca Aran Murphy, John Navone, Ben Quash, Patrick Sherry, Richard Viladesau, Rowan Williams, T. D. Gorringe, Trevor Hart, and Jim Fodor, among others.

3. The traditional language for this group is "neo-Arian," but Lewis Ayres, following Rowan Williams, has pointed out the problem of this term, which suggests continuity with the theology and person of Arius not borne by the evidence. That Eunomius and those sympathetic to his theology were labeled "Arian" speaks more to the way heresiological labels function: Writers could use them to taint the reputation of the

was also one of the powerful: His brother Basil was bishop of the important see of Caesarea, and he himself was also a bishop, though of a less important see, as was his good friend Gregory of Nazianzus. Together these three, known collectively as the "Cappadocian Fathers," set about Trinitizing the church. So the story goes.[4]

It is easy to extract these three men and name their importance as the Cappadocian Fathers because they wrote treatises, debated doctrines, convened synods, and attended councils. The further one goes into Nyssen's writings, though, the more one sees the loss such extraction entails. On the one hand, extracting them as the Cappadocian Fathers is a loss because it overly conflates the three men and glosses over differences, particularly in theological style and commitment.[5] On the other hand, titling them as the Cappadocian Fathers overemphasizes their agency and significance at the expense of others', especially that of their family members. In this second respect, the title inflates the aloneness, the uniqueness, the unrepeatability of their achievements. Yet Gregory was certainly not alone. Born into a wealthy, locally important family in Pontus, Gregory might deserve the distinction of belonging to one of the most significant Christian families

---

group in question and church historians and theologians could use them to give both coherence and disrepute to a group. In *Nicaea and Its Legacy*, Ayres writes, "In fact, it is virtually impossible to identify a school of thought dependent on Arius' specific theology, and certainly impossible to show that even a bare majority of Arians had any extensive knowledge of Arius' writing. Arius was part of a wider trajectory; many of his ideas were opposed by others in this trajectory: he neither originated the trajectory nor uniquely exemplified it. One further result of this polemical move was to hide the ways in which the theologies typified as Arian draw on a variety of theological trajectories and cannot be understood as springing from one source" (2). He addresses the label again later, speaking to the specific situation of Eunomius and the Cappadocians: "The habit is still widespread of calling this movement 'neo-Arian.' There are, however, significant differences between Arius' theology and that of Aetius and Eunomius, and neither ever appears to have made any claim on Arius' legacy. Their most persistent and important opponents, the Cappadocians, do not engage in an 'Athanasian'-style attempt to cast Aetius and Eunomius as the new Ariuses" (145). To make this point, he draws on Rowan Williams, *Arius*.

4. It is how the story goes, but Lewis Ayres has complicated this point, too. The First Ecumenical Council at Nicaea established the consubstantiality of the Son and the Father before the Cappadocians were born. Their role, as Ayres elaborates in various ways over the course of *Nicaea and Its Legacy*, was to articulate a pro-Nicene theological grammar—a way of making intelligible Nicaea's commitment to the divine difference in persons and unity in substance.

5. Christopher Beeley makes this point in his book on Gregory of Nazianzus. He writes, "Since the late nineteenth century Gregory of Nazianzus has been somewhat artificially grouped together with Basil and Gregory of Nyssa as the three 'Cappadocian fathers,' a designation that has tended to overstate their similarities and to obscure the sometimes painful differences that arose among them" (*Gregory of Nazianzus*, viii).

in history. His friend witnesses to the family's significance for the church. Upon the death of Gregory's mother, Emmelia, Gregory of Nazianzus wrote epigrams about her. In one, he "marveled" at "the wealth of her mighty womb."[6] In another, he exclaimed,

> Emmelia is dead! Who would have thought it, she who gave to life the light of so many and such children, both sons and daughters married and unmarried? She alone among mortals had both good children and many children. Three of her sons were illustrious priests, and one daughter the companion of a priest, and the rest were like an army of saints.[7]

"The rest" brought Emmelia's total to nine children.[8] They included Macrina and Naucratius, who would influence the development of Christian monasticism. Naucratius suffered an early death, but Macrina (c. 327–80) was a formidable influence on her family up through old age. As the eldest child, Macrina helped her mother raise her siblings, which meant that she loved them tenderly and rebuked them sternly. In his book about her, the *Life of Macrina* (*De Vita Macrinae*), Gregory testifies to her use of both parental modes.

BORING

Macrina is the hidden heroine of our story. It is gallingly familiar that a woman should perform the role of silent heroine enabling the rehabilitation a male hero performs. But how can we draw her out of hiding? Gregory of Nazianzus, too, wonders over Macrina's hiddenness. As he does with Emmelia, Nazianzen brings his poetry to bear on Macrina after her death. He writes, "The dust holds the illustrious virgin Macrina, if you have heard something of her, the first born of the great Emmelia. But who kept herself from the eyes of all men, is now on the tongues of all and has a greater glory than any."[9] The qualification "if you have heard something of her" belies the ending declaration of her surpassing glory and makes plain the impossibility that she is "on the tongues of all." We must understand Gregory of Nazianzus as describing Macrina's glory in the eschatological present, which means that there is a strong "not yet" to the way humanity may perceive the glory of the one who "kept herself from the eyes of all men." Not until

---

6. Gregory of Nazianzus, "Epigram 162."

7. Gregory of Nazianzus, "Epigram 161."

8. It is commonly claimed Emmelia had ten children, with only nine surviving infancy, but this has most recently been dismissed as an "overly literal" interpretation of *Vita Macrinae*'s claim that Emmelia's last son, Peter, was her "tithe." Pierre Maraval prefers the number nine, since all *Vita Macrinae* claims about Emmelia's children is that she had four sons and five daughters. Maraval, "Biography of Gregory of Nyssa," 104.

9. Gregory of Nazianzus, "Epigram 163."

every tongue has confessed the Lordship of Christ will they also celebrate the glory of Macrina.

Until then, Macrina, who occupied no position of power, who bequeathed to us no texts, meets us modern readers through her brother's texts. For Gregory of Nazianzus was not the only Cappadocian to take note of Macrina's hidden glory. Apparently troubled by her lack of renown, Gregory of Nyssa explains in the beginning of the *Life of Macrina* that if Macrina's life were to remain "veiled in silence," it would be a loss.[10] He conceives of his writing, then, as a kind of unveiling, and he takes pains to assure the reader that the Macrina she meets in his text is, indeed, Macrina the Younger of Annisa. All the stories in his text come from personal experience,[11] and he insists he delivers them in an unstudied and unstylized manner.[12]

One needn't doubt Gregory's truthfulness to know the difficulty of discerning the historical Macrina. It is difficult to discern Macrina's presence, for access to Macrina is always mediated by Gregory's compositions; she's a character in and of his memories, agendas, and debates. Nevertheless, Macrina, even as Gregory's character, exceeds Gregory's writerly purposes. At times she glimmers forth, reminding us that Gregory's rehabilitative quest is a form of fidelity to her—she who showed him the beautiful Bridegroom into whose arms she finally disappeared. But we are never sure which appearance and disappearance reveals Macrina, daughter of Emmelia and founder of the monastic life at Annisa. Many have tried to pin this Macrina down,[13] yet the lady always vanishes.[14] We pay homage to her absent pres-

---

10. I quote here from the translation of Anna M. Silvas (Gregory of Nyssa, *Life of Macrina*, 110). Virginia Woods Callahan, whose generally excellent translation I will use in my readings of the text, renders this passage with a less evocative phrase: "passed over in silence" (Gregory of Nyssa, "Life of Saint Macrina," 163).

11. ἡ πεῖρα διδάσκαλος ἦν (Trial was the teacher). Gregory of Nyssa, "Life of Saint Macrina," 1.18.

12. Gregory of Nyssa, "Life of Saint Macrina," 163.

13. One recent and impressively researched attempt is found in Silvas, *Macrina the Younger, Philosopher of God*. But her careful research and conscientious presentation also make clear to the reader how much conjecture necessarily comprises Silvas's narrative of Macrina's life. Another attempt is made by Morwenna Ludlow, who reviews various attempts to understand Macrina before deciding that she is "at least to some degree" a "literary construction" (Ludlow, *Gregory of Nyssa*, 214).

14. For a rich discussion of the problems and possibilities attending the recovery of female characteres from texts, see Clark, "The Lady Vanishes." To Clark's considerations, I foreground another reason for discovering "traces" of Macrina characters in Gregory's texts: Gregory the author is no more transcendent and self-enclosed than any of the subjects about whom he writes. He is constituted by those whom he loves. His subjectivity is inseparable from Macrina, to whom he discipled himself, whom he called teacher, whom he longed to present, whose death and life shaped his life. I will elaborate this anthropology in the fourth chapter.

ence in the life of her disciple Gregory and consider the ways in which he presents his memory of Macrina as issuing him both comfort and challenge.

If Gregory at times presents Macrina as his most significant teacher,[15] he refers to his brother Basil (c. 330–78/79) as his most distinguished—his only distinguished teacher, in fact.[16] Basil, after all, had studied abroad in Athens with much success. For Gregory, Basil was the "guardian of his oratory," his teacher, his father. Gregory's own father died when he was young (the early 340s), so Basil, as the eldest brother, became a kind of father to his siblings.[17] To most of them, at least: Basil was not a father to Macrina. Even her biological father could barely father her, as she used her father's own theology to convince him, against his plans, to let her remain unmarried. Then at his death, she transformed his conventional, patriarchally ordered household into a (more) egalitarian ascetic community. Macrina had a powerful and deeply rooted vision for Christian life—one more powerful than her father's and rooted before Basil's. If anything, Macrina was more of a parent to Basil than the other way around. Thus Gregory reports that when Basil returned from Athens, flush with success and "excessively puffed up," Macrina rebuked him and showed him an alternative to rhetorical competition. She displayed for him an ascetic life. She was not the only ascetic influence in Basil's life—between Athens and Annisa, Basil journeyed east to tour the ascetic communities—but she was a significant one.[18] The examples of Macrina, Naucratius, and the ascetic communities of the East (among other influences) enlivened Basil's commitment to monasticism, which he would live out in his construction of a poor hospice. Gregory followed his siblings' example by affirming such monastic commitments in his first text, *On Virginity (De virginitate),* which defended and eulogized Basil's monastic program. Gregory's undertakings as a young man show him to be ever the pupil of these two *didaskaloi.*

That Gregory referred to Basil as a teacher of distinction was more than a mark of brotherly pride. Basil had a remarkable education. After mastering grammar with his father at their home in Pontus, he went to Caesarea and Constantinople before traveling to Athens, then the center of philosophical and rhetorical education. Gregory of Nazianzus, whom Basil

15. See his narration of her importance in *Life of Macrina,* or his address to her as *didaskalos* (teacher) throughout *On the Soul and the Resurrection.*

16. Gregory makes this point in his letter to Libanius, the famous sophist and former teacher of Basil in Constantinople. Raymond Van Dam discusses Gregory's education and his letter in *Families and Friends in Late Roman Cappadocia,* 68.

17. Rousseau, *Basil of Caesarea,* 62.

18. After returning home and seeing Macrina, Basil toured the monastic communities in Egypt, Syria, Palestine, and Mesopotamia. Ibid., 72–73.

had met in Caesarea, was also in Athens, as, for a time, was Julian the Apostate, who would one day become emperor.[19] As emperor, he would issue an edict forbidding Christians from teaching pagan literature.[20] But in the 350s in Athens, Christians and pagans studied rhetoric and philosophy together. Two of Basil's most important educational influences in Athens were, in fact, Christian: his fellow student Gregory of Nazianzus and his teacher Prohaeresius. Named Athens's "unrivalled 'King of Rhetoric'"[21] Prohaeresius was deeply respected by Christians and pagans alike. Julian later tried to celebrate this rhetorical king with the appellate "honorary Hellenist," but in fact Prohaeresius's approach was more accurately Christian Alexandrian. He had an Origenistic approach to learning that claimed continuity between the *Logos* of God and the *logos* of human learning.[22] When Julian tried to protect Prohaeresius's teaching chair from his edict that Christians not teach pagan literature, Prohaersius voluntarily resigned, his resignation testifying to his refusal to split the *logos*.

Prohaeresius was not the primary Origenistic influence on Basil and Nazianzen. Two generations earlier, Gregory Thaumaturgus—the namesake for both Gregorys—had evangelized Pontus with Origenist Christianity. After their return from Athens, Nazianzen and Basil would live some years in ascetic retreat, compiling many excerpts from Origen for their *Philocalia*. Origen would also provide Nyssen with a subject for his studies, many years later, when he responded to Origen's *Commentary on the Song of Songs* with his own commentary on the same. In addition to the Jewish mystical thinker Philo of Alexandria and the inaugurator of the tradition known as "Neoplatonism," Plotinus, Origen was the most significant mediator of Plato to Nyssen.[23] The influence of these Platonists on Gregory is varied, but key aspects of their thought include Philo's negative theology and apophatic impulses, Origen's commitment to universal salvation as elaborated in his doctrine of *apokatastasis*, and Plotinus's descriptions of glimpsing Beauty itself.

But Gregory did not always take his Plato mediated. In *On the Soul and the Resurrection*, for example, Gregory not only models his dialogue on Plato's *Phaedo*, he also imports passages from the *Phaedrus* wholesale, barely modifies them, and plunks them into the middle of his text.

---

19. Van Dam, *Kingdom of Snow*, 181.

20. The year they overlapped was 355. Ibid., 161.

21. McGuckin, *St. Gregory of Nazianzus*, 60.

22. Ibid., 61.

23. Warren Smith nicely describes the influence of Origen on Gregory of Nyssa in *Passions and Paradise*, 8–9.

In addition to providing Gregory and his theological predecessors a framework for working out theological commitments, Plato also bequeathed to them skepticism about rhetoric. His criticisms of the fifth-century sophists became the *locus classicus* for philosophical critiques of rhetoric.[24] The sophists use rhetoric to render persuasive whatever side of an issue they choose, whether for sport or money. In this way, Plato claims, they operate only in the realm of opinion, which corresponds to the realm of becoming, appearance, and change.[25] They mystify for people the realm that philosophers seek to illuminate: the realm of knowledge, which corresponds to the realm of being, truth, and unity. It is a realm arrived at by dialectic. Yet many sophists were not so anti-philosophical as Plato suggests. They were instead a-philosophical. They were in the business of imparting rhetorical techniques and were content to let their students get their metaphysics elsewhere. The Cappadocians encountered both kinds of sophists. Basil and Nazianzen were educated in Athens during "the last florescence" of the rhetorical period known as the Second Sophistic (330–90).[26] In the centuries since Plato, the terms rhetoric and philosophy had acquired different meanings. For Plato, sophistry named the activity of orators who were paid to give speeches for political candidates. But as the free city-state declined, so did political oratory.[27] Sophistry moved into the classroom, where rhetoric was taught alongside philosophy, though different schools claimed one discipline as a subset of the other. Rhetoric and philosophy were elastic terms, with rhetoric able to contract to denote stylistic tricks or stretch to mean something like humanism or political virtue.[28] Similarly, philosophy could mean something as narrow as a particular set of doctrines belonging to a traditional philosophic school, or something as broad as what rhetorical humanism is supposed to name. It could also mean something altogether different, as when it identified a radical ascetic moralism and mysticism that defined itself against rhetoric.[29] It is this latter strain that characterized the philosophical life fourth-century Christians identified with Christianity, as will be evident in our reading of the *Life of Macrina*. This understanding of

24. In her book *Gregory of Nazianzus*, Rosemary Radford Ruether makes this point in the introduction, which helpfully elaborates the historical stakes of this conflict of rhetoric and philosophy (2).

25. In *Greek Rhetoric under Christian Emperors*, Kennedy describes sophistic rhetoric as a kind of play—someone would give an encomium to hair and then turn right around to deliver an encomium of baldness (35–37).

26. Ruether, *Gregory of Nazianzus*, 7.

27. Ibid., 4.

28. Ibid., 8.

29. Ibid.

philosophy as ascetic discipline cultivated skepticism about the prodigality of rhetoric.

Yet rhetoric, too, was figured as a kind of discipline, intrinsic to becoming a certain type of person—namely, a man. Maud Gleason argues in her book *Making Men* that rhetoric was a way to achieve and perform masculinity. She points to Galen, who exhorts men to nurture masculinity by navigating toward some mean between overly frequent exercise and a sedentary life. Too much exercise rendered one ill-fit for military or political life—no better than a pig, according to Galen—yet too little made one womanly. For achieving the appropriate level of activity, many doctors recommended the vocal exercise of rhetoric.[30] It has a number of benefits: Rhetoric exercises the chest and vital organs, increases yet purifies the body's vital heat, and restores the body from fatigue.[31] Most importantly, it increases the body's intake of breath or *pneuma*, which is taken in through the bronchial tubes and the pores.[32] Women, children, and eunuchs, in fact, cannot excel at oratory because their pores are too small to take in enough *pneuma*. (We see now that over- and under-exercising are both ways of being excessively bodily: Neither the overactive nor the inactive take in as much *pneuma* [breath, but also spirit] as the properly active.) But it was not just that women *couldn't* benefit from oratory: They *shouldn't* practice oratory, for public discourse, with its power to produce *masculinity*, was also policed as the province of men.[33] Rhetoric was something men could do and, through it, become more manly.

Rhetoric, then, was multivalent, presenting both problems and possibilities for the Christians in the late Roman Empire. However they might have railed against rhetoric, educated Christians of late antiquity could not help employing it. Ecclesial careers were steeped in rhetoric, beginning with the classical education accompanied by Progymnasmata—the textbooks that taught students the rhetorical genres and how to employ them—and ending, for those ordained, in a vocation that required regular homilizing. Thus we get the well-documented irony that some of the greatest rhetoricians of the late ancient world decried the dangers of rhetoric in their rhetorically skillful speeches. Writing about the three Cappadocian Fathers, George A. Kennedy puzzles over this paradox in his book *Classical Rhetoric and Its Christian and Secular Tradition from Ancient to Modern Times*:

---

30. Gleason, *Making Men*, 87.
31. Ibid., 88.
32. Ibid., 90.
33. Ibid., 98–100.

Virtually every figure of speech and rhetorical device of composition can be illustrated from their sermons, treatises, and numerous letters; they were also influenced by rhetorical theories of argumentation and arrangements, and probably by theories of memory and delivery as well, though direct evidence is lacking. Yet all three are repeatedly critical of classical rhetoric as something of little importance for the Christian, and none of them made, or even seriously attempted, a synthesis of classical and Christian rhetorical theory to describe their own practice. They were more successful in uniting Greek philosophy with Christian theology.[34]

The anxiety about rhetoric is present in Gregory of Nyssa's writing as well as Basil's and Nazianzen's, though he seemed to come to it later than his colleagues. Initially, at least, he seemed driven by a great thirst for Greek rhetoric and philosophy alike.

Who knows how long Gregory would have stayed in Athens had he been able to go? As the oldest son, it was Basil who received the privilege of the best education—yet Basil was not seduced into a life of teaching and learning in Athens. Had he stayed in Athens, Basil might have become the next Prohaeresius. He certainly had no shortage of opportunities to teach. But he was drawn back to his homeland after a tour of ascetic communities, and so in 356, he left Gregory of Nazianzus mourning his departure. Back on his native soil, he went first to Caesarea, where he taught. Among his pupils was his own brother Gregory of Nyssa. Then he went home to Annisa in Pontus, where Macrina met him with her rebuke.

During Gregory's stint as a student in Caesarea, Cappadocia, he received the training he would first put to use as a teacher of rhetoric. It was a career made possible by Julian's death in 363, when the 361 edict against Christians teaching Greek literature was rescinded. The scholarly consensus is that around this time, Gregory married—a status he seems to allude to in *On Virginity*.[35] Given his graphic description of grief upon the death of

---

34. Kennedy, *Classical Rhetoric*, 163.

35. The common evidence given for Gregory's marriage is *De virginitate* 3, when Gregory describes the good of virginity as no longer available to him, and Nazianzen's Letter 197, which refers to one Theosebia who is a companion to Gregory. The first does not seem to be either firm or unambiguous as evidence, and the second is discredited by Silvas. Drawing on Nazianzen's Epigram 164, she explains why Theosebia must be Gregory's sister and not (also) his spouse. She offers a more convincing argument for Gregory's marriage through her reading of Nazianzen's Epigram 161, which claims for Emmelia "sons and daughters married and unmarried" (υἱέας ἠδὲ θύγατρας ὁμόζυγας ἀζυγέας τε). She reasons that since the vocational virginity of three of the four sons is certain, the fourth—Gregory—must have been married. Perhaps an alternate reading

infants in *On Virginity* and his extended treatment of infant mortality in *On the Death of Infants (De mortuis infantibus)*, some scholars think Gregory might have had children that did not survive infancy. But there is no firm record that Gregory was married, much less fathered a child. We do know that he taught rhetoric, and that Gregory of Nazianzus famously chastised him in the 360s for preferring the title rhetor to Christian (thus echoing Plato's terms for his criticism of rhetoric).[36] At the time, Nazianzen, like Basil, was pursuing a vocation to the priesthood, for which he, also like Basil, was consecrated in 362.

Nazianzen's accusation might not have been entirely fair. Gregory was not uninterested in Christianity. He had been ordained as a reader and at one point may have been on a path to an ecclesial vocation.[37] It is not certain what derailed him. Perhaps it was simply that the splendor of pagan literature lured him in the wake of Julian's death. But perhaps his reasons can be illuminated by the events, years later, leading up to Basil's consecration as a bishop in 370. What exactly happened in the lead-up is unknown, but for some reason, controversy shrouded Basil's coming consecration. One of Basil's uncles—a bishop he referred to as a father—publicly criticized Basil, refused to support his episcopacy, and thereby precipitated a rift between the two men. The strain on Gregory is manifest in his response. He forged[38] a series of letters between Basil and the uncle to try to reconcile them.[39] This is certainly not Gregory's finest moment, but if Basil's complaints about Gregory's overeagerness to convene synods for reconciliation are any indication,[40] Gregory did not bear disharmony well. And if he could not bear disunity in his church, how much more difficult to bear disharmony that was *both* ecclesial *and* familial. He who wrote so often and so lovingly of his family let his anxiety over these feuding father figures lead him into foolishness. Of course Basil found out. And he was supremely irritated with his younger brother. Yet even after this incident, Basil did not think dishonesty part of Gregory's nature. Over the course of his letter rebuking Gregory, Basil escalates his accusation from simplicity—the insult he hurls at the beginning—to the ending declaration that Gregory has forgotten the

---

of this epigram could interpret "married and unmarried" not as referring to each group of sons and daughters but to the one group as a heterogeneous whole. Silvas, *Macrina the Younger*, 82n13, 81n6.

36. Gregory of Nazianzus, Letter 11.

37. Van Dam, *Families and Friends*, 69.

38. The word Basil uses in accusing Gregory is συμπλέκω, which means to braid together or intertwine.

39. Rousseau tells the story well. Rousseau, *Basil of Caesarea*, 6–7.

40. Ibid., 7.

ties of brotherhood and declared war on Basil.[41] In a letter written after this burst of hot fury (373), Basil offers a more cool-headed evaluation of his younger brother:

> He is quite inexperienced in ecclesiastical matters; and . . . although his dealings would inspire respect with a kindly man and be worth much, yet with a high and elevated personage, one occupying a lofty seat, and therefore unable to listen to men who from a lowly position on the ground would tell him the truth—what advantage could accrue to our common interests from the converse of such a man as Gregory, who has a character foreign to servile flattery?[42]

Political animal that he was, Basil achieved such administrative and ecclesial successes that he became known as Basil the Great to subsequent generations. Gregory did not have this same gift. Perhaps the reason Gregory initially avoided an ecclesial vocation was because he had determined he had neither taste nor aptitude for what Basil's modern biographer describes as "the sheer brutality of church politics."[43] Whatever the case, the year after Basil and Nazianzen were ordained priests, Gregory began teaching rhetoric.

Several years after these men had set out in their chosen vocations—and before any of them had become a bishop—famine hit Cappadocia. It was 368, and Eusebius, the bishop of Caesarea, was infirm. In two years he would die and be replaced by Basil, but at this point, he allowed Basil to function as acting bishop for the capital of Cappadocia.[44] As drought spread over the land, rivers dried up and agriculture was thrown into crisis. In her book on this famine, Susan Holman evokes the disaster: "Laborers began to starve. Schools closed down. The populace came to church to pray for rain. The poor who worked in the fields and wandered along the roads took

---

41. Basil's rebuke bears the marks of a strained and humiliated man: "At such a time as this you ought to have borne in mind that you are my brother, and have not yet forgotten the ties of nature, and do not regard me in the light of an enemy, for I have entered on a life which is wearing out my strength, and is so far beyond my powers that it is injuring even my soul. Yet for all this, as you have determined to declare war against me, you ought to have come to me and shared my troubles" (Basil of Caesarea, "Epistle 58").

42. Basil of Caesarea, Letter 215, quoted by Rousseau, *Basil of Caesarea*, 7–8.

43. Rousseau, *Basil of Caesarea*, 9.

44. Holman, *Hungry Are Dying*, 73. Caesarea's power was compromised when Cappadocia was divided by Emperor Valens in 372 into Primo and Segundo, with Caesarea the capital of the former and Tyana the capital of the latter. For more on the political and ecclesial intrigue surrounding this partition, see Van Dam's excellent article "Emperor, Bishops, and Friends in Late Antique Cappadocia."

on the appearance of living cadavers."[45] In the midst of this devastation, Basil was active in organizing relief efforts, which included, as the effects of the famine lingered on, the construction in 372 of a poor hospice, the forerunner to the modern hospital.[46] So influential was this hospice that Gregory of Nazianzus referred to it as the "new city."[47] Holman understands this newness as testifying to the largeness of the hospice, which shifted the population density of Caesarea and redrew the city boundaries.[48] But it seems likely that Nazianzen (also) connected such newness to the work of the Spirit who makes all things new. The poor hospice was a new city because it inaugurated a new, Spirit-given way of living with one another.

The poor-hospice was one way Basil sought to institutionalize heavenly living on earth. His monastic program was another. These initiatives became the occasion for Gregory's first theological text, *On Virginity* (370). Written at the request of the "most pious Bishop and father" Basil, *On Virginity* is the only public writing Gregory did before Basil's death (in 378 or 379), at which point he began releasing texts like waters from a dam. *On Virginity* also marked a turn toward ecclesial affairs that Basil would complete by appointing Gregory bishop of Nyssa in 372. Though Gregory was not circulating his texts widely in the early and mid-370s, as a bishop with a congregation he did have to preach. Many of the homilies we have today are from the time before Basil's death. Shortly after his appointment, for example, Nyssen preached on poverty and hunger to a region still suffering from the 368–69 famine. He also preached against usury, fornication, and, with remarkable force, against slavery.[49]

It was not long before his preaching was interrupted. Gregory had been the bishop of Nyssa for just four years—during the time that Basil complained of his ecclesiastical ineptitude—when a group of Basil's enemies, Eunomian bishops in Ancyra, Galatia, accused Gregory of embezzlement

---

45. Holman, *Hungry Are Dying*, 69.

46. Ibid., 74.

47. Ibid., 75.

48. Ibid.

49. Maraval, "Biography of Gregory of Nyssa," 114–15. J. Kameron Carter claims that Gregory's unequivocal stance against slavery surpasses even the early writings of the American-British abolition movement. The power of Gregory's abolitionism, according to Carter, is that it "expresses an exegetical imagination that reads against rather than within the social order" ("Interlude on Christology and Race," 231). Gregory did have one model for how one might live out a commitment to abolitionism in his older sister Macrina, who freed her slaves and invited them into her household monastic community. Of course, there are complex issues surrounding the agency of the former slaves of Annisa, but however imperfect Macrina's gesture might have been, it was an attempt at creating a community that provided an alternative to the slave-master relationship.

and irregular ordination. Gregory was arrested in the winter but fled. Basil intervened on his brother's behalf, asking that he be excused for fleeing on account of illness and requesting that his situation be handled according to ecclesiastical law—by a local (Cappadocian) synod rather than a foreign (Galatian) one. The request was granted only after it was reinterpreted. Gregory was deposed by a synod of Galatians and Pontians—foreign bishops that yet met locally in Nyssa, Cappadocia, in the spring of 376. Gregory was accordingly condemned to exile.[50] These conditions of exile were made possible by the Eunomian-friendly Emperor Valens, whose death in 378 was presumably the occasion for Gregory's return to Cappadocia. Valens died not long before Basil, and Gregory preached at his brother's funeral.

These two significant events around 378—Basil's death and Gregory's reinstallation as bishop—converged to accelerate Gregory's public life and legacy. He began by attempting to continue the legacy of his famed and busy brother. He completed Basil's *Hexameron* on the six days of creation by writing *On the Making of the Human (De hominis opificio)* in Easter 379. He played a significant role in the council at Antioch (379), which laid the groundwork for the Second Ecumenical Council, the Council of Constantinople (381). On his return from the council at Antioch, he went to visit Macrina, who was on her deathbed. Shortly after she died, her life became an occasion for two more works, the *Life of Macrina* and *On the Soul and the Resurrection*. He also wrote *Against Eunomius (Contra Eunomium)* during this time, thus continuing Basil's dispute with Eunomius. His brother Peter encouraged him to make this text public, despite Gregory's misgivings about the tenor of his reply.[51] Gregory went on to be an important actor in the Council of Constantinople, at which Emperor Theodosius I declared Gregory of Nyssa one of the bishops with whom one must be in communion to be considered orthodox. The council also entrusted Gregory with a mission to Arabia and a voyage to Jerusalem. It seems they were both failures.[52] But when he returned, he could focus more on writing. No longer charged with defending *homoousian* understandings of divinity or preserving ecclesial unity,[53] Gregory continued to pastor his church at Nyssa and set about creating the vast treasury of writings for which he is still studied today. These include the *Catechetical Oration*, the date of which is contested (it was some time in the 380s) and two of his most popular and so-called

---

50. The details, culled from Letters 225, 232, 237, and 239, are outlined in Maraval, "Biography of Gregory of Nyssa," 108.

51. Van Dam, *Families and Friends*, 72.

52. Maraval, "Biography of Gregory of Nyssa," 112.

53. Ibid., 113.

mystical works—*On the Life of Moses (De vita Moysis)* and *On the Song of Songs (In Canticum Canticorum)*, which are commonly considered his last. Scholars are not sure when he died, but his last recorded appearance was at a synod in Constantinople in 394.

There are several extant funeral orations Gregory of Nyssa gave in honor of others but no funeral oration given on his behalf. Though he was canonized along with Basil and Gregory of Nazianzus, he was not for many years given the acclaim they were. His brother Basil received the title "the Great" and Nazianzen became "the Theologian." These two were, along with Athanasius and John Chrysostom, named the four Great Doctors of the Greek Church in 1568. As for Gregory of Nyssa, he was represented much less frequently in mosaics and cited more seldom in theological and ecclesial literature.[54] John Calvin, for example, cited Basil extensively, Gregory of Nazianzus occasionally, and Gregory of Nyssa not at all.[55]

It is not as though history forgot Gregory. Certainly the Greek-speaking church remembered him. He was, after all, proclaimed the Father of Fathers at the Seventh Ecumenical Council, Nicea II in 787. But he simply was not appreciated as the other two Cappadocian Fathers were. One reason Gregory was not taken up into the theological stream in the West is that he was little translated into Latin. John Scotus Eriugena (c. 800–c. 877) should be greatly credited for the influence Gregory did have. Not only was Eriugena himself influenced by Gregory,[56] but he also translated *On the Making of the Human* into Latin. Even more: He also translated many of the works of fifth-century thinker Pseudo-Dionysius, whose writings bear the mark of Gregory's influence. Much of Gregory's influence in the West comes through Pseudo-Dionysius by way of Eriugena. Another stream of Gregory's theology is reaching current theological conversations through the rehabilitation and translation of seventh-century thinker Maximus the Confessor. Maximus, like Eriugena, bears Nyssen's legacy primarily through Pseudo-Dionysius. But Maximus was as little translated as Gregory, and scholars are just beginning to wade through his long and difficult corpus of Byzantine Greek theology.[57]

---

54. Meredith, "Influence of Gregory of Nyssa," 427.

55. Ludlow, *Gregory of Nyssa*, 35. Ludlow is drawing on the work of Lane, *John Calvin, Student of Church Fathers*, 84.

56. Balthasar claims Eriugena cites Nyssen with the same frequency that he cites Augustine. Balthasar, *Presence and Thought*, 15.

57. Paul Blowers is to be especially credited for his pioneering work both translating and intepreting Maximus; and the credit for whetting the contemporary appetite for more Maximus is (once again) Balthasar, particularly in *Cosmic Liturgy*.

The obvious next question, of course, is why Gregory was so little translated. Two suggested reasons are his ambiguity on the question of Christ's nature(s) and his universalism. On the first, Gregory himself predates the controversy over whether Christ had one nature or two, but his writings were used by both sides of that debate, which may have tinged his reputation as orthodox. On the second, he seems clearly to follow Origen in his commitment to universal salvation.[58] Not only was Origen censured for universalism (at a council of Constantinople in 543; a criticism ambiguously affirmed by the Fifth Ecumenical Council [553]), but Gregory's close association with Origen could not have made him an appealing Father to study when, in the century after his death, "Origenism" would become a pejorative theologians hurled to discredit one another's work. The Origenist controversy might have been the most significant factor in dampening interest in Gregory's work.

Interest reignited in the twentieth century. The mid-century *ressourcement* movement in Catholic theology deserves much of the credit. Committed to retrieving forgotten voices of the Greek Fathers, Hans Urs von Balthasar and Jean Daniélou in particular opened the field of Nyssen scholarship: Balthasar with his 1942 book *Presence and Thought (Présence et pensée)*, and Daniélou with his 1944 dissertation *Platonism and Mystical Theology (Platonisme et théologie mystique)*. Balthasar's opening declaration of his book is telling: "Only a very small number of initiates have read and are aware of Gregory of Nyssa, and they have jealously guarded their secret."[59] The few studies that had been done were made possible largely by the work of Werner Jaeger, who in 1920 began the *Gregorii Nysseni Opera*, an ongoing series that continues to provide critical editions of Gregory's works. Jaeger's work especially encouraged a tradition of German scholarship on Nyssen, of whom Walther Völker with *Gregory of Nyssa as Mystic (Gregory von Nyssa als Mystiker*, 1955) and Ekkehard Mühlenberg with *The Infinity of God according to Gregory of Nyssa (Die Unendlichkeit Gottes bei Gregor von Nyssa*, 1966) are mid-century pioneers. With the exception of Harold Cherniss's important book *The Platonism of Gregory of Nyssa* (1930), English scholarship came somewhat later. Rowan Williams's 1979 *The Wound of Knowledge* and Andrew Louth's 1981 *The Origins of the Christian Mystical Tradition from Plato to Denys* were among the first English theological works on Gregory to appear.

Since then, scholarship on Gregory has exploded. Sarah Coakley's volume *Re-thinking Gregory of Nyssa* (2003) brought together a number of

58. Meredith, "Influence of Gregory of Nyssa," 427.

59. Balthasar, *Presence and Thought*, 15.

fine scholars who worked on Gregory. The occasion for the volume testifies to the popularity Gregory had attained as an academic subject: No longer a hidden "secret" known to "a very small number of initiates," Gregory had become such a figure in the academic imagination that his persona now needed to be rethought.[60] The same year Coakley's book was published, one of the contributors to that volume released his own book drawing considerably on Gregory: David Bentley Hart published *The Beauty of the Infinite*. Hart writes systematic theology in the tradition of Gregory, yet in conversation with contemporary thinkers. He writes Nyssen theology in the same way theologians for years have written Augustinian theology. His work is also importantly about beauty, but I am not ready to draw these stories together just yet.

Story Two: Beauty of Antiquity, Modernity, and the Present

We move from one once-exile to another. Yet long before exile, beauty (and its linguistic relatives *belle*, *belleza*, *beauté*, and *Schöne*) was central to much intellectual and academic reflection. In the ancient Greek-speaking philosophical world, the progenitor of the term *the beautiful* was *to kalon*—which suggests fineness, nobility, and pleasure—and it occupied a proud position near *to agathon*, the good. With powerful images, Plato described *to kalon* as inspiring the growth of wings that enable divine ascent, as that in which one births virtue, and as representing for us immortal blessedness. Though we have no such poetic image of beauty from him, Aristotle was apparently no less insistent than his teacher on the importance of *to kalon*, which characterizes for him both virtuous actions—they are themselves *kalon*—and the reason the virtuous agent performs those actions—the virtuous person acts for the sake of the *kalon*.[61] Plotinus continued the high place of beauty in his philosophy when he gave it, along with the Good, as a name for the One, and described the beautiful as mediating between the sensible and intelligible worlds, drawing the beholder from the former to the latter and so awakening the soul to its true home.[62] The Plotinian trajectory continued

60. What this rethinking entailed, among other things, was the way Gregory was often cast in opposition to Augustine and the West.

61. Philosopher Gabriel Richardson Lear rigorously explores the significance of beauty in Plato in "Permanent Beauty and Becoming Happy in Plato's *Symposium*," and the significance of beauty for moral virtue in Aristotle in "Aristotle on Moral Virtue and the Fine."

62. For more on beauty in the thought of Plotinus, see the chapters on beauty in the recent books on Plotinus by O'Meara (*Plotinus*), Miles (*Plotinus on Body and Beauty*),

in the West, both through Augustine, who thematized beauty's importance in signifying God with the Latin word *pulcher*, and also through Pseudo-Dionysius, whose Greek works describing the importance of beauty in ascending to God were translated into Latin. These two thinkers dominated the Western philosophical and theological tradition throughout the Middle Ages, and medieval anxieties about and hopes for beauty were largely worked out in the vocabulary of their thought.[63]

So what happened? When did beauty cease to be central to theological and philosophical reflection, and what occasioned its decline? There were a number of transformations prior to the English word beauty, but determinative changes—changes that set up the break between beauty and academia—arrived with modernity. It is impossible to narrate this break well with a single narrative. To convey the multiple stories involved in beauty's loss in intellectual and academic status, I cluster together three different storytellers: Jerome Stolnitz, whose essay "'Beauty': Some Stages in the History of an Idea" is a classic for modern aesthetics, especially in the British tradition; Paul Guyer, the foremost contemporary interpreter of Kant's aesthetics; and Larry Shiner, whose book *The Invention of Art* situates the intellectual history of beauty and art in the messy milieu of material and social changes. Together, these three writers draw multi-textured histories that delineate beauty's place today.

In his 1961 article on the history of beauty, Jerome Stolnitz will (wisely) not single out one cause for beauty's exile from intellectual favor. He writes, "'[B]eauty' has receded or even disappeared from contemporary aesthetic theory. For, like other once influential ideas, it has simply faded away." If he refuses to name a single cause of this fading, he does not hesitate to supply

---

and Hadot (*Plotinus, or, The Simplicity of Vision*). For an excellent analysis of the differences in beauty and the beautiful in Plotinus's thought and a digestion of the important scholarship on it, see Rist, "Beauty, the Beautiful, and the Good."

63. This is not to suggest that there was a uniformity of opinion regarding beauty. Abbott Suger (1081–1151) and Bernard of Clairvaux (1090–1153) provide an interesting case of two thinkers devoted to Dionysian descriptions of beauty's role in mediating the sensible and intelligible realms, who nevertheless arrived at different practical conclusions. Where Suger devoted much of his career to renovating the choir of the abbey church of St. Denis (named in honor of Pseudo-Dionysius) so that it might accommodate pilgrims and testify to the beauty of God, Bernard of Clairvaux banished images from Cistercian abbeys and railed against the beautiful extravagances of abbey churches, declaring that such excessive material beauty distracted monks from the divine and that resources would be better devoted in care for the poor. He was more accommodating of ornament in cathedrals, where those less advanced in the spiritual life—and therefore more in need of material beauty to aid them—worshiped. For Suger's argument, see his *On the Abbey Church of St. Denis*; for Bernard of Clairvaux's, see his *Cistercians and Cluniacs*.

the century: the eighteenth. It was in that century, Stolnitz claims, that the modern aesthetic was born and beauty lost the venerable position it held in classical, medieval, and renaissance thought.[64]

Stolnitz describes beauty's gradual disappearance from aesthetics by focusing on a lineage of British thinkers. He justifies this decision by claiming British thinkers as the origin of aesthetics "as we [twentieth-century Europeans and Americans?] know it." They are for him "the prime movers in the demotion of beauty."[65] Before the eighteenth century, Stolnitz explains, treatises on artistic genres and the rules that govern them treated beauty as their unifying aim. Beauty was not just prior to but also instrumental in the development of fine arts.[66] Yet by the end of the century, beauty would have lost any capacity to perform such a unifying role, for it lost any unifying principle by which people could agree that something was beautiful. That is, beauty came to name, not a *thing*, but a person's *experience* of a thing. The story of British thinkers, Stolnitz thinks, dramatizes this story most sharply.

Bypassing the traditional starting place for British aesthetics—Lord Shaftesbury, also known as Anthony Ashley Cooper (1677–1713)—Stolnitz claims it is Joseph Addison (1672–1719) who provides "the first at all systematic statement in British aesthetics."[67] In an article published the same year as his history of beauty, Stolnitz argues that by introducing the concept of disinterestedness, Shaftesbury opened up a path for the pioneers of modern aesthetics to tread.[68] Shaftesbury himself, though, was too unsystematic[69] a thinker and too caught in an older way of seeing the world—where the good is identified with the beautiful and the beautiful can be identified by properties like proportion and harmony—to walk that path himself.[70] To understand modern aesthetics, then, Stolnitz directs attention to the first heirs of Shaftesbury's work.

Addison did not use the word *aesthetic*—it would be coined in a modern language by the German thinker Alexander Baumgarten in 1735—but he did, Stolnitz claims, "move towards the concept" by distinguishing a realm of pleasure distinct from the gross pleasures of sense and the refined

---

64. Stolnitz, "Beauty," 186.

65. Ibid.

66. Ibid., 187.

67. Ibid.

68. Stolnitz, "On the Significance of Lord Shaftesbury," 100.

69. Stolnitz quotes Shaftesbury rejecting system categorically: "The most ingenious way of becoming foolish is by a system" (Stolnitz, "On the Significance of Lord Shaftesbury," 100, quoting Shaftesbury, *Characteristics of Men*, 1:189).

70. Stolnitz, "On the Significance of Lord Shaftesbury," 105.

pleasures of understanding.[71] It was the pleasures of the imagination. Central to such pleasure was "disinterestedness," which entailed an ennobling self-forgetfulness distinct from the "lower," self-aggrandizing pleasure of possession. In Stolnitz's description of Addison's thought, the arts that were formerly found in genres determined by rules that aim for beauty were now unified by the way they provide pleasure of the imagination. Beauty, moreover, became just one form this pleasure could take. Such pleasure could also be "great," "novel," or "uncommon."[72] With Stolnitz's Addison, then, the pleasure of the imagination is inclusive of beauty, which is placed alongside other forms of this pleasure.

Where Addison made the pleasure of the imagination foundational to beauty, Alexander Gerard, according to Stolnitz, gave that honor to taste. For Gerard, beauty becomes one of several perceptions proper to taste, one among the ranks of novelty, sublimity, imitation, harmony, the ridiculous, and virtue.[73] Stolnitz notes that Gerard gives equal attention both to beauty and sublimity,[74] thus hinting at the growing importance of the sublime relative to the beautiful. Burke casts the decisive opposition between them. Stolnitz describes Burke's transformation of the beautiful and the sublime from distinct concepts to mutually exclusive ones.[75] Beauty entails pleasure, relaxation, melting; the sublime involves uneasiness, paralysis, horror. Where beauty is small and delicate, the sublime is vast and rugged.[76] Most importantly for Stolnitz's telling of Burke, the sublime entails an emotional intensity lacking in the beautiful, and such intensity evidences for Burke and many subsequent thinkers the greater significance of the sublime.[77] Stolnitz's

71. Stolnitz, "Beauty," 188.

72. Ibid., 189.

73. Ibid.,190.

74. Ibid., 191.

75. Ibid.

76. Ibid., 191–92.

77. Ibid., 192. In Morris's fascinating book *The Culture of Pain*, he describes the split between the beautiful and the sublime as echoing the distinction between pleasure and pain, so that the Burkean sublime becomes an aesthetics of pain. Morris describes two sculptures depicting Greek tales—a first-century BCE sculpture of the ill-fated seer Laocöon and an eighteenth-century sculpture of the fire-stealing Prometheus—and interprets the move from a beauty that can mix with pain to a beauty that cannot, that must be displaced by the sublime to draw near pain. He then writes, "Beauty in Burke's *Philosophical Enquiry* loses all its ancient classical and Christian links with heroism, knowledge, truth, virtue, and wisdom. It reappears as little more than a facile charm. . . . Beauty . . . stands completely stripped of any moral, cognitive, or spiritual power. It is merely an external arrangement of matter: 'some quality' in bodies" (215–16). Part of what I find so important about Morris' narrative is the way it emphasizes the sublime, not simply as invented to be beauty's inverse, but as an attempt to extract and separate

narration of Burke's thought highlights the way beauty becomes less important the more the sublime is elevated. Yet if beauty is on the decline, so is
pleasure: Not only does Burke introduce negative feelings into the aesthetic,
thus to Stolnitz's mind paving the way for the twentieth-century's valuation
of ugliness,[78] he also prizes the aesthetic concept productive of negative feelings more highly than the concept devoid of them. Cast opposite the dark
mystery of the sublime, beauty takes on an increasingly frivolous hue.

Accompanying the move in Addison, Gerard, and Burke to understanding beauty via the perceiver and her feelings, other writers discredit
the traditional principles for locating beauty: proportion, uniformity in variety, and utility. Under the scrutiny of British empiricism, Stolnitz claims,
these principles began to fade.[79] Francis Hutcheson (1694–1746) made a
valiant effort to correlate the traditional features of beauty with the experience of beauty by refusing to admit negative evidence: Sometimes, in making a judgment about beauty, people are swayed by pleasures and aversions
unrelated to beauty and so fail to respond properly to the beauty or lack of
beauty in an object.[80] But the old system was crumbling under the pressures
of empiricism. How could *proportion* explain the way flowers as a class are
more beautiful to us than vegetables are, though flowers come in all different shapes and proportions? Or *utility* explain why a turtle-dove is more
beautiful than a toad, though each are equally well-suited to their purposes?
By the close of the century, aestheticians were giving up on finding a single
formula for beauty. Stolnitz references John Donaldson's *The Elements of
Beauty* (1780) and Archibald Alison's *Essay on the Nature and Principles
of Taste* (1790) to illustrate the state of aesthetics by the end of the eighteenth century: Both works name the impossibility of reducing aesthetics
to a single principle.[81] The shift from identifying beauty by objective features to subjective states enabled a second shift that Stolnitz describes: from
its circumscription in an exclusive and aristocratic set of things, to naming potentially anything. Unbound from "the objective" that would tether
beauty to particular features, beauty becomes inclusive and democratic.[82]
(An irony of democratizing the set of things that can be named beautiful

---

what was formerly part of, or deeply intertwined with, beauty itself. In Plotinus, for
example, we find traces of the modern sublime and its relationship to the beautiful
framed in terms of the relationship of Beauty Itself (which is formless and ultimately
unnameable) to the beautiful.

78. Stolnitz, "Beauty," 193.
79. Ibid., 197.
80. Ibid., 195.
81. Ibid., 199–200.
82. Ibid., 200.

is that this democratizing became productive of its own kind of elitism, one that identifies a class of people rather than a class of objects.) Beauty comes to name that which arouses the feeling that something is beautiful, which is another way of saying there is no prior limitation on what may be deemed beautiful.[83] By the end of the eighteenth-century, aesthetics is well on the road to allowing the perceiver to determine whether something is beautiful.[84] An implication of this "Copernican revolution" of aesthetics is that beauty becomes a word that gives no information about an object. It becomes a "general term of approbation" of little use in intellectual discussion.[85] Not only is beauty at this point one aesthetic concept among others; and not only is it, with regard to the sublime at least, a less significant aesthetic concept; but it is also an increasingly vague and useless one. So Stolnitz accounts for the gradual disappearance of beauty from aesthetics in the twentieth century.

While Stolnitz is persuaded that his story of the British philosophers accounts for the twentieth-century demise of beauty, Immanuel Kant (1724–1804) was unconvinced that what these writers were doing was philosophy at all. He looked for the origins of aesthetics to the man who coined the term: Alexander Gottlieb Baumgarten (1714–62), who reworked the Greek word *aisthesis* in his dissertation to name the science of how things are known by the senses. It was 1735, and Baumgarten was twenty-one years old. Fifteen years later, he wrote *Aesthetica*, where he defined aesthetics as "the theory of liberal arts, lower gnoseology, the art of thinking beautifully, the art and analog of reason, the science of sensitive cognition."[86] In his own story of the origins of modern aesthetics, Paul Guyer begins with Baumgarten's definition. Guyer is a scholar of Kant, and, unsurprisingly, gives Kant pride of place in his account of eighteenth-century aesthetics. Guyer appreciates Kant for holding the importance of sense (the starting point of the empirical school dominant in early modern Britain) together with the importance of rationality (the starting point of the rationalist school dominant in early modern Germany).[87] The mediator between these two realms, for Guyer as for Kant, is the imagination, and Guyer describes the emergence of modern aesthetics riding on the back of the freedom of the imagination.[88]

---

83. Ibid.
84. Ibid., 201.
85. Ibid., 203.
86. Guyer, "Origins of Modern Aesthetics," 15, quoting Baumgarten, *Aesthetica*.
87. Ibid., 18.
88. Ibid., 16.

By identifying the freedom of the imagination as the center of modern aesthetics, Guyer finds a way to fold British, German, and even a French thinker into his story. To accomplish this, Guyer tells a story that is not predominantly about empiricists and rationalists responding to inadequacies in their own philosophical systems. It is about the struggle of all his thinkers—Shaftesbury, Hutcheson, Addison, Jean-Baptiste Du Bos, Baumgarten, and Kant—to locate experiences of art and beauty in the human subject. Shaftesbury is brought into the realm of modern concerns from which Stolnitz excluded him for two reasons: First, Guyer sees Shaftesbury as preparing the way for the rise of disinterestedness, and, second, Shaftesbury claimed that what people admire in appreciating order and proportion is really the creative intelligence behind them—"creative intelligence" foreshadowing, for Guyer, the importance of the "freedom of the imagination." Hutcheson founds his understanding of the "sense of beauty" on this philosophical work of Shaftesbury, and in Hutcheson's hands, this "sense of beauty" becomes an internal sense that is neither cognition nor volition.[89] Addison goes one step closer to the freedom of imagination. As we learned from Stolnitz, Addison makes the pleasures of the imagination central to (and, in fact, governing of) how he understands beauty. Du Bos is important to Guyer for the way he begins to articulate a freedom of the imagination in the arts.[90] Baumgarten, who is ambiguously related to these past thinkers, locates aesthetic perception in the cognitive faculty, but by contrasting the determinacy of logical representation with the indeterminacy of aesthetic representation, he prepares the way for Kant's articulation of aesthetic ideas as carrying real cognitive content yet remaining free from understanding's constraint. The indeterminacy of aesthetic ideas in this way preserves the freedom of the imagination.[91] And so modern aesthetics is organized.

Guyer's story is different from Stolnitz's because he includes different thinkers and aims to illumine a slightly different question. Stolnitz wants to address why beauty declined and so writes about the rise of aesthetics and the repudiation of the traditional principles of beauty. Guyer, on the other hand, wants to describe how modern aesthetics was born as a commitment to the freedom of imagination. Any story about beauty Guyer tells is incidental to that aim. Guyer has, in fact, criticized Stolnitz in the past for the way Stolnitz narrates changes in the formulations of beauty in the eighteenth century. He focuses his criticisms, not on Stoltnitz's article on

---

89. Ibid., 24–25.
90. Ibid., 29, 28.
91. Ibid., 36.

the British aestheticians, nor on his article on Lord Shaftesbury.[92] Guyer reserves the heft of his critique for a third article Stolnitz published in 1961, "On the Origins of 'Aesthetic Disinterest,'" and an article he published seventeen years later, "The 'Aesthetic Attitude' in the Rise of Modern Aesthetics." Guyer objects to the way that Stolnitz understands British disinterestedness as a distinct mode of perception that prefigured the twentieth-century "aesthetic attitude."[93] Following George Dickie's critiques of Stolnitz, Guyer maintains that the eighteenth-century theorists did not see disinterestedness as an aesthetic attitude that could be applied to any set of properties in an object. Guyer objects, then, not to the weak version of Stolnitz's argument—that there was in the eighteenth-century a movement in aesthetics from aesthetic properties to aesthetic perceiver—but to the strong version of it—that the eighteenth century yielded a distinct mode of perception called "the aesthetic" that replaced a set of objective or external properties. Guyer sees Stolnitz as appealing to this narrative "in defence of what [he] take[s] to be the proper approach to contemporary aesthetics," which is one based on aesthetic disinterestedness as a distinct mode of perception.[94]

Guyer's critique of Stolnitz reveals what is important about their narrations of beauty in modernity: They go some way to explaining (and justifying) trends in conversations about aesthetics today. Stolnitz sets up not only his own arguments for thinking about aesthetics via disinterestedness, but also applications and reinterpretations of aesthetics, for example, in conversations about nature, in which scholars like Emily Brady participate. Distinguishing it from indifference and detachment, Brady articulates the appeal of disinterestedness as a way of valuing an object aesthetically, beyond any purpose it serves or desire it satisfies.[95] Stolnitz's account of changes in the history of beauty thus helps to lay out the terrain of many contemporary conversations in aesthetics. Likewise, Guyer's emphasis on the imagination sets up the intimacy of imagination and aesthetics or beauty in contemporary conversations about beauty. Francesca Aran Murphy represents one such strand through her work in theological aesthetics. As she claims in her important work *Christ the Form of Beauty: A Study in Theology and Literature*, "Our ability to enter into the Incarnation [i.e., the form of beauty] is in proportion to our willingness to imagine realistically."[96] She

92. Guyer, "History of Modern Aesthetics," 25–60.

93. Ibid., 28. Stolnitz, "On the Origins of 'Aesthetic Disinterest'"; Stolnitz, "The 'Aesthetic Attitude' in the Rise of Modern Aesthetics."

94. Guyer, "History of Modern Aesthetics," 27.

95. Brady, "Don't Eat the Daisies."

96. Murphy, *Christ the Form of Beauty*, 1.

goes on to adumbrate the relationship between beauty and imagination, associating comprehending Christ as "transcendental beauty" with a capacity to "envisage the person of Christ in the light of imagination."[97] The imagination, then, provides "the human context" for how a person enters into the transcendental beauty that is Christ.[98] And the centrality of imagination to Murphy's reflections about beauty is made intelligible in part by the history Guyer recounts of imagination's growing importance in modern aesthetics.

If there are different inflections in the stories told by Stolnitz and Guyer, there are also instructive similarities. The thinkers in Guyer's story set out to describe the pleasure that beauty affords and so begin to articulate a faculty—the imagination—that apprehends that pleasure. But as the faculty of the imagination and its role are articulated, beauty becomes subordinate to it, and thinkers find that the faculty can apprehend other categories of aesthetics as well. In Kant's case, as in Burke's, the masculine sublime will become the most important of these other categories (though Guyer does not tell this part of the story). The freedom of the imagination, initially developed in service to describing beauty, becomes a more determinative category than beauty itself. Like Stolnitz, Guyer tells a story of beauty's subordination to a category in which it is primed to become marginal, and also like Stolnitz, Guyer sets his story in the eighteenth century.

As illuminating as Guyer's and Stolnitz's narrations of the rise of the aesthetic are, they tell only pieces of the story. The thinkers they describe are not, as it may seem in their essays, simply responding to other thinkers. Their intellectual moves are also attempts to make sense of social changes in the eighteenth century, and as they make sense of these changes, they open up cultural imaginaries for new possibilities. Illustrative of this possibility was an event at the end of the eighteenth century as important for the rise of modern aesthetics as any of these philosophers: in 1793, the Louvre Museum opened.

The Louvre was a solution to a problem caused by the French Revolution. As the revolutionaries sought to instantiate an order of liberty, equality, and fraternity free from the centuries of tyranny by church and crown, angry mobs attacked the symbols of the old regime. In his book *The Invention of Art*, Larry Shiner describes the iconoclastic fervor in the summer of 1793 in which nothing was safe from vandals: tombs of French kings, statues and portraits of royalty, the Notre Dame Cathedral.[99] Yet there were those troubled by such destruction. After the revolutionaries' assembly voted for a

97. Ibid., 9.
98. Ibid.
99. Shiner, *Invention of Art*, 169.

decree to destroy all signs of royalty in 1792, some people publicly worried about damaging old masterpieces. It was Pierre Cambon who proposed the creation of a museum as an alternative to destroying the symbols of the old regime.[100] The Louvre opened a year after the iconoclastic decree and displayed a collection of art objects from French royalty and former church property.[101] Shiner describes the logic of moving the pieces to a museum:

> By placing the suspect works in a museum, the assembly recognized that the museum would neutralize them. Once in the museum, monuments to royalty would lose their sacred power. They would cease to be symbols pointing beyond themselves and become merely art. Out of the crucible of the Revolution had come an institution that "makes" art, that transforms works of art dedicated to a purpose and place into works of Art that are essentially purposeless and placeless.[102]

As a building, the Louvre Museum itself bears the marks of this transformation. Before becoming a museum, it was, famously, a palace. The Louvre's shifting status from palace to museum marked the transition of the objects within it from art of the church and the royals to fine art, originally made in ecclesial and royal contexts. The Louvre was not the first museum, but it was one of the most important. Others quickly followed, and the institution of the museum instantiated a new way of thinking about art, one in which art can be removed from its traditional social, political, and religious purposes. In this way it is enabled by and expansive of the concept of disinterestedness that thinkers like Addison were developing with regard to beauty. Disinterestedness not only names the difference between beauty and "lower" forms of pleasure, but as it is institutionalized in the museum, disinterestedness precipitates the distinction between fine arts and crafts. The way Shiner describes this and other changing social and cultural formations both before and after the eighteenth century can help us fill out the story Stolnitz and Guyer tell about intellectual shifts around beauty.

The migration of the concept of disinterestedness from the philosophy of beauty to the realm of fine arts suggests the historical interrelation of the two categories, and indeed, the very genealogy of the term *fine arts* betrays this relation. Fine arts was first coined in the century Stolnitz and Guyer deem definitive for aesthetics. It was originally a French word *beaux-arts* (beautiful arts) that became fine arts or *polite arts* in English.[103] According

100. Ibid., 181.
101. Ibid., 180.
102. Ibid., 182.
103. Ibid., 81.

to Shiner, Charles Batteux made the first widely read attempt to delineate a set of arts as fine arts in his book *Les Beaux Arts Réduits à un Même Principe* (*The Fine Arts Reduced to a Single Principle*) (1746). In keeping the work on beauty at the time, Batteux distinguished from *beaux-arts* those arts that are associated with need or a combination of utility and pleasure. The *beaux-arts* aim only at beauty, and moreover require genius and taste.[104] Shiner's narration of Batteux's delineation of *beaux-arts* thus supports Stolnitz's claim that at the beginning of the eighteenth century, the fine arts were united by their common aim of the beautiful.

But Shiner explains that at the same time the term fine arts was born, the meaning of genius was also shifting. While in the beginning of the eighteenth century, it was generally believed that everyone had a genius for something, by the end of that century, genius was no longer something everyone had but was instead something only a few people could *be*.[105] Genius was not a thing to be perfected by reason and rule but entailed originality, inspiration, and imagination.[106] This new conception of genius, with its attendant traits of spontaneity and creativity, was associated with the artist, while rule, now divorced from genius, described the talent of the artisan, who worked not by inspiration but by calculation, who was associated with skill of the body rather than the spontaneity of the mind, and who imitated past masters and copied nature rather than creating and originating.[107] "Genius," then, helped render intelligible the division of fine arts and crafts, but as it did so, it also marked a tension with beauty. Stolnitz argues that the beautiful became more democratic and less aristocratic in the objects it might name—it ceased to refer to a predetermined class of objects or to be limited by any principles—but the *beaux-arts*, inasmuch as they were bound up with genius, were becoming increasingly elite.

Moreover, "fine arts" was differently gendered than "beauty." Shiner traces the way craft was feminized and marginalized as women's art, a process especially evident in the case of embroidery. Once treated as an art with the status of painting, the female-dominated activity of embroidery was increasingly dismissed through the fourteenth and fifteenth centuries as a "patient handiwork" for keeping noblewomen's hands busy. The dominance of women in embroidery was taken as evidence of its inferiority and grounds for consigning it to the category of craft—a category proven inferior to fine arts by the number of women within it. At the same time, the

104. Ibid., 83.
105. Ibid., 111.
106. Ibid., 112–13.
107. Ibid., 114–15.

male-dominated guilds of the higher status arts practiced excluding women more and more.[108]

The division between artist and artisan was generated and sustained not just by the intellectual work done in shifting conceptions of genius and the articulation of a new set of fine arts but also in the development of a new system of art. The old art economy was run by patrons, who often gave very specific instructions in commissioning a particular art piece, to the point even of determining, for instance, a painter's subject matter and colors. For one example, Shiner describes the way Shakespeare's plot outlines might be given to him. He then had to marry freedom and technique, autonomy and submission in his writing process. But in the new system of arts, the painter created for a free market, so that the success of an art object was not determined by its fittingness to a particular location and project but by standards internal to the art object itself.[109] The patrons were invisible and faceless, their dictates therefore more obscure. With no particular, concrete person to determine subject matter, originality was understood and valued differently, and this transformation in the status of "original" in turn informed the development of "genius."

But if the artist was increasingly valued for his originality, the opportunity for the artisan's originality was eroded by the Industrial Revolution. Shiner describes how the pre-Revolution intimacy of workshop life gave way to large workshops structured on a division-of-labor model. These new workshops were owned by merchants rather than master craftsmen, and mechanization increasingly replaced human skill. As less skill and training were required to perform smaller tasks under the model of division of labor and factory production, artisans became increasingly interchangeable. Gone were the days of long apprenticeships and investment in artisans. The social and economic value of the artisan was on the decline.

At the same time that artisans were losing autonomy, social status, and creative control of their crafts, artists were gaining ground in those very areas while acquiring a kind of spiritual status.[110] Institutions and venues developed to support and showcase the fine arts. The museum was one such eighteenth-century development, but Shiner also points out that except for theater and opera, all the fine arts institutions known to the modern world date from this time, including secular concerts and literary criticism, which allowed for art objects and productions to be appreciated (ostensibly) apart

---

108. Ibid., 44.

109. Ibid., 126–28.

110. Ibid., 197.

from their social function.[111] These institutions, moreover, generated a new public—one that was more anonymous and socio-economically diverse than the patrons, but nonetheless generally propertied and educated.[112]

The origins of this public in some ways predated the institutions it patronized. Hagiographies of the artistic genius like Giorgio Vasari's (1511–74) *Lives of Eminent Artists* prepared a high pedestal for artists, and suggested that "artistic genius" was different from the genius for shoemaking, for example, or weaving. In this way, it anticipated later formulations of genius. In the sixteenth and seventeenth centuries, art collecting and art criticism and theory developed, thus giving the bourgeoisie new ways of talking about the arts.[113] This literature around art prepared those who read it to become consumers of the arts. The development of the term fine arts and the consolidation of particular arts as *fine* was enabled by the growth of the bourgeoisie who patronized those arts—just as such development and consolidation was inextricable from the rise of factories, the market economy, and the impulse to preserve traditional gender roles.

Those crafts and artisans that were not displaced by factory products and less-skilled laborers were often shut into the domestic world of women and homes. Shiner references Schopenhauer's statement that women can have talent but not genius, and Ruskin's contrast of the man who discovers with the woman who sweetly orders, to illustrate the domestication of craft.[114] Thus, as new publics were created to legitimate and sustain fine arts and its geniuses, a new private was delineated where crafts were practiced by women as domestic activities that yielded ornament rather than art. The generation of fine arts was on the one hand enabled by the theorization of beauty, but on the other hand put in some tension with it by its gendering and elitism. We can trace here an emerging trend: masculine, sublime, fine, arts, and elite were clustered together in their opposition to feminine, beautiful, craft, and non-elite.

The separation of fine arts and beauty was complete in the twentieth century: Shiner describes a series of displacements, from beauty to the sublime to art, the last of which he specifies as "the idea of the self-contained work of art as creation."[115] The democratization and evacuation of beauty that rendered it a "general term of approbation" as described by Stolnitz, together with beauty's feminization, meant that it was no longer fit to de-

---

111. Ibid., 88.

112. Ibid., 94.

113. Morgan, "Art and Religion in the Modern Age," 25.

114. Shiner, *Invention of Art*, 200.

115. Ibid., 141.

scribe the spiritual heights of genius found in art. The masculine, weighty, and exceptional sublime was much more suited to the work of describing both spirituality and art. In his essay "Art and Religion in the Modern Age," David Morgan describes the sublime as "the most influential aesthetic idea in the spiritualization of art." Citing such artists as Caspar David Friedrich, Vincent van Gogh, Wassily Kandinsky, Piet Mondrian, Mark Rothko, and Barnett Newman, Morgan invokes Robert Rosenblum's work of tracing the "spiritually charged visual strategy" of certain artists "that culminates in the painterly gestures toward transcendence and sublimity."[116] Such gestures "dematerialize representation and infuse it with a heroic, mythical stature that readily recalls the theological discourse of the 'sublime' by theologian Friedrich Schleiermacher, the 'numinous' by Rudolf Otto, and the 'ultimate' by Paul Tillich."[117] In emphasizing the resonances of the sublime found in the fields of religion as well as art, Morgan points us toward work the sublime was doing outside of the world of art. At the same time that the sublime was helping to consolidate the fine arts as distinct from beauty, it was also birthing a new discipline for the academy: religious studies.

The organization of religious studies as an academic discipline was indirectly related to—and illuminative of—beauty's academic fate. Its relation to beauty comes principally by way of its relation to the sublime, which had been formulated as beauty's inverse by Burke and Kant. The sublime helped to make possible the academic field of religious studies, which began with the attempt to identify the *sine qua non* of religion. It was a move enabled by the theologian Friedrich Schleiermacher (1768–1834)—like Kant and Baumgarten, a German of a Pietist background—who located religion in a feeling of absolute dependence. This move was itself an attempt to release religion from the rationalist strictures of Kant's *Religion within the Bounds of Reason Alone*. While scholars have noted affinities between the sublime and Schleiermacher's "feeling of absolute dependence,"[118] the mark of the sub-

116. Morgan, "Art and Religion in the Modern Age," 37.

117. Ibid.

118. Robert Williams notes Schleiermacher's use of the sublime: "Schleiermacher maintains that there is a close resemblance between the feeling of the sublime and the feeling of utter dependence, and his description of the feeling of the sublime brings out the correlation of subordination of the subject with the dominance of the codetermining other. . . . [The feeling of absolute dependence] signifies a sense of creaturely dependence on the one hand, but on the other hand it combines the central elements of the idea of the holy, namely, awe and fascination at the object" ("Schleiermacher and Feuerbach," 439). The same scholar describes the continuity between Schleiermacher and Otto. He writes in a footnote: "Otto's account of Schleiermacher amounts to little more than a caricature. The preceding quotation clearly shows that the feeling of utter dependence combines not only a sense of creatureliness and dependence, but also a

lime is even more obvious in Rudolf Otto (1869–1937). Deeply influenced by Schleiermacher, Otto identified the holy as religion's *sine qua non* in his book *The Idea of the Holy*. The holy marks out a special kind of experience in the world that can be named religious, and so it can serve as a category for comparison across religions. Of course, as many scholars have pointed out, Otto's holy is derived from his own Christian background, and so Christianity enjoys a privileged place in his comparisons across religions.[119] Yet his holy is not merely Christian; it is specifically Lutheran Pietist (like Schleiermacher himself) and shaped by the lineage of German thinkers Otto was reading.[120]

The result of these influences is that the holy looks remarkably similar to the sublime. It entails excess, fearfulness, fascination, overpoweringness—and it stands in distinction, if not flat opposition, to the beautiful. In a footnote, Otto grants that the sublime is a "figurative analogical description" for divine transcendence, even as he insists that the sublime and the holy cannot be literally the same. He explains, trying to mark his distinction from Schleiermacher: "Religious feelings are not the same as aesthetic feelings, and 'the sublime' is as definitely an aesthetic term as 'the beautiful,' however widely different may be the facts denoted by the words."[121] Otto here admits the structural similarity of the holy to the sublime, which he describes as "widely different" from the beautiful. One writer sees in Otto's understanding of the holy a more explicitly hostile relationship to the beautiful than Otto admits, one of unmasking "the pretensions of the beautiful."[122] Whether Otto saw the beautiful as illegitimately pretentious is not clear, but he is quite clear that religion is not to find its analog in beauty. That kind of heavy-lifting requires the sublime, Otto's "figurative analog" for divine transcendence.

Otto was not the only twentieth-century writer to rethink the sublime in an explicitly religious framework. In her article "The Idea of the Holy

---

multifaceted sense of its object, combining both *mysterium tremendum* and the sense of fascination. Although Otto reached his position independently, it appears as if his contribution to the sense of the holy is largely one of assembling additional factual data, rather than isolating and describing structures" (ibid., 439n55).

119. See, for example, Lynn Poland's critique: "The apparatus of sublimity makes for flawed science of religion. As his critics all in various ways conclude, one difficulty is that Otto seems to think of *Das Heilige* as an inductive psychological study, while his defense of the sui generis character of religion actually assumes in advance a good deal of what it claims empirically to discover" ("Idea of the Holy," 195).

120. Otto, in fact, devotes an entire chapter to Luther in *The Idea of the Holy* and references Schleiermacher repeatedly.

121. Otto, *Idea of the Holy*, 42n1.

122. Poland, "Idea of the Holy," 195.

and the History of the Sublime," Lynn Poland describes the revival of the sublime in the early twentieth century "in more or less Kantian form" as a way "to reproduce and cure the anxieties of the period surrounding the First World War."[123] She lists three religious works published around the same time: Otto's *The Idea of the Holy* (1917), Barth's *Letter to the Romans* (1918), and Freud's *Totem and Taboo* (1913). Without necessarily naming the sublime, all three works, she claims, mark its influence in the way they privilege terror, discontinuity, and the uncanny.[124] Later religious studies scholars will attempt to dislodge the discipline from these theological moorings, but they, like those in art, were left with a discipline formed (or re-formed) with the architecture of the sublime. These two children of the sublime frequently share language with one another—some of which I explore in the fourth chapter—while their relationship also betrays a kind of sibling rivalry. Situating him in the tradition of Kandinsky and Schopenhauer, David Morgan gives an example of such sublime siblinghood when he quotes Clive Bell. "Art and religion are . . . two roads by which men escape from circumstances to ecstasy. Between aesthetic and religious rapture there is a family alliance. Art and Religion are means to similar states of mind."[125] Art and religion in Bell are, that is, alternative paths to the kind of transcendence represented in the sublime.

Art and religion's rivalry, however, lasted longer than their intimacy. In a recent essay for a symposium on art and religion, James Elkins wonders over the estranged relationship between them by describing an international art competition called Jesus 2000. Judging over a thousand entries from nineteen countries, Sister Wendy Beckett chose as the winner Janet McKenzie's *Jesus of the People*, which depicted Jesus as a black man with a woman's body and three background symbols: a halo (representing, as McKenzie explains, Jesus's holiness), a yin-yang (representing perfect harmony), and a feather (representing transcendent knowledge or the Native American Great Spirit). Elkins describes another entry where Jesus's body is modeled on a homeless man and also the artist's father, rendered also with the artist's own hair and her daughter's nose. This Jesus is wearing a baseball cap and standing on a country road with a dead-end sign in the background. The heavy-handed symbolism is too much for Elkins. Verbally handling these objects with the care of one barely concealing distaste, Elkins attempts a gentle understatement: "I think the conclusion of this history has to be that

123. Ibid., 184.

124. Ibid.

125. Morgan, "Art and Religion in the Modern Age," 35, quoting Bell, "Art and Religion," 68.

fine art and religious art have gone their separate ways."[126] In fact, the only place Jesus 2000 could have in contemporary academic art criticism is as camp, with critics who might find McKenzie's painting "so bad it's good."[127] Here he voices his criticism more strongly: "People in my profession consider such things as *Jesus 2000* untouchable."[128] "Serious art," he writes later, "has grown estranged from religion."[129] He has an explanation of why: "[T]o suddenly put modern art back with religion or spirituality is to give up the history and purposes of a certain understanding of modernism."[130] Elkins could more helpfully explain the lack of "seriousness" in the *Jesus 2000* art entries in terms other than their religiosity. These paintings seem suffused, for example, with limpid liberalism. But perhaps the more pressing problem with Elkins's analysis is that he misses the way *religion* is every bit as complicit in the modernism he wants to protect as *art*. The individualized, ordinary-person-glorifying, hierarchy-resisting, tradition-transgressing religion of these artists (or, should Elkins prefer, "artists") is precisely the kind of religion Elkins's modernism has enabled. And it is an approach to religion the category of the sublime has enabled by generating a *sine qua non* for religion—a tradition-crossing spectrum, a practice/belief-independent force to particular religions.

In addition to failing to see the modernism of the very category of religion, Elkins also fails to narrate the way contemporary art is skeptical of the religious sensibility of the art of high modernism. In other words, modern art was also indebted to the sublime to make its own religious claims for transcendence—a fact that much of the art world now finds embarrassing. No one—artist, "artist," judge, or critic—in Elkins's descriptions of the world of art, is seeking after the sublime. Art has repudiated such seeking almost as vehemently as religious studies. It has sought other means of understanding and redefining itself. Late nineteenth- and twentieth-century movements like the Arts and Crafts movement and Bauhaus sought to resist the distinction between arts and crafts and to revalue traditional crafts. Yet what it meant for these crafts to be valued—to receive recognition, interpretation, and funding—has been determined by the arts establishment. So rather than moving beyond the polarization of arts and crafts, these movements simply expanded the canon of what counts as art. Certain bowls that are displayed

126. Elkins, "How Some Scholars Deal with the Question," 70.

127. Ibid., 71.

128. Ibid.

129. Ibid., 72. In another text, Elkins writes, "Most religious art—I'm saying this bluntly here because it needs to be said—is just bad art" (*On the Strange Place of Religion*, 20).

130. Elkins, "How Some Scholars Deal with the Question," 22.

in museums are validated *as art* and by the arts establishment. They are set apart from bowls made merely as crafts, which continue to command lesser recognition and funding. Similarly, the "Outsider Art" popularized by Roger Cardinal's 1972 book of the same name initially appears to reject the art establishment by valorizing as artists those untrained in art institutions—especially the mentally ill, children, and "folk, self-taught, and naïve art."[131] Here shades of the repressed sublime return. This art is celebrated because it "gives one the sense of entering another world,"[132] taps into "automatic creativity"[133] and its origin in the "psychic elsewhere."[134] This begins to sound like the transcendent, the holy, or sublime that defies tradition and location. Yet these are only shades of sublimity (and it is, of course, still the art establishment that names something [Outsider] art). In general, the sublime has been pushed to the margins of the art world, to the annals of art history, along with religion.[135]

The fields of religious studies and art in the North Atlantic world consolidated for a time around the sublime because it described a reality that was ultimate, significant, and weighty. As those disciplines moved away from a category that began to be seen as crypto-theological, beauty remained at the margins. It remained, at least, at the margins of intellectual discussion—a status secured by its saturation of the marketplace. Beauty became synonymous with market desirability. It named a realm of products for sale that humans (women) could use to increase their own desirability; it named sections of newspapers and drugstores devoted to the same. Gone from academic journals and art institutions, beauty was increasingly discussed in women's magazines and advertising agencies. Cast as the frivolous feminine against the sublime's masculinity in the eighteenth century,

131. Beardsley, "Imagining the Outsider," 10. My thanks to Rosalind Carnes for introducing me to this phenomenon and bringing this book to my attention.

132. Ibid., 11.

133. Ibid., 12.

134. Ibid., quoting Cardinal, "Surrealism," 95.

135. In a call for papers for a recent conference sponsored by the Museum of Contemporary Art in Montreal and Concordia University, the conference organizers note that "the world of contemporary art seems to have preserved a form of discursive inhibition vis-à-vis the issue of religion." At the conference itself, art professionals from museums and universities expressed fear at what could happen to their careers should they try to publish themes from their conference conversations, and one person explained that much of the reticence around religion stems from a desire for contemporary art to distinguish itself from the high modernism of Kandinsky, Mondrian, and the like. Fourth International Max and Iris Stern Symposium: Art + Religion, Musée d'Art Contemporain de Montréal and Concordia University, Montreal, Canada, April 25–27, 2010.

twentieth century beauty lived into this identity with a vengeance. Beauty was the realm of cosmetics, the ornamental, the decorative. Its final form was inscribed into an idealized female body in whose image many women since have been carved. In the eighteenth century, beauty began to name the marginality of women in contrast to men. In the twentieth, it named another source of oppression: the impossible standard of Woman to which women were held.[136]

It was not a standard equally impossible to all women. In particular, it was not a standard equally (im)possible to all colors of women. In the North Atlantic—and especially in the United States—whiteness gained a privileged place in the beauty of Woman. Toni Morrison evokes the destructiveness of Woman's whiteness in her descriptions of young, black Pecola. She evokes the hatred, the isolation that bears on Pecola as her blackness is interpreted to her as ugliness. "Long hours she sat looking in the mirror, trying to discover the secret of the ugliness, the ugliness that made her ignored or despised at school, by teachers and classmates alike."[137] Morrison blisters beauty with her story of a girl destroyed by society's valuations of Womanly beauty. As beauty is marginalized within academia by being feminized, within the category of the feminine, black women are further marginalized by their *dis*-association from beauty. They are double-jeopardized. Marginalized for being women, they are also marginalized as women who fail to live up to the criterion (of whiteness) found in the ideal Woman.

Though the beauty of Woman is far from egalitarian, racial valuations of beauty have changed a little in the forty years since Morrison published *The Bluest Eye*. To the extent that the promise of beauty is extended to women of all colors, they are all targets for the net of the beauty market. This impossible standard of Woman was (is) sustained and masked by the realm of beauty products that promise its realization to female consumers. The explosion of and concomitant gendering of this industry is astounding: From the forerunners of the beauty industry in fragrances, soaps, and hair—marketed to and consumed almost equally by men and women—the beauty industry post-World War II had been almost completely feminized. By 1948, around 90 percent of women used lipstick and two-thirds used

136. In her landmark book *The Beauty Myth*, Naomi Wolf argues that "the beauty myth" grew stronger in the late twentieth century "to take over the work of social coercion that myths about motherhood, domesticity, chastity, and passivity, can no longer manage" (11). She traces how diet and skin care industries became "the new cultural censors of women's intellectual space" and provided a new model to arbitrate "successful womanhood" (11). As beauty ideals determined womanhood, money determined beauty ideals. When women moved into the positions and institutions of public power, beauty, Wolf argues, "*became* money" (21).

137. Morrison, *Bluest Eye*, 45.

blush.[138] In the boom of the cosmetics market, beauty became an industry. Its association with the market only assured beauty was derelict in academia.

In his book *The Invisible Dragon*, Dave Hickey describes the loss of a critical vocabulary of beauty through its relocation in the market. "If you broached the issue of beauty in the American art world of 1988," he writes, "you could not incite a conversation about rhetoric—or efficacy—or plea- sure—or politics—or even Bellini. You would instead ignite a conversation about the marketplace. That, at the time, was the 'signified' of beauty."[139] The problem with beautiful art was that it sells, just as advertising sells.[140] Yet Dave Hickey, himself an art critic, writer, and teacher, was able to publish his book about beauty and art in 1993, and the work's popularity meant that it was republished in 2009. He has not started a beauty revolution in the art world, but he has participated in a growing chorus of academic voices on beauty. These voices include Elaine Scarry, who has argued for beauty's positive relationship with justice;[141] Alexander Nehamas, who has argued that beauty is a pressing human concern;[142] and Wendy Steiner, who has argued for the importance of beauty in conceptualizing the subject-object interchange in art.[143] In a book that records conversations from a recent symposium of art historians and aestheticians, Steiner names herself and these other three as authors of "beauty books." These works, she claims, are engaged in a difficult task. She declares, "Figuring out what 'beauty' might mean at this point in history and why it is being so frequently evoked is anything but an exercise in nostalgia. It is forward-looking, sometimes al- most oracular, demanding an awareness different from that of a critic, an art historian, an aesthetician, or an arts practitioner."[144] Such oracular exercises were ventured recently in theology, a field rather hospitable to oracles, be- ginning in the middle of the twentieth century. It was then that two thinkers in particular began a theological rehabilitation of beauty.

Recent Theological Performances of Beauty

The two theologians who may be most responsible for recovering the theo- logical significance of beauty in the twentieth century came to their projects

138. Jones, *Beauty Imagined*, 134.
139. Hickey, "Enter the Dragon," 4.
140. Ibid., 8.
141. Scarry, *On Beauty and Being Just.*
142. Nehamas, *Only a Promise of Happiness.*
143. Steiner, *Venus in Exile.*
144. Steiner, "Aesthetics and Art History," 160.

independently. They are Hans Urs von Balthasar (1905–88), a name familiar from the previous discussion of scholarship on Gregory, and Jacques Maritain (1882–1973), a French Thomist with a long-standing commitment to the arts and several long-standing relationships with artists. These friends included his wife Raïssa, who was a poet, as well as the painter Marc Chagall and filmmaker and multi-artist Jean Cocteau. Such friendships established an important context for Maritain's discussions of beauty, and themes of art and beauty figure prominently in his early work *Art and Scholasticism* (1920) as well as his later *Creative Intuition in Art and Poetry* (1953). In these books, Maritain in some ways resists the dichotomization of art and craft—as well as the glorification of the artist that attends that opposition—while reaffirming it in others. The way he understands beauty is important to how he understands the right relationship between art and craft.

In his discussion of the arts, Maritain frequently refers to the Scholastic discussion of *ars*, which does not divide art into fine arts and crafts. In fact, many Scholastic examples of *ars* are what we would name today as crafts. So, at one level, he chafes against the modern restriction of *ars* to the fine arts. As he resists setting apart fine arts as laying exclusive claim to *ars*, so he also wants to resist fine arts' exclusive claim to beauty. Beauty can be found in arts that are not fine arts, and fine arts have a particular *kind* of beauty. To conflate fine arts and beauty, Maritain claims, vitiates both art *and* beauty. In this last claim, he finds disciples in the painter David Jones and in letter-cutter and engraver Eric Gill. Yet there is an important difference between these two disciples with regard to a distinction Maritain articulates between fine arts and crafts or "useful arts." David Jones embraces the distinction, offering his own interpretation of it as naming the "gratuitous" and the "utile," while Eric Gill ignores it.[145] The distinction is important for Maritain because while "useful arts" may be beautiful, they are not ordered to beauty in the way fine arts are. Fine arts objects "have an intelligibility which exceeds that of a mere thing."[146] It is an intelligibility born of the creative intuition that animates artistic making, and it grants the fine arts a special—and more important—kind of beauty than crafts. Yet the beauty of fine arts remains kin to the beauty of craft, for its creative intuition results, not from the artist aiming at beauty or any such spiritual ideal, but from his careful attention to the object that he makes. In this way, the best artistic making models the best craft making—that is why they are both examples of *ars*—even if crafts

145. Nichols, *Redeeming Beauty*, 137. In his book that follows the trajectories of all three men, it is important that Rowan Williams follows artist David Jones in embracing this distinction as significant rather than craftsman Eric Gill in rejecting it. I explore Williams's decision further in the second chapter.

146. Ibid.

do not possess the same intelligibility as fine arts. To create a fine art is not the work of a superhuman genius who peers beyond the veil of this world to some transcendent truth or ideal. It entails the much more human activity of attending carefully to the object right in front of one's eyes. The beauty present in fine arts reflects the humanness of its creation by presenting a beauty that is finite, that is, for Maritain, "limping." Maritain's move, then, is to resist the deification of the artist while retaining a more modest description of inspiration, to temper the polarization of fine arts and crafts while keeping them distinct, to claim beauty can be found outside of fine arts while naming a beauty special to such arts.

While Maritain wrote to rescue beauty from improper conflation with the arts, Balthasar wrote to return beauty from its devastating dissociation from everything else. He wrote about beauty, he claimed, for a world losing the capacity to perceive and respond to it.[147] Insisting that philosophy, religion, and theology have abandoned it in their imitation of the sciences, Balthasar wants to begin his systematics with beauty.[148] And he does. He produced a seven-volume set on theological aesthetics titled *The Glory of the Lord* that develops theology in light of the beautiful—the transcendental historically outshined, he claims, by her sisters the good and the true.[149] In so doing, Balthasar hopes to return to theology "a main artery which it has abandoned,"[150] for, as the magnitude of the seven volumes should attest, the beautiful, for Balthasar, is not an idiosyncratic lens or side concern of theology. Questions of beauty are at the heart of theological knowledge. Beauty is central to theology, not only because through beauty we see the true and love the good, but also because at the heart of Christianity is the conviction that Christ is the form of God, that it is "through form [that] the lightning-bolt of eternal beauty flash[es]."[151] It is a conviction born out of his retrieval of Christian voices in the tradition, Gregory of Nyssa among others.[152] But it is also a conviction that requires him to elaborate beauty in relation to the sublime. In an essay titled "Beauty and Revelation," Balthasar writes,

> And since the beautiful comprises both tension and release, and reconciliation of opposites by their interaction, it extends beyond its own domain and necessarily postulates its own opposite as a foil. The sublime has to be set off by the base, the

147. Balthasar, *Glory of the Lord*, 1:19.

148. Ibid., 17–18.

149. Ibid., 9.

150. Ibid.

151. Ibid., 19, 29, 32

152. See, for example, Balthasar, *Glory of the Lord*, 1:39.

noble by the comic and grotesque, even by the ugly and the horrible, so that the beautiful may have its due place in the whole, and that a heightened value may accrue from its presence. Yet all that the history of art and culture, archaeology, and sociology are mainly concerned with would be inadequate were it not polarized through the experience of the whole mystery of being and the origin of things, *mysterium tremendum et fascinosum*. It is this which has always been the unique real occasion of the great religious or "mythological" art of all people.[153]

When Balthasar invokes beauty's "own domain," he describes that domain as including both the sublime and the noble. Thus he grants the sublime its own aesthetic moment, but he names the category of which the sublime is a species, not as aesthetics, but as beauty. Balthasar's sublime is no longer coequal with (much less greater than) beauty. Not only does beauty name that which the sublime can instance, but beauty also transcends the sublime's domain to include its opposite. This kind of beauty therefore properly describes the *mysterium tremendum et fascinosum* of Rudolf Otto, whom Balthasar mentions by name at the beginning of this book. "Art" is the result of the mystery of being, and thus art and religion join as expressions of and responses to a particular kind of beauty. In Balthasar's retrieval of beauty for theological aesthetics, beauty is the proper location of art, the numinous, the sacred, the holy. He performs an expansion of beauty, not by eradicating modern terms and categories like the sublime, the numinous, and art (modernly understood), but by integrating them into the architecture of the beautiful.

Maritain and Balthasar are two of the most important and influential theological voices on beauty in the twentieth century, and their approaches to beauty have become paradigmatic for many writing in the emerging subfield of theological aesthetics.[154] The most important theologian of beauty to emerge in the new millennium is also one of the most important theological appropriators of Gregory of Nyssa: David Bentley Hart. Describing his work as "an extended marginalium on some page of Balthasar's work," he valorizes beauty as the name for a Christian metaphysics, in contrast to the postmodern metaphysics of sublimity found in critical theorists.[155] Hart shows that postmodern thinkers' insistence that there is no truth becomes their new truth, and in this way, they respond to one totalizing project by crushing

---

153. Balthasar, "Revelation and the Beautiful," 105.

154. Balthasar has been particularly influential, as the recent publication of the volume *Theological Aesthetics after von Balthasar* testifies. Balthasar-inflected voices like those of Francesca Aran Murphy and Ben Quash are especially prominent in the field.

155. Hart, *Beauty of the Infinite*, 27.

it with another.[156] Theological aesthetics names the alternative Hart outlines of accepting the inability of dialectics to produce or arrive at truth (in
continuity with postmodern thinkers) while yet rejecting postmodernity's
totalizing metaphysical assumptions.[157] In other words, for Hart, there is
truth, but it cannot be secured dialectically. We must be persuaded to it by
perceiving its beauty, for in Hart's metaphysics (as in Balthasar's and Maritain's), beauty is the transcendental that manifests being. It is a metaphysics
based on the infinite, ordered beautiful, not the chaotic, totalizing sublime.
So the move Hart makes with respect to the beautiful and the sublime is to
transform them from aesthetic categories to names for metaphysical commitments. The Christian can therefore not see them as having equal status.
The sublime, for Hart, is but a violence-begetting myth. Abandoned by the
disciplines of art and religious studies as crypto-theological, the sublime is
repudiated by this theologian as pseudo-theological. Hart then spends the
better part of his volume elaborating a *dogmatica minora* premised on beauty, demonstrating how beauty is central to theological reflection on Trinity,
creation, salvation, and eschaton. Hart thus retains the opposition between
the beautiful and the sublime but demonstrates the narrow enfolding of the
sublime in contrast to the capacious generativity of beauty.

Conclusion

These forays into Balthasar, Maritain, and Hart supply a taste of how others
have made compelling cases for the centrality of beauty to theological reflection.[158] Each of these thinkers participates in both modern and premodern
conversations about beauty, speaking into the specific contexts and concerns
of the former while reworking ideas from the latter. Jacques Maritain retools
contemporary understandings of art in relation to beauty by drawing from
Thomas and the Scholastics. Hans Urs von Balthasar reconfigures beauty's
relationship to the sublime by drawing from a chorus of Greek thinkers.
David Bentley Hart works in the tradition of Gregory of Nyssa to recast the
beautiful and the sublime as metaphysical alternatives. All of these thinkers
take seriously the history of beauty without being determined by it. In so

---

156. Ibid., 8–9.

157. Ibid., 150.

158. Theirs is a project that importantly diverges from many in the emerging subfield of theological aesthetics, where understandings of aesthetics sometimes take their
shape unreflectively from the historical process outlined in this chapter. The result
can be rooting beauty in categories that it precedes: the imagination, fine arts, and the
affective.

doing, they have attempted to show that beauty is not mere ornament, nor is it marginal to truth, goodness, or Christ. This book continues their work, though with different questions and different answers—yet with no less of a debt to them. In their good company, Gregory of Nyssa can speak to beauty in modernity.

2

Beautiful Bodies, Beautiful Words

SIGNS OF A RADICALLY TRANSCENDENT GOD

In late modernity, academic discussions of beauty bristle with tensions. Many scholars see beauty as peripheral to the questions constitutive of their discipline. Others insist on beauty's significance, but they cannot agree on its orientation to community, use, or desire, so that beauty can bear little weight. Drained of content, beauty has become vacuous, a "general term of approbation" that notes a subjective response such that recent attempts to recapture its significance raise the question of what conceptual work it can perform.[1]

In the last chapter, I rendered some historical roots for such divergences and evacuations by tracing moments in the history of "the aesthetic," the museum, fine arts, and crafts. I argued that we in late modernity inherit a "beauty" that was reborn in the distinction of fine arts from crafts and then set adrift as fine arts pulled away from a category that had been feminized, marginalized, and commodified. Though beauty initially distinguished the *beaux-arts* from the useful crafts, beauty has since that time been excluded from the critical vocabulary of art. Most recently, its exclusion has been ever so slightly softened, but that is to say only that the art world has opened some gaps in the electric fence.[2] Market-promiscuous beauty still rarely enters the

1. It was Stolnitz who referred to beauty as a "general term of approbation," as noted in the last chapter. Stolnitz, "Beauty," 203.

2. For a book that tries to explore the possibilities in some of those gaps (yet ultimately seems foiled by the fence), see Elkins, *Art History versus Aesthetics*. The book records a seminar in which one participant—philosopher of art Diarmuid Costello— captures the difficulty I am tracing. At one moment in the conversation, he claims that

sacred space of the art world. Yet despite this current distance, the one-time intimacy of beauty and fine arts lingers in contemporary invocations of and silences surrounding beauty. Beauty remains marked by the history of its association with the *beaux-arts* as surely as it remains stigmatized by its association with the market.

Such marks and stigmas become problematic when beauty is invoked by those who ignore its modern history—and thus fail to see beauty's inherited associations and assumptions—or by those who ignore its premodern history—and thus fail to imagine an alternative to those associations and assumptions. Though my purpose here has not been to provide historical analysis of the dozens of centuries for which people have written about beauty, I do want to take beauty's modern and premodern histories seriously by reflecting on two features that have been determinative of the distinction between fine arts and crafts and central to the architecture of beauty across both premodernity and modernity. They are *use* and *inspiration*. In the last chapter, I described how these categories helped polarize fine arts and crafts, where fine arts aligned with non-use (disinterestedness), inspiration, and mind, over and against the use (function), skill/rule, and body of craft. While these categories were challenged by artistic movements in the twentieth century, they have not been wholly overturned. And they remain deeply important to conversations around beauty.

Beauty's relationship to use was an issue that not only divided fine arts from crafts but was also itself recast by that division. "Disinterestedness" came to name one alternative by calling for beauty's repudiation of use. When it became the reigning paradigm for thinking about beauty, some thinkers reacted against it by wanting to rehabilitate use, which came from an old line of thinking and talking about beauty. Over and against a "disinterested" model of beauty, they called for a "functional" model. I want to show the advantages of both positions but will ultimately argue that disinterestedness and functionalism obscure more than they illuminate. Drawing from Gregory of Nyssa, I will propose a third approach: fittingness and gratuity. In proposing fittingness and gratuity as an approach to beauty, I do not mean to suggest them as essences that inhere in a thing called beauty. I

"beautiful," as a descriptor for an artwork, is simply interchangeable with "good." Then he reconsiders his statement. "Given that, these days, beauty is used as a way of deprecating a work, as when one calls it '*merely* beautiful,' which would amount to calling it empty. Beauty, when predicated of works of art, needs to be invested with meaning by further explanations and elaborations. On its own it's empty as a judgment about the work" (56). Later he invokes Kant to describe the way beauty names the response of the beholder and says, "Perhaps that is why I find the idea of beauty unhelpful as a *critical* term; because it tells you more about how a work disposes a viewer than about the work itself" (56).

43

mean to suggest a model for describing how beauty works and how we talk about beauty.

After displaying the way Gregory fills out the fittingness and gratuity characterizing beauty, I will turn from *use* to *inspiration*. While use concerns the relationship of the beautiful to the beholder and the world, inspiration concerns the relationship of the beautiful object to the beholder and world *in the process of its being made*. There is, then, something of an asymmetry in the breadth of the problems around use and inspiration. All kinds of beauty can be thought of by the categories of fittingness and gratuity (so I shall argue), but problems of inspiration pertain only to human artifacts. Yet I bring these two sets of beauty problems together, not only because they both press and are pressed by the separation of fine arts and crafts, but also because we can think about each set of problems better in light of Gregory's doctrine of God as radically transcendent.

Gregory's doctrine of God will be central to reflections on beauty in this chapter because Beauty, for Gregory, names God.[3] Reflecting on who God is, then, tells us something about what beauty is. I will explore and convey the centrality of God to Gregory's reflections on beauty by threading throughout the chapter a conversation between the thought of Gregory and that of Plato. As mentioned above, the point of this conversation is not to argue that Gregory's relationship to Plato was unmediated by the near-millennium of history separating them. It is, rather, to illustrate how Gregory's doctrine of God opens up possibilities for beauty unavailable to someone with otherwise similar philosophical commitments about beauty. Particularly important in this regard is how Gregory transforms Plato's image of a ladder, which initially frames his reflections on fittingness and gratuity, and how Gregory renders Plato's account of inspiration more consistent.

Throughout these explorations of use and inspiration, *bodies* and *words* continually recur, largely because they figure prominently in Plato and Gregory's accounts of beauty. In the case of words, discourses constitute important moments in learning to perceive beauty, and rhetoric-making is explained with paradigms of inspiration. As for bodies, they are contested sites of beauty in the thought of both writers, and through their alignment with skill and rule, bodies also negatively define certain models of inspiration. For Plato and Gregory, both bodies and words are extraordinarily dangerous and extraordinarily important. Descriptions of bodies and words are therefore bound up with Plato's and Gregory's most profound reflections on beauty.

---

3. I will use "Beauty Itself" to refer to beauty as a name for God.

For Gregory, bodies and words, like Beauty Itself, are most fully interpretable within his doctrine of God. Gregory's Beauty, as a name for a radically transcendent God, becomes paradigmatic for all instances of beauty, including bodies and words, fine arts and crafts.[4] It turns out that fittingness and gratuity are ways of describing the participation of beautiful objects in the radical transcendence and immanence of Beauty Itself. Such theological reflections on beauty do not take the shape that many modern conversations do on the same. Perhaps that is not surprising. But neither do his reflections, we shall finally see, take the same shape as Plato's, though the difference between these two is subtler. It will take us the course of the chapter to discern the nature and stakes of these differences, for we begin with where they are similar: in their resistance to functionality and disinterestedness.

Fittingness and Gratuity as an Alternative to Functionality or Disinterestedness

Of all the eighteenth-century articulations of disinterestedness, it was Immanuel Kant's that seeped most deeply into the discourses of art and beauty. Buttressing a model of beauty as utterly distinct from any concept of use or sensual pleasure, the Kantian notion of disinterestedness became the dominant criterion for making judgments about beauty.[5] I will call this model *disinterested beauty*. It is not a model that all scholars have found entirely

4. In writing about beauty, Gregory uses both *kallos* (the noun *beauty*) and *kalos* or *to kalon* (beautiful, the beautiful). It seems he often uses *kalos* or *to kalon* to refer to the beauty that participates in *kallos*, which, while not exactly unparticipated beauty, often denotes divine beauty. Further study across Gregory's corpus is required to characterize his use of these terms, but he seems to use them similarly in the beauty-centric text *Life of Moses*, though this verbal relationship is often obscured in Ferguson and Malherbe's translation, which renders *kallos* as beauty or the beautiful, and *kalon* and *kalos* as good, the good, excellent, or beautiful.

5. Some writers of art and beauty have found Kant more hospitable to function than the picture I will draw of his thought suggests. Most influentially, George Dickie works on Kant's understanding of purposiveness to recover a concept of function internal to Kantian appreciation of art and beauty, so that beauty names the appearance of a purposive design found in natural organisms and found analogously in art. Dickie provides this characterization of Kantian purposiveness, however, only to dismiss it as untenable. Moreover, Paul Guyer points out the way that Dickie mis-places purposiveness in Kant's aesthetic appreciation. The purposiveness Kant outlines refers to the subjective purposiveness of our cognition and the intentional purposiveness of artistic making. The analogy, then, flows the other way: We understand some natural phenomena by the analogy of art. Guyer is clear, however, that this has nothing to do with how Kant understands beauty: "We do not understand beauty in either nature or art on the basis of a prior conception of organic function, let alone its supposed distinctive appearance" ("History of Modern Aesthetics," 33).

satisfying. Some philosophers began to claim functional beauty as an alternative to disinterested beauty. These functionalists understand beauty in terms of use or purpose: a craft-like model of beauty that began challenging disinterestedness around the same time that crafts began challenging the hegemony of fine arts. The rise of crafts and the re-examination of beauty's relationship to function are indebted to the late nineteenth- and early twentieth-century Arts and Crafts movement, which sought to valorize the artisan in an increasingly industrialized world. One offshoot of that movement was the post-World War I German Bauhaus school, which sought to reintegrate fine arts and crafts into a total art in which form followed function.[6] The return of functionalism, then, has followed on the valorization of craft, much as disinterestedness developed in conversations about what set the fine arts apart from other arts.[7] These historical associations of disinterestedness and functionality with fine arts and crafts also name their limitation: their roots in an opposition that drastically limits the phenomena they can illumine. What can disinterestedness tell us about the beauty of craft? Or functionality about the beauty of fine arts, faces, or friendship? It is not impossible that these categories may shed light on such phenomena, but surely there are concepts better suited to it. If we want to find a way of naming the relationship between the beauty of fine arts and crafts, functionality and disinterestedness seem ill-suited to the task. But before I search for alternative concepts, I want to sketch moments in the history of these current ones.

The idea that the beauty of an object can be explained solely, principally, or partially by considering its function is an idea that dates at least back to the fifth century BCE. It was then that Xenophon's Socrates gave utilitarian beauty its most colorful formulation by insisting that a dung-basket well suited to its purpose was beautiful, whereas a golden shield ill-suited to its was not.[8] The association of beauty and use has an admirable

6. The founder of this school, Walter Gropius, framed Bauhaus as such a reintegration in his 1919 pamphlet for the Exhibition of Unknown Architects. At Bauhaus, they wanted "to create a new guild of craftsmen, without the class distinctions which raise an arrogant barrier between craftsman and artist" (Gropius, pamphlet for the Exhibition for Unknown Architects, Berlin).

7. Of course, this image is a bit clean for the historical reality. The Arts and Crafts movement, for example, was famously influenced by John Ruskin's writings on the relationship of beauty and art to a community's forms of production—though he was vehement that beauty was distinct from usefulness. Conflating the two, for Ruskin, confuses "admiration with hunger, love with lust, and life with sensation" (*Modern Painters*, 29).

8. Xenophon, *Memorabilia*, III.8.7. It is a position that contrasts with that of Plato's Socrates, who, in *Hippias Major*, rejects attempts to account for the beautiful by the useful as more laughable than the definition of the beautiful as a beautiful girl (297d).

pedigree, including such thinkers as David Hume, William Hogarth, and Adam Smith. But thinking of beauty in relation to utility fell out of favor as the model of disinterested beauty gained prominence. As articulated by Kant, disinterestedness means that an object is not properly appreciated aesthetically when it is appreciated for its use. The object must be appreciated "apart from concepts,"[9] which means apart from its specific relevance to the beholder—apart from sensuality and purpose. Neither determined by nor explicable through rules and concepts, Kant's judgments of beauty refuse assimilation to cognitive judgments. And neither defined by nor evocative of desire, Kant's notion of beauty resists assimilation to the agreeable. Kant locates the beautiful in a free play of the imagination and understanding. One virtue of this location is that it protects beauty from exhaustion by the beholder. There is a surplus to beauty that can never be captured by the purpose to which a person wants to put it. Kant's way of explaining this is to say that although judgments about beauty cannot be located in universalizable concepts, a person renders judgments of beauty in the universal voice (*allgemeine Stimme*).[10] That is, judgments about sensation are made in the particular—Canary wine is pleasant *to me*—but judgments of beauty suggest universal assent—that building is *beautiful*.

Kant dwells on the example of architecture in order to elaborate disinterestedness. In considering whether a building is beautiful, one puts aside questions about whether it functions to display power or facilitate great cooking. One does not consider whether it was made by the exploitation of others or how well it fits the need for which it was built.[11] More than

9. Kant, *Critique of Judgment*, 68–73.

10. Kant puts it this way: "If we judge objects merely according to concepts, then all representation of beauty is lost. Thus there can be no rule according to which anyone is forced to recognize anything as beautiful. We cannot press [upon others] by the aid of any reasons or fundamental propositions our judgment that a coat, a house, or a flower is beautiful. People wish to submit the object to their own eyes, as if the satisfaction in it depended on sensation; and yet, if we then call the object beautiful, we believe that we speak with a universal voice, and we claim the assent of everyone, although on the contrary all private sensation can only decide for the observer himself and his satisfaction. We may see now that in the judgment of taste nothing is postulated but such a *universal voice*, in respect of the satisfaction without the intervention of concepts, and thus the *possibility* of an aesthetical judgment that can, at the same time, be regarded as valid for everyone. The judgment of taste itself does not *postulate* agreement of everyone (for that can only be done by a logically universal judgment because it can adduce reasons); it only *imputes* this agreement to everyone, as a case of the rule in respect of which it expects, not confirmation by concepts, but assent from others" (*Critique of Judgment*, 51).

11. On this matter, Kant writes, "If anyone asks me if I find that palace beautiful which I see before me, I may answer: I do not like things of that kind which are made merely to be stared at. Or I can answer like that Iroquois Sachem, who was pleased in Paris by nothing more than by the cook shops. Or again, after the manner of Rousseau,

just insulating beauty from purely utilitarian conceptions of beauty, though, Kant wants to say that *use* is the wrong aspect for appreciating beauty. The beautiful is the "mere representation" of the object, the "pure disinterested satisfaction" that considers neither history nor use, sense nor purpose.[12]

Kant's insistence that an object's beauty not be tied to a purpose beyond itself mirrors his insistence that an action's morality is not derived from a source outside the human subject and requires that the human subject not be instrumentalized as a means toward a further goal. The non-instrumental nature of the judgments of beauty and ethics means that each can share something of the character of the universal: The universal voice in which aesthetic judgment is spoken gives it the appearance of universality so that the beautiful can represent the moral law in its universality. The self-effacement entailed in making disinterested judgments about beauty thus resembles the self-effacement of the categorical imperative in Kant's *Critique of Practical Reason*. The disinterestedness and universality of aesthetic judgment mean for Kant that beauty can be a symbol of morality. The divorce between beauty and use therefore has a larger role in his critical philosophy, though exactly what that role is remains debated.[13]

Schopenhauer expresses the divorce between beauty and use even more emphatically, claiming, "We rarely see the useful united with the beautiful. . . . The most beautiful buildings are not the useful ones; a temple is not a dwelling house."[14] In a discussion of trees, Schopenhauer goes one step further. Beyond claiming use has no place in explaining a thing's beauty, he additionally claims that useful things are rarely beautiful, that there is something about beauty that resists mingling with use. In such insistence, Schopenhauer and Kant buttress the category of fine arts emerging contemporaneously with disinterested beauty. In contradistinction to crafts, which are ordered toward specific purposes like covering feet or mixing batter or

---

I may rebuke the vanity of the great who waste the sweat of the people on such superfluous things. In fine, I could easily convince myself that if I found myself on an uninhabited island without the hope of ever again coming among men, and could conjure up just such a splendid building by my mere wish, I should not even give myself the trouble if I had a sufficiently comfortable hut. This may all be admitted and approved, but we are not now talking of this. . . . Taste is the faculty of judging of an object or a method of representing it by an entirely disinterested satisfaction or dissatisfaction. The object of such satisfaction is called beautiful" (*Critique of Judgment*, 38–39).

12. Ibid., 39.

13. There is an interesting body of literature exploring and debating other relationships between aesthetics and morality in Kant. See especially Cohen, "Beauty as a Symbol of Morality"; Guyer, *Kant's System of Nature and Freedom*; Guyer, *Kant and the Experience of Freedom*.

14. Schopenhauer, *World as Will and Representation*, 388.

decorating walls, fine arts serve no purpose of everyday life. That is why they require, so some argue, institutions set apart for their contemplation.

There is something about what Kant and Schopenhauer are striving after here that is important. There is a sense of disinterestedness that is important not to reject: the disinterestedness that opposes self-interestedness, narrowly understood. This kind of disinterestedness names the way, for example, a parent might in her best moments make decisions on behalf of a child. Such disinterestedness is not only perfectly consistent with purpose-lessness, but is itself a form of love that is even hospitable to certain kinds of desire. This kind of disinterestedness means something like unpossessivness, unselfishness, large-heartedness, generosity, and it identifies an important feature of beauty: that it can inspire a love that considers the interests of the beautiful one before one's own. But disinterestedness as it has come through the aesthetic tradition—the disinterestedness that stands for the evacuation of desire—is not necessary to protect the unselfishness of beauty.

Gabriel Richardson Lear elaborates the possibility for beauty both desiring and unselfish through Plato's account in the *Symposium* of the way beautiful things possess perfection ("immortally") and therefore elicit a desire that is not directed toward possessing a finite good for a specific amount of time. She writes,

> In this respect, then, Plato's account captures the intuition that when we experience something beautiful we step apart from or transcend our quotidian practical standpoint. We may believe that this phenomenon is best described by saying that aesthetic experience is disinterested. But stepping outside our ordinary, finite practical standpoint does not imply that we have stepped outside the practical standpoint altogether. For according to Plato, our desire for the good is infinite, although this is not something we ordinarily notice. Thus, it is no longer clear that we must find a disinterested aspect to proper appreciation of the beautiful.[15]

The way Lear describes a response to beauty that is not selfish and yet not evacuated of desire resonates with von Balthasar's reinterpretation of disinterestedness as God's splendorous display of the common cause of true love and true beauty.[16] It is because aesthetic disinterestedness makes it difficult to express this joining of love and beauty that I look to other terms to render their relationship.

---

15. Lear, "Permanent Beauty and Becoming Happy," 21.
16. Balthasar, "Another Ten Years," 213.

But it is not "love" that concerns functionalists in their critiques of disinterestedness. Whether because or in spite of Kant's explication of disinterestedness with the example of buildings, resistance to disinterested approaches to beauty has been brewing the longest in the field of architecture.[17] Most recently, philosophers like Roger Scruton and Allen Carlson have been working on architecture and functionality, and Carlson has also treated the adjacent field of agricultural landscape, thus linking architecturally grounded critiques of disinterestedness to critiques from another field growing in its hospitality to functional approaches to beauty: the environment.[18] Widening these efforts, Allen Carlson has joined with Glenn Parsons to retrieve functional approaches to aesthetics to displace the dominance of disinterestedness in modern conceptions of beauty.[19] While they are only two functional theorists among several, they are notable for the rigor and richness of their work as well as their attempt to describe the way function is involved in aesthetic appreciation across a range of fields: nature, architecture, artifacts, and fine arts. To do this, they develop a theory of functional beauty that describes an object's function based on its "selected effects." In the realm of artifacts, the formulation is this: "X has a *proper function* F if and only if Xs currently exist because, in the recent past, ancestors of X were successful in meeting some need or want in the marketplace because they performed F, leading to the manufacture and distribution of X."[20] They unpack how this criterion for discerning function works with the example of large-scale industrial farming. Responding to Ned Hettinger's argument that the communal or social uses and purposes of the industrial farm indicate that its function is to act as a "poison delivery system,"[21] Parsons and Carlson contend that the proper function of the industrial farm is

---

17. Walter Gropius, for example, was an architect, and some of the greatest successes of the Arts and Crafts movement were in architecture.

18. See, for example, Saito, *Everyday Aesthetics*.

19. Parsons and Carlson also trace a third theory of aesthetic appreciation: cultural models. While disinterestedness presumes a subject and object abstracted from their sociohistorical context, cultural models seek to understand art precisely in context. The example Parsons and Carlson cite is George Dickie's institutional theory of art, which holds that institutions determine what is art and how it is to be appreciated and criticized (*Functional Beauty*, 34–35). I do not treat it here for three reasons: first, because it is meant to illumine why something is called art, not why something is called beautiful; second, because Parsons and Carlson see it as paving the way for a potential return to functional beauty; and third, because I largely agree with it as a theory of art and find it compatible with fittingness and gratuity—as I will suggest later in the chapter.

20. Parsons and Carlson, *Functional Beauty*, 75.

21. It is an argument from Hettinger, "Carlson's Environmental Aesthetics," and it is expounded by Parson and Carlson, *Functional Beauty*, 87.

elucidated by the effect "by means of which its ancestors have passed muster in the marketplace."[22] Among the many ways industrial farms function, their *proper* function, according to Parsons and Carlson, is to deliver cheap food widely, and their aesthetic appreciation ought therefore to be indexed to the delivery of cheap food rather than the delivery of poison.

In the end, Parsons and Carlson affirm a weak version of functional beauty. Functionality, they say, is one important aspect of beauty but need not radically revise our understanding of the aesthetic. Whether the functional theory is strong or weak, to the extent it uses function to explain an object's beauty, it takes crafts (the useful arts) as its paradigmatic beauty rather than fine arts. While Parsons and Carlson prove that it is possible to write about the functional beauty of fine arts, they are able to do so by applying models they have culled from thinking about artifacts.[23] Fine arts and crafts, as they emerged as mutually defining ends of a polarity, model the similarly polarized disinterested and functional approaches to beauty.

At stake in functional and disinterested conceptions of beauty are different understandings of necessity. Disinterested theories of beauty locate necessity in the feeling that everyone *ought* to share one's judgment about the beautiful, thus evidencing the way a person does not experience a judgment about beauty as a desire particular to herself. Necessity, in disinterested approaches, is heard in the universal voice that names the way beautiful objects appear to a person *as beautiful*, not as beautiful *to me*.[24] Functional approaches to beauty locate necessity in the object's obedience to a set of rules governing the object's purpose. The constraint, then, is not

22. Parsons and Carlson, *Functional Beauty*, 88.

23. Moreover, Parsons and Carlson have some difficulty applying the selected effects model of functionality to artworks and settle on an affirmation of the plurality of uses for different artworks.

24. Kant says it this way: "But the *beautiful* we think as having a *necessary* reference to satisfaction. Now this necessity is of a peculiar kind. It is not a theoretical objective necessity, in which case it would be cognized *a priori* that everyone *will feel* this satisfaction in the object called beautiful by me. It is not a practical necessity, in which case, by concepts of a pure rational will serving as a rule for freely acting beings, the satisfaction is the necessary result of an objective law and only indicates that we absolutely (without any further design) ought to act in a certain way. But the necessity which is thought in an aesthetical judgment can only be called exemplary, i.e. a necessity of the assent of *all* to a judgment which is regarded as the example of a universal rule that we cannot state. Since an aesthetical judgment is not an objective cognitive judgment, this necessity cannot be derived from definite concepts and is therefore not apodictic" (73–74). Later he elaborates further what he means by "exemplary" necessity: "For the principle which concerns the agreement of different judging persons, although only subjective, is yet assumed as subjectively universal (an idea necessary for everyone), and thus can claim universal assent (as if it were objective) provided we are sure we have correctly subsumed [the particulars] under it" (76–77).

the appearance of universality, but the appearance of the object in relation to the purpose it serves.

These two approaches, of course, are not the only options for framing necessity. In his book *Grace and Necessity*, Rowan Williams formulates an understanding of necessity that counters functionalist approaches without falling into disinterestedness. Following Jacques Maritain, Williams locates necessity in obedience to the internal logic of an art object—an obedience that, when scrupulous, opens up a surplus of meaning in the art object. Williams in this reasoning retrieves Maritain's observation that fine arts have an intelligibility that comes from the creative intuition that animates artistic making, which itself requires not aiming for a transcendent ideal but attending to the demands of the object at hand. By locating necessity in a logic wholly internal to a particular artwork, Williams reclaims necessity from obedience to external rules like those of craft guilds or other extrinsic ends. Such reclamation protects the freedom of the artist and opens necessity up into the purposelessness required by disinterested theories of beauty. He frees necessity from purpose by introducing purposelessness, not merely in the act of appreciation, but in the act of creation. The freedom of the artist and the purposelessness of the art object yield a gratuity to art objects appreciated in the perception of beauty. Such freedom and gratuity are important for Williams because for him, the artistic act echoes God's perfectly free, perfectly gratuitous act of creation.[25] The gratuity yielded by scrupulous attention to internal necessity challenges a "vulgarized Darwinism" by refusing to represent the world-as-is as necessary.[26] "Internal" necessity thus protects against "external" necessity. In drawing purposelessness and freedom into the concept of gratuity, Williams distinguishes himself from a Kantian model by disentangling purposelessness, necessity, and freedom from disinterestedness. Williams's gratuity can coexist with desire in a way disinterestedness could not.

Desire is not the only difference between Williams's beauty and Kant's. The surplus generated by the artist's obedience to necessity is another way of naming beauty's transcendence, and it is inseparable, according to Williams, from beauty's woundedness. At one point Williams quotes Maritain, who writes, "A totally perfect finite thing is untrue to the transcendental nature of beauty. And nothing is more precious than a certain sacred weakness, and that kind of imperfection through which infinity wounds the finite."[27] As infinity that enters the world of the finite, beauty does not ter-

---

25. Williams, *Grace and Necessity*, 86.

26. Ibid., 156.

27. Ibid., 128. The metaphor of wound is one Gregory also picks up on in his

minate; there is a lack to it that evokes a longing, an "irritated melancholy."[28] Williams thus locates beauty's transcendence in an absence that is also an overflowing presence—a presence too full for the present. Such a transcendent beauty cannot be captured, Williams is certain, by functional models. Williams takes Eric Gill to illustrate a misappropriation of Maritain and a distortion of the role of grace in art. A sculptor and typeface designer associated with the Arts and Crafts movement, Eric Gill insisted, to Williams's dismay, that art be directed toward the good of a community with a shared ideology, and he challenged the distinction between arts and crafts.[29] Further, Gill disapproved of art as pure entertainment or purposeless end, which Williams sees as a betrayal of Maritain's commitment to the gratuity in art.[30] Where are the wounds in Gill? Williams asks.[31] Williams worries that Gill associates art too strongly with need and comes close to a "drastic functionalism" (an external necessity, for Williams) that undermines the graciousness of the artistic act. Williams concludes his book by reaffirming the importance of gratuity, insisting on the importance of human making as more than merely functional.[32]

Williams offers an important critique of functional models of beauty, yet what is elided in both Williams's repudiation of functional models of art and Parson and Carlson's retrieval of functional models of beauty is the extent to which functional beauty itself entails a kind of gratuity. Functional beauty is never merely functional. It is *exquisitely* suited to its function. A field is not beautiful simply because it fulfills the function of growing food. It may be beautiful if it is inter-cropped so the crops can give and take from one another the nourishment they need to live well. Or likewise: a knife is not beautiful simply because it can cut things. It may be beautiful because its weight is delicately balanced and its blade expertly curved for slicing so that every part of the knife seems perfectly suited to the purpose of cutting. Its absolute fittingness for cutting exceeds any general cutting need. Again, we might imagine a similar situation with a cup. There is no need for a cup that is perfectly shaped and balanced for the purposes of drinking. Most of us could drink out of an awkward or mediocre glass without real difficulty. The

---

Homilies on the Song of Songs and one that I will reflect on in the fourth chapter. "Wound" does important work for Gregory, but it never calls for the exclusion of need or function.

28. Maritain uses this phrase from Baudelaire in *Creative Intuition in Art and Poetry*, 128.

29. Williams, *Grace and Necessity*, 49.

30. Ibid., 53.

31. Ibid., 55.

32. Ibid., 160.

delicately crafted cup's perfect fittingness for my drinking from it, the way it is more excellently suited for drinking than I need it to be in order to drink out of, that it in this way exceeds my drinking purpose, is itself a gratuity.

In other words, while I think Williams's insistence on the significance of gratuity to art and beauty is right, such an insistence need not come at the expense of considering function's place within beauty. Moreover, to the extent that functional beauty itself entails gratuity, it cannot. Wrestling more with Gill could have helped Williams challenge Maritain's strong division between the internal necessity of an artwork and its external uses by interrogating what communal ideologies sustain the idea that an artwork has an internal necessity and how any particular internal necessity speaks out of and to commitments held by various communities and sub-communities. This is not to say that Gill himself operates with an especially sophisticated understanding of the permeability of internal and external, for in characterizing the fine arts as purposeless, he mistakes the way they have purposes proper to participation in certain institutionally sanctioned conversations. Those institutions are embedded in communities and cultures such that Gill's distinction between art directed toward the good of the community and art for purposeless ends softens once the wider contexts of purposeless arts are considered. He may or may not think they are directed toward good purposes, but they are purposes nonetheless. He also fails to see the way they have a beauty proper to those purposes. As Gill would acknowledge a beauty proper to, for example, a well-formed alphabetic letter—perhaps in the way it communicates clearly and expressively—there is also a beauty proper to fine art objects, perhaps in a luminous facility in the conversation in which the object participates. What makes the beauty purpose-fulfillment possible is a community with a shared set of commitments. But just as there might be beauty proper to these objects' purposes, there might be a beauty independent of those purposes. The brilliant glaze of a bowl has little to do with its capacity to hold fruit; the exquisite embroidery on a blouse says nothing about its suitability as clothing. The colors of the Matisse's *Harmony in Red* may be beautiful even for those uninitiated into institutionally sanctioned conversations the painting participates in. Surplus is located both in relation to function and completely outside of it. There is a beauty we may understand in relation to an object's purpose, but the object is not beautiful because it just fulfills that purpose, nor need *purpose* exhaust the way in which the object is beautiful.

The model of disinterestedness, in attempting to preserve the inexhaustibility of the object by the beholder, fails, like Williams, to recognize that function can entail gratuity, that function does not mean the subject's relation to the object exhausts the object. They thus try to preserve beautiful objects from such exhaustion and instrumentalization by trumpeting such mantras as "art for art's sake" and "no real purpose for art" in the realm of fine arts. Yet such mantras obscure the larger context in which objects and activities are always embedded. In disinterestedness, the beauty-beholder is effaced so that the illusion of objectivity—for disinterested theories of beauty always maintain such objectivity is illusory—can be maintained. But the insistent presence of disinterested theories of beauty have led to modern formulations of functional beauty that attempt to take context and beholder seriously by making beauty a utilitarian concept. Locked into avoiding one another's mistakes, these theories of disinterested and functional beauty are thus mutually reinforcing even as and because they are mutually excluding, much like fine arts and crafts.

Rather than treating the separation of fine arts and crafts as a site on which to negotiate the conceptual distinctions central to beauty and perception, I treat it as an important historical reality that can be freshly illumined by a conception of beauty founded on other terms. Gregory offers those other terms with the image of a ladder, with its horizontal rungs and vertical sides.[33] An object of beauty is as perfectly fitting and present as a rung is present to the foot and as perfectly gratuitous and future-pushing as the sides of a ladder, which beckon the climber ever upward, ever out of her present rung to the next, higher one. In other words, the sides of the ladder connect the lower rungs to the higher rungs as the gratuity of beauty connects the lower instances of beauty with the higher ones. The way the lower beauties lead to the higher ones is in their perfect fittingness, which opens up onto gratuity.

I propose that we think of *fittingness* instead of function both because it avoids the reductionistic, utilitarian ring of function, and because it suggests a wider nexus of relationships in which the object might be fitting. In so doing, it resists the strong and problematic divide of internal and external found both in Williams and Maritain's defense of fine arts and in Gill's valorization of craft. As it is not defined by an opposition of fine arts and crafts, fittingness might more usefully speak to both. It also provides ways of understanding paradoxical situations, such as how a thing can be both beautiful and unbeautiful at the same time. For example, Xenophon's golden shield might be quite ludicrous when one considers its fitness to serve as a shield, but once one considers it in a different context—perhaps

---

33. The ladder image is thematized with respect to beauty in Gregory's homilies on the Sermon on the Mount—homilies in which ladders and mountains interchange as images of ascent to God. The mountain provides an image of ascent in Gregory's *Life of Moses*, where beauty is found at the mountain's summit and beyond the summit. I treat these texts in chapter 3.

as a commentary on the war tradition—one might consider it quite beautiful, and its pointless golden radiance or intricate carvings might be integral
to that beauty.[34] Similarly, we can consider beauty both with regard to the
selected effects of the object at hand, as Parsons and Carlson wish to do,
without neglecting the communal and social purposes Hettinger found so
important. The category of fittingness allows us to invoke multiple levels
of context—the way a flower fits in a garden; the way that garden fits with
the landscape; the way the garden fits with surrounding community; and
so on. There are etymological reasons for considering the beauty through
fittingness as well. In arguing for the relationship between beauty and justice, Elaine Scarry points to the words' shared ground of *fairness*, which is
rooted (in European languages and in Sanskrit) in *fit*—"fit both in the sense
of 'pleasing to the eye' and in the sense of 'firmly placed,' as when something
matches or exists in accordance with another thing's shape or size."[35] To
speak of beauty in terms of fittingness, then, is to recover a historical line
that has not yet been wholly lost.

The historical line has been thematized in Greek as *to prepon* and in
Latin as *conveniens*, each of which has a history, though somewhat mixed, of
being thought together with the beautiful. The Greek, from the verb *prepō*,
suggests fittingness, properness, appropriateness, and is thematized by Plato
in relation to *to kalon* in *Hippias Major*, where he criticizes the idea that *to
prepon* could define beauty since *to prepon* speaks to contingent circumstances, while *to kalon* must speak to every circumstance. (Nevertheless,
something of the contingent and *prepon* appear, as we shall see, in Plato's
descriptions of the beautiful objects he encounters as he ascends to pure
Beauty Itself.)

Latin equivalents for *prepon* include *aptum* and *decorum*, but the word
that most often indicates beauty is *convenientia*, from the verb *convenire*,
literally a "coming together." Denys Turner explores the medieval theological use of this word in order to shed light on Julian of Norwich's use of the
Middle English "behovely." He describes *conveniens* as sharing something
of the character of necessity in the way "that it 'fits' against a background

34. It is interesting to wonder how fittingness relates to function in the case of
another famous golden shield in antiquity—Glaucus's shield in *The Iliad*. Meeting in
battle, two warriors, Diomedes and Glaucus, realize that they are from families bound
by a tie of friendship. They form a truce with one another and trade armor to honor
their ties. Yet Glaucus is described as having his wits stolen away, for "he traded his gold
armor for bronze with Diomedes, the worth of a hundred oxen just for nine" (Homer,
Iliad, Book 6, lines 281–82 [Fagles, 203]). Bronze is clearly the stronger metal, though
gold, of course, is rarer. How can we describe why this golden shield, even in the throes
of battle, is worth more (is more beautiful?) than the one made of stronger metal?

35. Scarry, *On Beauty and Being Just*, 91–92.

. . . which makes sense of it" (an interesting response to Plato's objection to *to prepon*) and yet remains contingent to the extent that it might have logically remained otherwise.[36] Such a description sheds light on the use of *convenientia* by Thomas Aquinas (who also ascribes to *conveniens* a version of the character of necessity) and Bonaventure, among many others, as they ask whether it is fitting that God would do a particular action.[37] It is exactly the kind of question Gregory of Nyssa asks with *to prepon* as he explores the Incarnation. How is it fitting that God would become human? What it means to posit something is *to prepon* of God in this way turns out to require a radicalization of *to prepon* in relation to beauty, for the God who is Beauty radicalizes our conception of fittingness.

Just as I suggest fittingness instead of function, I also suggest *gratuity* instead of disinterest. Gratuity does not refuse history and context the way disinterestedness does, and it does not efface the beholder. Disinterested approaches to beauty protect beauty from exhaustion by the beholder by claiming the beholder speaks in a universal voice rather than the voice of a particular person who can render the beautiful an instrument to fill his own desires and needs. To claim beauty as gratuitous is not to refuse a purpose or use to beauty; it is simply to claim that beauty exceeds any particular purpose or use to which a person puts it. Gratuity, further, requires rather than denies a specific relationship with the beholder. Though it precedes person, purpose, desire, and need, gratuity is always understood with reference to them and the way it exceeds them. Where disinterestedness protects the beautiful object's surplus of meaning by refusing to let an object's purpose illumine its beauty, conceptions of beauty's gratuity welcome purpose as

---

36. Turner, "'Sin is Behovely,'" 413, 416. Turner explains with the example of a Rembrandt painting, which could have been painted otherwise yet everything in the painting is "right, fitting, meet, must, beautiful, and, in a word, *conveniens*" (416). He continues: "So it is contingent, in the sense that you would have no sense of there being anything missing had we the painting without the patch of shading, and there is no antecedent requirement that it should be there in the bottom right-hand corner; but also it is 'necessary,' in the sense that the painting as it is sets up its own standards of expectation: we now know just how far a painting without that shaded patch would have fallen short of the quality of the one we have with it: when we look at the painting we can see that it has to be exactly as it is, but in a sense of 'has to be' that has nothing to do either with analyticity or with natural necessity" (416–17).

37. In the Treatise on Christ in the *Summa Theologica*, Thomas begins by asking whether the Incarnation was necessary for the restoration of humanity. Before answering in the affirmative, he distinguishes two senses of necessary: one in which an end cannot be had apart from the thing and the other in which an end is attained better and more fittingly by the thing. For more on "fittingness" as a mode of argument in Thomas, see Wawykrow, "Fittingness."

illuminative of beauty, and then also highlight the way the object exceeds that purpose.

In refusing to index beauty to disinterestedness, I follow a call Nicholas Wolterstorff issued to theological and philosophical aesthetics years ago in his book *Art in Action* and recently articulated in a more refined form in his contribution to *Theological Aesthetics after Von Balthasar*.[38] Identifying what he calls a Grand Modern Narrative of the Arts that argues art comes into its own through disinterested contemplation, Wolterstorff counters that narrative in five ways: first, by highlighting many of the historical details traced in chapter 1, such as the split between fine arts and crafts, artist and artisan; second, by pointing to many cases of religious artworks—altarpieces, for example, or icons—that disinterestedness cannot illumine; third, by relatedly pointing to *functions* these pieces serve, such as memorialization or worship; fourth, by pointing to the way that disinterestedness and the aesthetic are deeply implicated in political projects; and fifth, by insisting on a consideration of the social practice of artworks, which foregrounds the contexts and functions of art objects. Clearly, Wolterstorff's particular interest in his work on aesthetics is to discredit disinterested contemplation as the most valued mode of engagement with the arts, and beauty gets wrapped up in his critique to the extent that he fails to thematize a Grand Modern Narrative of Beauty along with his Grand Modern Narrrative of the Arts. What Wolterstorff has done for the arts in disentangling them from disinterestedness, I propose to do for beauty. "Fittingness" and "gratuity" will be important alternative categories for accomplishing that disentangling.

Functional beauty and disinterestedness each refer beauty to the concept of use to define beauty either positively or negatively. Each approach illuminates important features of beauty, but framed as competing options, they obscure beauty's true stakes by indexing it too strongly to use and evacuating beauty of desire. I have briefly sketched the possibilities of the alternative vision of beauty as *both* fittingness *and* gratuity for offering a richer account of beauty than *either* functionality *or* disinterestedness. The beauty described through fittingness and gratuity can account for the beauty of objects in terms of their purposes to particular individuals and cultures, the surplus entailed by purpose-oriented beauty, the particular beholder's relationship to the beautiful, and multiple levels of fit or purpose rather than one particular selected effect of an object. But these moves from functionality to fittingness and disinterestedness to gratuity are not just a vocabulary substitution. Fittingness and gratuity presume a different

38. Wolterstorff, "Beyond Beauty and the Aesthetic in the Engagement of Religion and Art."

subjectivity, divinity, and cosmology than function and disinterest, and I will unpack this difference over the course of the chapter. Fittingness and gratuity, moreover, characterize the way beauty works like a ladder for Gregory, while functionality and disinterestedness cannot provide such a characterization. With beauty framed by fittingness and gratuity, we can go deeper into Gregory's texts and cull from them characteristics of beauty that can fill out what fittingness and gratuity entail. By reflecting on strands of Gregory's presentation of beauty's relationship to rhetoric, I will tease out features of a fitting and gratuitous beauty that result when it is considered as Gregory considers it: a sign of divine presence that is also a form of divine presence. In considering beauty as a divine sign, I also want to explore the way the ladder, a prominent image in Gregory's descriptions of ascent both to God and Beauty, is also subverted as an image for both God and Beauty.

There is another advantage to thinking of beauty that is fitting and gratuitous. Disinterestedness and functionality appear to eschew aesthetic training. Disinterested models of beauty generally display beauty, not as objective, but as simply given in some sense. Because aesthetic judgments are made in a universal voice, training to perceive the beautiful is rendered invisible by the disinterested theorist. For the functionalist, in contrast, training can be visible, but it is always training into a particular object; the sense of beauty arises from the sight or knowledge of the object. The more one knows about knives, the more one can judge a knife's beauty. For a functionalist, a beholder might better appreciate the beauty of the field by, for instance, understanding its landscape and relationship to its place, but there is no training into beauty *per se* that helps a person appreciate beautiful fields. Without a space for reflecting on aesthetic training, these two models have difficulty accounting for how a person either comes to judge rightly or how she goes wrong in aesthetic judgment—why one person finds this building beautiful and another does not. Yet a Nyssenian approach to beauty can not only describe how a person makes problematic aesthetic judgments or why the same object may be beautiful in one culture and ugly in another; it can also accommodate the best features of both functional and disinterested approaches of beauty. It can describe a beauty that includes fitness to contexts and purposes, in continuity with functional approaches, and a surplus of meaning, in continuity with disinterested approaches. Gregory can help give an account, that is, not only of how judgments of something's beauty can go wrong and be trained but also how judgments about what beauty *is* can go wrong and be trained. For it is essential to Gregory's approach to beauty that it is always, inescapably trained. He has moments of presenting beauty as self-evidently attractive, a beauty that draws us to God, but I will keep those strands woven together with his descriptions of coming to perceive beauty rightly. For when the training and formation that develops a person's sense of beauty is ignored, so are the social forces and institutions determining such training and formation. The importance of keeping training in clear view, then, is bound up with the importance of keeping open the possibility of social critique, which I will explore in chapters 3 and 4. For now, as I turn to Gregory's texts, I want to ask: Where does the training into beauty begin?

Initiation: The Work of Rhetoric

Bodies, Words, and Worded Bodies:
How the *Life of Macrina* Reinterprets the *Symposium*

The *Life of Moses* is one of Gregory of Nyssa's most famous texts and also one of his most beauty-centric. In it, he responds to Caesarius' question about how to attain perfect virtue by inviting his reader(s) to pursue Christian perfection by imitating Moses's ascent up Sinai. To ascend Sinai is to climb to True Beauty, in order to enjoy it "face to face."[39] Beauty, then, is at the heart of Christian perfection.

The movement of ascent evokes Plato's description of the same, and like Plato, Gregory is concerned with how one begins such an ascent. He introduces this issue with the question, "How shall I place myself in the same rank with [one such as Moses], when I do not know how to imitate anyone so far removed from me by the circumstances of his life?"[40] His first answer in response to this question is to provide a *historia* of Moses's life. He dwells on the details of the scriptural account, explaining and augmenting them where it seems to him necessary. But at the end of his account, he returns to the beginning of Moses's life and asks, "How shall we as a matter of choice imitate this fortuitous birth of Moses?"[41] So grounded in the *historia* of Moses's life, Gregory provides in this second account of Moses's life a *theoria*, or a contemplation, of the significance of Moses's life. Like a good student of Alexandrian hermeneutics, Gregory commends spiritual exegesis to his reader. A person must allegorize Moses's life in order to imitate it, and Gregory does the difficult work of providing an allegorical reading for us. But he cannot do all the work for us. In the conclusion of the *Life of Moses*, Gregory summarizes what he has done:

---

39. Gregory of Nyssa, *Life of Moses* II.232 (Ferguson and Malherbe, 115).

40. Ibid., I.14 (Ferguson and Malherbe, 32).

41. Ibid., II.1 (Ferguson and Malherbe, 55).

> These things concerning the perfection of the virtuous life, O
> Caesarius man of God, we have briefly written for you, tracing
> in outline like a pattern of beauty the life of the great Moses so
> that each one of us might copy the image of beauty which has
> been shown to us by imitating his way of life.[42]

Gregory characterizes his method of reading as tracing the pattern of beauty
in Moses's life, a process the reader (Caesarius) is exhorted to replicate in
his imitation of Moses. In other words, Gregory has translated the beauty
of Moses's life in Scripture into a text that, presumably, makes beauty more
accessible to the reader so that he can make the further translation from text
to life. But generating a further text cannot ultimately solve the problem of
how to identify beauty such that it can be translated into a life. Or can it? If
one knows true beauty only by imitating Moses's journey up Sinai, how does
she acquire the sense of beauty required to read about Moses and translate
his beauty into her life? Relatedly, where does a person, blind and wounded
as she is, acquire the desire to imitate Moses in the first place? Where does
the training into beauty begin?

Where Gregory is elliptic, Plato is straightforward. Socrates famously
describes the teaching of wise Diotima, who lays out the ladder of beauty
that he recounts in the *Symposium*. She is unambiguous, though still doubtful that Socrates will be able to follow her advice. "The correct way for
someone to approach this business," she says, "is to begin when he's young
by being drawn towards beautiful bodies."[43] At first, if his guide leads him
correctly, he should love one body and in that relationship produce beautiful discourses. The teacher-guide then introduces the lover to the beauty of
other bodies, convincing him to regard the beauty of all bodies as one and
the same. Thus his passion for the particular body of stage one slackens, and
he is able to progress to the beauty of souls. The second stage requires the
first even as it also cures it.

Diotima's beauty-lover is not just a passive beholder. He must give
speeches. Diotima particularly connects the love of beauty with the production of beautiful discourses in two of the stages: in the love of the one
beautiful body, which I just quoted, and in the love of beautiful forms of

---

42. Ibid., II.319 (Ferguson and Malherbe, 136–37). With key Greek phrases: "These
things concerning the perfection of the virtuous life, O Caesarius man of God, we have
briefly written for you, tracing in outline like a pattern of beauty [τι πρωτότυπον ἐν
μορφῇ κάλλους . . . ὑπογράψας] the life of the great Moses so that each one of us might
copy the image of beauty which has been shown to us [μεταγράφειν τοῦ προδειχθέντος
ἡμῖν κάλλους τὸν χαρακτῆρα] by imitating his way of life [διὰ τῆς τῶν ἐπιτηδευμάτων
μιμήσεως]."

43. Plato, *Symposium* 209b (Gill, 46–47).

knowledge. At this latter point, the lover will look upon the "great sea" of beauty and in a boundless love of knowledge give birth to discourses and ideas both beautiful and magnificent.[44] Beauty, then, is first identified in beautiful bodies and then acts as a midwife for discourses, just as the notoriously ugly Socrates serves as a midwife for wisdom in *Theaetetus*. The metaphor is almost complete: Beauty is the midwife and discourses are the children. The missing link comes earlier in Diotima's teaching: That with which the person is pregnant is (not discourses but) a desire for immortality. All humans are pregnant, Diotima explains, either in body or soul. Those in body pursue immortality through having children, those in soul through honor and virtue. Both need to encounter a beautiful body to give birth.

The analysis here is deeply gendered, for the one—the man—pregnant in body seeks a woman with whom he can give birth to immortality through bearing children, while the man pregnant in soul seeks a beautiful (male) body with a beautiful soul who can discuss what is necessary for a good man.[45] Women here are doubly displaced. On the one hand, attributing pregnancy and the honor of child-bearing to the man displaces women. Yet pregnancy of the body is not even the right kind of pregnancy by which to pursue immortality. Pregnancy of the soul is. For the *men* united by soul-pregnancy bear immortal "children" of honor rather than the less desirable human, mortal children born by partnership with women. The result of such children is the rise of cults to honor these men.[46] Ultimately the hope is that the men will progress from giving birth to images of virtue like honor and fame to giving birth to virtue itself, which they can do after seeing Beauty. Thus Plato puts into the mouth of his most famous female character a reinscription of male as soul, virtue, and immortality, on the one hand, and female as body, mortality, and death, on the other. Pregnancy, moreover, becomes the business of men, for it is a man's pregnancy that gives birth to immortality in either body or soul, and the presence of a woman only signifies that the immortality is of an inferior kind.

Women, as David Halperin notes in his essay "Why is Diotima a Woman?" have been abstracted away in the *Symposium*. They are tools to think with, present in the text to help Socrates reflect on the "feminine" attributes of procreativity and receptivity, which Socrates then claims as part of his male philosophical ego. Woman has been annexed to man, her presence as abstraction and memory secured and rendered safe by the absence

44. Ibid., 210d (Gill, 48).

45. Man: ἀνήρ rather than the gender-neutral ἄνθρωπος.

46. Men: again, a form of ἀνήρ.

of any particular woman.[47] Even the girl flute player is sent away before the philosophical conversation begins, echoing the *Phaedo* in which Socrates sends his wife Xanthippe away to converse with his male friends before he dies. There are more generative possibilities for women at other points in Plato's writing—possibilities opened by his prioritization and de-gendering of the soul—but these possibilities here are not only unexplored, they are foreclosed by the alignment of male with soul over and against the female and body.[48]

Plato definitively subordinates body to soul in Diotima's analysis of immortality, but then he also emphasizes the importance of body in beginning the ascent to Beauty. Like Plato, Gregory also initiates training into beauty with beautiful bodies. If the *Life of Moses* exhorts its reader to apprentice herself to Moses, following him up Sinai to find true beauty, it also gives the reader a beautiful Moses. So beautiful is he, according to Gregory, that his beauty twice saves his infant life: once in causing his parents to draw back from obeying Pharaoh's orders to kill male babies and then again in moving Pharaoh's daughter to draw him out of the Nile.[49] His beauty is named a final time at the end of Gregory's first narration of his life, where the reader is assured that time had not diminished Moses's beauty: "Always remaining the same, he preserved in the changeableness of nature an unchangeable beauty."[50] It is a passage that resonates with Diotima's similar description of beauty as neither increasing nor diminishing, nor ever changing.[51]

But where Plato has no place for fleshly, mortal women in the rise to Beauty—unless she is invoked, like wise Diotima, as memory—Gregory foregrounds his sister Macrina and her beauty in his *Life of Macrina (Vita Macrinae)*. As female, her beauty is dangerous in a way that Moses's is not. Where Moses's beauty saves his life and gives evidence of his virtue, Macrina's threatens her pursuit of virtue by making her a highly attractive marriage prospect. Anticipating the problems her beauty will generate in his narrative, Gregory troubles her womanhood before mentioning her beauty, acknowledging that a woman is the subject of his narrative but querying

47. Halperin, "Why Is Diotima a Woman?" 149–51.

48. One interesting moment of gender equality occurs in Plato's *Republic* 454E, when Plato explains that there is no essential difference in nature between men and women. This anthropological point is made in the course of a political one: Women should, like men, serve as guardians for the city. Women may be handicapped by physical weakness, but virtue resides in the soul, and because the soul is neither male nor female, women can equally exhibit the virtue requisite for guardianship.

49. Gregory of Nyssa, *Life of Moses* I.16, I.17 (Ferguson and Malherbe, 33).

50. Ibid., I.76 (Ferguson and Malherbe, 50).

51. Plato, *Symposium* 211a (Gill, 48–49).

whether one who has so risen above nature ought to have such a nature-derived term applied to her. Womanly beauty is dangerous, seductive, and in competition with the life of virtue—in this text, primarily because of men who are fleshly and worldly. While Plato spiritualizes Diotima as a memory, Gregory spiritualizes Macrina to an almost angel-like status. Her bodily beauty remains, yet Gregory's Macrina refuses to be identified with the possibilities it offers; spurning marriage, she seeks a greater beauty, a better immortality.

Macrina is not the only beautiful body in the *Life of Macrina*. The text teems with beautiful bodies: Emmelia, Naucratius, and Vetiana are all described as beautiful. These beautiful bodies intertwine with the beautiful rhetoric in and of the text, and the work they do illuminates what beauty is for Gregory and how the apprehension of true beauty begins.

The first beautiful body of the text is Macrina's mother Emmelia, who maddens suitors with her famous blooming beauty. The text hints darkly at the threat these mad suitors pose: the possibility of violence and of her being carried off. Orphaned and recognizing this danger, Emmelia abandons her decision to remain a virgin and chooses a suitor-protector wisely: one known for his uprightness, who could be a guardian to her. The first child she bears with him is Macrina, a girl even more beautiful than herself, her youthful beauty rendering her a marvel to her homeland and surpassing the capacity of painters to represent it. Macrina tries to conceal her beauty, but like her mother, she, too, is swarmed with suitors. Unlike her mother, she has no choice to make. Her marriage is her father's choice; yet, fortunately for Macrina, her father is a man practiced in discerning the *kalon*. Gregory at this point draws the first explicit connection between *logos* (word, speech, reason, argument, account) and beauty in the *Vita*. Her father's ability to discern the beautiful means he chooses for Macrina a suitor with great rhetorical ability, one who uses this ability for the good—as Gregory emphasizes, to argue lawsuits on behalf of the wronged. The suitor gives his reputation for *logos* like a wedding gift to the family.[52] Two different beauties are discerned here. The first (a beautiful body) is obvious, despite attempts to hide it, while the second (beautiful words) requires some discernment, despite no attempts to obscure it. That is, Macrina's beauty is discerned

---

52. "Her father (he was wise and considered outstanding in his judgment of what was good) singled out from the rest a young man in the family known for his moderation, who had recently finished school, and he decided to give his daughter to him when she came of age. During this period, the young man showed great promise and brought to the girl's father (as a cherished bridal gift, as it were) his reputation as an orator [τὴν διὰ τῶν λόγων εὐδοκίμησιν], displaying his rhetorical skill in lawsuits in defense of the wronged" (Gregory of Nyssa, "Life of Saint Macrina" 4 [Callahan, 165–66]).

by the suitors, though she tried to conceal it, while her father discerns the beauty of the suitors—and the beauty he sees is the beauty of the *logos*. Macrina's father acquired his practice in discerning the *kalon* through his own career as a *sophistikes* (sophist, rhetor).[53]

When her fiancé dies before the wedding, young Macrina seizes her opportunity, elaborating a theology of the resurrection that would make any further betrothal an act of infidelity. She can now live in virginity, and when Macrina's father dies, Emmelia and Macrina pursue the monastic life together, protecting their lifestyles by managing their beauty with great modesty. Her own life refuses containment by the small and inferior place Plato's Diotima grants women in the pursuit of Beauty. Macrina will not help men "pregnant in body" bear children destined for death. She pursues a life of chastity, which opens up her access to the beauty of *logoi* (and, ultimately, the *Logos* who is Beauty Itself). In Gregory's *On the Soul and the Resurrection (De anima et resurrectione)*, as in the *Life of Macrina*, it is also Macrina's wit and wisdom (her *logos*) that helps both Gregory and herself through a potential stumbling block to Christian virtue: excessive grief over the death of Basil and Macrina's own impending death. Macrina's virtuous life is correlated with, safeguarded in, and evidenced by, not her beauty, as Moses's is, but her *logos*, which she develops from Scripture. Still, Macrina is depicted as beautiful and so is Emmelia. They are objects of desire who lend their desirability to Christ through their devotion to him.

For Macrina and Moses, words and rhetoric both displace and draw on the beauty of their bodies. Macrina's own words and reasoning displace her beauty in determining her life trajectory, even as the beauty of her body and the possibilities such beauty promises for her augments the desirability of the life she chooses. In Gregory's rhetorical construction of Moses, the beauty of Moses's body is both represented in and displaced by Gregory's writing about his beauty. The same is true of Gregory's brother Naucratius.

The next beautiful body in *Life of Macrina*, Naucratius, excels in his beautiful body as well as his swiftness, his strength, and his capacity for everything, including rhetoric.[54] He is never called a rhetor, like Macrina's betrothed, nor a sophist, like Macrina's father, nor is he ever described as working with *logoi*, but at the age of twenty-one, he gives a public hearing that deeply moves the audience.[55] Rather than pursue a promising career,

53. Gregory of Nyssa, "Life of Saint Macrina," 21.12.

54. In his beautiful body: σώματος κάλλει.

55. Gregory of Nyssa, "Life of Saint Macrina" 8.3, 8.6 (Callahan, 168). Gregory does not seem to attach much significance to the distinction of rhetor and sophist. They seem to mark vocational differences. Much more important to Gregory's understanding of a vocation that tracks in words is what the person does with his word-making.

though, Naucratius is led by some divine providence to renounce these possibilities and is drawn by some great impulse of thought to a life of solitude and poverty.[56] Beauty functions for Naucratius similarly to how it functions for Macrina. As beauty for Macrina represents those worldly possibilities she gave up (of marrying well), so for Naucratius beauty functions as a sign of his great abilities more broadly, of which his capacity for rhetoric represents the worldly possibility he forsook (a career in rhetoric). Both give up the possibility for worldly greatness in order to pursue monastic lives—Macrina's in community and Naucratius's in solitude.[57]

The next beautiful body is Vetiana, a companion of Macrina whose beauty also functions to signify what she has given up. Then there is a Bridegroom, whose beauty will become important to the production of inspired discourses. But the final beauty in the *Life* is, once again, Macrina's. Like Moses, Macrina is beautiful in death. And like the beauty of youthful Macrina, dead Macrina's beauty cannot be concealed. Gregory and Vetiana place Emmelia's dark mantle over Macrina, but her beauty is luminous, shining through the mantle like rays of light. "But even in the dark, the body glowed, the divine power adding such grace to her body that, as in the vision of my dream, rays seemed to be shining forth from her loveliness [*kallous*: from beauty]."[58] The text never lets the reader leave the beauty of bodies. It continually returns to them, the final instance of a beautiful body the most compelling, pointing not to possibilities for worldly acclaim, but to divine power and grace. Macrina's beauty remains bodily but has been transfigured into a sign of divine presence. While it was always a sign of divine presence for one such as Gregory, who had eyes to see it, it is now a sign of divine presence for everyone. As such, it is no longer dangerous in the sense of tempting sexual response. Her body points to God. Even the once-cancerous breast that was hidden from doctors is laid bare for Gregory, also a sign of God's grace.

That bodily beauty can function as a sign of divine presence might seem to elevate the beauty of bodies above their role in the *Symposium*,

---

Macrina's betrothed proves his worthiness by arguing lawsuits for the wronged. The word *logos* has a more specific set of valences, which I will continue to unpack.

56. By some divine providence: θεία τινὶ προμηθείᾳ. By some great impulse of thought: μεγάλῃ τινὶ τῆς διανοίας ὁρμῇ. Gregory of Nyssa, "Life of Saint Macrina" 8.7–10 (Callahan, 168).

57. Basil is described as *kalon* as well, but in a sense that has little to do with his body. He is the common *kalon* (honor, nobility) of the family.

58. Gregory of Nyssa, "Life of Saint Macrina," 32.8–12 (Callahan, 186). ἡ δὲ ἔλαμπε καὶ ἐν τῷ φαιῷ, τῆς θείας, οἶμαι, δυνάμεως καὶ ταύτην προσθείσης τὴν χάριν τῷ σώματι, ὥστε κατὰ τὴν τοῦ ἐνυπνίου ὄψιν ἀκριβῶς αὐγάς τινας ἐκ τοῦ κάλλους ἐκλάμπειν δοκεῖν.

where they are a stepping stone to greater things, a rung on the ladder to be crossed and left behind. But if Gregory has elevated beautiful bodies by naming their capacity to signify divine presence, he has also taken away their great significance as necessary for the initiation into Beauty. While beautiful bodies are not the lowest rung on the ladder to Beauty, for Gregory neither are they on the ladder at all.

The narrative of Gregory's stories does not proceed as a Platonic narrative should. Readers are invited to pursue the beautiful Macrina, but the beautiful bodies of *Life of Macrina* do no favors to any of the characters who pursue them *qua* beautiful bodies. Emmelia's husband, though practiced enough in discerning the *kalon* to choose a good suitor for Macrina, is never represented as one who ascends great heights in the love of wisdom and vision of beauty. (If he had, presumably he would have been able to choose for Macrina the greater beauty of virginity, which Macrina herself preferred.) And Macrina's suitor dies away, nameless as her father is in this text. Macrina's beauty is different from that of Plato's beautiful body because her beauty is at a remove from the reader. The reader is not exhorted to encounter her beautiful body outside the text any more than the reader is invited to begin her ascent to beauty with any particular body she finds beautiful. No, the reader is not directed toward the beautiful body she is to pursue, and she is not invited to access that body outside the text. Macrina's body, like Moses's, remains rhetorically constructed—a worded body—and Gregory's provision of beautiful, worded bodies to initiate the ascent to Beauty is one aspect of a complicated relationship he constructs between words and bodies in *Life of Macrina*. What is important for Gregory as a stepping stone to Beauty in this text is not physical beauty but rhetorically represented physical beauty. Gregory wants initiation into the Beautiful to begin with rhetoric, not bodies.

At the same time, beautiful bodies do not disappear in the ascent to Beauty for Gregory, and the production of beautiful discourses ends up not just leading the speaker to beauty but making her beautiful. Macrina's bodily beauty bookends her narrative, and as her youthful beauty transmutes into the perfected beauty of her death, she speaks beautiful words in an attempt to assuage the grief of those listening to her. Producing beautiful rhetoric clarifies Macrina's bodily beauty as a divine sign. Where Plato's Diotima describes the initiation into Beauty as beginning with one body, producing beautiful discourses for that body, and then opening up into multiple bodies before leading to the immaterial beauty of souls, practices, and institutions, Gregory collapses those first stages all into rhetoric. Plato needs the initiate first to encounter one beautiful body because one learns to love in the concrete and then to translate the beauty of a body into words and to locate it in multiple bodies for her to see beauty as an intellectual (that is, spiritual or immaterial) property. But Gregory uses rhetoric, which is concrete, sensory, and intellectual all at once to perform this work for him of moving a subject from focusing on the sensory world to attending to the intellectual one. Rhetoric commends the soul and other beautiful sensory objects without ever leaving behind its sensuality. As spiritual yet also inescapably bodily, rhetoric acts as an important mediator between the two realms of beauty.[59] In this way, rhetoric echoes in beauty the place the human occupies in Gregory's cosmology, bridging the purely spiritual and the purely material, the divine and the earthly.[60]

Woven throughout descriptions of Macrina's bodily and rhetorical beauty are descriptions of Psalm-singing. The Psalms occupy a significant place in the *Life of Macrina*. Gregory attempts to model Macrina's holy serenity as she dies by exhorting the grief-stricken maidens attending her to Psalm-singing. The women then sing Psalms all night after Macrina's death, filling the place with their voices and so alerting the community of their holy mother's death. The more people who join, though, the more wailings and weepings punctuate the singing of the Psalms. Gregory, meanwhile, makes funeral arrangements determining how the Psalms should be sung at the ceremony (in a harmonious and rhythmic manner, as in chorus singing). The Psalms sustain the mourners through their procession into the church, but as their voices still for prayer, weeping overwhelms them. With Gregory according the Psalms a prominent role in the emotional and spiritual life of Macrina's community, it is unsurprising that he devotes a slightly later— though still early—text to their inscriptions. Equally unsurprising in light of the *Life of Macrina* is his determination to understand their effectiveness as rhetoric. As he analyzes them, Gregory finds a paradigm for how rhetoric should work.[61]

59. In this way, rhetoric performs a mediating role for Beauty Itself similar to that of the soul for Plotinus. For more on the status of soul as mediating the intellectual and sensory realms in Plotinus's metaphysics, see Miles' chapter on the soul in *Plotinus on Body and Beauty*.

60. For more on the place of the human in Gregory's cosmology, see *On the Making of the Human* (*De hominis opificio*), especially secs. 2.2 and 16.9.

61. Gregory understands the text of the Beatitudes in similar terms, as he describes it in his later work *Homilies on the Beatitudes*. For reasons I hope will become clear, I am reserving that text for chapter 3, when I will consider it in light of Gregory's Christological commitments.

Describing Perfect Rhetoric: *On the Inscriptions of the Psalms*

The *Life of Macrina* is a rich text that yields interesting twists on Plato's ladder. As one of Gregory's earliest texts, it discloses more transparently than some of his later ones how Gregory negotiates his relationship to pagan philosophy. At this early point in his career, Gregory is working out how to think about the education and training he received as a wealthy male with his Christian commitments to Scripture and asceticism. The next two texts to which I attend are also early texts, and like the *Life of Macrina*, they also show the scars of Gregory's wrestling with his education. They are *On the Inscriptions of the Psalms* and *On Virginity*, and they are particularly concerned with his rhetorical training. At the point of writing these works, rhetoric is still a problem for Gregory. His friend Gregory of Nazianzus has accused him of preferring the title rhetor to Christian, making clear to him that he has failed to find his measure as either, and Nyssen is trying to work out what it means to embrace both. As he becomes more comfortable with the possibilities and limitations he identifies in rhetoric, it disappears as a theme in his later works. (Rhetoric is also, as we shall see, surrounded with other, perhaps more powerful entrances to beauty. As Gregory begins to thematize the importance of the sacraments in perceiving beauty, rhetoric loses its special place as the singular entry-point to beauty—a shift I explore in chapter 4.) While I do not think Gregory ever leaves behind the importance of rhetoric, he does not make rhetoric an occasion for reflection in his later texts as he does his earlier ones. These early works are especially helpful as sources for how Gregory thought rhetoric was functioning in his thought.[62]

---

62. Brian Daley produced a vigorous translation of Letter 11. He captures Nazianzen's moment of chastisement and the question he puts to Gregory well: "Why have [you] turned your hand to salty, undrinkable literature, and wish to be called 'rhetor' rather than 'Christian'? We prefer the second of these names to the first, thanks be to God! Now don't you suffer this sickness any longer, my good friend. Sober up, late as it may be, and return to your senses; explain yourself to the faithful, explain yourself to God, and to his altars and his mysteries, from which you have distanced yourself! Don't speak to me clever, artificial phrases such as these: 'What, then? Was I not still a Christian when I practiced the rhetorical art? Was I not a believer when I associated with the young?' Perhaps you may even call God to be your witness! But the answer, my good man, is 'Not at all!' Or if we even grant part of what you should say, 'Not at all as much as you should!' Why shock others through what you now are doing, when they are naturally more inclined to evil than to good? Why give them the opportunity to think and say the worst about you? Perhaps it is a lie—but what need is there to prompt it? One does not live simply for oneself, after all, but also for one's neighbor; it is not enough to persuade oneself, if one does not also persuade others" (Gregory of Nazianzus, Letter 11, 174).

It is important that Gregory reflects on rhetoric with regard to the Psalms, for that book is the only one he names besides Proverbs as appropriate for novices entering the life of virtue. We have no commentary from Gregory on Proverbs, which is *primarily* for novices, but we do have this commentary on the inscriptions of the Psalms, which speaks to people at all levels of the life of virtue, *including* beginners.[63] How Gregory's text on the Psalms describing initiation into the life of virtue is therefore instructive for the place rhetoric has in Gregory's thought.

On the Inscriptions of the Psalms begins with turning from evil to good. There is a kind of conversion that must happen, and Gregory believes the Psalms enjoin a person to conversion. Before he describes how, Gregory deploys a strategy of his own to convince the skeptic (and explain to the Christian) why she should read or hear the Psalms in the first place. He identifies the virtuous life with blessedness,[64] which he claims as the purpose of the virtuous life.[65] So far Gregory might sound like many ancient philosophers, but he then identifies blessedness with the divine nature, claiming it alone is properly called blessed,[66] while human blessedness refers to humanity's divine likeness and requires participation in the divine nature.[67] The Psalms, then, set forth a sequence in teaching that describes the way to acquire this blessing that is also virtue and divinity.[68] Here Gregory describes the Psalms as a kind of guide to the philosophical life that yields God-like virtue and happiness.

But Gregory does not rely on something as general as the appetite for happiness to perform a task as tricky as conversion. Instead, he turns to the text of the Psalms to name how the Psalms perform that task, how they can move a person from general admiration for the life of virtue to "being in" virtue.[69] They do this by presuming that in the ubiquitous desire for happiness, the person untrained in the ways of virtue will use sensory pleasure as her criterion for pursuing happiness. The psalmist uses rhetorical tech-

---

63. See Heine's introduction to his translation for Origen's influence on Gregory in the *Inscriptiones*, particularly for how Gregory follows Origen in seeing Proverbs for the beginner, Ecclesiastes for the intermediate, Song of Songs for the advanced, and Psalms for them all. Gregory of Nyssa, *Gregory of Nyssa's Treatise on the Inscriptions of the Psalms*, 75. Hereafter cited as *On the Inscriptions of the Psalms*.

64. The word he uses is *makarios*. It is a word that means happiness, and it is also the word used in the Beatitudes.

65. Gregory of Nyssa, *On the Inscriptions of the Psalms* I.1.5 (Heine, 84).

66. Ibid., I.1.6 (Heine, 84).

67. Ibid., I.1.6, I.1.7 (Heine, 84–85).

68. Ibid., I.1.7 (Heine, 84–85).

69. Ibid., I.2.9 (Heine, 85).

niques that appeal to the senses to train a person into more sophisticated criteria for happiness the way a physician uses honey to sweeten bitter medicine.[70] One way such "sweetening" happens is through the musicality of the Psalms, by which the Psalms provide pleasure to the least educated: "even to women and children."[71] Gregory writes of such musicality providing an obvious pleasure in the Psalms:

> The reason we meditate on them with pleasure is obvious to everyone. For one might say that it is the singing of the words which causes us to go through these teachings with pleasure. On the other hand, even if this be true, I insist that we must not overlook what is not obvious. For the philosophy that comes through the singing seems to hint at something more than what most people think.[72]

There is a movement from the obvious pleasures of sensuality to the non-obvious pleasure of spiritual health. As mediating the sensory and the intellectual, rhetoric that rightly uses the sweetness of its sensory pleasures can train a person to meditate on more than she knows and so impress upon her the philosophy of the text that she may be transformed. It is crucial that rhetoric be deployed in the proper way, though, and Gregory goes to great pains to distinguish a music that obscures meaning (artifice) from a music, like the psalmist's, that brings out its intention.[73] Unlike the heavy-handed musicality of the lyric poets (as Gregory describes it), who add music onto words as something external and separate, the psalmist entwines music without design, music that is sympathetically ordered to the words, so that it reinforces and sweetens the words as sauces sweeten a nourishing meal.[74] It is the difference between a music that masks, that manipulates by wresting attention away from the words, and a music that clarifies by helping to elucidate the libretto. There is a kind of fit Gregory demands between lyric and melody.

In appealing to the sensuality of the hearer, the Psalms can train the intellectual perception of the hearers. According to Gregory, the psalmist uses at least two rhetorical strategies to move the hearer further along the path to virtue. The first deploys praise of virtue and censure of vice to attract

---

70. Rhetorical training was itself quite physical in late antiquity. It required physical exercise and discipline to master deep vocal tones, proper breathing, appropriate stances, and harmonious gestures. Van Dam, *Kingdom of Snow*, 184.

71. Gregory of Nyssa, *On the Inscriptions of the Psalms* I.3.23 (Heine, 91).

72. Ibid., I.3.17, I.3.18 (Heine, 87–88).

73. Ibid., I.3.25 (Heine, 129).

74. Ibid.

desire to the holy and produce hatred of evil.[75] The second—an important extension of praising and censuring—praises the examples of lives, for such examples "produce a certain intensification of the disposition of the soul and an obvious steadfastness, since hope attracts the soul to honour which equals that of the best, and hostile comment on those who have been censured trains the soul to flee and avoid similar pursuits."[76] Through these examples, not only is desire cultivated but discernment is trained, as one learns to move beyond the criterion of sense perception and develop a fuller sense of sight.[77]

Gregory compares the hearer of such discourse to an art object in process. He vividly describes the "orderly arrangement" of the work of a sculptor, how the sculptor breaks the stone she is to work with away from the rock, smoothing the protrusions and rough edges, hollowing out parts of the stone, and polishing it to produce the image of the model in the stone.[78] The Psalms similarly follow a certain order, which results in the hearer becoming a work of art. As Gregory describes how the Psalms work on us, he describes them as tools deployed through the agency of the Word.

> In the same way since our entire nature has become stone, as it were, through our propensity to what is material, the Word which is hewing us in relation to the divine likeness proceeds methodically and orderly to the end of the aim. First it separates us, as it were, from the attached rock (I mean evil, of course), to which we have been attached by participation. Then it trims off the excesses of the material. After this it begins to form that which lies within in relation to the likeness of the aim, by stripping off those things which hinder the representation. And thus it scrapes and polishes our understanding by means of more delicate teachings of ideas. Then, by means of the forms of virtue, it forms Christ in us, in accordance with whose image we existed in the beginning, and in accordance with which we again come to exist.[79]

75. Ibid., I.2.11 (Heine, 85–86).

76. Ibid., I.2.12 (Heine, 86).

77. Ibid., I.2.14 (Heine, 86).

78. Ibid., II.11.133 (Heine, 163–64).

79. Ibid., II.11.134 (Heine, 164). He appears to be reworking the following Plotinian passage: "Withdraw into yourself and look. And if you do not find yourself beautiful yet, act as does the creator of a statue that is to be made beautiful: he cuts away here, he smoothes there, he makes this line lighter, this other purer, until a lovely face has grown upon his work. So do you also; cut away all that is excessive, straighten all that is crooked, bring light to all that is overcast, labour to make all one glow of beauty and never cease chiseling your statue, until there shall shine out on you from it the godlike

The Psalms' perfect order and arrangement make them ideal tools in sculpting a person to become an image of Christ. The rule governing their perfection is likened to the rule governing a sculptor producing a sculpture. Gregory, then, uses the model of an art, a *technē*, to describe how the Word works through Scripture via its rhetoric to conform a person into Christlikeness. Gregory here describes the work of rhetoric with respect to divine agency, highlighting, as he does, that the creature's agency and virtue is nothing in and of itself; it is always founded in the agency of the Word. But Gregory's hearer is never simply an empty vessel to be filled with divine power. The very way he finds structure in the Psalms—the very way he describes how the Psalms work—manifests a commitment to understanding how the humanity of the person is engaged in her redemption. The place of rhetoric in these works represents an interesting twist on Plato: Whereas for Plato, the production of beautiful discourses moves a person from admiring beautiful bodies to a more abstract or intellectual beauty found in souls and practices, for Gregory, whose ascetic commitments preclude multiple encounters with beautiful bodies—and ideally no encounter at all—hearing discourses is more important than producing them. Or perhaps "production" has been reinterpreted to include praying texts already written, as in the Psalms. Hearing and praying these texts provides sensory delights that lure her into contemplation of their intellectual treasures, which, in turn, translates into a life lived virtuously.

The sensory is ambivalent in Gregory's text and fraught with danger. On the one hand, Gregory aligns the senses with evil when he declares evil to bring joy to the senses and virtue joy to the soul.[80] On the other hand, Gregory approvingly describes the psalmist sweetening virtue for the senses. Sensory pleasure, moreover, is often indistinguishable from the lowest kind of beauty, sensory beauty. The two can be reliably distinguished, as virtue can, only by their ends.[81] Sensory beauty is distinguished from sensory pleasure by its capacity to open up onto and lean toward intellectual beauty. While sensory pleasure terminates, sensory beauty has the capacity to yield higher beauty. But even right judgments that beauty is present must continually be revised. Gregory writes,

> It is as if someone born at night should judge the darkness in
> which he was nurtured and grew up to be a great good, but later,

---

splendour of virtue, until you shall see the perfect goodness surely established in the stainless shrine" (*Enneads* I.6.8–9 [MacKenna, 54]).

80. Gregory of Nyssa, *On the Inscriptions of the Psalms* I.4.27 (Heine, 92). "Evil, on the one hand, brings joy to our physical senses, but virtue brings joy to the soul."

81. Gregory of Nyssa, *On the Inscriptions of the Psalms* I.6.44 (Heine, 98).

when he has participated in the beauty of the open air, he despises his former judgment saying, "I used to prefer the darkness to which I was accustomed to such sights as the sun and stars and every beauty in heaven because I was ignorant of that which is superior."[82]

The image here is remarkably similar to Plato's cave in the *Republic*, melded with his invocation of the ladder in *Symposium*, but with a subtle difference. The mistake is not in loving the night or the lower beauties of the dark but in thinking those beauties to be the greatest, in preferring them to all other beauties. Where Plato's ladder-ascender in the *Symposium* despises bodies when he ascends to souls, Gregory's dark-dweller despises his *judgment* preferring darkness, not the dark itself. Light may be a superior kind of beauty, but that does not mean darkness is not beautiful itself.[83] Gregory describes a process, not of repudiating initial judgments about beauty, but revising them. This initial sensory beauty occupies a precarious place in Gregory's thought, especially in his early thought, but he cannot escape it as he constructs a model of training, for he holds sensory pleasure to be the common denominator across humanity.

One result of these different models of relationship to "lower" beauties is that Gregory need not banish poets from his ideal state. Plato articulates in the *Republic* three worries about poetry: 1) that it is at a third remove from truth—imitating appearances of virtue and truth;[84] 2) that it appeals to the inferior, non-rational part of the soul, thereby "arous[ing], nourish[ing], and strengthen[ing] this part of the soul and so destroy[ing] the rational one;"[85] and 3) because of this, poetry corrupts even decent people by training us to indulge rather than master our grief, to enjoy rather than despise evil.[86] Plato, of course, is himself a poetic, myth-making philosopher, and his harshest critiques of poetry (the second and third critique above) may be read as critiques of particular poems that Gregory and Macrina also worried about.[87] Yet inheriting a book of poetry as a sacred text—and the privileged text in monastic living—caused Gregory to thematize the possibility

82. Ibid., I.6.46 (Heine, 99).

83. Darkness, in fact, has a complex role in Gregory's thought, particularly in his apophatic descriptions of ascent in the *Life of Moses*.

84. Plato, *Republic*, 598d, 600e.

85. Ibid., 603 a/b, 605b.

86. Ibid., 605 d/e.

87. Near the beginning of the *Life of Macrina*, Macrina's mother, Emmelia, decides it better that one so tender study Scripture rather than the indecent, passionate, and weak characters of Greek poetry. Gregory of Nyssa, "Life of Saint Macrina" 3 (Callahan, 165).

for virtuous poetry in a way Plato did not. In Gregory's reinterpretation of Plato's dark cave, he addresses the first objection by de-polarizing the beauty of darkness and the beauty of light, the beauty of imitation and the beauty of the imitated. Imitation is entirely recast, both in his presentation of saints' lives for *mimesis* (it is possible, for Gregory, to instantiate the virtuous man, not just the emotionally uncontrolled man, in poetry), and in his recon-figuration of the material and the spiritual. Gregory's de-polarization of imitating beauty and imitated beauty is part of a larger movement of recon-figuring the beauty of the sensory and the intellectual, an opposition that sustains Plato's second objection and thereby feeds his third. The way the poetry of the Psalms appeals to the lower part of the soul does not preclude them from appealing to the higher; it is, instead, the means by which they appeal to the higher. The Psalms, in this way, are both good and pleasurable, a case that the Plato of the *Republic* does not treat.[88] Near the end of his speech against the poets, Socrates says:

> But you should also know that hymns to the gods and eulogies to good people are the only poetry we can admit into our city. If you admit the pleasure-giving Muse, whether in lyric or epic poetry, pleasure and pain will be kings in your city instead of law of the thing that everyone has always believed to be best, namely, reason.[89]

The good poetry that Plato does admit, then, is poetry that does not yield (to) pleasure, a different understanding of poetry than Gregory's pleasure-yielding, divine Psalms. For Gregory, pleasure and pain can be *logos*-form. That is, pleasure can participate in beauty (though it need not) and therefore illumine, train towards, lead to the beauty of reason. In this way, the sensory and the intellectual can have a friendlier relationship in Gregory than they sometimes seem to share in Plato.

While remaining ambivalent to the sensory as such, the sensory that is properly ordered often takes a place of honor in Gregory's writings. Gregory offers in *On the Inscriptions of the Psalms*, for example, images of humanity's beginnings and ends that are physically exuberant. Before the fall, angels and humans were as two cymbals sounding, joining in praise to God.[90] Now they are separated by sin, but one day, they will sound again. They will also dance again.

---

88. He has happier things to say about this possibility in the *Phaedrus*, as we shall see, and he elsewhere describes music as linking beauty and pleasure, the good (sub-stance) and the pleasant (form). *Hippias Major* 298A, *Laws* Book 2 659D.

89. Plato, *Republic* 607A (Grube and Reeve, 1211).

90. Gregory of Nyssa, *On the Inscriptions of the Psalms*, I.9.117 (Heine, 121).

For there was a time when the dance of the rational nature was one, and looked to the one leader of the chorus, and, in its movement in relation to his command, interpreted the choral song in relation to the harmony exhibited thence. But, when sin occurred, it put an end to that divine concord of the chorus, when it poured the slipperiness of deceit at the feet of the first humans who used to sing in chorus with the angelic powers and caused the fall, wherefore man was separated from connection with the angels. Because the fall put an end to this conjunction, there is the necessity of many hardships and labours by the one who has fallen, that he might again be restored, once he has prevailed against and overthrown the sentence that was imposed upon him by the fall, and has received the divine dance as the prize of his victory over the opponent.[91]

Sin tripped the praising one, turning him away from singing and dancing and landing him in a world for which hard labor was necessary. Praising God through the Psalms, we remember our beginnings and hope for our ends. Through the Psalms, we become the creatures we were made to be. Though we are not free from the slippage of sin—the danger never disappears—Gregory wants us to look to this dance as the end to which the virtuous life is headed. It is toward such a hope that his later works tend more and more, exploring how a resurrected body and incarnated Savior inform Christian attitudes toward physicality.

Gregory's attitude toward physicality and the sensory is bound up with how beauty's fittingness and gratuity work on beauty's beholder. The ladder works as an image for learning to apprehend true Beauty in the works of Plato and Gregory of Nyssa because beauty is for them both fitting and gratuitous. Fittingness and gratuity can describe the way the beautiful object enables a process of ascent. It invites the beholder to itself in its fittingness, and trains the initiate into thicker, higher beauty still with its gratuity. This general picture of how fittingness and gratuity work to structure beauty as a ladder is complicated by a number of factors, not least of which is the issue of the multiple levels of context for fittingness. For example, if the new context casts an unfavorable light on the lower beauty, the movement to higher beauties can look like a movement away from lower beauties.

With this possibility is introduced the ambivalence toward the sensory and the physical that initiates the novice into her ascent to beauty. It is particularly evident in the case of Plato, who describes the second stage of perceiving beauty, wherein one sees the beauty of multiple bodies, as curing one of the first, wherein one perceives and loves the beauty of a single body.

91. Ibid., II.6.60 (Heine, 138–39).

For Plato, a person needs a guide to encourage him to respond to the one beautiful body by producing a discourse and then introducing him to the beauty of multiple bodies. The guide shifts the context for the novice by giving him a new vantage point from which she can perceive the first beautiful body. The beauty so perfectly fitting in one context—and eliciting of an erotic attachment and a beautiful discourse, which seem such perfectly fitting responses—becomes less fitting once introduced into the larger context of the multiple bodies of beauty, as do the initial responses of eros and discourse. The first beautiful body one encounters might be the most surpassingly fitting form of a human body the novice has yet seen (a sentiment perhaps expressed in exclamations that the beloved is her ideal woman or man), so that beauty itself seems to inhere in that particular person. The guide has the trickiest work to do in the move away from the attachment to one beautiful body because here the process of ascent is paradoxical. To climb past the multiplicity of beautiful things to see one, true beauty, the novice must first pass from the one beautiful body to the many. The novice must move from the one to the many in order to move from many to the one.

The guide helps the novice through this trickiness by helping her to perceive the gratuity of beauty. The guide trains the novice into beauty's gratuity by teaching him to respond not only in a way, for Plato, fitting for a beautiful body (erotic attachment), but also in way that recognizes that beauty yields a surplus of meaning. Training the novice to respond to the beautiful body by a beautiful discourse helps her to recognize in beauty that which she cannot exhaust. It helps her to perceive, that is, the gratuity in beauty, that which surpasses her desires and needs. But that gratuity is not in itself enough to propel her into another level of context for beauty. She still needs the guide to point out to her the multiple beautiful bodies so that she knows beauty does not inhere in the first body. At that point it is still the fittingness of beauty that she responds to, seeing the way the first body, seen in the context of multiple bodies, is not as singularly beautiful as she first thought. Her initiation into beauty requires constant redirection in these initial stages, until she learns to respond to the ascending rhythm of fittingness and gratuity—the fittingness drawing her to the present rung's beauty, its gratuity lifting her to the next—as the guide intervenes to introduce her to the right instantiation of beauty at the right moment.[92] As she ascends,

92. Unlike *On the Inscriptions of the Psalms*, *On Virginity* does speak of a guide in the ladder of ascent. Gregory's guide in this text, however, functions differently from Plato's guide in the *Symposium*. Gregory's guide is much less active. Rather than intervening to introduce new kinds of beauty, Gregory's guide makes sure his student stays on the path he began rather than wandering off (ch. 23 [Callahan, 70]). The guide,

her appreciation of the previous rungs diminishes. She regards the "beauty of body as something petty" and is no longer bound by "low and small-minded slavery" of attraction to lesser things.[93] At the penultimate stage, seeing the beauty of forms of knowledge she produces many magnificent discourses, a process that "develop[s] and strengthen[s]"[94] him to see the final beauty. The vision of Beauty Itself is of a beauty that "always *is*" without being beautiful in one respect but ugly in another. There is no context from which to revalue Beauty. It is the final context; it is that which gives all beautiful things their character.

Gregory offers another variation on fittingness and gratuity. In Gregory's descriptions of encountering beauty, the same basic rhythm of fittingness and gratuity pull the initiate up the ladder, but he relies for ascent less on the new levels of context to disclose diminished fittingness of the present level and more on the gratuity of the present level to disclose the beauty that exceeds it. For Gregory, the movement is not away from lesser beauties but a movement deeper into their beauty, with the result that new beauty is discovered. Gregory does not disparage the physical or sensory quite as much as Plato, which we might explain as follows using the terms of fittingness and gratuity: Gregory sees fittingness and gratuity as manifestly internally related to one another even at these early stages. A person learns the beauty of the subject by pursuing the beauty of the rightly constructed rhetoric. This is what distinguishes (mere) sensory gratification from beauty for Gregory: Beauty opens infinitely up, while sensory pleasure absent beauty terminates. The musicality of a rhetoric ordered to its subject is beautiful and never worthy of disdain. The Psalms are never unbeautiful, no matter how far a person advances. The rhetoric worthy of disdain is one improperly ordered to its subject, that fails to *fit* its subject—to yield graciously to it so that the rhetoric itself yields gratuity—*that* rhetoric terminates in pleasure (at best). It is in retrospect, having glimpsed a true beauty, that a person can make this judgment about unworthy rhetoric. For Gregory, new levels of context help a person to recognize untrue beauty, but they do not lead to the disdain for the "lower" beauties that preceded "higher" ones. The higher

moreover, turns out to be more of an exemplar, "someone to whom we can look, [who will] let us sail securely through the storm of temptations" (73). Most scholars interpret this guide to be Basil since Gregory at the beginning of his text promises at the end of his discourse to refer "to our most reverent bishop and father as the only one capable of teaching these things" (7), but there is good reason also to interpret that figure as Christ—and possibly both. What is importantly different from Plato is that Gregory's guide turns out to teach more by leading a life that discloses truth rather than any sort of didacticism. Gregory of Nyssa, "On Virginity."

93. Plato, *Symposium* 210c/d (Gill, 48).

94. Ibid., 210d (Gill, 48).

beauties do not leave behind the lower ones because the higher is a deepening of the lower and because Gregory understood the movement not as one of disdaining previous levels of fittingness but as pursuing the beautiful object in its gratuity.

It is not that beautiful rhetoric—even a rhetoric in which words and content graciously fit—guarantees proper ascent: Not all who read the Psalms are saved, and Socrates—working with all of his skill to produce a rhetoric that will win Phaedrus to the philosophical life—fails in his efforts, leaving Phaedrus enamored of his style rather than his subject.[95] Phaedrus responds by fetishizing beautiful speeches rather than loving them, and precisely in this response of cutting speeches off from their purpose and context—a response that would seem to be the ultimate respect for the gratuity of their beauty—he denies the gratuity of speeches by refusing to let words be more than words or speeches be more than speeches. Phaedrus becomes an illustration for the way the disinterested appreciation of beauty trivializes rather than elevates the beautiful object. A person must be trained to recognize the subject to which the musicality is fitting, and responding rightly to beautiful rhetoric further requires that her life learn to fit the subject.

So then, just as there is a response to beautiful rhetoric that denies its capacity to facilitate ascent, so there is a kind of rhetoric that, though perhaps an occasion for ascent, one disdains as one ascends to greater heights of beauty. This is a rhetoric not properly ordered to its subject, that fails to fit its subject and so does not properly draw on the fittingness and gratuity of beauty to move a person up the ladder. We can understand the kind of rhetoric that fails to initiate a person into the Beautiful and why that failure happens by turning to a text in which Gregory thematizes rhetoric as a primary concern.

Imitating Perfect Rhetoric: *On Virginity*

The Psalms are an especially effective text for initiating people into the life of virtue via rhetoric, for the Word wields them as the Word's own instrument. But other texts can perform that work as well. Gregory himself attempts to

---

95. There is not, of course, perfect alignment in how to interpret the end of the *Phaedrus*, but I am persuaded by Drew Hyland's account of Phaedrus's failure. Hyland points to Phaedrus's lack of interest in understanding Socrates's speech; his query about what Socrates will say to Lysias; Socrates's exclusion of Lysias in his final prayer (in contrast to his inclusion of Lysias in his early palinode); Socrates's curt reply to Phaedrus's request for inclusion in the final prayer ("let's go"); and what was known of Phaedrus's later involvement with scandals as evidence that Phaedrus remains unconverted. Hyland, *Plato and the Question of Beauty*, 118.

model such delighting and luring in another early text—the one, in fact, considered his earliest—*On Virginity*, a text most scholars agree was designed to support Basil's monastic program. As a rather transparent meditation on Gregory's vocation as a Christian rhetor, *On Virginity* begins by reflecting on its own aim and form. In the opening sentence, Gregory states his goal to be creating in the reader a desire for the life of virtue to which the life of virginity acts as a door.[96] The problem Gregory identifies for himself as a writer is how to present the "lofty form" of virginity that "is prized by all those who discern the beautiful in purity" to those who do not yet discern the beautiful.[97] He considers his method:

> Since advice, in itself, is rather slow to persuade, and since a person who is urging another on to something beneficial does not easily influence him by a mere word without first exalting that towards which he is urging his listener, our discourse begins with a eulogy of virginity and ends with advice.[98]

The mere word of *On Virginity* presages the "mere writing" in the *Life of Moses*. Where the mereness of writing is overcome in the *Life of Moses* by the splendor of the tabernacle, the "mere word" in *On Virginity* must be overcome by proper encomium. Though Gregory worries at the power of words to equal the grace of virginity,[99] for the benefit of others, he determines to "say a few words because of the necessity of establishing in all men a belief in the power of the One who enjoins virginity upon us."[100]

In Gregory's worries about crafting rhetoric appropriate to his subject, one of his most pressing concerns is that in trying to embellish his subject, he will denigrate it. As in his piece on the Psalms, Gregory worries about a rhetoric that presumes to add something to its subject. People who compose extensive speeches of praise in an attempt to add something to virginity not only fail in their purpose, they accomplish its opposite by rendering virginity an object of suspicion. It is only "for things on the lower level" that the *logos* "through its clever praise, adds some fantasy of greatness."[101] A problem with the admiration evoked by speeches of praise is that they draw attention to the cleverness and sophistication of the speaker as much as to the subject. The praise of virtue must proceed differently. The right way to

96. Gregory of Nyssa, "On Virginity" intro. (Callahan, 6).
97. Ibid., ch. 1 (Callahan, 9).
98. Ibid., intro. (Callahan, 6).
99. Ibid., ch. 2 (Callahan, 10).
100. Ibid., ch. 2 (Callahan, 12).
101. Ibid., ch. 1 (Callahan, 9).

praise virtue is to make clear that it is beyond praise; that is how the speaker creates a speech that resists fetishization. As the psalmist wisely refrained from a musical rhythm and verbal pitch that had a design and artifice of their own, so Gregory refrains from any praise that embroiders his subject rather than disclosing the beauty of its form. Gregory's concern is one about fittingness, but his problem is about how to formulate a rhetoric fitting to a subject that is so divine, so grace-filled, so *gratuitous* as virtue. The answer is that rhetoric must not pretend equality to virtue; it must consciously point beyond itself, and its beauty will derive from its so pointing.

Rhetoric, for Gregory, reveals truth by removing obstacles rather than by constructing its own edifice. Gregory's vision of training into truth, beauty, and goodness is an un-training: Adam had the three close at his hand and deliberately turned away, and so learning to see beauty involves removing the impurities that cloud that original sight.[102] An embellished rhetoric represents, for Gregory, an overweening human agency that attempts to wrest control from God. It is both repellent, and if our goal is praise of God, doomed to failure. Gregory's stated vision of beautiful rhetoric requires that rhetoric not be overweening, that it not instantiate the grasp to have more than it holds or be more than it is. The gratuity of beauty means that the beautiful rhetoric yields to its object, that in fitting with its object, it gives its object graciously rather than hurling it. Any attempt to wrest beauty toward one's own purpose inevitably distorts it.

Midway through the text, Gregory gives a different version of these problems of representing virtue in rhetoric when he names the problem of praising beauty. Gregory reflects on his deployment of rhetoric when he writes that perhaps the treatise "has gently led us through examples to the thought of transforming ourselves to something better than we are . . . ."[103] In this middle section of the eulogy (chapters 10–12), Gregory returns to his ambivalence about the capacity of rhetoric to represent divine things. This time, though, he worries less about rhetoric's capacity to represent the desirability of virtue and more about its capacity to render apparent beauty. Just before Gregory voices the possibility his treatise has led the hearer/reader into greater virtue, he wonders how a treatise could possibly make a person see the beauty he does not already see for himself. He writes: "Any verbal explanation of light is useless and idle for the person blind from birth, because it is not possible to visualize the brilliance of the sun through the ear. In the same way, each individual needs his own eyes to see the beauty of

---

102. Ibid., ch. 12 (Callahan, 42–46).
103. Ibid., ch. 11 (Callahan, 41).

the true and intelligible light."[104] Gregory identifies at least two reasons why words are inadequate to Beauty. The first is that they are unnecessary for the one who already sees Beauty and useless for those who "are still immersed in material matters."[105] The second is that the person who sees something "in which fantasy is mixed with beauty"—if that person is "not sufficiently trained in distinguishing between the beautiful and the not beautiful"—will think a beautiful thing is beautiful according to its own nature rather than seeing beyond the "matter in which the beauty is encased" to the true beauty, the "intelligible beauty."[106] Let us set to the side for a moment this Plotinian vision of beauty and consider what Gregory writes about rhetoric. Rhetoric cannot make beauty apparent to the one still deeply attached to material things, and if that rhetoric uses fantasy—Gregory's word for praise extrinsically overlaid onto the subject—it is in danger of confusing a person even more deeply about how to locate true beauty. Rhetoric, then, must work on the desire of the person in order to work on her vision, and it must work on that desire by avoiding false or extrinsic forms of praise.

At the beginning of Gregory's ladder to Beauty and prior to the initiate apprehending the larger context of Beauty is the inviting musicality of the Psalm, the soul-melting perfection of Plato's beautiful boy, the soaring rhetoric of the gifted orator. It is beauty the initiate perceives without reference to any particular purpose or function and with a minimally trained context. The beautiful body is the space for Plato where natural desire comes to fit with the possibility for spiritual uplift and the only context it presumes is other bodies. Rhetoric is the space for Gregory where sensory pleasure meets true beauty, and its only context for fittingness is other words. That is why rhetoric is so dangerous. It can seduce the uninitiated into glorifying words as ends in themselves or into valorizing any number of ways of being and seeing in the world. It is also dangerous because, as Gregory describes in *On Virginity*, the uninitiated has at best a tenuous grasp of the difference between pleasure and beauty.[107] Mistaking the first for the second, the initiate will fail to discover the great and diverse realm of beauty. The reason why it is easy for the initiate to make this mistake in the first place, though, is because the task of distinguishing sensory beauty from pleasure is subtle indeed. It may be that it can be done only in retrospect, once the initiate follows where that sensory beauty leads. Then she can discern what kind of sign that beauty/pleasure is. (It may be that she never finally knows.) So

104. Ibid., ch. 11 (Callahan, 38).
105. Ibid., ch. 10 (Callahan, 36).
106. Ibid., ch. 11 (Callahan, 39).
107. Ibid.

then, while a person can and certainly often does make the initial judgments about beauty without reference to what that beauty points toward, such judgments are less accurate than those made with a broader perspective—a new level of fittingness—regarding what beauty is and how it signifies.[108] We now have a more specific way to distinguish between Plato and Gregory on the subject of "lower" beauties: While Plato will claim that appreciating higher beauties evokes disdain for the lower beauties one formerly admired, Gregory will maintain that if an object is truly beautiful, its beauty with respect to the aspect for which it was appreciated will hold up even as one discovers other beauties or even aspects under which it is ugly. To discover that a thing's beauty does not hold up is to discover that it is, in fact, not beautiful but merely *pleasurable*. An object, then, can be *either* truly beautiful in one respect and ugly in another *or* merely pleasurable in one respect and ugly (or beautiful) in another.

In *On Virginity*, Gregory works to craft a rhetoric so perfectly fitting its subject that the rhetoric, in the gratuity of its excessive fittingness, might groom desire for that subject. But the reader does not initially know what his true subject is. Ostensibly about virginity, Gregory's speech initially promises immortality and ends in praise to the Christ he names the Crucified One. His use of rhetoric to cultivate desire for the Crucified One indicates his high opinion of both the power of rhetoric and the possibilities for perception yielded in the process of ascent. How he harnesses such potency is instructive.

After praising the life of virtue and virginity as beyond the capacity of words to represent it, Gregory begins trying to cultivate desire for that life by taking up Diotima's description of how people pursue immortality.[109] That might seem like a good place to start, for Diotima subordinated

---

108. Many ancient writers—and almost all contemporary ones—are skeptical about associating beauty with what they call the lower senses. There is good reason for such skepticism, I think, in that the beauties of sight and sound more obviously represent a kind of transcendence in their immanence because the seen or heard object can be at more of a remove to the perceiver. The presence of an object to some senses and its absence from others (especially touch and taste) suggest a kind of spiritualization of the seen and heard object that likens it to the spiritual beauty that is the goal of ascent. But Gregory provides us with the basis for a different approach to the senses in his doctrine of the spiritual senses, all of which yield to and give information about Beauty Itself. We will explore this further in chapter 4, when we will also consider how these spiritual senses extend rather than supplant the physical senses, which suggests that all physical senses have some capacity to perceive beauty, even taste, the sense that requires the internalization of the perceived object.

109. As in *On Virginity*, Gregory also begins *On the Soul and the Resurrection* by assuming the natural desire to avoid death, which becomes the starting point for philosophical reflection (i.4).

the pursuit of immortality according to the body to immortality pursued according to the soul. Diotima describes the attempt to secure immortality through posterity as inferior to securing it through honor and virtue because the children it bears, though they themselves may have children, are yet mortal. Gregory goes one step farther: He describes such an attempt as utterly vain. Death attends even the most fulfilling marriages, and the happier the marriage, the greater the pain of loss.[110]

But Gregory is not recommending an erotic liaison with a noble man, nor is he recommending the immortality pursued by acquiring fame and honor. That kind of immortality—fame-and-honor immortality—ultimately has nothing to do with a person's actual mortality—"mortal man remains mortal whether he is honored or not;"[111] and it conflicts with immortality through children since career ambition and child-raising are difficult to reconcile, even though having children often gives rise to the desire for achievement and financial success. Gregory is instead recommending only Plato's highest form of immortality: immortality pursued according to the Beauty-beholding soul, which gives birth not to the images of virtue like honor and fame, but to true virtue. As the way to pursue such immortality, Gregory recommends virginity, which opens up a different space for women than Plato's philosophy does. He interprets the verse in Timothy that women will be saved through childbearing to mean that life and incorruptibility are born to the one united through participation in the Spirit. Gregory writes, "The virgin mother who begets immortal children through the Spirit truly rejoices and she is called barren by the prophet because of her moderation."[112] The "virgin mother," though, is not only a metaphor, in the way that male pregnancy is a metaphor in Plato. For Gregory, there is a virgin mother who limits the activity of all death. Gregory writes:

> Just as at the time of Mary, the Mother of God, death who had been king from the time of Adam until then, when she was born, was shattered, being dashed against the fruit of virginity as if against a stone, so in every soul which through virginity

---

110. Gregory of Nyssa, "On Virginity" ch. 3 (Callahan, 12–13). In reading Gregory's arguments about marriage and immortality as responding to Plato's arguments in the *Symposium*, I am following the work of Ton H. C. van Eijk and offering an alternative way to Mark Hart's recent attempts to see Gregory's anti-marriage arguments as ironic and Valerie Karras' attempts to identify a fourfold hierarchy involving marriage, virginity and the "spiritual versions." Van Eijk, "Marriage and Virginity, Death and Immortality"; Hart, "Gregory of Nyssa's Ironic Praise"; Hart, "Reconciliation of Body and Soul"; Karras, "A Re-evaluation of Marriage, Celibacy, and Irony."

111. Gregory of Nyssa, "On Virginity" ch. 4 (Callahan, 22).

112. Ibid., ch. 13 (Callahan, 48).

rejects life in the flesh, the power of death is somehow shattered and destroyed, since it cannot apply its goad to them.[113]

Mary's virginity becomes paradigmatic for all Christian virginity. It is the fruitful virginity that enables all other virginity to participate in God. Gregory writes near the beginning of the text: "For what happened corporeally in the case of the immaculate Mary, when the fullness of the divinity shone forth in Christ through her virginity, takes place also in every soul spiritually giving birth to Christ . . . ."[114] A person can pursue immortality and virtue through virginity because Mary was the virgin who was also the mother of Christ. Motherhood thus is not denigrated as a second-tier path to immortality, though neither is it unqualifiedly praised. It is Mary's virginity and corporeal motherhood that enables the virginity of subsequent Christians to become also the spiritual motherhood of Christ.

As Gregory works to cultivate a desire in the reader to become a spiritual mother, he uses some of the techniques he identified in *On the Inscriptions of the Psalms*: praise and censure and the description of exemplary lives, including Elijah, John, Christ, Miriam, and Mary.[115] Similar to Gregory's identification of the way the Psalms use the sensual appetite to stimulate the intellectual appetite, Gregory works in *On Virginity* by subtly shifting the object of desire. Gregory begins with what Plato has identified as the ubiquitous desire for immortality, and he shows how children and fame fail to achieve that immortality. After showing how these pursuits fail (his chapters 3 and 4), Gregory then argues that virginity achieves peacefulness (chapter 4), freedom from external disturbances (chapter 5), and tranquility (chapter 6). It avoids crucifixion by worldly pleasures (chapter 5). Into these arguments, Gregory weaves the desire for God, who is associated with the same benefits as virginity, for God is immortal, unchangeable, impassible.

Then Gregory begins to focus more explicitly on the desire for God. The terms of death and immortality give way to the vocabulary of Christ and paradise. We are told that the goal of virginity is not to gain immortality but to see God (chapter 11), that the reason virginity is not associated with death is because it participates in Paradise (chapters 13 and 14), and that the virginity that ultimately limits death is not ours but Mary's (chapter 14). Gregory redirects the natural desire for immortality to a place where it can be fulfilled, and that place is paradise, where we enter because of Christ through Mary. In subsequent chapters, Gregory embeds the desire for

---

113. Ibid., ch. 4 (Callahan, 49).

114. Ibid., ch. 2 (Callahan, 11).

115. Spiritual motherhood is a theme explored further with the figure of Macrina in chapter 4.

virginity into another larger story of the unity of virtues, and the desire now enfolds into itself desire for the virtues more generally.[116] Gregory shows the beauty of immortality to be more perfectly disclosed in the beauty of the virtues. Rather than disdaining the beauty of immortality, the initiate learns to love it more by loving immortality *in* virtue.

It is here, with the characters of Miriam and Mary, that Gregory reintroduces death. The prototype of Mary, Miriam beats a tambourine, which is dead skin and represents her virginity, thus illustrating that virginity is *nekrosis somatos*, deadness of the body.[117] Gregory has progressed from arguing against marriage by highlighting its associations with death to arguing for a virginity that includes within it a kind of death. Here is the first sense that aversion to death must be chastened by the desire for virginity; avoiding death is not the highest good. God is the highest good, and Gregory's next chapter elaborates that theme by discussing how both spiritual virginity and spiritual marriage are implicated in love for God.[118] Gregory can now return to marital love, invoking love of one's spouse as a paradigm for how one is to love Christ, the incorruptible Bridegroom. Thus, marriage, like virginity, has been put in service of the greater good of drawing near Christ. Virginity is initially valorized for avoiding death, then further valorized for conquering it, and then thrown into the shadow of a greater good. The desire for Christ overtakes the desire for virginity as the primary desire on which the text focuses. Gregory continues to disclose new levels of context that reinterpret previous levels of beauty, not by revealing previous instances of beauty to be less fitting in the new context, but by revealing them to have a surplus revealed by the new context. Immortality becomes more beautiful in light of Christ, not less. And Christ is loved, not by leaving behind the love for immortality, nor by claiming it to be unbeautiful, but by following the beauty of immortality into its deeper beauty disclosed in the beauty of Christ.

Then in the final chapter of *On Virginity,* while urging his readers to embrace the life of virtue, Gregory refers to Christ by a new name. It is at the very end of chapter 23 that Christ becomes the Crucified One. Reversing the previous metaphor of crucifixion to worldly pleasures as something to be avoided, Gregory refers to crucifixion here as what it means to eschew worldly pleasure.[119] The final reference to crucifixion comes in Gregory's ending exhortation:

116. Gregory of Nyssa, "On Virginity" chs. 15–18 (Callahan, 51–60).
117. Ibid., ch. 19 (Callahan, 60–62).
118. Ibid., ch. 20 (Callahan, 62–64).
119. Ibid., ch. 5 (Callahan, 28).

> We want you to be one of those crucified with Christ, to stand
> beside Him as a pure priest, to become a pure sacrifice in all pu-
> rity, preparing yourself through your holiness for the presence
> of God, in order that you yourself may see God in the purity of
> your heart according the promise of God and our Savior Jesus
> Christ, to whom is the glory and the power forever and ever.
> Amen.[120]

The final desire, that toward which Gregory's text moves, is not an immortal self but a crucified self. Gregory's rhetoric works on the hearer's natural desire to avoid death and reworks it through a series of associations, dissociations, praises, censures, and shining exemplars to produce a desire to follow a Christ who bore death—the Christ he calls not the Resurrected One but the Crucified One.

The Crucified One names the final form of virtue—that which Gregory worried about representing at the beginning of the text—and beauty, that which Gregory worried about in the middle of the text. To desire virtue and perceive beauty is to desire and perceive the Crucified Christ. Rhetoric does the work of helping a person not only understand the relationship between beauty and the Crucified Christ but to transform her desire to include the Crucified One as well. Following the beauty of immortality, loving it deeply, takes one, for Gregory, to the Crucified Christ, who yet stands in some continuity with immortality. The way Gregory uses rhetoric (and specifically scriptural, homiletic, and liturgical rhetoric) to initiate a person into a life capable of perceiving beauty (a life of desiring God and of pursuing virtue) indicates the reception of the art of rhetoric, of the words of God, and of the desire for God that is internal to a person's humanity. That is, her sensuality, her rationality, and her current spiritual state are all important to her conversion. To answer the previous question raised about the hermeneutics of the *Life of Moses*: yes, generating another text can, for Gregory, help resolve how a person perceives the beautiful, for texts and rhetoric are a person's best hope for beginning her ascent to Beauty. Rhetoric is a powerful force in Gregory's thought. Insulating his reader from the dangerous beauty of a lover's body, Gregory nonetheless exposes him to the likewise dangerous beauty of words. That is why, in both *On Virginity* and *On the Inscriptions of the Psalms*, Gregory worries about how to make and use rhetoric properly.

The thematization of beautiful objects and ideas as a ladder discloses one important way in which each stage is both fitting and gratuitous. Each stage is both an increasingly perfect sign for the divine and also marks the presence of the divine. We might think, for example, of the body of dead

120. Ibid., ch. 23 (Callahan, 75).

Macrina, with its luminous beauty, clearly pointing to God even as it comes itself to manifest her sanctity. As a sign for the divine, Macrina's body is especially fitting. It points perfectly to God at the moment of death, unavoidably invoking the death of the Bridegroom whose beauty enamors her, and pointing to the promise his death enabled. She loved her Bridegroom, and it is fitting that she should point so unmistakably towards the one her soul loved. But there is a gratuity in the very one she points toward, and as a remarkably fitting sign of that divinity, Macrina must herself represent that gratuity. She does, too, in the unconcealable light streaming from her body. The gratuity of beauty suggests God's transcendence to the world; its fittingness, God's immanence. This is how the ladder works: An object's fittingness draws the beholder to itself while its gratuity points her beyond it, to a new object and a new framework in which to understand an object's fittingness. This framework, too, will fail to exhaust the beautiful object, which continues to point to the One present in all things yet beyond all things.

Macrina is both an object and a subject for Gregory. As she in the moment of her death acquires a beauty that is a near-perfect sign of the divine, so in the moments before her death, she attains the vision at the ladder's top. The image Gregory offers of a person who has climbed the ladder is the dying Macrina perceiving the beauty of the Bridegroom. The proper response to such beauty, as exemplified by Macrina, is not to put it to any kind of use, but to offer a discourse of praise, doxology, for to Gregory's mind, praise is the proper response to true beauty because it is the praise of the one who is Beauty in whom our beauty participates. He performs this response himself in *On Virginity*, where he first praises the beauty of virginity, then praises virtue as the perfection of virginity, and at last ends in doxology to the Crucified Christ, who is the perfect form of virtue. It is through such praise, moreover, that Gregory perceives the possibility for others to begin to glimpse this beauty, which is why he states as the purpose for his encomium the cultivation of desire. The praise that issues forth from the sight of True Beauty thus becomes itself a site of beauty that can introduce the uninitiated into an ascent. The great Beauty is gratuitous, exceeding any purpose the beholder might devise. She can only respond to such gratuity by receiving and imitating it, by, as Plato writes in the *Symposium* and Gregory picks up on in *On Virginity*, giving birth, especially to virtue and to discourses. The gratuity of Beauty is echoed in her children, who communicate something of this grace as well. When beauty inspires virtue and desire for virtue, beauty's gratuity comes to us as divine grace.

But in *On Virginity*, this first text of Gregory's, he does not have an entirely consistent view of rhetoric and beauty worked out. His vision of beauty at this point is still very Plotinian, as evidenced by his distinction between "the matter in which a thing is encased" and its true "intelligible beauty." At the same time, Gregory tries to hold this strong sensible/intelligible distinction together with the Christian doctrine of a God who created all things, even matter itself, *ex nihilo*. This commitment leads him to a slightly different conclusion he voices several paragraphs later when he discusses beauty and evil: "Every creation of God is beautiful and not to be despised and whatever God has made is exceedingly beautiful."[121] In his late works, Gregory integrates these commitments into a coherent unity, as he works out a much more sophisticated relationship between "higher" and "lower" forms of beauty, which we will review in chapter 3, just before we review his more complex configuring of the beauty of the sensible and intelligible realms in chapter 4.

As there are inconsistencies in his account of beauty in *On Virginity*, so there is a significant moment where he espouses a view of rhetoric that belies his strategy of working internally to a person's humanity. It is a moment where producing rhetoric is a process external to the gift and capacities of the human. That moment comes in a description of seeing beauty that is also a description of the making of rhetoric, for he describes David (to Gregory, the author of the Psalms), as known especially through the Psalms:

> The one who does see it through some divine gift and unexplainable inspiration is astonished in the depths of his consciousness; the one who cannot see will not realize what he has missed. . . . We have not devised the particular verbal expressions for that beauty. There are no verbal tokens of what we are seeking. . . .
>
> When [the great David] was once lifted up in thought by the power of the Spirit, he was, as it were, divorced from himself and saw that incredible and incomprehensible beauty in a blessed ecstasy. But he did see it as far as it is possible for a man to do so when he is released from the limitations of the flesh and comes to the contemplation of the incorporeal and intelligible through thought alone. When he wanted to say something worthy of what he had seen, he sang out that song which all men sing: "Every man is a liar." [Ps 115:2] That is, as our treatise shows, that every man who commits his interpretation of the ineffable light to words is really a liar, not because of any hatred of the truth, but because of the weakness of his description.[122]

At this moment Gregory describes seeing Beauty as a gift that cannot be captured in words and must divorce a person from his humanity and his

121. Ibid., ch. 12 (Callahan, 42).
122. Ibid., ch. 10 (Callahan, 36–37).

flesh. The inspiration for creating things such as the Psalms—things, that is, which possess a beauty more like the true Beauty than almost anything else—is understood in contrast to flesh, materiality, humanity, and, paradoxically, words themselves.[123]

While Gregory in this moment in *On Virginity* presents divine inspiration in a neo-Platonic vein, he later revises this position as he meditates more on the significance of the body in such pieces as *On the Soul and the Resurrection* to cohere with the vision of rhetoric and human making he embodies at other moments in the text. Even by the *Life of Macrina*, in fact, Gregory offers an alternative model of inspiration in the figure of his sister Macrina. Gregory describes her inspired discourses in terms very different than he here describes the psalmist's psalm-making, though the Psalms, of course, constantly reappear, reminders of the work that inspired discourses can do.

Inspiration: The Work of Making Rhetoric

Marsilio Ficino: The Beginnings of the Inspired Arts

Gregory's characterization of Macrina, unlike his description of the psalmist, illustrates a version of divine inspiration that celebrates humanity, skill,

---

123. It is a version of inspiration that strongly echoes moments of the flesh-escaping inspiration in the *Enneads* such as this one: "Many times it has happened: lifted out of the body into myself; becoming external to all other things and self-encentered; beholding a marvelous beauty; then, more than ever, assured of community with the loftiest order; enacting the noblest life, acquiring identity with the divine; stationing within It by having attained that activity; poised above whatsoever within the Intellectual is less than the Supreme; yet, there comes the moment of descent from intellection to reasoning, and after that sojourn in the divine, I ask myself how it happens that I can now be descending, and how did the Soul ever enter into my body, the Soul which, even within the body, is the high thing it has shown itself to be" (Plotinus, *Enneads* IV.8.I [MacKenna, 334]). Or found in humanity-denying moments of inspiration in Iamblichus' *Divine Mysteries,* such as this: "This is the greatest proof: many are not burned even though fire is applied to them, for the fire does not touch them because of their divine inspiration. And many, though they are burned, do not respond because they are not living the life of a [mortal] creature. And some, while being pierced with spits, have no awareness of it, and others, while striking their backs with sharp blades, do not feel it. Still others, while stabbing their lower arms with daggers, are completely unaware of it. Their activities are in no way human—for the inaccessible things become accessible to those possessed by a God. . . . From these examples it is clear that those inspired by the Gods are not conscious of themselves; they live neither a human life nor an animal life according to sensation or impulse, but they have taken in exchange a more divine life from which they are inspired and perfectly possessed" (Iamblichus, *Divine Mysteries,* 110.4–111.2; quoted in Shaw, *Theurgy and the Soul,* 82).

and flesh, even as it also traces their limits. In order to make visible the significance of Gregory's achievement and the beauty of his interpretation of Plato, I want to travel forward a thousand years to another great reader of Plato: Marsilio Ficino. Attending closely to Plato's texts, Ficino offers a plausible though different interpretation of Plato's inspiration than Gregory. Discerning how Ficino arrives at this reading—what he highlights, what he elides—will help make plain the stakes of Gregory's own inspiration and the differences in the pictures of divinity girding different formulations of inspiration.

Ficino translated Plato into Latin for a West that had lost all but a handful of Plato's dialogues. He published the *Phaedrus* together with several other translations of Plato's texts in 1484, some sixty years after the dialogue had been partially translated by Leonardo Bruni, who had rendered the beginning of the *Phaedrus* on love and beauty but stopped before the discussion of rhetoric and philosophy.[124] It was enough to raise controversy. In the wake of Bruni's 1423 translation, a debate swirled around pederasty and sexual love in the dialogue. Almost five decades later, the controversy stilled with the death of the primary interlocutors, and Ficino reintroduced the work with a long preface that became the first three chapters of his commentary on the text. Hearkening to the immortal pregnancies of the *Symposium*, he begins: "Our Plato was pregnant with the madness of the poetic Muse, whom he followed from a tender age or rather from his Apollonian generation. In his radiance, Plato gave birth to his first child, and it was itself almost entirely poetical and radiant."[125] The "poetical and radiant" "first child" Ficino references is the *Phaedrus* itself. Ficino named it first-born because both he and Bruni counted it as Plato's first dialogue,[126] an opinion with a pedigree tracing back to Diogenes Laertius and likely reinforced by the theme of youthfulness in the work.[127] But Ficino understood its status as a youthful production to have particular significance, for he related Plato's youthfulness to the description of divine inspiration he found in the work, connecting the poetry of the work to the tenderness of Plato's soul—and

---

124. His translation stopped at 257C, which is just after Socrates's hymn to love and before he discusses rhetoric (Ficino, *Marsilio Ficino*, 5). His translation no doubt contributed to the reading of the *Phaedrus* against which I will argue later, wherein the arguments about poetry are understood in isolation from the arguments about rhetoric.

125. "Plato noster poetice Muse, quam a tenera etate immo ab apollinea genitura sectatus est, furore gravidus, primum peperit liberum totum pene poeticum et candidissimum candidissimum" (Ficino, *Marsilio Ficino*, ch. 1.i, 72).

126. Ibid., 8.

127. Ibid., 9.

thus his receptivity to the Muses. Socrates's invocation of a tender soul was key to Ficino's reading of divine inspiration in the *Phaedrus*. Ficino explains:

> To achieve poetic madness (the madness that may instruct men in divine ways and sing the divine mysteries), the soul of the future poet must be so affected as to become almost tender and soft and untouched too. The poet's province is very wide, and his material is varied; so his soul (which can be formed very easily) must subject itself to God. This is what we mean by becoming "soft" and "tender." If the soul has already received alien forms or blemishes because of its ability to be formed too easily, then it certainly cannot be formed in the meantime by the divine forms.[128]

Despite describing poetic madness as an achievement, Ficino's overriding characterization of divine inspiration is passive. It is something that happens to the poet. The poet's responsibility is to be tender and soft and subject herself to God, and it is then that she can be formed by God. Youthfulness is important to inspiration because the young soul has had less exposure to things that might corrode it.

Age gives nothing to poetry, for Ficino, because poetry is not a skill someone develops over time. This is an understanding of poetry Ficino is convinced he finds in Plato. Ficino writes in a letter, "We agree that the truest assertion of our Plato is that *poetry* is derived not from art, but from some kind of madness."[129] "Art" here is not the modern sense of fine arts, but a cognate for the Latin *ars*. Ficino defined it earlier in that letter as "an appropriate rule for making things."[130] Ficino here refers to a passage in the *Phaedrus* in which Socrates describes the madness that is possession by the Muses. In this passage, Socrates says, "But if a man comes to the door of poetry untouched by the madness of the Muses, believing that technique alone will make him a good poet, he and his sane compositions never reach perfection, but are utterly eclipsed by the performances of the inspired madman."[131] The poet's significance as an inspired madman is explored theologically by Ficino: He who is touched by madness heaven-sent will himself ascend to heaven. Ficino writes, "Through the power of divine madness man is elevated above human nature and enters the divine sphere.

---

128. Ibid., 82.

129. Ficino, *Epistolae*, I (Op. 1561, p. 634; quoted in Tatarkiewicz, *History of Aesthetics*, 3:111). "Consensimus verissimam esse illam Platonis nostri sententiam. Poesim non ab arte, sed a furore aliquo profisci."

130. Ibid. "Ars est recta efficiendorum operum regula."

131. Plato, *Symposium* 245 (Gill, 48).

Divine madness is the enlightenment of the rational spirit by which God restores the fallen soul to the heights."[132] In his book tracing poetic madness in the Romantic age, Frederick Burwick refers to Ficino's formulation of divine madness in *On Divine Madness (De Furore divino* 1457) as "reaffirm[ing] naïve mystical receptivity to divine ventriloquism."[133] Poetry requires passivity before the divine so that a person can become a conduit for the divine: This is Ficino's understanding of inspiration. It is this understanding of poetic inspiration that underwrites his still further elevation of the poet as a "god upon the earth" *(deus in terris)*.[134] Ficino thus elaborates a doctrine of poetry that is aligned with madness, inspiration, and God-likeness and opposed to rule, skill, and human making. If this division sounds familiar, it is because Shiner similarly narrates the split between fine arts and crafts centuries later and because the polarity sustains eighteenth-century contrasts between the beautiful and the sublime.[135]

In his three-volume *History of Aesthetics*, Wladyslaw Tatarkiewicz describes the way inspiration becomes central to Ficino's understanding of the arts. Naming inspiration as the source of all acts of creation—poetry and painting alike—Ficino displaces skill and rule as the unifying characteristics of the arts and proposes a new criterion: similarity to poetry. Tatarkiewicz writes, "The distinguishing feature of arts like music or painting is not that, like the other arts, they are governed by rules, but that like poetry they are moved by 'madness' and inspiration. In the history of the concept of art this was an important turning point."[136] Inspiration, as Shiner explained, was central to the genius that produced fine arts. The arts that were later called the fine arts, Tatarkiewicz claims, Ficino called the inspired arts.[137] The understanding of inspiration Ficino culled from the *Phaedrus* thus helped sustain the division between fine arts and crafts.[138]

132. In Ficino's *Commentarium in Convivium*, as quoted in Tatarkiewicz, *History of Aesthetics*, 3:111. "Divino autem furore super hominis naturam erigitur et in Deum transit. Est autem furor divinus illustratio rationalis animae, per quam Deus animam, a superis delapsam ad infera, ab inferis ad supera retrahit."

133. Burwick, *Poetic Madness*, 3.

134. In Ficino's *Theologica Platonica*, as quoted in ibid., 22.

135. See chapter 1 for a discussion of Shiner's thesis.

136. Tatarkiewicz, *History of Aesthetics*, 3:105

137. For more on the development of the concept of inspiration and the role of genius in that process, see Brann, *The Debate Over the Origin of Genius during the Italian Renaissance.*

138. "Poetic madness" or inspiration continued to undergo important shifts after Ficino, of course. Among these was its radical opposition to reason. The irrationality of poetic madness became particularly important under the intellectual reign of the rationalists. While Baumgarten identified aesthetics as a form of understanding

Ficino found support for his reading of inspiration displacing skill in the *Phaedrus* through the *Ion*, which also connects a kind of artistry with a kind of madness.[139] It is a move that sinks his reading of the *Phaedrus*, for the *Ion*'s madness differs significantly from that of the *Phaedrus*. The *Ion* opens with Ion of Ephesus having just won first prize at a contest for rhapsodes. He specializes in declaiming Homer and boasts that there is no one who speaks Homer's lines more beautifully, nor speaks more beautifully about the poet. Socrates engages him, demonstrating Ion's ignorance of poetry in general, as well as his ignorance of the particular crafts Homer describes. He proposes to reconcile Ion's great skill as a rhapsode together with his ignorance about poetry and the subjects of Homer by suggesting that Ion has no knowledge himself but is, when singing Homer, inspired by a Muse.[140] Such inspiration would enable Ion to speak out of divine gift rather than mastery.[141] It is not a compliment. Socrates mocks divinely inspired poets, disguising his mockery in garments of praise. He says of a lyric poet named Tynnichus, who has an uneven corpus,

> I think the god is showing us . . . that these beautiful poems are not human, not even *from* human beings, but are divine and from gods; that poets are nothing but representatives of the gods possessed by whoever possesses them. To show *that*, the god deliberately sang the most beautiful lyric poem through the most worthless poet.[142]

The dialogue ends with Socrates coaxing Ion into agreeing with this view of his own work. He says,

> If you're really a master of your subject, and if, as I said earlier, you're cheating me of the demonstration you promised about Homer, then you're doing me wrong. But if you're not a master of your subject, if you're possessed by a divine gift from Homer, so that you make many lovely speeches about the poet without knowing anything—as *I* said about you—then you're not doing

that rationalists missed because it was below reason, thinkers like Herder and Goethe wanted to identify artistic creativity as a capacity outside reason's province because it was too high. For more on the changing significance of poetic madness in the Romantic age, see "Introduction" (1–17) and "Genius, Madness and Inspiration" (21–42) in Burwick, *Poetic Madness*.

139. When Ficino arrives in his commentary at the section on madness, he specifically mentions reading the *Ion* and the *Symposium* together (ch. 4.ii; Ficino, *Marsilio Ficino*, 84, 85).

140. Plato, *Ion* 533d–534a (Woodruff, 941–42).

141. Ibid., 534c–d (Woodruff, 942).

142. Ibid., 534e–535a (Woodruff, 942).

me wrong. So choose, how do you want us to think of you—as a *man* who does wrong, or as someone *divine*?[143]

Ion decides that it is lovelier to be thought divine, and Socrates responds, "Then *that* is how we think of you Ion, the lovelier way: it's as someone divine, and not as master of a profession, that you are a singer of Homer's praises."[144] Even in the last exchange Socrates playfully placates Ion, letting him determine whether or not he acts by divine inspiration, making it difficult to know how seriously Plato takes this formulation of divine inspiration. Throughout the work, Socrates seems sometimes ironic, sometimes serious.[145] The one thing Plato does seem intent on demonstrating is that the emotional power of Ion's work signifies no great understanding on Ion's part.

Ion is a ridiculous character—superficial, ignorant, boastful. At one point he brags of his great skill in inciting the emotions of his audience while he himself is far from lost in the play. He watches his audience shrewdly to discern whether his performance will bring in the money. Ion says, "You see I must keep my wits and pay close attention to them: if I start them crying, *I* will laugh as I take their money, but if *they* laugh, I shall cry at having lost money."[146] The *Ion*, then, is a tricky text to support an exalted understanding of the inspired artist because Ion the exalted artist is himself portrayed as shallow and money-grubbing. Ion might declaim Homer more beautifully than anyone, but that beauty has been distorted by our knowledge that Ion himself trades on emotional manipulation to line his pockets. It is money, together with acclaim, that motivates his inspired performance, not beauty giving wings to the soul. He is far from the beauty-loving ascender of the ladder to the vision of True Beauty described in the *Phaedrus*. Ion is just the kind of emotion-stirring, ignorant artist Socrates worries about in his decision to banish the poets in the *Republic*.

The *Ion* is an early text for Plato,[147] and it is possible Plato had not himself worked out his relationship to divine inspiration at that point. If Plato does believe that the *Ion* accurately portrays how (a form of) artistic inspiration works, then it is clear that he cannot endorse such inspiration,

143. Ibid., 542a (Woodruff, 949).

144. Ibid.

145. There is a tradition of reading the *Ion* as ironic that includes Goethe. For more on interpreting the *Ion*, see Ferrari, "Plato and Poetry"; Halliwell, *The Aesthetics of Mimesis*; and Ranta, "The Drama of Plato's *Ion*."

146. Plato, *Ion* 535e (Woodruff, 943).

147. Halliwell, *Aesthetics of Mimesis*, 39, makes this point citing Brandwood's *The Chronology of Plato's Dialogues*.

for it is utterly divorced from understanding and directed toward emotional manipulation. It is also a vision of inspiration that contrasts with the inspiration described in the *Phaedrus*, which is a form of both love (not emotional manipulation) and knowledge (not ignorance). This is the inspiration that is the right response to true beauty. Ion is a character who separates art from truth, and a model of inspiration for which he is normative can easily lead to conceptualizing an aesthetic independent of the true and the good—as the Romantic conception of inspiration did in Shiner's telling and as Plato goes to great lengths to prevent in the *Phaedrus*. The attempt to read inspiration as a univocal concept across *Ion* and the *Phaedrus* will only mystify its significance in both texts. It is important as we consider inspiration in Plato that we mark the differences between the two texts.

Ficino's Occlusions: Poetic-Rhetorical Agency in the *Phaedrus*

There are, indeed, two important moments occluded in Ficino's reading of the *Phaedrus*, and I want to trace these occlusions to show the material that informs Gregory's reading of the dialogue, as exemplified by the figure of Macrina. The first omission concerns how Plato describes the divine madness of the lover's response to the beloved—a madness that gives rise to beautiful *logoi* in both the *Phaedrus* and the *Symposium*. Upon seeing the beauty of the beloved, the soul does not just "soften," as Ficino says, but, in a passage teeming with metaphors of both male and female sexual desire, the soul's plumage also "grows hot" as "nourishing moisture" falls upon the stump of feathers, causing it to "swell" and "grow from its root," leaving the soul in a state of "ferment and throbbing" as the emanations of beauty "flood in upon it."[148] In other words, the way divine madness possesses the soul is by causing the soul to grow wings on its wing stumps and by inspiring it to the activity of flying (an activity which is properly its own); it does not displace the soul's agency with that of another. Plato's metaphors weave together active and passive descriptions of the soul's agency, so that the soul is both acted upon and acting. In Ficino's commentary on this passage, by contrast, it is not the soul that has wings, but love, and the soul receives an "influx" of beauty or perhaps, Ficino qualifies, it is an influx of love. The soul is thereby reformed and transformed as in the *Phaedrus*, but Ficino's description accords the soul no agency at this point, in contrast to Plato's complex description of activity and passivity.[149]

---

148. Plato, *Phaedrus* 251 (Hamilton, 58). Hyland, *Plato and the Question of Beauty*, 83.

149. This is not to say that Ficino has no doctrine of the soul's activity in redemption.

The second occlusion is particularly significant insofar as Ficino reads the *Phaedrus* as itself the product of divine inspiration and poetic making, of a radiant Plato pregnant with the divine Muse. There is good reason for reading the *Phaedrus* as the product of poetic making, for the text is filled with hymns, prayers, and myths.[150] But if it is poetry, it is not *only* poetry, and the passage on technique and madness that Ficino makes so much of must be read together with one on rhetoric and philosophy, for while it certainly might be more, the *Phaedrus* is not less than a philosophical work. It is a poetic-philosophic work. There is another reason to read the passages about technique/madness together with those about rhetoric/philosophy. They present parallel arguments. They are not often read together. Bruni, we may recall, translated only the part of the *Phaedrus* that treated poetry, love and beauty, stopping before the exploration of rhetoric and philosophy. But it is not insignificant that poetry, love, beauty, philosophy, and rhetoric all appear in the same piece.

Socrates begins his argument against understanding rhetoric as mere technique by describing it, like the poetry described earlier in the work and like the rhapsodies of *Ion*, as a performance.[151] Rhetoric, he insists— as he had insisted about poetry—cannot be mastered by technique alone. In fact, Socrates has constructed a whole argument for why no art can be mastered by just technique. Socrates gets Phaedrus to admit that the person who thinks he is a doctor because he knows particular techniques used by doctors, though he knows not when or why to use them, is mad. He *rages*, Socrates prompts Phaedrus to claim, using *mainomai*, the verb form of

---

Jörg Lauster, for one, claims that Ficino displays a strong commitment to the activity of both God and the human in salvation—in contrast to many other Renaissance humanists who emphasize the activity of the human at the expense of God ("Marsilio Ficino as Christian Thinker," 54, 63–64). It is simply to note that when he speaks of artistic inspiration, Ficino reverts to language that renders the human passive. It would be an interesting study to identify precisely why and where that shift in the accent on divine agency happens in Ficino's impressively large corpus.

150. Of course, as we know from the *Republic*, hymns to the gods do not represent the kind of poetry that worries Plato. It is not the emotionally wrought and wreaking poetry that corrupts rational souls. On the note of different styles, some readers of Plato, particularly late ancient ones, took the variety of styles as evidence of Plato's youthfulness in composing the *Phaedrus*. Allen writes, "Whereas Diogenes Laertius referred in the first instance to the youthfulness of the *Phaedrus*'s theme, others, such as Dicaearchus, had censured its youthful style, characterizing it as 'turgid' and 'overwrought' (*phortikos*), or, more positively, with Olympiodorus, as 'dithyrambic' (following Socrates himself at 238D2–3)" (Allen, "Introduction," in Ficino, *Marsilio Ficino*, 11).

151. Plato, *Phaedrus* 269d–70a (Hamilton, 88–89).

mania.[152] As the doctor must have some knowledge of medicine, so the musician must know something about harmony, and the successful rhetorician must have some knowledge of truth. Every *technē* presupposes a kind of knowledge, and every form of knowledge corresponds, for Plato, to a metaphysical reality. The medical arts require knowledge of health and wellness; the musical arts require knowledge of the musical of the spheres (for music itself was a metaphysical reality for Plato and many ancient writers); and the rhetorical arts require knowledge of truth. Or, as Socrates puts it later in the *Phaedrus*, as medical *technē* requires knowledge of the human body, rhetorical *technē* requires knowledge of the human soul.[153] Philosophy, it turns out, is not a nice addition to rhetoric but intrinsic to the art of rhetoric itself. No person can be a rhetor without it—at least not a good rhetor. (The problem of loving speeches more than philosophy gets extended treatment in *The Sophist*.) Socrates's discussion of rhetoric began with the problem with Lysias' speech on love, a speech Socrates deemed wrong and poorly organized. Now, many speeches later in the dialogue, it is clear that those two faults were not unrelated.

In the argument about poetry, Socrates maintains that technique absent *mania* fails to become good poetry, and in the argument about rhetoric, that technique absent philosophy is itself a form of madness that fails for all forms of art. Any art presupposes knowledge, and the aspiring artist/artisan is obligated to acquire that knowledge. Ficino passes lightly over these passages, spending remarkably little space on them and not relating them at all to the work of Socrates over the course of the dialogue. By emphasizing only the technique-and-madness section and not the technique-and-philosophy section, while also formulating madness in terms of receptivity, Ficino shades the activity of artistic making as properly passive.

Ficino's failure to give serious consideration to Socrates's speech on rhetoric echoes the much graver error of Phaedrus in his eponymous dialogue. Socrates tries to persuade the would-be lover to philosophy by pointing to philosophy as the practice grounding a person in the metaphysical reality presupposed by rhetoric. It is an attempt that comes on the heels of several failed efforts to point Phaedrus to philosophy. Phaedrus has gone awry on the ladder of beauty in the *Phaedrus* by loving speeches as philosophy just as Alcibiades has in the *Symposium* by loving bodies as souls. What began as a discussion of speeches and loving them moved to the content of the speeches (love and how it is a proper response to beauty and especially beautiful bodies) and then back to speeches and rhetoric. The dialogue's

---

152. Ibid., 268c (Hamilton, 86).
153. Ibid., 270b–c (Hamilton, 89–90).

shifting subject is the result of the diverging ways Socrates and Phaedrus love speeches: Socrates loves them as a way of philosophizing and rising to true beauty, while Phaedrus loves them for themselves, as things to possess and proliferate. Ficino, even if he does not unpack what it means for rhetoric to be an art that requires philosophy, thus downplaying the agency involved in producing a piece such as the *Phaedrus*, at least properly projects Plato's larger picture of a movement up toward Beauty and virtue.

In fairness to Ficino, it is not as if Plato is entirely consistent on the point of Socrates's agency. In transitioning to the "true art of rhetoric," Socrates acts as if he cannot remember or claim responsibility for his speech. Offering to unpack what the genuine art of rhetoric and its opposite look like, he says,

> Well, by a lucky accident the two speeches provide an example of how a speaker who knows the truth can make fun of his hearers and lead them astray. My own belief, Phaedrus, is that the local divinities are responsible for this; or it may be the interpreters of the Muses, the sweet singers overhead, that have been kind enough to inspire us, since for my part I lay no claim to any proficiency to the art of speaking.[154]

The passage is quite possibly ironic, for certainly Socrates is famously proficient at the art of speaking and working with much more of a design than he will admit here. Whether Socrates is "mak[ing] fun of his readers" at this point is difficult to say. What is clear from the dialogue is that Socrates does acknowledge his proficiency in the art of speaking—implicitly in his criticisms of Lysias and explicitly in his hymn to Love[155]—and that he is at the same time inspired. Nevertheless, there is a strong tradition of taking this passage straightforwardly, as Ficino does. It is an important passage for Ficino:

> Now, [Socrates] says, he cannot recall whether he had himself defined love; and justly, for he had defined it when he was inspired with the divine frenzy. Now, as if he were someone different, he cannot remember doing so. That he had defined it correctly and thereby defeated Lysias, he attributes to the wonderful favor of the local divinities. Here he mentions mercurial Pan, the leader of clever and mercurial Nymphs. Dionysus, the

154. Ibid., 262d (Hamilton, 76).

155. Socrates says, "This speech, dear God of Love, I offer to thee in reparation as the best and finest palinode that my powers can devise. . . . Deal kindly and graciously with me, and do not in anger take away or impair the skill in the science of love which thou has given me" (Plato, *Phaedrus* 257a [Hamilton, 66]).

Muses, Pan, and the Nymphs have all inspired Socrates: Diony-
sus gave him the gift of escaping from his intelligence, the Muses
gave him poetry, Pan, eloquence.[156]

Ficino's reading of Plato here once again describes inspiration as an effacement of the inspired's agency. While this understanding of poetic agency
does not do justice to the *Phaedrus* as a whole, Ficino's non-ironic reading
of Socrates's own effacement of agency might be right. It might be, that is,
that Plato has introduced a moment of inconsistency into the *Phaedrus*'s
generally complex portrayal of inspiration as active-passive, for even if Plato
can portray poetic agency as active-passive, he does not have the theological commitments to sustain such a position. He lacks the robust doctrine
of God it would require—one which Gregory has and which I develop in
the fourth section. Socrates's speech must either be the work of his own
proficiency in the art of speaking or the work of Muses—not both. At the
moment of Socrates's "memory lapse," the image of agency he draws on is
one in which the Muses inspire Socrates by his intelligence and leave him
no memory of the work performed through him. He was merely a vessel for
their activity. If this moment of describing poetic agency as passive helped
generate Ficino's reading and Romantic understandings of inspiration, other
moments in the *Phaedrus* helped birth a reading that configured rationality
and inspiration, human and divine activity differently.

Macrina as Inspired Rhetor

Gregory of Nyssa did not produce a commentary on the *Phaedrus*, but he
had certainly studied it. The Platonic charioteer is an image Gregory repeatedly invokes, especially in *On the Soul and the Resurrection*, where he also
recapitulates *Phaedrus*'s argument against rhetoric as mere skill, supplant-
ing Plato's place for philosophy with one for Scripture.[157] The charioteer is
central to his anthropology as well. Also featured in *On the Soul and the
Resurrection* are passages from the *Phaedo* about the soul; Gregory modifies them only by changing "body" (*sōma*) to "flesh" (*sarx*) before putting
them in.[158] When the *Phaedrus* argues so insistently that a rhetorician must
know souls, one wonders if Gregory's borrowing works to display Macrina's
fitness as a rhetor. Such fitness is displayed other ways as well. In *Life of*

---

156. Ficino, *Marsilio Ficino*, ch. 39, 201.

157. For an analysis of how the Platonic charioteer functions in *On the Soul and the
Resurrection*, see Smith, "Macrina."

158. *Phaedo* 81A–D gets imported into "chapter 6" of *On the Soul and the
Resurrection*.

Macrina, she produces beautiful *logoi*; she hymns a prayer and chants her Psalms. She is, in fact, the poet-rhetor that Socrates (and also Plato) is in the *Phaedrus*. But she is not youthful and neither does she have an innocent soul, if by innocent we mean inexperienced. She has helped her mother raise children, buried her parents and at least two siblings, and by Gregory's accounts, deeply loved her community of women, her family, and her God. Her soul has known too much life to be innocent—but it is yet virgin. Macrina's virginal soul has waited diligently, wittily, and increasingly ardently for her Bridegroom. Her soul-virginity is maintained by her virginity of body, which has taught her how to live into and wait for the eschaton. In contrast to Ficino's image of the young, impressionable poet, Macrina is old, so old she is near a natural death, and wise, too wise to be impressed by ideas and people who attempt to persuade her away from pursuing her love. She knows philosophy, but she studies Scripture. And throughout the *Life of Macrina*, Gregory describes her as inspired. Her inspiration comes from one of the beautiful bodies of the text: the Bridegroom. He enters near the end of the text as she is very near death. As her fever spends her strength, her fervor increases for her Bridegroom.

> The day was almost over and the sun was beginning to set, but the zeal in her did not decline. Indeed, as she neared her end and saw the beauty of the Bridegroom more clearly, she rushed with greater impulse toward the One she desired, no longer speaking to those of us who were present, but to that very One toward whom she looked with steadfast eyes. Her couch was turned toward the East and, stopping her conversation with us, for the rest of the time she addressed herself to God in prayer.[159]

Having seen the beauty of her beloved bridegroom, Macrina, like a Platonically trained lover, breaks into a beautiful discourse, a hymn to her beloved. She prays. She gives praise to the one who freed her from the power of death, whose Holy Cross signifies the protection of life against the Enemy, and whom she has loved since infancy. She asks to be brought safely to her Beloved and begs, like Socrates did to Love, forgiveness for her sins, commending her soul to the hands of her lover and her sacrifice to the lover's face.

While disinterested beauty presumes a response evacuated of desire, gratuitous beauty evokes love, and the love that responds to Beauty is a delight-filled love that powers a desire into and through that Beauty—an epectatic love, the love of a woman for her Bridegroom. As the epectatic love of a virgin soul for her Bridegroom, the desire elicited by gratuitous

---

159. Gregory of Nyssa, "Life of Saint Macrina," 179–80.

beauty does not attempt to hoard or exhaust because it is a desire structured by respect—reverence even—and because it is ordered to an inexhaustible object. She therefore responds with doxology.

But Macrina does not just produce a beautiful discourse for her Bridegroom; she manifests his beauty in her own body. Having resolved to engage in philosophical meditation until the end of her life, Macrina's gaze and emotions are so wholly directed toward the Spirit (which is to say, the one who reveals the Bridegroom), that she manifests that pure, undefiled love of the Bridegroom.[160] It is a beauty that will be made still more radiant in her death, even as it will point all the less ambiguously to God.

The Macrina who produces this beautiful discourse (and is elsewhere said to produce beautiful *logoi*[161]) does remarkable things with *logoi*. She deploys philosophy and arguments (*logoi*) in comforting Gregory about Basil's death, revealing to reason (*logos*) the divine providence concealed in human events. Such capacity is the gift of God, for she speaks as inspired (literally, bearing God) by the Holy Spirit.[162] So inspired, her words lift Gregory *almost* outside his human nature and set him in the heavenly realm, the rhetoric doing what good rhetoric should do according to Gregory: conveying him to the Spiritual. Gregory is careful here to insert the "almost," a modification of his description of David's inspiration in *On Virginity*. Another interesting difference between the two descriptions of inspiration is that it is not the maker of discourses who is set in heaven but the hearer. Macrina as rhetoric-maker bears God in her humanity, revealing God's providence to reason. It is Gregory, whose life has not prepared him as Macrina's has prepared her for such God-bearing and God-revealing, who is taken to the limits of his humanity by her disclosure of God.

The fever, meanwhile, eats at Macrina's body, though it never pushes Macrina into madness or at all distracts her from contemplation. This is not a fever that compromises Macrina's consciousness, bleeding into madness and enabling ecstatic declarations and mystical visions. It is a fever that underscores Macrina's supreme rationality. Macrina does not waver in her philosophizing but instead, by reasoned reflection, explains the nature of the soul, the purpose of death, and the hope of the resurrection. Here again, Gregory describes her as inspired:

> In all of this, she went on as if inspired by the power of the Holy
> Spirit, explaining it all clearly and logically. Her speech flowed

160. Ibid., 179.

161. Ibid.

162. Inspired (bearing God) by the Holy Spirit: θεοφορουμένη τῷ ἁγίῳ πνεύματι. Gregory of Nyssa, "Life of Saint Macrina" 17.26–27 (Callahan, 175).

with complete ease, just as a stream of water goes down a hill without obstruction.[163]

This time the word for inspired is something like "en-spirited," and the Spirit works with her *logos* rather than displacing it. In fact, her *logos* flows with perfect ease from the Spirit. By using the comprehensive *logos* rather than the more specific *rhema* (word), Gregory suggests that Macrina's words are not mere instruments of a higher power but that she in her very rationality is working with the Spirit, for by now, *logos* has acquired multiple valences over the course of the dialogue.

Gregory has gone to great lengths to describe how Macrina's *logos* functioned on multiple occasions, ways it was deeply connected to her way of life, faith in God, and scriptural reasoning. Not only does Gregory narrate several rhetors in the text (their father, Macrina's betrothed, Naucratius, Basil, Gregory himself), but both the conversation that prompted Gregory to write the narrative of Macrina and the narrative itself are described as *logos*.[164] It is a *logos* likened to that of the great Thecla, with whom Macrina shares a secret name.[165] When Macrina's parents raise the *logos* of marriage with her after her fiancé dies, she in turn deploys *logoi* in pushing the subject aside.[166] She is a persuasive woman: She persuades Basil away from self-glory toward poverty and manual labor.[167] She persuades her mother to turn their home into a monastery and receive their servants (slaves) as sisters.[168] She also uses her *logos* and *logismos* (reasoned reflection) to oppose the whelming tides of passion at the deaths of Naucratius, her mother, and herself.[169] Macrina can even render in her *logos* the secret mysteries that defy human rationality, as when she reveals by her *logos* the divine providence hidden in the death of Basil.[170] (It is the inspired *logos* that accomplishes this feat and results in the momentary heaven-residence of Gregory's soul.) After she counsels Gregory back from despair at Basil's death, she continues

163. Ἐν οἷς ἅπασιν ὥσπερ ἐμπνευσθεῖσα τῇ δυνάμει τοῦ ἁγίου πνεύματος πάντα διεξήει σαφῶς τε καὶ ἀκολούθως, ἐν εὐκολίᾳ πάσῃ τοῦ λόγου ῥέοντος καθάπερ ἐκ πηγῆς τινος ἀπαραποδίστως πρὸς τὸ πρανὲς φερομένου τοῦ ὕδατος (Gregory of Nyssa, "Life of Saint Macrina" 18.18–22 [Callahan, 176]).

164. Gregory of Nyssa, "Life of Saint Macrina" 1.10, 1.14, and 1.19 (Callahan, 163–64).

165. Ibid., 2.27 (Callahan, 164).

166. Ibid., 5.6, 5.16 (Callahan, 166).

167. Ibid., 6 (Callahan, 167–68).

168. Ibid., 7 (Callahan, 170–71).

169. For more on Macrina as a figure of hope that stems the tide of grief, see Smith, "A Just and Reasonable Grief"; Smith, "Macrina."

170. Gregory of Nyssa, "Life of Saint Macrina" 17 (Callahan, 173).

in her efforts to disperse his grief at her own death, until her beautiful words are cut short by her tortured breathing.[171] With this reminder that her *logos* is ever-embodied, Macrina whispers one last inspired discourse: the prayer to her Bridegroom. She prays forgiveness for sins of thought, word (*logos*), and deed and then her tongue is burned dry, silencing her capacity to utter further *logoi*.[172] Though the text continues for several more sections, there is no further mention of *logos*. The only *logismos* is Gregory's, and it loses its balance to be submerged in the swollen river of his grief, leaving him to weep for his dead sister.[173]

When Gregory describes Macrina's *logos* flowing from the Spirit, the web of associations her *logos* has acquired in the text is taken up in that inspiration, recalled rather than displaced in the inspired speech. In that moment, Macrina's agency is elevated rather than effaced. As it is taken up in this web of associations it is also dissociated from certain ideas and sculpted in particular ways. This is a form of inspiration that ends in ecstasy precisely by privileging the *logos* above passion, for in disciplining passion by a Scripture-tutored *logos,* Macrina learns to see, move toward, and manifest the True Beauty, for whom her love is greater than any human attachment. When passion yields to the Scripture-tutored *logos,* the *logos* yields Bridegroom-directed love in such a way that, governed by the *logos,* Macrina manifests love.[174]

A second way Gregory clarifies *logos* is with regard to *technē*. Where Socrates disparages technique absent inspiration in poetry and technique absent philosophy in rhetoric, Gregory registers his own critiques of technique alone through the figure of Macrina. In *Life of Macrina,* her philosophical *logos* is contrasted with the technical *logos* of a Basil who has just returned from Athens, puffed up with his accomplishments, and the profane *logos* that refuses submission to Scripture. In *On the Soul and the Resurrection,* Macrina contrasts Aristotle's "technical reasoning" about the soul, which leads him into the error of naming the soul as mortal, with the proper reasoning that is governed by Scripture.[175] She worries that technique alone can lead someone to argue equally well for any position, whereas a Scrip-

171. Ibid., 22.13 (Callahan, 179).

172. Ibid., 24 and 25 (Callahan, 181).

173. Ibid., 26 (Callahan, 182).

174. It must be, however, Scripture-tutored *logos*. At one point in the narrative, the youngest brother, Peter, whom Macrina raised as her own, is said to look down on profane studies—or, more literally, the business of words—from the outside perspective (τῆς περὶ τοὺς ἔξωθεν τῶν λόγων ἀσχολίας ὑπεριδών). Gregory of Nyssa, "Life of Saint Macrina" 12.22, 30 (Callahan, 172).

175. Gregory of Nyssa, *On the Soul and the Resurrection* 3.8 (Silvas, 189).

ture-tutored *logos* can guide one to truth.[176] "Technical sophistication" of argument is called, Macrina notes, foolishness by the apostle.[177] As a rhetor, Macrina refuses technique alone, exemplifying Socrates's exhortation that rhetoric not be divorced from philosophy, and when she hymns a prayer, it is by the inspiration of the Holy Spirit, thereby integrating poetry and inspiration. But Macrina is never a poet without also being the good rhetor, for her inspiration does not displace her philosophy but consummates it.

Inspiration does not displace Macrina's *logos* because the agency of the one who inspires her does not displace her own agency. God most often works, for Gregory, internally to the human. Gregory sketches a beautiful literary representation of these agencies in the case of Naucratius's inspiration described earlier, wherein he is led by some divine providence and is drawn by some great impulse of thought.[178] The "by" reflects Gregory's double-use of the dative of agency in this passive construction to give two subjects—their doubleness highlighted by the repetition of "some" (*tinos*)—in describing Naucratius's decision to begin the life of solitude and poverty. Gregory illustrates literarily what is difficult to express expositionally: both God and Naucratius are fully the author of Naucratius's action. Beautiful Naucratius is inspired to render his life a beautiful sacrifice by an agency that is fully his and yet also more than his. This picture of divine and human agency recalls the passive-active imagery of the soul gaining wings in the *Phaedrus* and reinforces the image of the *logos* elevated rather than gagged in Macrina's moments of inspiration. It is very different from the bound agency of the poet in Ficino's depiction of inspiration as a kind of divine ventriloquism. As God works internally to the humanity of a person in learning to perceive beauty through rhetoric, so too does God work internally to the person in generating the rhetoric of beautiful discourses. The question of what kind of God can work in this manner takes us to the next stage of inquiry.

Participation: The Beauty
of a Radically Transcendent God

Throughout Gregory's descriptions of receiving rhetoric—in which God draws a person to Godself—and making rhetoric—in which a person creates a thing of beauty that may draw others to Godself—he assumes a God who works internally to the human without ever displacing the human.

176. Ibid., 3.13–14 (Silvas, 190).

177. Ibid., 3.10 (Silvas, 190).

178. By some divine providence: θείᾳ τινὶ προμηθείᾳ. By some great impulse of thought: μεγάλῃ τινὶ τῆς διανοίας ὁρμῇ.

I want to expound Gregory's doctrine of God that sustains such descriptions. So grounded, I can ask what possibilities for understanding artistic inspiration such a theological commitment allows. As I outline the role of inspiration with respect to fine arts and crafts, I propose a more Nyssenian understanding of inspiration that is a species of participation. This version of inspiration as participation will enable me to explore the role of a fitting and gratuitous beauty in fine art, as well as the difference between the artist and the saint. While I do not argue against the distinction between fine arts and crafts—which I take to name historical realities if not ideological essences—I argue that inspiration is the wrong category to distinguish them from one another, for understanding the fine arts as the inspired arts sustains a problematic picture of the divine. Finally, I return to fittingness and gratuity by considering how Gregory's doctrine of God requires a beauty that is fitting and gratuitous rather than disinterested or functional. But I go beyond finding new reasons for supporting the fittingness and gratuity that I argued for in the beginning of the chapter and explain how Gregory's invocation of Beauty to name a radically transcendent God gives Gregory a richer and more radical account of fittingness and gratuity than Plato can manage without it. Here we will discern the stakes of a radicalized fittingness and gratuity and how they transform the image of the ladder.

Gregory's Doctrine of God: Transcendence and Immanence

Properly formulating God's transcendence and immanence is central to Gregory's theology. Gregory's descriptions of divine agency working internally to human agency are enabled by his strong commitment to working out the implications of the radical transcendence of God, and Gregory stresses the radicality of God's transcendence by formulating it in terms of God's complete immanence. As he often found himself in disputes with the neo-Arians, his argument about God's transcendence frequently took the form of citing the Incarnation as, far from compromising the transcendence of God, offering its best proof. Paradoxically, Christ's wondrous miracles and displays of power are less persuasive evidence of Christ's divinity *because* they are the sort of things we expect divinity to do; miracles display power that strikes us as continuous with the power displayed in the creation and sustenance of the universe. But this comfort with a kind of ordinary transcendence evidences for Gregory how circumscribed our notion of God's power is and how weakly we have worked out the implication of creation. As he claims, the fact that God was able to descend to the materiality of humanness without ceasing to be God is evidence of a "power which is not bounded by circumstances contrary to its nature"—a transcendence so radical it requires no contrary to exclude.[179] It is a transcendence, moreover, that realizes the implications of the claim that God is the creator and sustainer of all. The incarnation should not be strange, Gregory argues, for the one who accepts *creatio ex nihilo*.

> For when he considers the universe, can anyone be so simpleminded as not to believe that the Divine is present in everything, pervading, embracing, and penetrating it? For all things depend on Him who is, and nothing can exist which does not have its being in Him who is. If, then, all things exist in him and he exists in all things, why are they shocked at a scheme of revelation which teaches that God became man, when we believe that even now he is not external to man?[180]

The radical transcendence evidenced in the Incarnation was already assumed in God's creation of the world from nothing, for God is the sole and complete author of all. There is no demiurge mediating God's relationship to the world, nor is there *nous* to shield God from all that is not-God. God's relationship to creation is immediate and direct. How could the divine nature, then, be compromised by flesh? God made flesh and keeps it in existence at every moment.

Gregory takes his argument still further: Though God is uniquely present in the Incarnation, God's radical transcendence also means God is equally present to all creation. Gregory argues that because everything is unworthy of God, nothing is unworthy of God (except evil, which is the nothing that signifies complete unworthiness). He elaborates:

> For every created thing is equally inferior to the Most High who, by reason of his transcendent nature, is unapproachable. The whole universe is uniformly beneath his dignity. For what is totally inaccessible is not accessible to one thing and inaccessible to another. Rather does it transcend all existing things in equal degree. Earth is not more below his dignity, and heaven less. Nor do the creatures inhabiting each of these elements differ in this respect, that some have a direct contact with his inaccessible nature, while others are distant from it. Otherwise we could not conceive of the power that governs the universe as equally pervading all things. In some it would be unduly present, in others it would be lacking. Consequently, from these differences of more and less, the divine nature would appear to be composite

179. Gregory of Nyssa, "Address on Religious Instruction," 300–301.
180. Ibid., 302.

and inconsistent with itself, were we to conceive of it in principle as remote from us while it was near some other creature and easily accessible by his proximity.[181]

The problem with the Arians, Gregory argues, is not that their view of God's transcendence is too high, but that it is too low. The Arians think that creatures at the top of the hierarchy of being approach worthiness of God more than creatures farther down in the hierarchy. In such a conception of God, they fail to grasp the radical ontological gap between divine and non-divine. It is a gap presumed in the doctrine of creation, wherein nothing can compromise the difference between Creator and created, between the former's independent existence and the latter's dependent existence. This infinite abyss between divine and non-divine means that any creaturely gain in worthiness counts but as nothing before this great, equalizing divide. God's divinity need not be sanitized from the touch of the non-divine, for God's divinity is not of such a kind that it can be compromised or polluted by creation. But creation's dependence also means that it exists at every moment in and by and through God's sustaining activity. The ontological gap, then, not only names the infinite farness of God but the infinite nearness, too. The best statement of God's radical transcendence is God's utter immanence to all things, and God's utter immanence is possible because God is radically transcendent.

The Incarnation is, for Gregory, the best illustration of God's radical transcendence, yet it also clarifies what radical transcendence does *not* entail: pantheism. To say that God is immanent to all things does not mean that God is reducible to all things, and the Incarnation (like the Temple) raises the need to distinguish among different *presences* of God. God is not present in the saint the same way God is present in Christ; while the death of God in Christ saves, the death of a martyr does not. The presence of God in Christ is absolute and without remainder. The presence of God in another person is always located in a relation of dependence of that person on God.

Kathryn Tanner draws on Gregory of Nyssa among others to work out a commitment to God's radical transcendence in terms of a relationship between human and divine agency she calls non-contrastive. In her book, *God and Creation in Christian Theology*, Tanner traces at one point how Christian theological understandings of non-contrastive agency developed the various Hellenistic options, which opposed God's transcendence to God's direct involvement in the world.[182] One option characterizes God as the most powerful being among beings, the top of the hierarchy of being.

181. Ibid., 305.
182. Tanner, *God and Creation*, 39.

Such a being was above humankind in the way that the best, most just, most powerful being transcends beings of ordinary goodness, justice, and power. In other words, God was at the top of the spectrum of being. It is not difficult to understand how such a being might be involved in the world, but this kind of being is transcendent only in a limited extent. This God is, like humans, a species of the shared genus of Being.[183] A second option refuses this characterization of divinity as a being among beings by understanding it as the separate realm of being, which exists in contrast to the realm of becoming. This kind of divinity is characterized by its unlikeness to humans, which protects the transcendence of God but mystifies the possibility of God's involvement in the world, for God and world are understood as logical contraries.[184] Tanner associates various Platonic writings with each of these positions. She identifies a third option with a failed effort by Plotinus to understand divine agency as transcending the language of opposition with the world. It succeeds as non-contrastive to the extent that Plotinus wants to name the One as the undifferentiated ground of all being, but it fails to the extent that Plotinus understands the One's involvement in the world via an emanationist scheme, by which the One only directly affects the *nous*. Such a scheme "protects" the One's transcendence from direct involvement in materiality, but such protection reinvokes the contrast the One is supposed to exist beyond. A Christian account of transcendence, by contrast, understands God as directly and unmediatedly responsible for all creation. As Gregory puts it, God cannot be nearer the heavens than the earth; God transcends all creation in equal degree.

That God is the ground of all Being who exists immediately near each creature precisely by infinitely transcending all of them opens up this "non-contrastive agency" whereby God's agency is beyond all opposition to our own. Because God is not a being among beings, God does not compete with humans for space. God's activity does not crowd out human activity. And similarly: Because God is the infinitely near source of all being and ground of all activity, human activity exists only in and by divine activity. Far from competing with human activity, divine activity enables it as it exceeds it. As God's transcendence is not compromised by God's immanence to the world, neither is human agency compromised by the divine agency immanent within it. God's freedom breaks transcendence and immanence out of their opposition and so enables human freedom to coexist with divine sovereignty.[185]

183. Ibid., 39–40.
184. Ibid., 40–42.
185. I am exploring non-contrastive agency as preliminary to thinking about

This understanding of non-contrastive or non-competitive agency, then, is important for (at least) three reasons: 1) It elaborates the doctrine of God's radical transcendence, which resolves the apparent opposition between God's transcendence and God's involvement in the world (also framed as the opposition between free will and divine sovereignty). 2) It is implied in the doctrine of *creatio ex nihilo* and the ontological gap such creation entails. 3) It explains how God could be incarnate without compromising God's divinity. Non-contrastive agency is a theological commitment with stakes in theological anthropology, creation, and Christology, and it is therefore a commitment with which theologians ought to take particular care to keep faith. I want to consider, therefore, what possibilities for thinking about the role of divine inspiration in the creation of art (including rhetoric) are available to a theologian determined to work out non-contrastive agency.

Inspiration as Participation

Human and Divine Agency in Inspiration

By now, it should be clear that I find Gregory's conception of inspiration to be more compelling than Ficino's. But Ficino himself never explicitly violates non-contrastive agency. It is no violation of divine transcendence for a poet to rhapsodize by God's power alone any more than it is for a rock to speak. Divine agency can act exclusive of human agency in the human without threatening non-contrastive agency. It *would* violate the principle of radical transcendence to say that a poet's agency must be bound *in order* to allow God to speak through him, for that would posit human agency as a limiting factor for divine agency. Divine agency must not be reduced to the gaps in human agency. Ficino, however, neither argues that divine activity requires human passivity nor thematizes poetic madness as a model for God's working in the world.

It is possible, after all, for inspiration simply to name those occasions when divine agency works without human agency. Though certainty about divine inspiration in such cases would remain elusive, the mark of inspiration would be the absence of the poet's own skill and her simultaneous production of a beautiful discourse—as in the case of Tynnichus in the *Ion*.

---

possibility for inspiration—that is, for the work of the Holy Spirit in us. Tanner herself has recently discussed the implications of non-contrastive agency for pneumatology in the seventh chapter of her latest book *Christ the Key*, though her concern is to articulate the kinds of religious authority enabled by different models of how the Holy Spirit works.

Inspiration would name the free choice of God to act through the human without human agency. (It is arguable that the appeal of mythologizing certain musicians, painters, and writers as Outsider Artists—usually: children, the institutionalized, and the untrained—turns in part on a Ficino-like appeal to the artist as receptive to divine inspiration that works outside human skill.) The problem with such understandings occurs when divine inspiration conflates with divine presence so that its opposite is divine absence or the merely human. We find just such slippage in early modern understandings of the human, which separate her from the realm of nature and separate both nature and culture from the divine. Then Ficino's divine inspiration is recast, not in continuity with a God who grounds all activity, but in discontinuity with a world that ticks by its own power.[186]

Such a transformation in cosmology takes Ficino's triangulation of divine inspiration, lack of human skill, and the poet as *deus in terris*, and identifies a corresponding abjected triangle of lack of divine inspiration, presence of human skill, and mere humanity.[187] The work these triangles end up doing, then, opposes the presence of God with the presence of human skill. The practiced craftsperson is not a "god upon the earth" as the poet is, for his skill marks the presence of his human-making and therefore the absence of divine-making. Ficino's polarity of the inspired arts and the non-inspired arts, when read through the later transformations of nature and culture, implicitly invokes a God whose transcendence is compromised by working through human skill rather than instead of it.[188] But a commitment to understanding God as radically transcendent means that God grounds all human activity, so that it is not only impossible that God's activity be threatened by human activity, but that human activity is impossible outside the divine activity grounding and enabling it. While human activity need not be present in, say, the production of beautiful discourses, divine

186. For more on the transformations of nature and culture from early humanists and Renaissance thinkers through the early seventeenth century, see Dupré, *Passage to Modernity*, 42–50.

187. Part of what is tricky in Ficino is that in some works he exalts the artist as acting analogously to the divine in the act of creation—thereby exalting the artist as skilled—and sometimes insists that the artist's own skill has nothing to do with such creation. In insisting on humanity's fundamental openness to God, Ficino draws no fast lines between human and divine agency, either in art or redemption.

188. It would be theologically sound to name the poet a "god upon the earth," not because the poet's lack of skill enables a more active divinity, but because the poet's absence of skill renders God's presence visible in a way it is normally difficult to perceive. But this interpretation of the poet's god-likeness fails to find its way into Ficino's descriptions.

activity is always present. Thus, two poles define the spectrum for theologically sound models of human and divine agency in inspired making.

- *Model at Pole 1: Fully engaged divine activity, zero human activity.*[189] The basic architecture of this model of inspired-making could accommodate both Ficino's description of inspired making and Plato's in the *Ion*. Where Ficino describes the poet as a god upon the earth, Plato characterizes the inspired rhapsode as a buffoon. In reality, inspiration of this variety says very little about the inspired one, for the inspired activity reflects entirely on God. Taken as exhaustive of human making, this model presumes a rather low view of the human as a creature lacking efficacy and powers properly her own, as an empty shell that creates only by conducing the divine. Yet this model can also be taken to describe only a particular type of human making, as in the veil of Veronica, which is described as bearing the image of Jesus's face without any human skill rendering it. Regardless of whether the inspired making this model illustrates marks a vast realm or a tiny one, the model's theological integrity depends upon a careful distinction between divine inspiration and divine activity. Slippage between the two generates a problem similar to the one of Ficino's legacy, wherein divine activity is located in the absence of human activity and not the presence. This model remains theologically responsible when couched in an understanding of human agency that is always already happening within divine agency.

- *Model at Pole 2: Fully engaged divine activity, fully engaged human activity.* The model of inspired making on the other pole presents a version of human agency that is fully responsible for the product of inspired making, even as divine agency is also fully responsible. This non-competitive co-responsibility—responsibility, that is, that is not divided up to be shared but is attributed to each agent fully and on different levels—is made possible by a strong commitment to understanding God's agency as non-contrastive. This model works because God's creative activity enables a creature to become more fully what she is; God's creative activity is the *only* way a creature can become more fully what she is. Because God grounds the creature's activity,

189. While I do not think inspiration ought to name what is distinctive about fine arts, I also do not think we ought to do away with a concept of inspiration altogether. It could even explain something about how both fine arts and crafts are made. In what follows, my concern is to outline a domain of possibilities for understanding inspiration given a commitment to the non-contrastive agency of God. By engaging in this exploration of inspiration, I will also position myself to distinguish more helpfully between fine arts and crafts.

God can work internally to the creature without compromising her freedom. Thus divine inspiration can include human freedom and human skill.

These two models of inspiration resemble the two views of how the Spirit works that Tanner articulates in *Christ the Key*. There she describes a view of the Spirit who works "instantaneously and directly," without mediation, "in exceptional events;" and another in which the Spirit works "gradually," "through the usual fully human and fully fallible" processes of "ordinary life."[190] In the same way that I have argued Model 1 inspiration works to secure a kind of divinity for art and artist, Tanner suggests that the vision of the Spirit's work as unmediated secures a kind of divine (unquestioned and unquestionable) authority. She ultimately argues that embracing the mediation view of the Holy Spirit's work can de-polarize the two views and generate a fuller picture of the Spirit's work that includes the immediate and mediate.

But while such descriptions of the Spirit's work make sense as a way to talk about authority, what makes the second model of inspiration *inspiration*? How does it describe how inspired making is set apart from other kinds of making? In short, it does not. It only describes how divine and human agency are configured in inspired making, but it leaves open the question of what makes such activity inspired. As we have been working within a Platonic scheme with Ficino, Gregory, and Plato, I suggest that we understand inspiration with reference to participation. Gregory follows the tradition of Plato, Christianized by Justin Martyr, reiterated by Irenaeus, and developed more extensively by Origen, of understanding creaturely existence and perfections through participation in God. Participation is a deep and frequent theme in Gregory's writings. It describes both how we exist and how we perfect our existence, for God is every perfection: life, goodness, beauty, truth. To the extent that ones lives or is virtuous or beautiful or true, one participates in God.

This basic schema—wherein one possesses a perfection to the extent that she participates in it—can be found in Plato, but Gregory makes an important modification of Plato and his heirs in Middle Platonism and Neoplatonism. Where Platonic schemas used participation primarily to describe the relation of the sensible world to the intelligible world (this chair exhibits chairness because it participates in the form of a chair), Gregory grounds participation in a distinction more fundamental to his thought: that of creation and Creator. Creation gains its existence and reaches its fulfillment in and through participation in the Creator. In David Balás's study

---

190. Tanner, *Christ the Key*, 274.

on participation in Gregory of Nyssa, he concludes that Gregory's modification of participation means that where later Platonism uses participation to
generate a hierarchy of divine beings, Gregory uses participation precisely
to exclude an intermediary between Creator and created.[191] Gregory uses
participation to mark the immanence and transcendence of God—or as Balás says, "the absolute distinction, but also gratuitous union, between God
and the spiritual creatures."[192] The creature's participation in the transcendent God means that she is ever dependent on God, that she never possesses
a divine perfection by nature or by identity but only as received. In this
way, participation affirms the distinction between Creator and creation. Yet
in the creature's participation in the Creator, Gregory maintains that the
transcendent source both remains unchanged and is fully present in the
participating creature, "as the efficient and especially the exemplary cause
of the shared perfection, and as known, loved, and enjoyed in a constantly
increasing measure."[193] The theme pervades Gregory's writings, though it
changes as Gregory develops his understanding of God as infinite.[194] As he
thematizes God's infinity, Gregory develops his corresponding notion of
epectasy, where the creature ever expands, growing always deeper into God
and her capacity to love.

While all activity is grounded in God and therefore also participates
in God, not all activity participates in the same way or to the same degree.
At the beginning of *On the Inscriptions of the Psalms*, we might remember,
Gregory exhorts the reader to the goal of blessedness, which is attained by
becoming blessed through participation in the blessed nature, which is God.
Not all activities equally attain to this blessedness. While God's perfection is
unparticipated and infinite, creaturely perfection is participated and limited
and therefore admits of degrees of more and less. We might say, then, that
while God is equally near all things, not all things are equally near God. Virtue, the name for blessed or divine activity by the human, is the foremost,
and virtue can be present, in some form at least, in any non-sinful activity.
The way a person makes supper, for example, or a cup, or the way a person
declaims Homer, can embody virtue. One can engage in those activities in
such a way as to participate more or less in the divine nature. The aim of
the activity is also important to understanding what kind of participation
happens. Activity that has as its aim, for example, truth, participates in God

191. Balás, *Metousia Theou*, 163–64.

192. Ibid., 163.

193. Ibid. See also 31–32, 60, and 140 for more on this theme.

194. Though this last clause represents my own view that Gregory's understanding of *metousia* changed over the course of his writings, I largely follow David Balàs's
discussion of participation in *Metousia Theou*.

in a way qualitatively different than activity that takes as its aim, say, making a good cup, or making money, or taking first prize at the rhapsode festival. A person is inspired when she participates in God in such a way as to produce a work that discloses a deep truth or splendorous beauty, for Truth and Beauty name God, and to participate deeply in them is to participate deeply in God. This understanding of inspiration as participation means that inspiration is no longer entwined with fine arts models of making, and it opens up different possibilities for how both fine arts and crafts might be inspired.

Inspiration in Fine Arts and Crafts

While I do not want *inspiration* to distinguish fine arts from crafts, it may be the case that fine arts conduce more than other arts to inspired participation. They are, after all, marked by participation in an institutionally sanctioned conversation, where those institutions are the university, the museum, and to a lesser extent, the gallery.[195] *Conversation* is here both analogical and literal. It is analogical in the sense that artworks do not literally speak ideas back and forth, though they do respond to one another. Yet their conversation is made literal both at the level of critics, who themselves respond to artworks by trading in words and ideas, and at the level of the artists themselves, who are trained in art schools into the process of speaking about their works as much as they are trained into making them.

Such conversations, either literal or analogical, may be frivolous or profound, and much of the time, the artists might not see themselves as engaging in a process of disclosing Truth. But because they are engaged in conversations, they are communicating ideas, and some of these ideas are truer than others, and *some* of them are deeply true. The conversations in which the fine arts objects take part have different subjects, and many art objects take multiple subjects. Some of these want to express the horror of a particular situation; others want to push the limits of what is accepted as art; some are social commentaries; some are explorations of particular colors

195. While I would not want to call this a definition of fine arts, it is broadly characteristic and inclusive of fine arts as disparate as "performance art," ready-mades, Beethoven, and Velázquez. It picks up on the insights of both Jacques Maritain and Rowan Williams that such arts are communicative, and it also allows for a piece to become fine art long after it has been made, by being made part of this conversation through subsequent pieces commenting on it. For "institutional conversation" characteristic of fine arts to be refined into a definition, I would have to attend to several difficulties, not least of which is the increasing diffusiveness of "the gallery." For more on the difficulty of defining fine arts institutionally given the emergence of alternative gallery spaces, see O'Brien, "New Alternatives"; Joyce, "Neutral Grounds/Fertile Territory"; Snow, "Show and Sell."

and the way color works. Some are all of those things. Most conversations reach for some kind of truth, and we can say that to the extent that a work is successful, the artist is participating in Truth, which is to say, God. So we might identify inspiration through, for example, the intensity of human suffering in war represented in Picasso's painting *Guernica* or the viscerality of grief expressed in Martha Graham's dance *Lamentation*. We might want to say that these artists are inspired if we believe they are disclosing a deep truth, which is to say, they are participating in God. Like Gregory's descriptions of the beautiful Psalms, the music of which opens up into their truth, perhaps the work of these artists open up for us some feature of reality.

It must be said that such conversing is not intrinsic to art as such. Inasmuch as art is the product of any skilled human making, art may or may not participate in a conversation. But fine arts have developed in such a way that they are sustained by and inseparable from institutions that legitimate their own presence and train, vet, and understand fine artists through conversation and writing about art. Apprenticeship into an artistic discipline need not involve learning to comment on the discipline or other art in the discipline through one's own art. This is traditionally true of the world that has come to be called craft. The silversmith simply learned to make good candlestick holders; the cobbler learned to make good shoes; the carpenter learned to make good chairs; etc. The chair did not, traditionally, comment on the chairs that came before it. It was made to be sat on. Many chairs today are still made for that purpose (most of them by machines), but sometimes chairs are made as comments on the chairs that came before, or sometimes they are later interpreted as such. Such chairs are often displayed in museums or galleries so that their "commentary" can be discussed.[196]

So how can crafts—these non-conceptual arts—be inspired? Let's take a step back and assess where we are in the conversation. The understanding of inspiration I am outlining—as a deep participation in God—so far suggests that some fine arts are inspired, but not all. I have not outlined ways in which non-fine arts might be inspired. They may also be inspired to the extent that they are beautiful, for Beauty, too, names God. Before unpacking ways in which crafts might participate in beauty, though, I should clarify two things.

---

196. This was the dilemma of the Arts and Crafts movement: the Arts and Crafts makers were too deeply implicated in the institutions of university and museum to escape their status as fine art. Their "crafts" were commenting on the status of the museum and its works, and it was, as such, incorporated into the museum and made to be fine art. The movement may have succeeded in redrawing some of the lines around art and craft, but the opposition itself remained.

First, I want to clarify that thinking of fine arts as characterized by participation in conversations mediated by the university, the museum, and the gallery is importantly different from Arthur Danto's famous insistence that art is defined by art theory. I distinguish my Nyssenian approach from his approach on two important points. Contrary to Danto, I maintain that art theory does not, in the abstract or in and of itself, constitute an object as art. It is art theory as mediated by the institutions of university, museum, and gallery that does this work; an art object is not an art object apart from these historically located, socially contextualized, power-brokering institutions. Part of my divergence here with Danto can be traced to his insistence that despite the importance of historical particularity, art is an essence for him that has been unfolding across time.[197] In contrast, I am presenting an understanding of fine arts as inescapably historically constructed. There is no inevitability about the way fine arts has emerged.

I also diverge from Danto in the way he understands art theory in opposition to the aesthetics of the art object. He points to the visual identicalness of Warhol's *Brillo Boxes* and the Brillo boxes sold in stores to say that what distinguishes *Brillo Boxes* is art theory, which means that art is finally about theory rather than aesthetics. I want to propose, instead, that because of fine art's participation in these conversations, we learn to see such art objects differently. We learn to see the bowl differently in light of the conversations in which it participates in a way similar to the lover seeing her beloved as beautiful. She does not just see that he is plain but know that he is good and kind and worthy; her knowing that he is good and kind and worthy—a knowledge that takes the form of love—transforms the way that she sees him. She has learned to see him as beautiful. I am proposing an understanding of sight in which sight is inescapably trained. It is not merely given, nor can it be reduced to a material, physical reality cleansed of all association with the spiritual-intellectual. The material and intellectual interpenetrate in such a way that proper sight must be ordered to the material-intellectual reality—a concept thematized by Gregory in his doctrine of the spiritual senses, which I unpack in chapter 4.

The second thing I want to clarify: inasmuch as Truth, Goodness, and Beauty all name God, for Gregory (and are likewise convertible for Plato), it

197. On this point, Danto writes, "As an essentialist in philosophy, I am committed to the view that art is eternally the same—that there are conditions necessary and sufficient for something to be artwork, regardless of time and place. I do not see how one can do the philosophy of art—or philosophy period—without to this extent being an essentialist. But as an historicist I am also committed to the view that what is a work of art at one time cannot be one at another, and in particular that there is a history, enacted through the history of art, in which the essence of art—the necessary and sufficient conditions—are painfully brought to consciousness" (*After the End of Art*, 95).

might seem as if I am failing to distinguish properly between artist and saint. While both the great artist and the saint deeply participate in God, they do so differently. We human beings are fragmented selves that have learned to lead fragmented lives. That is, the great artist who produces truthful (and therefore, in some sense, beautiful) works might yet be less than morally virtuous, for to the extent that we (especially as unsanctified) live fragmented lives, the artist can participate in goodness as an artist without necessarily transforming her whole person. Truth, beauty, and goodness cannot be fragmented, but people can. The artist can participate in Truth *qua* artist without necessarily leading an honest life because the unsanctified self is a fragmented self.[198] Not only is the artist's self (often) fragmented, but the piece can itself be fragmented in that it might participate in beauty or truth in one respect but not in another.

One example of fragmented participation for Gregory is Plato's *Symposium* or *Phaedrus*, where Plato was able to lay out a piece substantially right, according to Gregory, in its approach to beauty, even though they presumed a view of divinity unacceptable to Gregory. Or similarly: Gregory thought the *Phaedo,* known in the ancient world as *On the Soul*, so beautiful that he wanted to rewrite it as a Christian version. To that end he produced *On the Soul and the Resurrection*, and he imported certain passages from the *Phaedo* directly into his work, even as he reworked its philosophy to give a higher place to the body. For Gregory, Plato's works thus marked a deep participation in truth or beauty, though one that was fragmented, in that it left behind important doctrines about God or materiality or the resurrection. Similarly, rhetoric that is beautiful (not merely sensorily gratifying) may be put in the service of less than noble ends. We might consider, for example, a speech calling soldiers to participate in an unjust war. The speech may be quite beautiful, even if the action to which it calls the hearer is not. Such a speech would be ordered to its subject in that it is written in the proper register, but it is less than fully beautiful because it valorizes an action that is less than beautiful, good, or true.[199]

198. I am making a point here similar to Iris Murdoch, who says, "Art is a human product and virtues as well as talent are required of the artist. The good artist, in relation to his art, is brave, truthful, patient, humble" (*Sovereignty of Good*, 84).

199. This view, expressed particularly in *On Virginity* and *On the Inscriptions of the Psalms*, contrasts subtly with Plato's presentation of rhetoric in the *Phaedrus*, wherein rhetoric has much less independence from philosophy or philosophical rightness, if any. It was not just that Phaedrus misjudged the correctness of Lysias's argument but that Phaedrus was wrong to love the form of Lysias's speech, for Lysias's argument was manifest in the very organization of the speech. Further, when Socrates delivers his own "wrong" speech about love, the speech is not a lie but simply an incomplete truth.

This fragmentation in participation—particularly the fragmentation between self and work—marks the difference between an artist and a saint. To the extent a person is sanctified, she leads an integrated life, participating in God with her whole self.[200] (Although, the saint does not disclose the whole of God, and the saint's particular gifts and talents are not eradicated but heightened through such participation.) Witness Gregory's depiction of Macrina. Macrina's participation in God is so full, so integrated that not only could she produce wholly beautiful, truthful speeches, but she herself takes on the beauty of God, radiating divine beauty like rays of light. While Macrina had always been beautiful, years of increasing participation in God clarified her beauty until it streamed from her unconcealed, an undeniable revelation of God. This remarkable transformation is enabled by Gregory's doctrine—not yet fully developed at the point in his life when he wrote *Life of Macrina*—of a self that is not a stable unit but continues to grow, eternally, into and through the infinite God.[201] The self is not a vessel to be filled for Gregory, but an ever-extending wayfarer into the never-exhaustible God. This idea is thematized in Gregory's later writings as the doctrine of epectasy. I explore some implications of this doctrine in the fourth chapter, but for now it is important to understand that epectasy means there is no horizon for participation in God. A person can always go deeper, for the more deeply a person participates, the greater capacity she has for participation. This commitment to an epectatic notion of the self makes the commitments of the second model of divine inspiration all the more important for Gregory. Human making is characterized by human agency's dependence on and direct relation to divine agency, which continues to expand human activity to live into its own eschatological end. Making beautiful discourses is part of the sanctification and growth of the self. It is right that beauty expand into this infinite, epectatic journey into the God who is Beauty, for the fittingness

---

He discloses love as madness without revealing that madness can be divine and good. Socrates's second speech, wherein he discloses the full truth of love, is also manifestly more beautiful, ending with the famous hymn to love. Plato of the *Phaedrus* represents a form and content that align in their participation (or lack of participation) in the beautiful. However, it is possible to argue that Plato of the *Republic* has worries about the misalignment of beautiful form and true content.

200. This is not to say, obviously, that the saint will be capable of producing great works of art equal to that of the artist. She does not, simply by being a saint, receive all the gifts of human making.

201. For more on participation in the infinite God and how it forms, modifies, and displaces Gregory's understanding of deification, see Russell, *Doctrine of Deification*, 223–32.

and gratuity that characterize beauty have an inherent dynamism to them, in contrast to, say, the static distance of disinterestedness.

Transcendence and Immanence, Fittingness and Gratuity

From meditating on the beauty of the saint, we now return to meditating on the beauty of God. For, in describing the inspiration that is participation in truth or beauty as participation in the divine and in naming beauty as a sign of the divine, I raise the question of what it means for beauty to represent something of the character of God. What does it mean for beauty to be, not just continuous with, but in some way disclosive of the divine? And what does such disclosiveness suggest for how we are to think about beauty? I want to suggest that fittingness and gratuity characterize a beauty that signifies the divine in a way a beauty conceived as functional or disinterested cannot. As fitting and gratuitous, beauty signifies and partakes in the God who is immanent and transcendent, thus witnessing to and cohering with Gregory's doctrine of God. The shift to fittingness and gratuity is warranted not just by the way disinterestedness and functionality fail to account for the experience and judgment of beauty, but also because they fail as theological descriptions of a God who is Beauty. They are, to be fair, usually proposed by people who do not necessarily believe that beauty is divine, but if we take seriously Gregory's commitment to a God who is both Beauty and radically transcendent, we must not only give serious consideration to understanding beauty as fitting and gratuitous. We must also radicalize that fittingness and gratuity in ways that Plato could not.

After all, the very context for Gregory's discussion of radical transcendence is a question of fittingness. Gregory's *Address on Religious Instruction* is framed as a response to the Arian objection that it is unfitting that God would become human. The argument Gregory refutes is that because humanity is unfitting of God, the human Christ is clearly not fully God. Throughout the text, Gregory uses "to fit" (*prepō*) and "the fitting" (*to prepon*), among other words (like *axios* or worthy) to argue that the Arians are wrong. Not only is it not unfitting that God would become human, but it is, in fact, perfectly fitting. Most of his ink is spilled over this first, defensive argument, by which Gregory invokes God's transcending of all things to show how Gregory's Arians have an altogether wrong understanding of divine fittingness. God can be perfectly immanent as humanity without compromising God's divinity—the Incarnation is not *unfitting*—precisely because God radically transcends all things. Having radicalized descriptions of divine fittingness with his descriptions of radical transcendence, Gregory goes on to make his positive argument: The one fitting (*prepon*) thing that remains is that God would come to the aid of those who are in need. What is fitting of God is love and particularly the form of love that is mercy. It is this love that goes out to those who are in need, this love that can be perfectly immanent in suffering because it radically transcends all things, that discloses the fittingness of a God who is Beauty. Disinterestedness and functionality are woefully inadequate to this radically transcendent God to whom the mercy of the Incarnation, the mingling with flesh, is both perfectly fitting and utterly gratuitous.

Rowan Williams points out that functional theories of beauty fail to remember the transcendence of beauty (and, thus, implicitly, of God). Williams thinks it important to remember the beautiful object yields a surplus that points beyond itself and any particular purpose it might have.[202] But disinterested models have a similar problem. In focusing exclusively on a beautiful object's capacity to transcend its setting, uses, and communities, disinterested theories of beauty forget beauty's presence to creaturely life, society, and apprehension. Disinterested theories of beauty focus on beauty's transcendence. That is why Kant described beauty as a representation of the numinous moral law and divorced it from any relationship to the human body (sensuality) or a community (use or purpose). But as a signifier for a Creator who directly created and remains infinitely near creation, such a vaporous description of beauty is inadequate. We would expect that as God transcends creation while remaining immanent to it, Beauty would also remain true to such transcendence and immanence, pointing to God's beyond-ness while celebrating the particulars of God's nearness. Moreover, such beyond-ness and nearness are not in tension with one another. As

202. Williams is on this point remarkably similar to Simone Weil, who merged Plato's privileging of desire together with Kant's insistence on disinterestedness to arrive at a beauty that works on the self while refusing integration into the everyday. She writes, "Beauty is the only finality here below. As Kant said very aptly, it is a finality which involves no objective. A beautiful thing involves no good except itself, in its totality, as it appears to us. We are drawn toward it without knowing what to ask of it. It offers us its own existence" (Weil, "Forms of the Implicit Love," 105). Weil here expresses the way beauty is for her a force of *necessity*. By eschewing any purpose in the world, beauty represents the perfect necessity, the only purpose: God. Because necessity is perfectly immanent—it points to no future, no purpose beyond—it represents the one who is the eternal present, the one who absolutely transcends all purpose. While Weil captures—eloquently, poetically—the way the beautiful has its own agency, she ignores or binds the agency of the beholder. Beauty draws; we simply are drawn. It offers; what can we do but receive? She commends passivity to humanity. It is because Gregory's version of God's transcendence is not heavy—not the totality of the universe but something altogether beyond universe—that Gregory's version of beauty need not eschew purpose, nor be described as a force of necessity.

God's utter immanence to all things discloses God's radical transcendence, so the very perfection of beauty's fittingness expresses itself as gratuity. And conversely, as God's radical transcendence is evidenced in God's utter immanence to all things, so beauty's absolute gratuity is seen most clearly in its perfect fittingness at all levels of context, creaturely and divine.

While disinterestedness and functionality each find their coherence in suppressing the other,[203] fittingness and gratuity are mutually enriching, though such enrichment might not be immediately apparent. Like transcendence and immanence, gratuity and fittingness might initially seem to be at odds with one another. Where gratuity suggests no warrant, cause, or justification, fittingness suggests complete suitability, appropriateness, and properness. Fittingness suggests a symmetry that gratuity wholly thwarts. Yet understood within the framework of radical transcendence, they, like transcendence and immanence, open onto one another. The Beauty that appears as excess works internally to a person, so perfectly fitting to her humanity that there is gratuity in this perfect fittingness, as Beauty's perfectly fitting internal workings transform a person, causing her growth in Beauty so that she becomes an expanded and sanctified version of herself, fit for new kinds of internal workings.

While Plato at times describes a version of fittingness and gratuity that open onto one another, his descriptions of the novice's introduction to beauty indicates a version of fittingness and gratuity often at odds with one another. The initiate first responds to the beautiful body erotically, then rhetorically, then learns to prize the body less highly, then disdains the valorization of bodies at all. The fittingness of a particular beauty and the proper response to it are left behind as one responds to the gratuity of its beauty, its invitation to deeper depths and higher heights. Consequently, the initial sites of beauty are often celebrated in Plato *only* for their gratuity, only for the way they enable the novice to transcend them and move on to the Beauty that transcends all beauties.

But Gregory's Beauty remains immanent within beauties even as it transcends all of them. While a beautiful object may be beautiful in one respect and ugly in another, if it is truly beautiful in that one respect, it should not, in that respect, call forth disdain. (One might disdain a rhetoric that is deployed to less than noble ends but still admire the beauty of the words—the respect in which it is beautiful. Maybe Martin Luther thought

---

203. While one person may construe functionality and disinterestedness as alternative theories of beauty applicable to different objects—say disinterested models of beauty illumine fine arts and functional models illumine crafts—they must be suppressed, at least, with regard to the same object. For disinterestedness precisely requires, according to Kant, refusing the criterion of use.

something like this when he rehabilitated drinking songs as Christian hymns. The songs themselves are not irredeemably tainted by their less noble aspects.) A radically transcendent God who is Beauty will not allow us to leave behind less complete visions of beauty or ever claim them as unbeautiful or worthy of disdain. They remain disclosive of the God who called all things out of nothing and holds all creation in existence. Objects may be beautiful in one respect and ugly in another due to finitude, fallenness, or seeing the object under different aspects.

The image of the ladder is thus insufficient in two respects: first, in the way it suggests leaving behind lower rungs; and, second, in the way it suggests a singular entry-point and path to a vision of Beauty Itself. While rhetoric remains an important and powerful site of initiation into seeking beauty, it is not the only point, nor is it the most powerful. In the chapters that follow, I continue to explore the importance of rhetoric to the beauty-seeking life, but I add other entry-points as well, so that one way of envisioning all possible ways of entering the life of beauty-seeking would be with the image of an exploding star. There are as many entry-points as there are instances of beauty, though some of these, we shall see, are more potent than others. The ladder will be taken up into fuller, richer accounts of a Beauty-seeking life. As the ladder is an image that links God and Beauty in Gregory's writings, drawing together fittingness and gratuity with immanence and transcendence, so does the subversion of the ladder speak to the identification of these descriptions.

Though he allows for many different ways of learning to love Beauty, Gregory is most interested in displaying lives that have succeeded in that purpose extraordinarily well. Macrina is one such Beauty-lover. Gregory discloses his account of beauty and his doctrine of God in Macrina's relationship to the beautiful Bridegroom, whom she longs for, sings to, and worships. The Bridegroom is the Beauty who evokes love, elicits praise, and discloses God. The act of disclosure suggests a God immanent to the world; in the act of elicitation, a God transcendent to it; and in evocation, it names the distance between the transcendent God and the immanent God as God.

Conclusion

With the case of Macrina's Bridegroom, we move discussions of beauty and the doctrine of God into a discussion of Christology. Perhaps the most profound case of how fittingness and gratuity open rather than foreclose one another is found in Gregory of Nyssa's paradigm case for radical transcendence: the Incarnation. It is because of God's absolute surplus, God's perfect gratuity with respect to the human that God's incarnation as human is perfectly fitting. God's gracious excess allows God to be internal to the human, even *as* human. Such gratuity does not exhaust the fittingness of the Incarnation—Gregory has many more things to say about the role of humanity in the universe in *On the Making of the Human (De hominis opificio)*—but it does open up into a fittingness that works against Arian critiques.

But thinking about the gratuity and fittingness of Christ raises the difficult questions about kenosis, the Cross, and eschatology. If Beauty is God, then what does that mean for a Christ who had neither form nor majesty? Or what does it mean that Christ will come *again* in glory to judge the quick and the dead? Where was Christ's glory in the first coming? Was it perceptible? These questions are pressing us towards the next chapter, where we explore how Gregory's Christological ordering of beauty shifts the broad picture I have laid out so far by helping identify the place(s) of ugliness and poverty in it. The ladder cannot bear the weight of ugliness and poverty, and as we explore beauty's relationship to them, we will also sift Gregory for hints about what to do with this image.

3

Rotting Bodies, Bleeding Words

THE BEAUTY OF THE WORD MADE FLESH

Elizabeth Costello has been invited to speak at a small liberal arts college. The engagement is an endowed lectureship, and though she is famous as a feminist novelist, she has chosen to speak about non-human animals and the cruelty humans inflict on them. Her knowledge of this cruelty horrifies and alienates her from the otherwise kind-seeming humans among whom she lives and speaks. In her lectures, she can only perform and confirm the isolation of her horror. By the end of her visit to the college, Costello's speech—in both her lectures and her conversations—has left her fatigued and hopeless, a weeping old woman cradled in her son's arms as they pause on the way to the airport.

Costello is a fictional character J. M. Coetzee imagined as the heroine of his two-part novella *The Lives of Animals*, delivered as the Tanner Lectures at Princeton University in 1997–98.[1] The story has inspired several philosophical reflections, including a powerful essay by philosopher Cora Diamond, who reads Costello as illustrating problems of philosophical skepticism: that is, as illustrating a problem skepticism treats regarding the knowledge of another's pain and the problems in its treatment of this problem.[2] At one point Diamond (following Stanley Cavell) writes that it

1. The two parts, "The Philosophers and the Animals" and "The Poets and the Animals," have been collected together with the responses from some of the original responders in Coetzee, *The Lives of Animals*. The two parts have also been included in Coetzee's novel *Elizabeth Costello*.

2. Diamond's essay, in fact, has been collected and republished as the inaugural essay in a volume of philosophers' reflections on Coetzee's story: Cavell et al., *Philosophy and Animal Life*.

125

is characteristic of philosophy that it misrepresent our reality: philosophy *deflects* reality.[3] She concludes her essay by noting "how much the coming apart of thought and reality belongs to flesh and blood."[4]

The "difficulty of reality," for Diamond, includes beauty as well as horror, for beauty, too, can "shoulder" one out of ordinary life toward the incomprehensible, the astonishing, the strange.[5] Beauty, horror, goodness, death: they can all instance the difficulty of reality for their "not being fit-table in with the world as one understands it."[6] The question of *fit* and fit-tingness will return in this chapter, but I want to start, not with the way beauty is like horror in instancing a difficulty of reality, but with the way it is like philosophical language in its resistance to reality's difficulties.

The problem of the way beauty and horror elude philosophical correct-ness—their evasion of linguistic representation—is inseparable for Gregory from the (other) central problematic of this chapter: beauty's relationship to privilege, ugliness, wealth, and horror. What is it about both philosophi-cal language and the beautiful that they seem inadequate to what Diamond names "the difficulty of reality?" Might we imagine a way for language to be in relationship to horror, or beauty to be in relationship to ugliness? Given modern art's readiness to treat horror and explore ugliness, it might seem counter-intuitive that beauty's estrangement from these difficulties of reality has roots in beauty's role in delineating the fine arts.[7] Yet that appears to be so, largely because fine arts defined for beauty an aloof social space to occupy long after the fine arts abandoned beauty as their aim.[8] In dis-sociating beauty from use, the beauty articulated on the paradigm of the fine arts not only gave beauty a certain (disinterested, inspired) shape, it also associated beauty with certain audiences and patrons and dissociated

3. Diamond, "Difficulty of Reality," 11.

4. Ibid., 26.

5. Ibid., 12.

6. Ibid., 14.

7. This is not to say that the premodern history of the relationship between beauty and poverty is not fraught. But the terms of the dispute are very different, in that pre-modern criticisms from, for example, Bernard of Clairvaux that money spent adorning an abbey church would be better spent on the poor, never presume that the leisure or training of bourgeois life is required to appreciate the beautiful, or that appreciating the beautiful makes one ignore or hate the poor. In the case of Bernard of Clairvaux, he was much more comfortable with beauty that was democratically available (in the churches built by bishops) than with beauty available only to the elite (such as the abbey churches whose excesses he decries). For the details of his critique, see Bernard of Clairvaux, *Cistercians and Cluniacs*.

8. This history of beauty's relationship to fine arts is explored in chapter 1, and an al-ternative understanding of beauty's relationship to the fine arts is outlined in chapter 2.

it from others—particularly, those without the leisure and means to occupy themselves with non-useful objects—thus opening beauty up to an eventually devastating critique.[9]

The contemporary version of this critique is at least vaguely familiar to many of us. It is an important part of why many scholars stopped writing about beauty: for many, beauty's relation to wealth, education, and privilege smelled sour. As critics traced its ties to social heights, beauty fell ever faster, ever further from academic favor. Alexander Nehamas discusses a gentle version of their critique in the distinction between "popular arts" and "high arts," which—together with the oft-implied claim that beauty belongs to the latter—renders beauty vulnerable to accusations it breeds class hatred. He gives an example:

> Imagine . . . that Thomas Kinkade's *Dogwood Chapel* seems to me as beautiful as van Gogh's *Church at Auvers-sur-Oise* seems to you and that both of us experience the pleasure these works produce in the same amount of time. How can we now distinguish between the upper regions and the lower depths? How does the thrill I get from Kinkade differ from your admiration of van Gogh? . . . If the experience of beauty is already complete, no sophisticated analysis can affect it, and the aesthete's urbane appreciation begins to look like a deceitful version of the lowbrow's sentimental bliss.[10]

A worry of the popular art/high art distinction is that the difference between *thrill* and *admiration*, between Kinkade and van Gogh, polices the class divide—that beauty, in other words, turns out to signify and serve a certain class status. It is the unwashed masses who find Kinkade appealing, while we, the properly cultivated elite, disdain Kinkade and prefer van Gogh. It does not really matter in this scenario whether beauty is objective or subjective. Either way its value is dubious and raises a starker version of

---

9. The social ramifications of the dissociation of beauty from use are particularly pronounced in an early moment of Immanuel Kant's *Critique of Judgment*, when he distinguished between the pleasant and the beautiful. "As regards the interest of inclination in the case of the pleasant, everyone says that hunger is the best sauce, and everything that is eatable is relished by people with a healthy appetite; and thus a satisfaction of this sort shows no choice directed by taste. It is only when the want is appeased that we can distinguish which of many men has or has not taste" (44). Kant thus excludes the hungry (analogously understood) from judgments of beauty about that for which they are hungry. It is only those people who lead lives that are not governed by want, by the necessity want imposes, who have the freedom to make aesthetic judgments. The capacity to judge the beautiful is thus restricted to a class of people who can afford lives of satiation.

10. Nehamas, *Only a Promise of Happiness*, 17.

Nehamas's question: Why should we care about an elitist value like beauty when there is so much poverty in the world—especially if beauty serves to cast the poor away and out of sight? It is a question that haunts—that *should* haunt—contemporary retrievals of beauty.

It is also a question that contributed to silencing academic discussion of beauty.[11] In an essay that appeared seven years before his book with the Kinkade/van Gogh scenario, Nehamas describes beauty as "the most discredited philosophical notion."[12] Nehamas links beauty's exile to its "embarrassing" association with the bourgeois. He invokes Pierre Bourdieu to note the bourgeois origin of aesthetic judgments as well as the "quasi-bourgeois mode of existence" (that is, prolonged education) required to make them properly. Nehamas here is drawing on *Distinction: A Social Critique of Taste*, in which Bourdieu points to the aesthetic's rejection of bodily, immediate pleasures for higher, intellectual ones as constitutive of taste.[13] As aesthetic pleasures migrate away from the body and into the intellect, they increasingly require an intellect trained into proper disembodiment (which is to say, into the denial of embodiment) to appreciate them. That is, they require training into a subjectivity capable of rendering such rarefied aesthetic judgment. There are two different problems, then, with this subjectivity: First, it signifies class status, and its absence marks as excludable those who fail to render "correct" aesthetic judgments. Second, such subjectivity cannot properly see and attend to those outside of one's (elite) social situation. Since beauty was identified as an aesthetic category, it is entangled in the particular class problems of the aesthetic.[14]

Terry Eagleton argues for an even deeper association between the bourgeois and the aesthetic in his book *The Ideology of the Aesthetic*. The aesthetic, Eagleton argues, was constructed in and for the political hegemony of the middle class, and it nurtures a subjectivity that serves that political/social order.[15] It claims autonomy while introducing means of repression. This

11. Just about the same time that Nehamas's essay came out, Elaine Scarry identified in her 1999 book *On Beauty and Being Just* two criticisms of beauty that drove it from the academy: that it distracts attention from wrong social arrangements and that the gaze it elicits is destructive (objectifying, rapacious). The critique of beauty as bourgeois bears analogy with this first critique.

12. Nehamas, "An Essay on Beauty and Judgment."

13. At times this has, complicatedly, involved downgrading beauty to the status of a "lower" aesthetic pleasure in favor of the "higher" aesthetic pleasure of the sublime. For example, in Kant, the beautiful is elaborated as the charming, the decorative, the feminine in contrast to the weighty aesthetic value of the religious, masculine sublime.

14. For more on the history of beauty's formulation as an aesthetic category, see chapter 1.

15. Eagleton, *Ideology of the Aesthetic*, 3.

double-movement toward autonomy and repression is possible because the aesthetic's status as self-regulating and self-determining provide the bourgeoisie with a model of human subjectivity even as the aesthetic inscribes social power into the bodies of those it subjugates by regulating taste.[16] At the same time that the aesthetic generates and polices the social order, it also provides the means for its subversion, for the functionlessness of the aesthetic, Eagleton argues, resists the processes of instrumentalization central to capitalism.[17] The picture Eagleton paints of the political work done by and to the aesthetic in modernity raises the question of whether the aesthetic is irrevocably locked in a sometimes friendly, sometimes antagonistic relationship with the bourgeois—a relationship that, however fraught, is yet definitive of the aesthetic. Is there a way of recovering an aesthetic uncharged with the politics and battles of class? As Nehamas, Eagleton, and Bourdieu help us to see: not in this world.

After all, the rich—always a relative term—own more things called beautiful. They comprise more of the people deemed beautiful, and they possess more power to determine what object, situation, or person deserves to be considered beautiful. Those who do not share the rich's judgments about beauty are marked as inferior, and those who are inferior are often those with limited access to educational institutions or material wealth. Simone Weil powerfully frames the problem of beauty's implication in wealth by inverting the terms. "The horror of poverty," she claims, "is essentially a horror of ugliness."[18] The disquieting suggestion of Weil's statement is that the horror of ugliness generates or sustains horror at those who are poor, that it imagines the poor as contaminants of the beautiful. Beauty must always be discussed, then, with an eye toward the class disdain and exclusions it is capable of generating. Fitting for whom?, we must ask. Who benefits from beauty's gratuity? What kind of world does beauty help to consolidate?

Beauty's deep implication in social power echoes Diamond's concern that language cannot but serve a privileged position, one that cannot treat the fullness of death and horror. We cannot ignore the class-policing power of beauty or the horror-deflecting work of language. But I shall argue in this chapter that Gregory presents us with a beautiful language (a double problem) that nevertheless resists its own privilege. Gregory's theological commitments demand such resistance: For Gregory, as the profoundest beauties participate in Beauty Crucified, so the truest language speaks from the fleshly *Logos*, which such language works to render apparent.

16. Ibid., 9.

17. Ibid.

18. Weil, "Forms of the Implicit Love," 106.

This language never idles; it does not luxuriate in the leisure of privilege. Gregory's beautiful language makes plain its own power; it takes seriously the capacity of beauty further to marginalize the socially powerless and to serve the privileged. Yet he attempts to do the opposite.

Gregory can help us learn to attend to the exclusionary capacity of beauty, to see its political power, yet without insisting that we discard beauty. He will, however, work to re-form our vision of the beautiful, for Gregory conceives a beauty that breaks out of its enclosure in the rich. He can help us do the same in two ways. First, by providing new contexts of fittingness against which objects, people, and situations can be evaluated, Gregory disrupts and reconditions the subjectivity of the rich. Toward this end, he interprets sites that wealth has deemed beautiful to be, in fact, ugly, and sites wealth has abandoned as ugly to be both ugly *and* beautiful. Second, and related, Gregory insists on beauty's deep association with ugliness and invisibility. For Gregory, beauty is rarely found far from ugliness, and any search for an ugly-free beauty on this side of eternity bristles with the danger of self-deception and class-enclosure.

This is not to say that Gregory himself transcended class. Certainly his own social stratum wore the purple-bordered toga, and he benefited from access to the greatest education of the day. But his meditations on beauty—particularly his Christological meditations—articulate a vision of beauty that resists assimilation to the rich by tracing beauty's deep implication in poverty, suffering, ugliness, and invisibility. Retrieving Gregory's vision for beauty recasts what is beautiful and how beauty is discussed. Such a retrieval therefore has political implications, for it trains a person into a way of seeing—and thus a subjectivity—that resists class hegemony.

Ugliness and invisibility will not only help us think about the relationship of beauty to the rich and the poor; it will also help us to reflect more deeply on divine immanence and transcendence. In tracing the involvement of beauty in ugliness and invisibility, I will note both continuities and discontinuities with the vision of beauty I culled from Gregory in the previous chapter. On the one hand, beauty's implication in ugliness and invisibility will de-throne and reinterpret the image of a ladder that saturates Gregory's writings discussed in the last chapter. Yet, on the other hand, the significance of ugliness and invisibility will help us to expand the discussion of radicalized fittingness and gratuity. It will, moreover, help us to extend Gregory's sense of how rhetoric works, how it trains us into beauty while attending to the ugliness of pain and suffering. This is to say that the relationship between the beauty described in this chapter and the beauty of the last chapter echoes the relationships between Gregory's doctrine of God and Christology. Here, then, we move deeper into the Trinitarian character of beauty. For Gregory, the Incarnation transforms the way a person approaches God while also extending what a person knows about God through creation. That is, *creatio ex nihilo* implies that God could be incarnate without compromising God's divinity, for, as discussed in the previous chapter, *creatio ex nihilo* demonstrates 1) the fundamental goodness of creation; 2) the radically equalizing abyss between creation and Creator; 3) the absolute dependence of all creation on God; and, therefore, 4) the infinite farness and nearness of God to creation. But *that* God is incarnate is something definitively new with respect to creation. And the Incarnation transforms how we locate God in the world. Where *creatio ex nihilo* and radical transcendence speak to an undifferentiated presence of God in the world, the Incarnation is the supreme case of differentiated presence. In the same way that the Incarnation is both new and an elaboration of the possibilities inherent in creation (it is possible, that is, because of the radical transcendence *creatio ex nihilo* identifies), as Gregory argues, so beauty's implication in ugliness, invisibility, and affliction are both distinct from and entailments of the suggestions present in radical fittingness and gratuity. Attending to the newness and familiarity of ugliness and Incarnation will help us retain Gregory's ladder while also noting its limitations.

Strains on the Ladder

Gregory's repeated invocation of a ladder to describe how a person perceives Beauty Itself presses the question of beauty's implication in social hierarchies. The image of a ladder, of course, also serves as a frequent image of social hierarchy and is used, with disdain, to describe attempts at class mobility, as in a social climber. But Gregory's ladder of beauty cannot be mounted with the same ease (or difficulty) as a social ladder, for the structure of Gregory's ladder renders impossible ascent through purely muscular effort. There are discontinuities in his ladder, particularly near the vision of Beauty Itself. These discontinuities echo and transform those of the Beauty ladders in two of Gregory's most influential sources, Plato and Plotinus.

None of these three thinkers has a vision of a ladder with evenly-paced rungs and unbroken verticality. For Plato, love falls away in the vision of beauty. The child of Poverty and Resource, Love is the force that compels a person up to see higher beauties, and so once one reaches Beauty Itself, there is no more poverty and no need for canny Love seeking his way into greater resource. Upon arriving at the vision of Beauty, the viewer forever knows it; it becomes her epistemological possession. Knowing now what it is to see Beauty Itself, she can produce true virtue rather than images of virtue. There is continuity, then, in the movement from images of virtue to true virtue, but it is the kind of continuity that entails the disdain for lesser beauties that we traced in the last chapter. Most importantly, love, the engine of ascent and beauty's other half, falls away once the climber sees Beauty Itself, generating a significant discontinuity in Plato's ladder, though not necessarily one that impedes the climber.

For Plotinus, it is not love that falls away in the vision of Beauty (also called the One) but intellection. Love cannot be left behind, for the One is love by being pure gift. But the One who is Beauty is also unknowable. It is thought, then, that the climber leaves behind, and since the Beauty that is the One cannot be epistemologically grasped, it is unsurprising that it cannot be epistemologically possessed in the way that Plato's can. The climber works hard, and the vision comes or it does not. The last rung of the ladder can be neither achieved nor willed; the final vision requires waiting.[19] Upon seeing Beauty Itself, the climber who looks back on materiality appreciates it only by seeing through it to spiritual beauty, which is where true beauty lay. Pure materiality is something like a corpse. Not only, then, is there a strong discontinuity between the material and intelligible realms, but there is a strong discontinuity between the final vision of the One and other intelligible beauties—a discontinuity named by the way a person speaks of the beauty of the One and all other beauty only equivocally.[20]

Gregory is similar to Plotinus on the point of what falls away—intellection but not love. He also has two important theological commitments through which to explore his ladder's discontinuity: epectasy and apophasis. These commitments elaborate Gregory's understanding of God as infinite, and that infinity occasions both joy and sadness. The way infinity causes joy is a subject for the next chapter. The way it causes sadness is bound up with the finitude of the creature, who as finite and creaturely cannot attain her deepest desire of seeing God. Balthasar notes that for Gregory, "There is a sadness in the creature, who knows that it will never see God as he is for himself."[21] Both in the *Life of Moses* and the *Homilies on the Beatitudes*, Gregory describes this sadness as "despair" at not being able to see God face

---

19. Andrew Louth reads the passage in the *Symposium* in which the beholder sees Beauty Itself "on a sudden" (εξαιφνες) to point similarly to a waiting for the Beautiful to reveal itself (*Origins of the Christian Mystical Tradition*, 13). Nevertheless, he also emphasizes a contrast with Philo by claiming the unpossessibility of the vision of the One for Plotinus as "a rare and fleeting phenomenon" (48).

20. Plotinus takes beauty as his central theme in *Ennead* I.6 and V.8, though beauty is a motif throughout his writings.

21. Balthasar, *Presence and Thought*, 104.

to face.[22] God's infinity means that the creature never possesses a vision of God. There is no last rung of the ladder to achieve, no beatific rest. But the transformation the creature undergoes in death and resurrection enables her to encounter God in a different way: by eternally journeying through God. This is epectasy,[23] and though it is not fully elaborated until Gregory's later texts, versions of it appear even in his earliest text, *On Virginity*. There the one ascending to God "arrives" by following the Crucified One. The resurrection opens up the possibility of a kind of encounter with God, though the possibilities of the encounter are ever-chastened by the status of the creature as creature.

The infinity of God also suggests the inadequacy of words and concepts for describing God. Gregory's understanding of the inadequacy of language suffuses his texts and is most famously described in *Against Eunomius (Contra Eunomium)*, where he insists that words and concepts can never attain the fullness of God. This is apophasis, an understanding of language's limits that he shares, with some differences, with Plotinus. Together, apophasis and epectasy draw out the implications of an infinite God in such a way that Gregory's ladder is unlike any ladder available on earth. It is an endless ladder where arriving is understood both as entering a space of unknowingness and also as continuing to follow.

Because we cannot perceive God in God's infinity before our bodies have been resurrected into a new life in which we can infinitely journey, there is discontinuity between our pre-resurrection experiences of beauty and the experiences of beauty that will be made available to us. Gregory has two primary ways of describing the discontinuity between earthly and divine beauty. When he describes them relative to God the Father, he speaks of the discontinuity as one of invisibility. When Gregory discusses the discontinuity relative to Christ, he speaks of ugliness. But what is more puzzling than Gregory marking ugliness and invisibility as discontinuities separating us from God is that, in another sense, Gregory wants to recover ugliness and invisibility as *continuities*. The ugly, invisible, and beautiful end up intersecting in the divine. Gregory, then, not only describes the deep continuities between higher and lower beauties, as traced in the previous chapter; he also wants to extend and describe such continuity through beauty's connections to ugliness and invisibility.

To discern more exactly what Gregory is doing with beauty and the image of the ladder, I will turn to a series of texts, all later than those of

22. Gregory of Nyssa, *Life of Moses* II.220 (Ferguson and Malherbe, 112); Gregory of Nyssa, *On the Beatitudes*, homily six (Hall, 66).

23. Jean Daniélou coined the term *epectasy* in his book *Platonisme et theologie mystique* to describe the self's ever-expansion through the never-ending God.

the previous chapter, in which Gregory reflects upon ugliness, invisibility, and beauty. Two of these texts—the two that will claim the most space in what follows—are written in a genre I did not treat in the last chapter. They are sermons. The homiletic genre is particularly important given the weight Gregory accords rhetoric in training people into the perception of beauty, for the homily is a genre of teaching and exhortation. In reading those homilies, I attend to Gregory's use of language to train his hearers into new contexts of fittingness and new ways of perceiving. Such attention will set me up to return to Coetzee and the problem of philosophical language meeting the difficulty of reality, which will help further qualify the Christological shape of Beauty.

On Things Unseen and Unseemly

Invisibility and Poverty: *Homilies on the Beatitudes*

Mountains interpret ladders that in turn redescribe mountains in Gregory's interweaving of images in his *Homilies on the Beatitudes*. Each of the eight homilies—on the eight Beatitudes in Jesus's sermons—begins with a brief meditation on a mountain (homilies one, three, six, and seven) or a ladder (homilies two, four, five, and eight), thus textually layering Sinai on the Sermon's mount together with the ladders of Jacob and Plato. It is not just that he discusses ascent; Gregory figures the Beatitudes themselves through these tropes of ascent. They are arranged like a ladder (homily two); they point the way up the mountain (homily three); and most often, they are themselves the mountain-ladder by which we ascend to the blessedness that is God (homilies four, five, six, and eight).[24] Gregory has other names for the summit as well, including "ineffable and inconceivable good," "essential grace and wisdom and power," "true light," "fount of all goodness," "authority transcending the universe," "sole object of love," and—importantly for

---

24. For example: "I think the arrangement of the Beatitudes is like a series of rungs, and it makes it possible for the mind to ascend by climbing from one to another" (Gregory of Nyssa, *On the Beatitudes*, homily two [Hall, 32]). "After these the Word leads us toward higher places and points us by the Beatitudes to a third successive high point" (homily three [Hall, 39]). "The Word, who leads us by the hand towards the upper parts of the ladder of the Beatitudes, the same who, as the prophet says, has set in our heart the goodly ascents, when he takes the next step forward, after the steps already achieved he proposes to us a fourth similar 'ascent'" (homily four [Hall, 47]). "In this case also the elevation of the Beatitudes, one above another, prepares us to approach God himself, the truly blessed one who stands firmly above all blessedness" (homily five [Hall, 57]).

our own inquiries—"indescribable beauty."[25] How to see the God who is Beauty is an important sub-theme in these homilies, and I will focus my own exploration of it in homilies one, three, five, and six—homilies for which sight and the problem of seeing God are most explicitly thematized and intertwined with another important theme of the homilies: poverty. To ask how to see beauty, for Gregory, is to ask how to see God, which is to raise the dual problems of God's invisibility and insistent identification with poverty. Here we delve into our exploration of beauty and the difficulty of reality by asking: What does it mean for Beauty to be invisible to humans? What does it mean for Beauty to identify with poverty?

The ascent described in the *Homilies on the Beatitudes* is not the same ascent Gregory describes in *On Virginity* or the *Inscriptions of the Psalms*. Those ascents address both the advanced and the beginners—even ones who have not yet turned to virtue or to God. The *Homilies on the Beatitudes*, by contrast, speak to disciples. Gregory trumpets his opening call, "Who then among those gathered here is such as to be a disciple of the Word and to go up with him from the low ground away from the hollows of lowly thoughts to the spiritual mountain of sublime contemplation?"[26] Gregory addresses "those gathered here," presumably his congregants, who are ready to consider discipleship to the Word. These people need to learn how to ascend, and they need their desire increased for the ascent—but they already have some commitment to ascending to God. Gregory therefore begins his address to them with a fairly elaborated theological vocabulary, assuming his congregants believe that they are fallen and that the Word is redeeming them.

Fallenness, in fact, is introduced as a topic for discussion fairly quickly. After naming God as the all-good, all-gracious, all-illuminating, all-beautiful one, Gregory proceeds to unpack divine blessedness with the case of human beauty. As the derivative beauty of a portrait is to the beauty of the living human, so the image of God that is the human is to the first beauty that is the blessedness of God. Having lost our secondary beauty due to sin, we must be redrawn. In his first homily, Gregory writes,

> In the case of pictorial art the artist might say to the untrained that a face is beautiful if it consists of physical parts of a certain kind, with hair of such a kind and roundness of the eyes and lines of the eyebrows and set of the cheeks and all the individual points which together constitute beautiful shape. In just the same way the one who redraws our soul to make it resemble

25. Gregory of Nyssa, *On the Beatitudes*, homily one (Hall, 24–25).
26. Ibid., homily one (Hall, 23).

the only Blessed One will in his discourse outline each one of the things which draw us toward blessedness, and he says at the outset, "Blessed are the poor in spirit, for theirs is the kingdom of the heavens."[27]

So Gregory understands his homilies to be meditations on the ascent to the Blessed One who is indescribable Beauty and whose blessedness is both an analog for human physical beauty and the perfection of moral or spiritual beauty. To ascend the Beatitudes is to draw near Beauty Itself while becoming beautiful oneself. And the way one begins such ascent, Gregory claims in the first homily, is to be poor in spirit.

To embody spirit-poverty is to imitate God in one of the only ways we can: God's humility.[28] Certainly, Gregory makes clear, we cannot hope to imitate God in divine impassibility or incorruptibility. Again and again Gregory marks God's elusiveness to humanity, particularly in Gregory's homily on the third beatitude, *Blessed are the sorrowful, for they shall be comforted.* What is sorrow but the deprivation of a good? And what could be more sorrowful than the deprivation of the Good Itself? Gregory meditates on humanity's capacity to "look upon the truly Good," which causes sorrow when afterwards a person turns to "the poverty of human nature"[29] and realizes what a remove she is at from the Good.[30] The problem of poverty, already invoked in the first homily, continues to return, but in this third homily, Gregory wants to problematize the vision he claimed one could have of the Good. Gregory turns to Plato's imagery to ask what "light might be by which this dark cave of human nature is not in our present life illuminated."[31] What light, indeed, for the Good—the God—Gregory desires to see is invisible. "How then is it possible, and by what mental processes, for such a good to come under our view, that which is contemplated but not seen . . . ?"[32] The desire to behold the Good suggests what is "unattainable" and "incomprehensible."[33] In this life, at least, we seem doomed to sorrow.

But the problem is worse than sorrow. In his homily on the fifth beatitude (*Blessed are the pitiful, for they shall be pitied*), Gregory claims that sin

---

27. Ibid., homily one (Hall, 25).

28. Anthony Meredith notes that there is a shift in Gregory's thought marked here between imitating God and imitating Christ; see his "Gregory of Nyssa, *De beatitudinibus*, Oratio 1," 98.

29. Poverty of human nature: ἡ πτωχεία τῆς ἀνθρωπίνης.

30. Gregory of Nyssa, *On the Beatitudes*, homily three (Hall, 42).

31. Ibid., homily three (Hall, 43).

32. That which is contemplated but not seen: τὸ θεώμενον καὶ μὴ βλεπόμενον. Ibid.

33. Ibid.

results from errors of perception. He writes, "[I]f evil were presented stark to people, and were not overlaid with the appearance of the good [or beautiful] mankind would never have defected to it."[34] In the mis-appearance of evil as the good, the Good's absence thus generates a problem about beauty. Gregory reiterates his hope that texts and rhetoric might help us to see it rightly, to "learn the true beauty" and so "be reformed accordingly."[35] But such possibility for reformation seems a meager hope, as Gregory ends this homily by exhorting his audience to forsake the promise of wealth and the beauty of stylish dress (the beauty we see) for the Beauty that has not yet been revealed (the beauty, it seems, we do not see). Gregory paints a vision of the eschaton:

> When the one who reigns over creation reveals himself to the human race, majestically seated on the exalted throne of his glory, when around him appear the countless myriads of angels, yes, when the ineffable kingdom of the heavens becomes visible to every eye, and over against it are revealed the dread torments, and in between stands the whole human race, those who lived from the first creation until the consummation of the universe . . . —if that person's works bring him forward with cries of praise and gratitude from those who have benefited, confidently resplendent before the Judge, will he value that good fortune by the standards of material wealth?[36]

This vision of God as resplendent, as revealed in God's beauty, is what we *will* see, Gregory promises us, but it is not what we see now—despite Gregory's narration of it in the present tense. This vision is the appearance of the good as the good; in this vision we will see the true beauty and glory of God, and seeing that beauty truly, we will be relieved of the greatest cause of sin: wrongly perceiving evil as good. But as this rhetorical vision is only a promise for the future, it seems that for now we are doomed not only to sorrow but to sin as well.

Humanity's plight worsens still. Gregory's head spins in vertigo as he surveys humanity's situation from the peak of the sixth beatitude: *Blessed are the pure in heart, for they shall see God.* Here is the desperate paradox of humanity's situation: Eternal life is to see God, yet no one can see God and

---

34. Appearance of the good: καλοῦ φαντασία. Ibid., homily five (Hall, 58). That Gregory uses *kalos* instead of *agathos* here helps make sense of his statement that follows: "We ought to be aware of the meaning of the text before us, in order that we may learn the true beauty of the thought it contains and be reformed accordingly" (58).

35. Gregory of Nyssa, *On the Beatitudes*, homily five (Hall, 58).

36. Ibid., homily five (Hall, 64–65).

live—and no one has seen God.[37] All of this Gregory knows from Scripture, and he swirls the paradox round and round, meditating on what it means that humanity is separated from the very life that it needs. We are surrounded by death. There is death for those who do not see God and death for those who do. Our problem with perception is not just a problem of sorrow and sin; it is a problem at the very heart of life itself. Where in other writings Gregory thematizes a hope for rhetoric, Gregory similarly places here some hope in sublime concepts and principles to make God visible in God's operations. "Sublime" ideas like power, purity, and immutability can help "[bring] God into view" and lead our thoughts upward, "[impressing] upon our minds the representation of a divine and sublime concept."[38] There is hope, then, that such representation is possible, but even before Gregory introduces such hope he has chastened it by claiming that the divine nature "transcends all conceptual comprehension."[39] Representations must likewise be transcended, however powerfully they might communicate the divine to us. Beauty is here a difficulty of philosophy in the way that Gregory presents it as a difficulty of reality: It eludes grasping at all sides.

Gregory frames the problem of God's presence and absence in conceptions of and terms for the sublime somewhat differently at the beginning of homily five when he describes the beatitudes as a kind of Jacob's ladder that prepares us to approach God in Godself—even while God is also standing firmly on the ladder.[40] There is some way in which God is present on the ladder, but God is finally, not just at the end of the ladder, but above the ladder. We are on a ladder to ascend to God when God both transcends the ladder, such that ascent is futile, and is present on the ladder, so that ascent is ridiculous. What does this mean for trusting the beauty we see? What does this mean for our hope of seeing the Beauty not yet revealed?

Taken by itself, the paradox of seeing God who is Beauty is a murky one. Gregory seems always to be extending a hope and then snatching it away, making clear how much we need to see God and then expressing how impossible it is to see God. But Gregory threads through this lament a hope that reframes his paradox. At the same time that Gregory meditates on the nearness and farness of God in terms of God's invisible, life-giving, life-taking glory, he also meditates on the nearness and farness of God in terms of the infinitely rich Word made poor for our sakes.

---

37. Ibid., homily six (Hall, 66).
38. Sublime: ὑψηλός (elevated, noble). Ibid., homily six (Hall, 69).
39. Ibid., homily six (Hall, 68).
40. Ibid., homily five (Hall, 58).

These meditations on the Word alternate with the meditations on the invisible God. From the first homily, when Gregory begins to lay out the paradox of seeing God, he also begins pointing a way forward. And from the first sentence of that homily, Gregory assures us that, rather than hovering watchfully over the ladder or standing statically on the ladder, the Word is climbing with us. The invitation to ascend the mountain of the Lord is not an invitation to follow the Word's precepts alone. It is a call to "go up with" the Word who blesses those who "climb up with him" and "accompany him."[41] The journey to behold God is one in which God the Word remains in solidarity with us, teaching us how to climb by example and words, offering us the company of a fellow-climber. It is by both example and words that we learn the ladder's first rung of being poor in spirit. The Word who commends spirit poverty is the same Word who offers the best model of it: Setting aside riches, the Word embodies the humility that is spirit poverty by becoming poor for our sakes.

Even in the case of humility, imitation of the Word is complicated by the differing situations of the Word and humans, which are (obviously) neither identical, nor even particularly analogous. Where the Word possesses wealth as properly the Word's own, we only play-act at our power and riches. In a colorful passage, Gregory chastises a healthy youth for his vanity:

> Are you not ashamed, you little clay doll, soon to be dust, blown up like a bubble with your own momentary puff, full of pride, all swollen with inflamed delusion and inflating your mind with empty conceit? Do you not see at each end the limits of human life, how it begins and where it ends? Yet you glory in your youth, you look to the blossom of your fresh years, and you boast of your full bloom, because your hands are strong for lifting, your feet agile for jumping, your curls blow about in the wind, the first beard lines your cheek, and because your clothes glow bright with purple dye, and your dresses of silk are embroidered, with embroidery of wars or hunts or legends. Yes, perhaps you look even to your shoes, carefully polished with blacking and smart with extravagantly stitched lines, yet do you not look at yourself? I will shew you your reflection, who you are and what you are.[42]

We little clay dolls have difficulty imitating the beauty of the Word as revealed in the Word's humility, first, because our eyes are absorbed with the purple dye on our robes and second, because, as we shall see, the robes are

41. Ibid., homily one (Hall, 23).
42. Ibid., homily one (Hall, 28).

not even our own. Thus we cannot divest ourselves of them the way the Word can divest the Wordself. The rhetorical color continues as Gregory makes good on his promise to show his imagined interlocutor who he is and what he is. From a higher vantage point up the mountain, Gregory can see that the roles of wealth and power people inhabit are just that: theatrical roles, which are to be inhabited without the actor ever forgetting that he merely acts.

> Who will convince those in this position that they differ not a whit from those in shows on the stage? These wear a mask artistically crafted and a purple robe shot with gold, and they proceed in a chariot; and yet no disease of pride gets into them as a result, but what they were in their dignity before the show, they keep the same state of mind unchanged during the display, and are not upset afterwards when they get down from the chariot and take off the costume. Those however who strut on the stage of life because of their imperial office take into account neither what is shortly before or shortly after, and in just the same way that bubbles expand as they are blown up, these people are roundly inflated by the loud proclamation of the herald; they plaster over themselves the shape of some other personality, switching the natural features of the face into something unsmiling and daunting, and they contrive a harsher voice, one made to resemble an animal in order to terrify the hearers. They stay no longer within the bounds of human nature, but assume divine power and authority. They believe they have sovereignty over life and death because to some of those who are judged by them they give the sentence of acquittal, while others they condemn to death; and they do not even consider who is truly the sovereign of human life and determines both the beginning of existence and its end. Nevertheless this alone should have been enough to restrain vain conceit, the sight of many rulers even during the performance of their reign snatched from their very thrones and carried out to their graves, and for them lamentation has replaced the cries of the heralds.[43]

The key, for Gregory, is not to see this present life as a lie to be refused. A king must govern, after all, and such governance might entail representing his people by wearing gold and purple and jewels and crowns. But it is important that the king not confuse his role with his person, for at the end of the short day that is this life, the man who played the king will hang up his crown and be brothers and sisters with those who played his servants.

---

43. Ibid., homily one (Hall, 29–30).

This present life deceives us only when we refuse to see its larger context. Youthful beauty turns to conceit only when a person fails to recognize that she is hurtling towards death and decay. Recognizing our theatrical roles as roles helps us to inhabit them better, so that our faces do not become conformed to our masks.

Imitating the humility of Christ, then, involves recognizing we are different from Christ, for we do not set aside what is properly our own but instead realize that sovereignty over life and death is an illusion created by a failure to see our origins and ends.[44] We do not *possess* our gold; still less do we possess our own life. Such a realization should help even the king entangled in "that mistaken masquerade of government" to give "equal respect to all members" of humanity and embrace spirit-poverty in imitation of the one who became poor because of us.[45]

Seeing the eschatological setting of the present life means not just that one inhabits one's role lightly, but that one inhabits it *differently*.[46] That is because in his call to spirit-poverty, Gregory refuses to let material poverty become invisible. He nears the conclusion of the homily with some stern words about not forgetting the "other word" about poverty—also in Matthew—in which Jesus tells the rich young ruler to sell all of his possessions and give them to the poor. This poverty "chimes in" with the blessed spirit-poverty of the beatitudes, and in the end, the two are not easily separable. "The one who shares the part of the pauper" also "takes the part of the one who impoverished himself because of us."[47] So sharing the Word's poverty, such a one will also share his wealth, for, "The one who for us became poor reigns over all creation. If therefore you share poverty with the impoverished, you will surely also share his kingdom when he reigns."[48] Reversing

44. Ibid., homily one (Hall, 30).

45. Ibid.

46. Gregory is also concerned that virtue not be defined in such a way that only the rich can possess it. He returns to the privileged position of kings in his fourth homily, which concerns the blessedness of the just: "The saving Word belongs equally to the whole human race, and not every human being is in the situations described; it is for a few to be a king or a governor or a judge, to have power over finance or administration, and the majority are in an inferior and subordinate position. This being so, how could it be accepted that that is true justice, if it is not accessible on equal terms to the whole race? For if equality is, according to the secular account, the goal of the just, and superiority implies inequality, there is no way that the account of justice deduced can be considered true, since it is directly refuted by the unfairness of real life" (*On the Beatitudes*, homily four [Hall, 48]).

47. Gregory of Nyssa, *On the Beatitudes*, homily one (Hall, 31).

48. If therefore you share poverty with the impoverished, you will surely also share his kingdom when he reigns: Οὐκοῦν ἐὰν πτωχεύσαντι συμπτωχεύσῃς, καὶ βασιλεύοντι συμβασιλεύσεις. Ibid.

the move of those interpreters who spiritualize away the material poverty of the Lucan beatitudes, Gregory materializes the spiritual poverty of this Matthean beatitude.[49] Ascending with the Word, Gregory tells us, requires that we descend with him, sharing poverty with him and the paupers. Poverty and glory are bound together, both characterizing the Word who was made flesh. Gregory wants to point out in this first homily that a person cannot access the one without accessing the other.

The politics embedded in this first homily are strange. While calling government a "mistaken masquerade," he yet bows to the importance of participating in it. The good king performs power relations he knows to be false (he is *actually* no better than his fellow humans; he has no *real* sovereignty over life and death) but does so without ever forgetting their falseness and ephemerality. He performs these false relations in an attempt to undermine them and bring power structures closer to the eschatological truth of humanity's relations. Whether Gregory thinks governmental powers will ever display the truth of our brother-sisterhood is doubtful, but he does not require abandoning participation in government. He recommends not withdrawal from society but an estranged engagement in it. Power is not to be refused but used to move towards brother-sisterhood, and in this way, social power can be properly leveraged to help disclose the Beauty that will be all in all—a theme we will see return again in other of Gregory's homilies.[50]

In addition to speaking of those materially disadvantaged, Gregory invokes poverty in this first homily to imply that all humanity partakes universally in a kind of poverty that is the human nature. (It is a kind of poverty for the Word, at least.) He makes that point explicit in his third homily in his discussions of the dark cave of human nature and the infinite distance between the ineffable Good and the poverty of human nature. This theme of the universal poverty of human nature returns again in the fifth homily. The homily on the pitiful, where sin is equated with wrong perception, links the poverty of human nature with material poverty and sets them together against the image of God's coming glory.

The call to pity, like the call to humility, is also a call to deification.[51] Gregory begins by talking about the virtues of pity. Once again distressed

---

49. It is something of a puzzle how a king might continue wearing purple and gold yet live as a kind of pauper. I wonder if it might look something like a pope who wears fine vestments for his liturgical and ecclesial duties while sleeping on a hard floor at night.

50. I have explored this passage and its use of theater in greater length in "The Mysteries of Our Existence."

51. Gregory of Nyssa, *On the Beatitudes*, homily five (Hall, 58).

by the inequalities in the human situation, Gregory extols mercy as "the only way to make efforts to cure the distress of one's neighbor" for in pity, one "loving[ly] self-identifies with those vexed by grievous events."[52] In this double-movement of self-identification and cure, Gregory presents material poverty as something to be embraced and ameliorated. But it is not just material poverty that Gregory is concerned to pity. In this homily that connects sins with the errors in perception wrought by humanity's inability to discern the divine from evil, Gregory claims we should pity our own souls. We have fallen prey to the "raving, savage masters" of wrath and pride, licentiousness and greed.[53] We do not pity ourselves because we do not recognize ourselves, Gregory claims, and at this point he paints the eschatological vision of a person standing before the glory of God. Gregory emphasizes once again the Word that we imitate in our pity of others, for the Word voluntarily took on our own miseries in order to assuage them. The Word went forth in a solidarity that was also salvific. Our movements of "self-identifying" and "curing" imperfectly imitate such salvific solidarity in an attempt to live into the call to imitate Christ. But at the same time, by insisting that we pity ourselves and our own plight, Gregory reminds us that we are not Christ, that we are exiled, helpless slaves to tyrannical masters and do not even recognize the horror of our plight. Relative to Christ's beauty, we are ugly, and to the extent that we fail to recognize that ugliness, we mis-perceive ourselves.

The contrast of divine power and human poverty may sound as if Gregory is feeding the masculinist trap articulated by Sarah Coakley in her feminist analysis of *kenosis*, the self-emptying of Christ, particularly as articulated in the hymn of Philippians 2.[54] What is problematic for Coakley is a description of *kenosis* as the self-emptying movement from the pre-existent substantial *Logos* to the Incarnated Christ—a movement from invulnerable omnipotence to vulnerable limited power. Such a reading is both implausible for Coakley on Pauline or pre-Pauline terms, inasmuch as the notion of a substantial pre-existence of Christ is not developed at the time of the Philippians hymn; and undesirable for the way it is embeds a description of divine power as *opposed to* weakness, vulnerability, and the abnegation of worldly (or "masculinist" or "bullying") power. Against such a description, Coakley wants to argue for a *kenosis* in which Christ chooses never to have worldly forms of power, in which divine power is perfectly concurrent with

---

52. Ibid., homily five (Hall, 59).
53. Ibid., homily five (Hall, 63).
54. See Sarah Coakley's important essay "*Kenosis* and Subversion."

self-effaced humanity.[55] She wants to suggest instead "true divine 'empowerment' occurs most unimpededly in the context of a *special* form of human 'vulnerability'" that is learned and imaged through the patient silence of contemplative prayer—a silence that can build the prophetic voice.[56]

I think we can read Gregory in ways resonant with—if not quite assimilable to—Coakley's descriptions of *kenosis*. At least, he does not advance the masculinist description of power that worries her, for though Gregory does read *kenosis* through his commitment to a pre-existent *Logos*, we might understand that *Logos* to be always already involved in the self-emptying and receiving that is entailed in Trinitarian love.[57] While Christic *kenosis* is the movement from pre-existent to Incarnated *Logos*, in such *kenosis* the *Logos* does not perform an action out of character with (or unbefitting of) itself. The *kenosis* of the Incarnation, that is, expresses the on-going *kenosis* within the Trinity; it is therefore a further revelation of the divine. Gregory himself does not make this explicit argument, but it is suggested both in his arguments about Incarnation revealing the kind of power (non-contrastive transcendence) possessed by a God who created from nothing—explored at the end of the last chapter—and in the arguments we will continue to explore in this chapter that the Incarnation's self-emptying reveals for us what it means to say that God is love. It is also what it means to say that the Incarnation is the revelation of Beauty Itself. The kenotic self-emptying of Christ, while entailing an impoverishment in the movement of the divine into human, is yet not a departure from God's Godliness but a way of expressing the Trinitarian love at the heart of Godself. That is the first reason Gregory need not fall into the masculinist trap. The second is that Gregory is much too complex and subtle in his invocations of richness and poverty.

The relationships among humanity, poverty, and Christ are multi-layered. In humanity's sinfulness and relative to the wealth of the glory of God, we humans are the poor. And God in Christ became poor for us, both by laying aside divine glory and by taking up material poverty. Because of Christ's material poverty, those without material possessions or wealth are

---

55. Coakley, "*Kenosis* and Subversion," 31.

56. Ibid., 33, 35.

57. For more on this approach, I recommend David Bentley Hart, who learned from Balthasar, who himself attended closely to Karl Barth's comments on beauty. At one point, Hart writes, "The Son goes forth because going forth is always already who he is as God, because all wealth and all poverty are already encompassed in his eternal life of receiving and pouring out, his infinitely accomplished bliss and love, his apatheia; and so he is hidden in being manifest and manifest in being hidden: he is the God he is in his very divestment and in his glory, both at once, as the same thing, inseparably. Because God is Trinity, and always gives and goes forth toward the other" (*Beauty of the Infinite*, 322).

the poor who have a special solidarity with Christ. Yet all humanity is called to imitate Christ in the move both to assuage poverty and be in solidarity with it. These movements presume and generate shifting categories of "poor" and "rich." As the one who came as a human, Christ is poor; as the one who will reign at the last judgment, Christ is rich. As those disadvantaged by the material inequalities of the human situation, the materially disadvantaged are poor; yet as those given Christ's special solidarity, as those participating in the poverty of the one who is coming in glory, they are rich. All humans *qua* their humanity participate in the poverty of Christ's human nature, yet the more deeply a person participates in poverty—recognizing her spiritual poverty and setting aside her material wealth—the more she imitates and participates in the great wealth of God in Christ. The way "poor" and "rich" shift point to the constant tension in this homily between the God of poverty and the God of glory. Gregory tries to bring the eschatological glory of Christ together with the Incarnational divestment by presenting both before our mind's eye at once. Gregory's moves suggest that if we could see God's glory together with God's poverty, we might ourselves respond rightly to material wealth and poverty.

The shifting categories have another set of effects as well. They generate contrasts between and continuities throughout "rich" and "poor" that give new contexts for seeing those materially wealthy and un-wealthy. These shifting categories reform our understanding of what is fitting for the rich and poor, training us into a vision of the beautiful by reshaping the way we perceive fittingness and gratuity relative to poverty. They illustrate the ridiculousness of materially advantaged humans claiming superiority due to their riches because rich and poor alike own nothing before the God to whom all wealth truly belongs and who is alone ontologically rich. Even while undermining the unequivocal claim of the materially advantaged to the title "rich," these shifts also model what one who is "rich" ought to do with her riches: give her wealth away, as Christ does. As for the poor, they find themselves suddenly given special identification with Christ through Christ's insistent presence in and as the poor (an insistence that shouts for social disruption), though they also find themselves linked with both the rich and Christ in their shared poverty of human nature. While rich and poor stand together in their unlikeness to God, they also stand together in their likeness of Christ. God's gratuitous action toward the poverty of nature and of materials establishes a way to think about fitting human actions in a world of poverty and wealth. God's free choice to display God's radical transcendence by becoming a creature while remaining the Creator breaks open the insulated class enclosures of rich and poor as contexts for beauty. Even as beauty cannot be beholden to rich-poor enclaves, the categories of rich and poor cannot, as Christ's identification with the poor attests, be ignored in assessments of beauty. We must see these categories in order to see the movement toward (and out of) poverty that occasions beauty.

But Gregory's troubling and recovering of the categories of rich and poor as contexts for beauty do not address the larger problematic of how it is we humans can see the God we so desperately want to see. In this way, perceiving Beauty Itself remains a problem. It is the next homily, the sixth, where Gregory foregrounds the issue of sight. In this homily about how the pure in heart see God, Gregory formulates the harshest version of his paradox about seeing God—the one where death attends both seeing and not seeing God. Toward the end, he resolves this paradox by distinguishing two types of sight. One requires "understanding the nature which transcends the universe"—clearly, an unattainable sight for Gregory, at least in this life.[58] The other is union with God through purity of life. That is, Gregory redefines purity as itself a kind of vision. Even though we cannot see God, we learn to know God by becoming like God. This "answer" seems hopelessly circular in a collection of homilies in which Gregory has argued that wrong perception causes most sin. The sight deemed so important and complicated in terms of poverty and wealth seems at this point to be abandoned in Gregory's redescription of sight as a kind of non-sight. The Christological hope may offer a way forward through these homilies, but after the hope takes us through the Christ who is rich and poor, trying to help us see God in humility and poverty while remembering God's coming glory, it seems to fade in this declaration of a visionless sight. The hope of seeing God in Christ is subdued by the reality that we do not yet live in the eschaton, that we have not been resurrected into the end time, that Christ has not yet come again in glory.

Veils and Tricks: The Catechetical Oration

The Catechetical Oration offers a different perspective on the problem of seeing the rich-poor Christ. It is the perspective of the devil. Gregory articulates the devil's perspective in the same speech in which he discusses the radical transcendence of God in terms of Incarnation.[59] In fact, Gregory discusses both the devil's perspective and God's radical transcendence in the same breath. He sets up the problem at the beginning of the *Oration* when he offers a Trinitarian reflection on the relationship of the Word to the Father. The Word, Gregory tells us, is the Word *of* the Father, yet is distinct *from*

58. Gregory of Nyssa, *On the Beatitudes*, homily six (Hall, 72).

59. See my discussion at the end of chapter 2.

the Father. The Word derives subsistence from the Father, yet the Word's subsistence is the Word's own. Gregory explains the way the Word is neither identical with nor independent of the Father, locating oneness in their shared nature and distinction in their unique subjects. What this means, Gregory explains, is that the Word can manifest the attributes of God.[60] It is, indeed, appropriate that a word manifests—and given Gregory's understanding of theological language, it is also inevitable that words distance and conceal.[61] In the same way that such disclosure and concealment is internal to the property of a word, so it is intrinsic to an image, and their simultaneous manifestation and hiddenness generates paradoxical relationships with words and images. One can see such paradoxes in Gregory's insistence that, on the one hand, humanity was "created as the image of the archetypal beauty"—after the image of Christ, the Image of the Father—and that it yet may seem "unbefitting" (a form of *prepon* references fitting) that God would become human.[62] It might actually seem that God could quite fittingly join the humanity who discloses the beauty of the One to the One who reveals the Beauty that is God. But image and word both suggest a difference from that which they represent, and that difference in the case of humans and Christ is marked by an infinite abyss. Humans do not image Christ in the same way that Christ images the Father. There is great heterogeneity within the category of "image." It is therefore possible to say both that humanity is the image of God and that it is unfitting that God would become human.

It is possible to say it—but Gregory does not. Accusations of unfittingness come from the "Jews and the Greeks" (and more proximately, for Gregory, the Eunomians) who fail to see, according to Gregory, the radical

---

60. Gregory of Nyssa, "Address on Religious Instruction," 272. Gregory writes, "This Word, however, is different from Him whose it is. For in a way it is a relative term, since 'the Word' certainly implies the Father of the Word. For there cannot be a word without its being someone's word. . . . We acknowledge God's living Word as active and creative—a doctrine the Jew does not accept; and we admit not distinction in nature between the Word and Him from whom it comes. In our own case we say that a spoken word comes from the mind, and is neither entirely identical with it nor altogether different. For by being derived from something else, it is different and not identical with it. Yet, since it reflects the mind, it can no longer be thought to be different from it, but is one with it in nature, though distinct as a subject. So the Word of God, by having its own subsistence, is distinct from Him from whom it derives its subsistence. On the other hand, by manifesting in itself the attributes to be seen in God, it is identical in nature with Him who is recognized by the same characteristics."

61. In Gregory's textual debates with Eunomius, he famously names the limits and proper uses of words, particularly with regard to God. For more on his intricate arguments, see the translation and rich set of studies in Karfíková et al., *Contra Eunomium II*.

62. Gregory of Nyssa, "Address on Religious Instruction," sec. 5 (Richardson, 275).

transcendence of God. They do not grasp that "the omnipotent nature was capable of descending to man's lowly position is a clearer evidence of power than great and supernatural miracles" or that God's descent to the human without ceasing to be God is a display of transcendent power.[63] All this we saw in the previous chapter. What is additionally interesting is that the way Jews, Greeks, and Eunomians fail properly to see the divine nature in Christ is similar to the way the devil also fails to see Christ rightly. Gregory describes the devil's failure as one in which he interpreted the miracles Christ performed to account for or disclose fully the kind of power this man Jesus had. The power he saw in the miracles thus lured the devil into wanting Christ as his own (captive) without making plain to him who Christ was. Gregory explains the devil's perception:

> But how can we recount in detail each of the gospel miracles? When the enemy saw such power, he recognized in Christ a bargain which offered him more than he held. For this reason he chose him as the ransom for those he had shut up in death's prison. Since, however, he could not look upon the direct vision of God, he had to see him clothed in some part of that flesh which he already held captive through sin. Consequently the Deity was veiled in flesh, so that the enemy, by seeing something familiar and natural to him, might not be terrified at the approach of transcendent power. So when he saw this power softly reflected more and more through the miracles, he reckoned that what he saw was to be desired rather than feared.[64]

Appearing to the devil as human was both necessary for the devil to see God—for the devil could not directly behold God—and strategic on God's part. The devil could be lured by Christ's displays of power without being fearful that the power was transcendent. The mistake the devil makes in perceiving Christ, then, is that he takes the miracles of Christ to exhaust the power of Christ rather than be the "soft reflection" of power they actually were. God's flesh veiled the power that would give God's identity away. But it is not just that this veiling is both the means of disclosure and concealment; it is also that God discloses Godself in the very *way* that God veils, in, that is, the perfections disclosed by such veiling. Gregory claims,

> Through the covering of the flesh the divine power is made accessible, so that the enemy will not take fright at God's appearing and so thwart his plan for us. All God's attributes are at once displayed in this—his goodness, his wisdom, and his justice. That

63. Ibid., sec. 24 (Richardson, 300–301).
64. Ibid., sec. 23 (Richardson, 300).

148

he decided to save us is proof of his goodness. That he struck a bargain to redeem the captive indicates his justice. And it is evidence of his transcendent wisdom that he contrived to make accessible to the enemy what was [otherwise] inaccessible.[65]

The Incarnation, then, is and was intended as a profound act of disclosure, teaching us the abiding goodness, wisdom, and justice of God. Nevertheless, Gregory continues to return to his certainty that God intended for the devil to misrecognize God, that God "veiled himself in our nature" so that as with a "greedy fish," the devil would "swallow the Godhead like a fishhook along with the flesh, which was the bait."[66] Once the devil had swallowed God and made God internal to death, hell, and sin, God could conquer the darkness with God's divine, sun-like radiance. Of course, the intention of putting out a bait is always to deceive, and Gregory admits that "in a way it was fraud and deception of God . . . not to show his naked [*gymnos*] deity."[67] But in a much better way, in a higher way, the Incarnation was not deception but "a crowning example of justice and wisdom," for the devil not only got his due (presumably, because the deceiver was himself deceived) but was also given more than his due by being taken up into a higher aim.[68] In enticing the devil to swallow God, God saves the devil.[69]

There is something unseemly (perhaps unfitting?) about imagining God involved in tricks. But let us press further into how God's dealings with the devil were, for Gregory, both trick and non-trick in order to get at what it might mean for Gregory to call them tricky. To do so, we might return to some of Gregory's favorite imagery and imagine the cave-dwellers of Plato's famous allegory. Suppose these cave-dwellers have already heard about the world where the sun shines and everything has color and multiple dimensions. They have heard about it—and they hate it. Maybe they are afraid or resentful or lazy or all of the above, but they hate this world of light that their former cave companions descend, torch in hand, to tell them about. They have taken to holding captive, even murdering, such story-telling one-time companions, angry that the companion is disrupting the familiar world of the dark. By this point, the cave-dwellers have heard many stories of the world outside the cave, and they have learned to hate the one who made what they have heard is called sun, the one who is, as their former companions say, Light Itself. Light Itself, watching the cave-dwellers reject storyteller

65. Ibid.

66. Ibid., sec. 25 (Richardson, 301).

67. Ibid., sec. 26 (Richardson, 302).

68. Ibid., sec. 26 (Richardson, 302–3).

69. Ibid., sec. 26 (Richardson, 303).

after storyteller, decides to visit these cave-dwellers, to rescue them from their small, dark lives of hate and fear. Knowing that going to them in the fullness of glory, Light would only blind the cave-dwellers, plunging them deeper into a world of darkness, Light takes on flesh. Like the former cave companions, Light descends, torch in hand, to the cave. Light fully expects to be mistaken as a former cave companion. Light, in fact, knows that such a mistake admits a nearness to the cave-dwellers that the glory of Light would have rendered impossible. In this way, Light tricks the cave-dwellers in order to bring them light. As expected, the cave-dwellers hold Light captive and even attempt to murder Light. But once there as captive, inhabiting their life and their home, Light enters their darkness, dispelling it from within the cave so that the dwellers recognize the cave as a cave, shadows as shadows, the former companions as friends, and themselves as murderers; and with these recognitions, they have already begun the journey out of the world of the cave. And so through this trick they are un-tricked. Any pedagogy for such a person as one of our hate-filled cave-dwellers (or the devil) can only be a trick, for they are incapable of receiving the truth as anything but tricky. Receiving the truth, after all, requires becoming the kind of person that can recognize herself as filled with untruth.[70]

The kind of trick God played on the devil was neither intended ultimately to deceive (it was a trick for the express purpose of un-deceiving), nor was it a lie. It would have been a lie had God hidden in flesh, had Light climbed into a human body like Greeks into a Trojan horse. But God did not hide in flesh. God took on flesh as God's own. God did something new, something unexpected, something God had never before done. A being who thinks she knows God exhaustively, who believes God is determined by God's past revelations, is vulnerable to tricks in her attempts to interpret present divine activity. (We, too, are vulnerable to being tricked by failing to look for the new thing God is doing.) It would have been a lying trick if God had represented Godself as something God was not. But God's trick was to do something infinitely more powerful and creative than the devil could conceive. The greatness evidenced by the Incarnation, in fact, becomes the

---

70. Wittgenstein considers a similar interpretation of a related issue. Puzzling over why, if Scripture is warning "of a terrible danger" it would "go about telling . . . a riddle whose solution will be the warning?" Wittgenstein writes, "But who is to say that the Scripture really is so unclear? Isn't it possible that it was essential in this case to 'tell a riddle'? And that, on the other hand, giving a more direct warning would necessarily have had the *wrong* effect?" (*Culture and Value*, Remarks from 1937, 31). I take Cavell to be working out this same theme when he says of King Lear, "And in the case of Lear, I know in a general way what he has to reveal about himself in order to acknowledge Cordelia as his unjustly banished daughter, viz., that he is her unjust banishing father" (*Claim of Reason*, 429).

theme of Gregory's address. God's trick was an unanticipated move: The Word *became* flesh.[71]

God's descent into the devil like a hook into a fish points not just to the way God dispels deception from the belly of the Deceiver. It also, for Gregory, points to the way no darkness will remain when God's salvation has come to fullness. God will be all in all, for Gregory. Even the instantiation of evil and hell and sin must be conquered by the almighty goodness of God. In this act of salvation, the devil will recognize God rightly, for the way to recognize God, as Gregory had said earlier in his oration, is to see God's benefits. Gregory writes,

> Do you ask the reason why God was born among men? If you exclude from life the benefits which come from God, you will have no way of recognizing the divine. It is from the blessings we experience that we recognize our benefactor, since by observing what happens to us, we deduce the nature of Him who is responsible for it. If, then, the love of man is a proper mark of the divine nature, here is the explanation you are looking for, here is the reason for God's presence among men. Our nature was sick and needed a doctor. Man had fallen and needed someone to raise him up. He who had lost life needed someone to restore it. . . . He who was shut up in darkness needed the presence of light. . . . Were these trifling and unworthy reasons to impel God to come down and visit human nature, seeing humanity was in such a pitiful and wretched state?[72]

To recognize God is to be loved by God and recognize the love of God toward oneself. Recognition and love are deeply intertwined for a God who is Love. To see God is to see the love of God toward us in our need—to see,

71. In a meditation on divine pedagogy, Kierkegaard takes a similar tack in his tale of the king who loved a lowly maiden. Troubled that he could not be assured the maiden was happy in his love if he came to her as a king, he determined that she could only be happily loved by someone obscure. This and many other worries about their possibility for understanding, love, and happiness caused the king great sorrow and convinced him he could not appear to the maiden as a king if he wished to win her love. Yet to appear as a lowly subject himself and later to disclose himself as king would be deception, and the king could not bear the thought of deceiving his beloved or risking her wrath. The king decides to appear as a servant—yet "this form of a servant is not something put on like the king's plebian cloak, which just by flapping open would betray the king . . . but it is his true form. For this is the boundlessness of love, that in earnestness and truth and not in jest it wills to be the equal of the beloved." To win the maiden's true love, the king must not simply appear as a servant but take on servanthood as his true form (*Philosophical Fragments*, 26–32).

72. Gregory of Nyssa, "Address on Religious Instruction" sec. 15 (Richardson, 290–91).

as Gregory puts it, the benefits of God. To see God is to be saved by God, and so to see God is to see oneself in need of saving. The Incarnation that tricked the devil was the saving-act that made possible the impossibility of the devil seeing God.

But sight is incomplete as long as salvation is incomplete, and to recognize God through God's benefits is not to see God in God's self. It is to see dimly through a darkened glass. And the hope Gregory extends to us in the *Homilies on the Beatitudes*—that though we cannot see the invisible God we might yet see the God made flesh in Christ—has also been complicated, for it seems the right vision of Christ is not simply given. The devil (like the Eunomians) makes plain to us that we look on Christ without fully seeing him. To see Christ is to see God coming in love to save the wounded. To see rightly the Christ who is God, then, one must rightly see the wounded. It is similar to the conclusion just drawn from the *Homilies on the Beatitudes* that to see Christ is to recognize one's own poverty. To see Beauty is to see one's own poverty (and perhaps one's ugliness) transformed through the abundant poverty of Christ. Gregory makes clear in this next set of homilies what these statements mean: Perceiving the beauty of Christ requires right attention to the ugliness of affliction.

The *Prosopon* of the Afflicted: Sermons on the Love of the Poor

The setting has special importance for interpreting these homilies on the love of the poor. From 368 to 369 there was a devastating famine in Cappadocia. Gregory's brother Basil had started a poor-hospice, which has commonly been called the first hospital.[73] In this poor-hospice, as in Gregory's

---

73. See Susan Holman's detailed discussion of the famine in *The Hungry Are Dying*, 64–98. Holman points to the best-known version of the famine and Basil's organized response to it, which is found in Gregory of Nazianzus's panegyric of Basil. He writes, "There was a famine, the most severe one ever recorded. The city was in distress, and there was no source of assistance, or relief for the calamity . . . but the hardest part of all such distress is the insensibility and insatiability of those who possess supplies. For they watch their opportunities, and turn their distress to profit, and thrive upon misfortune. . . . Such are the buyers and sellers of corn, who neither respect their fellows, nor are thankful to God, from Whom comes what they have. . . . But . . . by his word and advice [Basil] opened the stores of those who possessed them, and so, according to the Scripture, dealt food to the hungry, and satisfied the poor with bread, and fed them in the time of dearth, and filled the hungry souls with good things. And in what way? for this is no slight addition to his praise. He gathered together the victims of the famine with some who were but slightly recovering from it, men and women, infants, old men, every age which was in distress, and obtaining contributions of all sorts of food which can relieve famine, set before them basins of soup and such meat as was found preserved among us, on which the poor live. Then, imitating the ministry of Christ, Who, girded

Sermons on the Love of the Poor (*De pauperibus amandis*), poverty, hunger, and disease are tightly interwoven, almost inseparable, and when Gregory speaks of "the poor" in these sermons, he often means the lepers, the starving, and the otherwise marginalized once-members of society.[74] Here we examine two short sermons on the love of the poor, one called *On Good Works* (*De beneficentia*) and the other called *On the Saying, "Whoever Has Done It to One of These Has Done It to Me"* (*In illud: Quatenus uni ex fecistis mihi fecistis*).

These two sermons on the love of the poor follow sermons in which Gregory exhorted his congregation to fast. As he turns to the importance of caring for the poor, he tells his congregation that the reason why they fast is to remember—in their bodies as well as their minds—the passion of Christ, who submitted to insults and violence before being nailed to the Cross. Fasting, for Gregory, is a way to share in the suffering of Christ, to remember the fleshly pain by which Christ saved the world. In so doing, a person battles the sin of gluttony and becomes more like Christ. But fasting is not enough to become like Christ. Gregory tells his congregants that the other side of their gluttony is others' starvation. The hunger of poverty and the gorging of wealth are "two contrary" but related evils. It is clear Gregory is addressing the rich in this sermon because he speaks of moderating the zeal of one's cooks and relieving the weary hands of one's cupbearers.[75] But all that is only to recapitulate his previous sermon. Having addressed the wealthy's gorging, Gregory turns to the starvation of the poor. He launches into his subject with a ferocious critique: "What good does it serve you to observe a strict frugality at home if you unjustly steal from the poor? What kind of piety teaches you to drink water while you hatch plots and drink the blood of the man you have shamefully cheated?" They are strong words from one who does advocate drinking the blood of the one humanity shamefully treated.[76] It is not long before Gregory turns to this one, "the Lamb" who was insulted, brutalized, and nailed to the Cross.[77] There are

---

with a towel, did not disdain to wash the disciples' feet, using for this purpose the aid of his own servants, and also of his fellow servants, he attended to the bodies and souls of those who needed it, combining personal respect with the supply of their necessity, and so giving them a double relief" ("Pangegyric on St. Basil," 407).

74. For "the poor," Gregory uses both πτωχοι and πένητες.

75. Gregory of Nyssa, "'On the Love of the Poor' 1: 'On Good Works'" sec. 453 (Holman, 193). Hereafter cited as "On Good Works."

76. Gregory of Nyssa, "Address on Religious Instruction," 318–21.

77. Gregory communicates the brutality through ῥαπίσματα (received blows) and καθυβρίζω (was treated spitefully).

others who live a life Gregory terms brutal.[78] They "hide in the cracks of walls like owls" and drink from the spring "like animals."[79] As Christ was bestialized as the Lamb who was slain, so the afflicted are bestialized as hiding owls and spring-drinkers. In Gregory's *Address on Religious Instruction*, he claims we drink the blood of Christ that we might live; here Gregory describes his congregants as possessed by a lust for blood that drives them to drain life from the poor.

No sooner has Gregory sketched the image of the poor as dehumanized than he juxtaposes that image with another. Those who see the poor only as bestialized need to look closer. Upon considering who the poor are, the viewer will discover they bear the face (*prosopon*: person, representation, mask, character, countenance) of our savior.[80] That is, the poor both bear the Savior Christ's *prosopon* and themselves save the rich. Gregory writes,

> The Lord in His goodness has given them His own countenance in order that it might cause the hard-hearted, those who hate the poor, to blush with shame, just as those being robbed thrust before their attackers images of their king [on coinage] to shame the enemy with the appearance of the ruler. The poor are the stewards of our hope, doorkeepers of the kingdom, who open the door to the righteous and close it again to the unloving misanthropists. . . . For the deeds done to them cries out to the one who fathoms the heart in a voice clearer than the herald's trumpet.[81]

The poor here are those who open the door to the kingdom of God. From their bestialized position in cracks of walls, they are elevated to those with the right to supreme judgment. So holy are the poor, that even other poor should attend them.[82] As in his *Homilies on the Beatitudes*, Gregory slips into a kind of eschatological trance, envisioning the Son of Man escorted by thousands of angels and sitting on a throne of glory. He imagines the eschatological judgment, describing it in present tense as the separation of the sheep from the goats who respectively enjoy the kingdom or receive punishment by fire.[83]

Gregory is not innovating in his juxtaposition of the images of the poor bearing Christ's face and Christ's eschatological separation of sheep

78. Brutal: ἄγριος.

79. Gregory of Nyssa, "On Good Works" sec. 457 (Holman, 194).

80. Ibid., sec. 460 (Holman, 195).

81. Ibid.

82. Ibid.

83. Ibid., sec. 460–61 (Holman, 196).

and goats. He is reading Matthew 25:31–46 and commenting on its own descriptions of the same. But Gregory does not want his congregants to hear a contrast between the present position of the poor and their future revelation in glory. He wants them to hear it all in present tense. See these poor who have been dehumanized? They are the ones who are Christ, who are judging you for your lack of love, who hold your hope in their judgment.

Gregory does not dwell on the image of judgment but moves on to describe another aspect of God that provides new motivation for loving the poor. For it turns out that beneficence, the subject of this sermon, finds its first and final meaning in God. Gregory reminds his congregants of God the Creator:

> It is God Himself, who in the first instance manifests Himself to us as the author of good and philanthropic deeds: the creation of the earth, the arrangement of the heavens, the well-ordered rhythm of the season, the warmth of the sun, the formation, by cooling, of ice, in short, all things, individually, He created not for Himself—for he had no need of such things—but He maintains them continually on our behalf; invisible farmer of all human nourishment, He sows at the opportune moment and waters the earth skillfully. . . . You see, God is the original designer of good deeds, nourishing the starving, watering the thirsty, clothing those who are naked.[84]

God both gives God's face to the poor, the hungry, and the naked and is the original caregiver to the poor, the hungry, and the naked. In tending to the poor who bear Christ, those who give imitate the God who loves the poor—and all of us are poor before God because all of us receive our existence, our nourishment, our water from God. Gregory continues invoking humanity's equalizing ontological poverty before God by capitalizing on the equality such poverty presumes. As when Gregory describes the reality surrounding the roles of power we play in his *Homilies on the Beatitudes*, so here he describes humanity as "brothers" and claims that as such, we should "reap an equal part of the heritage."[85] Look, brothers, at the wolf and the dog: even they will share the carcass they find. A brother who refuses to share his heritage is worse than these animals.

A refusal to share one's heritage entails overindulgence in pleasures, which are not disconnected, as Gregory explained at the beginning of his homily, with depriving the poor. Beasts again become a mediating third

84. Ibid.
85. Ibid., sec. 465 (Holman, 197).

between rich and poor, as Gregory describes how the rich can avoid usurping the inheritance of the poor.

> Do not make yourself a destroyer of absolutely all living things, whether they be four-footed and large or four-footed and small, birds, fish, exotic or common, a good bargain or expensive. The sweat of the hunter ought not to fill your stomach like a bottomless well that many men digging cannot fill.[86]

The one who "devises clever traps" so that he can eat every kind of animal he sees exhibits the kind of bloodlust that will not rest content in "temperate relaxation" but will bestialize the bodies of the poor. The poor, meanwhile, "[drag] themselves along painfully," with "amputated feet," perhaps "crawling" or "mutilated" or with "gouged out" eyes.[87] Where are the rich who might give them food? At their loud banquets of excess, unable to hear the cries of the poor over the raucous music and "cackling of bawling laughter." When the poor beg more loudly, the rich treat them worse than their own animals: they set their dogs on them. Gregory moves quickly between the images of the poor and the rich:

> Accordingly [the poor] retreat, the beloved of Christ, who embody the essential commandment without having gained one mouthful of bread or meat, but satiated with insults and blows. And in the den of Mammon, some vomit up their meal like an overflowing vessel; others sleep on the table, their wine cups beside them.[88]

Bestialized or not, the poor are not painted as the disgusting ones in this tableau. Gregory's rhetoric reaches a climactic pitch, his intensity growing as if he himself wants to shout through the loud and bawdy banquet of the rich.

> If God sees these scenes—and I am sure He does—what fatal catastrophe, do you think, does He hold in store for those who hate the poor? Answer me! Or do you not know that it is to this end that the holy gospel shouts out and testifies with scenes of horror and dread?[89]

Gregory continues at this pitch for several sentences before he breaks it with a quieter call to "consider these things reasonably" by contemplating our

---

86. Ibid., sec. 465 (Holman, 198).
87. Ibid.
88. Ibid., sec. 468 (Holman, 198).
89. Ibid., sec. 468 (Holman, 199).

transience, our ephemerality, our death. We ought to be like the psalmist, who longs to know the moment of his death so that he might know in what way he is lacking. The psalm-singer does not see God in a darkened glass.[90] "He perceives the king of kings and judge of judges as clearly as in a mirror . . . ."[91] By longing to know his death, by trying to understand the shape of his life through attention to the moment it ends, the psalmist sees God. With this breathless mystery, Gregory ends his first homily.

Having left his congregation to ponder the mystery of the God-seeing psalmist, Gregory opens his second sermon on the love of the poor by picking up the theme of vision. He begins in his eschatological trance. "Again I hold before my eyes the dreadful vision of the return of the kingdom . . . ."[92] This sermon is even less restrained than the one that preceded it. The themes of vision, of eschatological judgment, of Christ's identification with the poor, of the poor as bestialized, all return more explicitly and dramatically. But the opening eschatological image blazes with wealth and power: A king sits formidably on a "magnificent" "throne of glory." The eschatological image "impresses upon [Gregory's] soul" such that "no reality seems at all urgent."[93] No reality seems more urgent because, as it turns out, this is no mere trance-induced glimpse into the future. "He who comes is always present."[94] Mystified by Christ's simultaneous presence and absence, Gregory asks, "If He is with us, why does he announce his return as if he has been absent?"[95] In such a thought, Gregory claims he "runs ahead" of himself.[96] There are other matters he must address first.

The principal matter is describing how one might avoid eschatological destruction. We do so by throwing "ourselves with zeal into the path of

90. Or in a more literal translation of 1 Cor 13:12, *darkly through a mirror* (δι'ἐσόπτου ἐν αἰνίγματι). While the Corinthians passage emphasizes the indirectness of looking at a mirror, as opposed to the possibility of direct sight in the eschaton (*now* a mirror, *then* face to face), Gregory's sermon, by contrast, emphasizes the wondrousness of seeing the one who surpasses all in a mirror. Holman tries to capture this wondrousness by including "clearly" in her translation, though there is no exact reference for the word in the Greek.

91. As clearly as in a mirror: ἐνοπτρίζω [literally: see as in a mirror]. Gregory of Nyssa, "On Good Works" sec. 469 (Holman, 199).

92. Gregory of Nyssa, "'On the Love of the Poor' 2: 'On the Saying, "Whoever Has Done It"'" sec. 472 (Holman, 199). Hereafter cited as "Whoever Has Done It."

93. Formidably: φοβερῶς [fearfully; forms of this word are used six times in the brief opening vision]. Gregory of Nyssa, "Whoever Has Done It" sec. 472 (Holman, 200).

94. Gregory of Nyssa, "Whoever Has Done It" sec. 472 (Holman, 200).

95. Ibid.

96. Ibid., sec. 473 (Holman, 200).

God . . . who holds himself bound to the attentions that we render to the needy."[97] For it is not just that the poor have Christ's face but that Christ says, "I was hungry, I was thirsty, I was a stranger, naked, sick, a prisoner."[98] To care for the poor is to care for Christ, to "see for yourself the realization of the good news."[99] Gregory reads the poor into the story of the Good Samaritan and then brings them before the mind's eye of his audience as even more explicitly bestialized. Their "frightful malady has changed them into beasts," barely recognizable as humans. "These people who yesterday stood upright and looked at the sky are here today, bending to the earth, walking on four feet, practically changed into animals. Listen to the rasping wheeze that comes from their chest. Thus it is that they breathe."[100] At the same time that Gregory describes the afflicted so gruesomely, he excoriates the rich for the form their horror takes, for failing to recognize the afflicted as brothers. Yet such horror can be useful to the rich—and can also be cured—if the rich consider the fall from health to affliction in humans against the infinitely greater descent from "the king of celestial bliss" to "stinking and unclean flesh."[101] The Incarnation is thus a balm for the rich's horror, which Gregory re-forms by following the bestial images of the poor with an insistence that the afflicted are no different in their nature from the satiated rich. Reshaping the horror of the rich, Gregory does not want them to lose their horror, because he wants the satiated rich fully sensitized to the material reality of the afflicted. Thus Gregory insists that the rich should see the "wandering men who are scattered along our roads like cattle foraging for a little nourishment, clothed in wretched rags" yet see them also as "man born in the image of God, entrusted with the governance of the earth and rule over all creatures."[102] The holiness and horror of the afflicted mingle with the holi-

---

97. Ibid.

98. Ibid.

99. Ibid.

100. Ibid., sec. 476 (Holman, 201).

101. Ibid.

102. Ibid., sec. 477 (Holman, 201). Gregory deploys this same juxtaposition between the image of God a human bears and her animalization by fellow humans to render the horror of slavery in his fourth homily on Ecclesiastes: "I got me slaves and slave-girls. For what price, tell me? What did you find in existence worth as much as this human nature? . . . How many obols did you reckon the equivalent of the likeness of God? . . . How too shall the ruler of the whole earth and all earthly things be put up for sale? . . . But has the scrap of paper, and the written contract, and the counting out of obols deceived you into thinking yourself the master of the image of God? What folly! . . . If you are equal in all these ways, therefore, in what respect have you something extra, tell me, that you who are human think yourself the master of a human being, and say, I got me slaves and slave girls, like herds or goats or pigs" (*Homilies on Ecclesiastes*, 74–75).

ness and horror of the Incarnation and Crucifixion. The rest of humanity is taken up in this horror and holiness through the afflicted with whom they share humanity and the poverty of humanity, and also through Christ who shared humanity with all humans and his face with the afflicted.

So far Gregory is dramatizing and elaborating themes already present in the first sermon but with more graphic detail. Here he pauses to distinguish the kind of graphic detail he is giving, and he does it by contrasting it with another kind of graphic detail, one which does not allow the afflicted their own sense of horror at their situation, for in it "necessity overrides the horror that they give themselves." Isolated from the community, the afflicted form their own society and get bread the only way they can.

> Can you distinguish their gloomy dances? Do you listen to their plaintive songs? How do they arrive to make a parade of their infirmities and give the crowds the spectacle of their crippled bodies? Macabre jugglers, exhibiting their diverse mutilations! Making sad melodies and gloomy chants, poets of a unique type of tragedy where without any need of new subjects, they fill the stage with their own misfortunes.[103]

They do these things because they are "pressed by hunger." Gregory confesses himself "filled with alarm" by this "atrocious spectacle," "deeply upset" by the image of the afflicted "dragging themselves along the road, half-dead yet supremely human," their bodies "rotting like carrion."[104] But even as he attends to the poor, he reserves his horrified ire for the way they show their distress to bargain for food. Powerless to save themselves, the afflicted become complicit in their own dehumanization, turning their suffering into the entertainment of the rich.

> What then? Is one not sinning against the natural law by reducing this person's suffering to theatrical phrases, treating the disease with a speech and remembering it with a ballad? Is it not necessary rather to let our compassion and love for one another shine forth radiantly in action? There is a difference between words and action as great as the difference between a painting and the reality.[105]

To save themselves from starvation, the afflicted turn their sufferings into sources of fascination and morbid pleasure for the satiated. In so doing, they translate their sufferings into the world of the satiated, where the

---

103. Gregory of Nyssa, "Whoever Has Done It" sec. 477 (Holman, 202).

104. Ibid., sec. 480 (Holman, 202).

105. Ibid., sec. 480 (Holman, 203).

subjectivity of the satiated is preserved at the expense of the afflicted, and the mutual need for healing remains unexpressed, misrepresented. This is a use of language that mystifies reality.

The right use of language is the language that galvanizes toward action; it establishes community with the afflicted, who, Gregory reminds us yet again, are Christ and bear human nature.[106] Why ostracize them? Do you fear their contagion? Gregory counters that there is no medical evidence that leprosy is contagious, and that the contagion the lepers do have is the contagion of holiness, which the rich should hope to catch. By healing their bodies of ulcers, hunger, and suffering, the satiated can themselves be healed of their greed and sin so that they may be received by them into the kingdom.[107] Admitting that it is indeed hard to master a natural aversion to such ugly suffering, Gregory presses his congregants nonetheless to do just that. "Are we, with so much at stake, going to choose the pleasant, smooth path and beat a retreat in the face of the steep path of virtue?"[108] You will cure your aversion, Gregory claims, by simply "persevering in exercise of care for the sick."[109] Like all forms of exercise, it will be difficult in the beginning but enjoyable, even "sweet" in the long-term. And such care for the sick is "profitable for the healthy."[110] Gregory explains why: "For it is beautiful for the soul to provide mercy to those who have fallen on misfortune."[111] With this call to action, Gregory moves into an extended metaphor exhorting his congregants to set sail safely and avoid shipwreck to arrive at the promised land.[112]

The beauty here is the act of charity, participation in the saving love by which we know God. This is a kind of "seeing God" described in the sixth homily on the Beatitudes, a seeing that is a union of God. But it is a union that also makes God visible. To provide mercy for those who have fallen on misfortune is to make visible the Christ who in mercy gave up life and glory for the humanity who had fallen and to do so by tending those who bear the *prosopon* of Christ. The glory of God is disclosed through the taking up of material poverty and spiritual poverty into this act of charity, which is described as unqualifiedly beautiful.

Regarding Christ's veiling and unveiling of the glory of the Father, we have learned that Christ unveils God's glory only when seen in and as

106. Ibid., sec. 484 (Holman, 204).

107. Ibid., sec. 483–84 (Holman, 204).

108. Ibid., sec. 488 (Holman, 205).

109. Ibid.

110. Sweet: ἡδύς. Ibid., sec. 488 (Holman, 206).

111. Ibid.

112. Ibid.

the love going out toward poverty. It is a formulation of love interestingly evocative of yet different from Socrates's formulation in the *Symposium*, where Love is not divine but is the child of Poverty and Resource. Socrates's Love cannily seeks resources to escape the exigencies of his own situation. Plotinus's love, which is the emanation of the One who is ontologically rich to ontologically impoverished matter, enables the One to give to the poor without ever touching the poor. Such conceptions of love are blind to the Incarnation, for the Incarnation says that the divine *became* poor (*contra* Plotinus) because the divine *is* love (*contra* Plato). For a person to see Christ go forth in poverty to seek and save the materially and ontologically poor is to see the God who comes to save her, just as the psalmist sees God when he sees his own neediness at death, just as the devil sees God when God is saving him.

The love that makes God visible is care-filled attention to ugliness. The ugliness this love attends is the dehumanization of the afflicted—an ugliness never separated from the beauty of the afflicted, and it is never separated from the beauty of the afflicted as Christ and as humans in the image of God. To see God requires seeing the half-dead human dragging herself along the road, the starved lepers foraging for food like cattle, the ostracized sick hiding owl-like in cracks of the walls. And these afflicted must not be sources of entertainment. They must be seen in their full humanity and Christ-likeness. Gregory works against rendering poverty either invisible or normal. To see poverty is to respond with the care the afflicted need and with the hope that the afflicted might yet heal the materially advantaged sin-sick, whom they might one day let into the kingdom. The response of hope and care is the act of charity to which Gregory commends his audience. It is here, in this place where soul-sickness meets body-sickness, bloated greed meets decaying limbs, blood-lusty meets hunger-wracked, that we find beauty. This beauty, which discloses the glory of the God who goes out toward the poor and becomes the poor, is a flash, a momentary glimpse of the glory we will see once we have arrived in what Gregory calls the promised land.

Gregory's beautiful homiletic rhetoric works to train his audience into a context of fittingness—the one who became poor for our sake—while also identifying a simultaneous context of definite unfittingness—juxtaposing humanity and God-imaging with beasts and worse than beasts. The afflicted are and are not beautiful. They are beautiful by bearing the image of God and representing and participating in the poverty of Christ. At the same time, affliction is not itself beautiful. This is the difference between Christ and all other afflicted humans: Christ's affliction is itself beautiful because it is overcome and taken up into Christ's glory. Christ's wounds still mark the resurrected Christ but they testify to the defeat of death. The wounds of the afflicted await such glorification. While the sharing of the afflicted in the poverty of Christ points to Christ's glory in which they participate, their affliction also displays their need for Christ's glory. They bear Christ yet stand in need of Christ. Such need puts them in an intimate relationship with Christ while also marking the distance from Christ, much like the intimacy and distance between an infant and her parent. That is, the infant is held near to the parent because she is distant from her, because she has none of the parent's capacities to feed, soothe, and care for herself. What Gregory makes clear in these sermons is not that the beautiful entails the ugly—the animalization of a human body is in no way beautiful—but that on this side of the eschaton, finding what is beautiful requires attending to what is ugly. The beautiful and the ugly can reference the same object, looked at in the context of Christ's coming in glory or the context of the exclusive banquet of the satiated. In this world, the beautiful and the ugly are so intimate that attempts to find a "beautiful" sanitized of the ugly often degenerates into little more than an unblessed rage for order—or a sentimental ignoring of the conditions of life. Attempts to purge the world of un-beauty can only yield ugliness. It is not that finding beauty apart from ugliness is impossible (perhaps one can imagine our exquisitely functional cup), but that the greater and the more profound the beauty, the greater the ugliness in which it is implicated, for the profoundest beauties participate in eschatological Beauty, which is to say, the One who is Beauty Crucified.

Furthermore, an attempt to find a beautiful unmixed with the ugly is in danger of becoming a love for beauty that disdains the suffering of this world. Such a search can never yield the love Gregory describes in his *Homilies on the Love of the Poor*: a love that seeks ugliness to enfold into its life-saving beauty—the love that Gregory describes as beautiful at the end of his *Homilies*. This, then, is one side of the paradox that to see God is to be unified with God: Participating in the God who is love makes God visible to the world. There is another side to the paradox, which Gregory develops in one of his last works, the *Life of Moses*. There he will develop the *kinesis* of seeing: seeing God and union with God are both ways of describing a movement into God.

The Seeing That Is Not Seeing: *The Life of Moses*

The primary issue concerning seeing beauty in the *Life of Moses* is not that it requires attending ugliness but that it requires seeing darkness in a way not-unrelated to how our shadow-dwellers learn to perceive darkness. Like the *Homilies on the Beatitudes,* Gregory's *Life of Moses* is themed around ascending a mountain: Sinai, in this case. The reader of this *Life* is supposed to imitate Moses in his climb, which, like that of the *Homilies on the Beatitudes,* is also an ascent that clarifies sight. But in Gregory's telling, at the peak of Sinai, just when Moses should, according to ascent narratives, catch his glimpse of Beauty Itself, he instead finds himself enrobed in a dazzling darkness. He is in the presence of the invisible and incomprehensible God. He *sees* the invisible God, and it is a "seeing that consists in not seeing."[113] The darkness marks the unknowability of the divine essence, and so the move up Sinai progresses from unknowingness to knowing the knowable to knowing the unknowability of the unknowable. Moses sees the vastness of God's unknowability, for the divine cannot be likened to anything known by humanity, and every concept about God risks idolatry. Yet this encounter with God's unknowability is stages beyond the encounter with one's own unknowingness. Moses's intelligence, Gregory tells us, lets him "slip in where God is," and the place where intelligence meets God "is called *darkness.*"[114]

Gregory does not leave his reader in this apophatic moment. After the encounter of darkness, a river of images floods the text, beginning with the heavenly tabernacle and succeeded by the earthly tabernacle, priestly vestments, and stone tablets. Image replaces image, as in a dreamscape, until finally Gregory confesses that there is no end in sight. Darkness is not the summit of Sinai, for Moses "at no time stopped in his ascent, nor did he set a limit for himself in his upward course."[115] Gregory writes this as he meditates on the paradox of seeing God, which he frames differently here than the invisibly glorious God of the *Homilies on the Beatitudes* or the deferred paradox of the present-absent Christ in the sermons on the love of the poor. "How does someone who Scripture says saw God clearly in such divine appearances—*face to face, as a man speaks with his friend*—require that God appear to him, as though he who is always visible had not yet been seen . . . ?"[116] In this description, God is not the invisible God but "he who is always visible."[117] Gregory is meditating on Exodus 33, which claims both that God spoke to Moses face to face like a friend (33:11) and presents God saying to Moses, in response to Moses's request to see God's glory, that no one can see God's face and live (33:20). Gregory suggests that there are

---

113. Gregory of Nyssa, *Life of Moses* II.163 (Malherbe and Ferguson, 95).

114. Ibid., II.169 (Malherbe and Ferguson, 97).

115. Ibid., II.228 (Malherbe and Ferguson, 113).

116. Ibid., II.219 (Malherbe and Ferguson, 111).

117. Ibid., II.219 (Malherbe and Ferguson, 95).

different presences God may have in one's life and different forms of visibility. And no human can bear face-to-face visibility.

According to Gregory, Moses is in despair that what he seeks "cannot be contained by human life."[118] So God makes a way for Moses: "Still, God says, there is a place with himself where there is a rock with a hole in it into which he commands Moses to enter. Then God placed his hand over the mouth of the hole and called out to Moses as he passed by."[119] Moses can see the back of God but not God's face, a scriptural description that Gregory explains as more fittingly contemplated spiritually than literally.[120] Gregory reads in the text a distinction between seeing the face of God and seeing the face of God in glory. Though Moses talks with God daily face to face, he can only catch back glances of God's glory. Such glances, however, suffice that, like Macrina, he glows with divine glory.

The glory of God—the Good Itself[121]—is not something a person ever definitively sees. Moses at no time stops in ascent because his desire for God is not satisfied—this thirst, no matter how he fills himself, refuses to be slaked. It is here in the discussion of never-ending progress, not in the description of Sinai's peak, that Gregory describes beauty. Moses's ever-expanding thirst allows him to partake according to God's true being, rather than according to his capacity. Such an experience, Gregory claims, "belongs to the soul which loves what is beautiful," the soul who wants to enjoy Beauty "face to face," who is drawn by hope "from the beauty which is seen to what is beyond."[122] And there is always a beyond for "the Divine is by its very nature infinite, enclosed by no boundary. If the Divine is perceived as though bounded by something, one must by all means consider along with that boundary what is beyond it."[123] The boundaries of one image give way to the boundaries of the next image; the next is described as higher, but it is only higher because of all the images that have come before it. That is, while initially some aspects of beauty were legitimately higher than others, after a certain point, the images are higher only because they add to a repository of images. To behold God is no longer to stop and see, as one looks at a painting. Seeing the back of God means that to behold God is "to follow God

118. Ibid., II.220 (Malherbe and Ferguson, 112).

119. Ibid.

120. Ibid., II.223 (Malherbe and Ferguson, 112–13).

121. Ibid., II.225 (Malherbe and Ferguson, 113).

122. Ibid., II.231 (Malherbe and Ferguson, 114); II.232 (Malherbe and Ferguson, 115); II.231 (Malherbe and Ferguson, 114).

123. Ibid., II.236 (Malherbe and Ferguson, 115).

wherever he might lead."[124] The vision of God consists in "never [being] satisfied with the desire to see" God.[125] We cannot face God, Gregory concludes, because we must follow God, and such following is a gift. Gregory writes, "You see how it is so great a thing to learn how to follow God, that after those lofty ascents and awesome glorious theophanies virtually at the end of his life, the man who has learned to follow behind God is scarcely considered worthy of the grace."[126] The one who so follows God beautifies herself such that she reveals the archetype that she images.[127] That is what has happened to Moses, and Gregory exhorts us to follow Moses in our effort to follow God. Through such following, we, like Moses, may attain the goal of the virtuous life: "to be known by God and to become [God's] friend."[128] The singular, Moses-like pursuit of Beauty thus ends in friendship with God.

Mystical, apophatic journeys such as the one in the *Life of Moses* risk assimilation to the powers of this world, for in their focus on the hereafter and beyondness of God, they risk rendering invisible the social structures of the present. Gregory protects against this danger in two ways: He does not let the apophatic moment become absolute but follows it with descriptions of unceasing images that characterize a never-ending journey into God. A person must never stop following God, and no social structure is a worthy place to rest. Rather than a journey that ends in a mystical union with God, implicitly blessing the social structure within which such union is possible, Gregory's call to journey unceasingly through God continually exposes social structures anew. How it exposes them is part of the second point: Gregory contextualizes this apophaticism by surrounding the *Life of Moses* with homiletic calls to social action. The beautiful is implicated in ugliness, and so is the eschaton in present social structures. The eschaton becomes manifest through the present structures of this world as light enters a room through slatted blinds. That is why kings must govern with an eye toward this light, to adjust their governance to let in as much light as possible. Gregory makes clear in his homilies on the love of the poor and on the Beatitudes that to follow God is to imitate God's love, God's going forth in poverty, and to see God is to see God in the poor and in the act of love by which the afflicted and the satiated are mutually healed. Following God is participating in the saving love of God. What the *Life of Moses* adds

124. Ibid., II.252 (Malherbe and Ferguson, 119).
125. Ibid., II.239 (Malherbe and Ferguson, 116).
126. Ibid., II.255 (Malherbe and Ferguson, 120).
127. Ibid., II.318 (Malherbe and Ferguson, 136).
128. Ibid., II.319-20 (Malherbe and Ferguson, 136-37).

to this understanding is the equation of sight with discipleship. The glory of God is always ahead of us; we can only catch glimpses of the glory trailing God's back. Purity is not a metaphor for seeing God; it is a form of sight that extends our physical sight beyond its capacity. We will explore what this sight is in the next chapter. But for now we have discerned that we can only see God's reflected glory by imitating God in humility, spirit poverty taking us to material poverty. Becoming the friend of God requires becoming a friend to the afflicted.

Taken as a cluster, these texts point to a number of ways that Gregory reworks the image of a ladder. First, he problematizes the idea of a summit or endpoint to the ladder. For Gregory, we never overcome our creatureliness such that we can take God in at a glance, so God's infinitude relative to our finitude means that we must keep moving through new perceptions of God's beauty. There is no final moment of resting and seeing the Beauty that is God. To see God is to follow God. Hope draws the soul continually from beauty seen to beauty beyond. Second, the vertical imagery gives way to horizontal imagery. At some point, Gregory stops talking about ascent in the *Life of Moses*. He leaves behind the image of Sinai and extends outward, like Joshua's spies, seeking the hope of the promised land that is the hope of Christ.[129] The spies, modeling faithfulness for the reader, drink the blood of the grapes, which Gregory takes as signifying the Passion. This hint that there is something about Christ that undermines the ladder is confirmed in the homiletic texts, which subvert the ladder image by claiming that the Image of Beauty Itself is to be found by attending the ugliness and horror of affliction. Lesser beauties cannot be simply left behind, and neither can ugliness. The other side of the claim that to see God is to be united with God is that there is no final vision of God. Because we are creatures and God is the Creator; God can only be seen as we move through the infinity that is God. This way of seeing God is not the same as seeing flashes of God's glory, but it provides the context for such flashes. Seeing is not simply a metaphor for following, nor is it displaced by following. Balthasar considers this paradox by explaining that representations of God in God's manifestations are God in Godself without exhausting God. Calling the representations of God "the subjective limit of the object that is itself limitless," Balthasar claims that manifestations of God, though veiled, are not detached from God. He writes, "In other words, we cannot say either that we see God or that we do not see him. . . . 'Seeing' therefore is the very *movement* that surpasses the intelligence, whereas the (static) *content*, on the basis of which desire surges

---

129. Ibid., II.268 (Malherbe and Ferguson, 136–37).

up, is precisely not the vision."[130] Together, what the seeing-flashes-of-glory (self-manifestations of God) and seeing-as-following amount to is an acceptance that we live in between the times: that we have the first-fruits of the resurrection in Christ but await the resurrection of the dead, that Christ has been raised but can be mistaken for a gardener or a stranger.

Seeing the Savior as Seeing the Saved

With all the ways Gregory problematizes the ladder as an image central to describing how a person accesses beauty, why retain it? Besides its presence in the literature most formative to him—Scripture and Plato—the ladder communicates for Gregory the effort of ascent and the panoramic view of the world one acquires while ascending. As one moves toward Beauty Itself, she can look back on lesser beauties of the world and see them from a different vantage. And, of course, the ladder communicates the fittingness and gratuity central to reflection on beauty.

To think about a beauty adjacent to or even mixed with ugliness calls into question what it means to think of beauty as fitting, for what could be less fitting to beauty than ugliness? And what could be less gratuitous, less of a surplus than a beauty mixed with the ugly? But we must remember that Gregory's fittingness and gratuity are not Plato's. They are transformed as beauty names and participates in a radically transcendent God. As God's radical transcendence means that God requires no contrary to exclude, so, too, beauty's radical gratuity cannot be limited by the ugly.[131] The Incarnation advances upon this relationship to point to a special kind of beauty found in ugliness. The afflicted ones dragging themselves along the road—how can one avoid thinking of the half-dead man in the story of the Good Samaritan?—are ugly and beautiful. The way their body has rotted, been dehumanized, and been made to figure death is ugly, yet the way they image Christ as humans and particularly as materially deprived humans, is beautiful. Even more, the act of charity in which they participate transforms them into the supreme eschatological beauty that is being revealed. Similarly, Gregory does not cease from exposing the ugliness of the rich's greed that

130. Balthasar, *Presence and Thought*, 99.

131. Strictly speaking, ugliness does not limit beauty because ugliness names a deprivation of beauty. But what I am trying to explore here is the way that the ugliness that names a deprivation of beauty due to poverty or suffering is also the occasion for a particular participation in the beauty of Christ. As God can join to what is not-God (can become, that is, a creature that is human, suffering, and poor) without ceasing to be God, so beauty can join to what is not-beauty (can saturate poverty and suffering) such that that which is poor and suffering is taken up into the beautiful.

lurks within the splendid gold and purple cloaks they wear. It is the multiple levels of fittingness that enable the beholder to perceive the way beauty can contend with, saturate, and transform that which is (also) ugly. An object can be ugly in one aspect but remain beautiful in others, as the rich are corrupted by greed, the poor bestialized by hunger, yet both still image God. For beauty rests on objects differently, which speaks to the multiple levels of fittingness that describe an object's existence in the world. One can see a person as the image-bearer of God; as decaying and degenerating towards death; as performing a life-saving act of charity.

Gregory's reflections on the Incarnation are not dissimilar from other theologians' reflection on the Crucifixion. A parallel might be helpful here in highlighting the relationship to beauty and ugliness in Christ. In particular, there are interesting resonances between Gregory's approach to beauty and Richard Viladesau's recent interpretation of the significance of Balthasar's "analogy of beauty." Drawing on Barth's insistence that creaturely understandings of the beautiful must rediscover themselves in divine beauty, Viladesau describes Barth and Balthasar as presenting a "converted" sense of beauty that can include even the Cross.[132] The Cross challenges Christians "to re-think and to expand our notion of what is beautiful, and indeed of the 'beauty' of God itself."[133] The "transcendent . . . 'light'" of God must also include "the abysmal darkness" of the Crucified—must, that is, "heal and expand on our human sense of beauty" but yet "not contradict it."[134] Viladesau wants to recover a "contrast theology" that preserves evil as evil in the crucifixion even while also articulating the coexistence of the beautiful and the good. Contrast theology's place in earlier Christian writers was to elaborate, for example, how the Cross might be ugly physically but beautiful morally.[135] In Viladesau's version of contrast theology, the Cross "only has beauty as the expression of an act of love; and love is 'beautiful,' theologically speaking, precisely because it is finally not defeated, but victorious."[136]

Gregory, too, has a vocabulary for thinking about beauty and ugliness coexisting in a contrast theology, but by grounding the contrast theology in the broader event of Incarnation rather than focusing primarily on Crucifixion, he reflects not only on the aspect of suffering but also on poverty. The beauty of Christ in Christ's poverty transfigures the face of the poor without

132. Viladesau, "Beauty of the Cross," 137. Viladesau treats these same themes in more historical detail in his books *The Beauty of the Cross* and *The Triumph of the Cross*.

133. Viladesau, "Beauty of the Cross," 137.

134. Ibid., 137, 142.

135. Ibid., 142, 140.

136. Ibid., 143.

erasing the ugliness of the way we let one another starve. The rich-poor Christ builds on the possibilities suggested by radicalized fittingness and gratuity, which suggest that beauty may exist near ugliness without ceasing to be beautiful. As discussed in the previous chapter, something may be beautiful in one aspect and ugly in another. But with Christ we learn that the paradigmatic beauty, Beauty Itself, cannot be found apart from ugliness. Thus, while *creatio ex nihilo* gives the doctrine of a God in which radicalized fittingness and gratuity tell us that Beauty holds all things in existence; and while sin and finitude might suggest that the things Beauty holds in existence are in some respects ugly and therefore that beauty might mingle with ugliness; the Incarnation displays the way beauty *does* mix with ugliness, the way Beauty Itself is found in the movement toward poverty, affliction, and the divestment of glory. In other words, the Incarnation reveals for Gregory not just that beauty may happen to be near ugliness, but that beauty's nearness to ugliness is constitutive of its beauty. That is the new thing done by Christ, the infinitely rich one who became ontologically poor, the God who identified with the poor of the world. It is this identification with the poor that associates Christ with ugliness, for it tells us what Incarnation means.

This is how we know what it means that God became Incarnate: God dwelt in a world of sinfulness and poverty, and God did so not as one separate and unscathed, but as one whose life was deeply implicated in that world, so that God gave God's own face to the ones suffering poverty and was crucified by the sinful structures governing the world. In this way, both Matthew 25:31–46 and the crucifixion tell us something about what Incarnation means and why it can be implicated in poverty and ugliness. In Christ we see beauty's life mingled with ugliness, a mingling that will continue until Christ is revealed in glory, until the hungry are fed, the thirsty are slaked, and the naked are clothed. This side of the eschaton, then, there will always be a beauty that mingles with ugliness, and charity, the most profound beauty we learn to perceive, cannot be found apart from ugliness. Beauty resists class-enclosure because charity resists it, because beauty often mingles with the ugly or the unseemly, and because the deeper one pushes toward Beauty, the more one is formed by a vision of the world in which we are brothers and sisters rather than royals and servants. It is a vision that will be realized, Gregory tells us, when Christ's glory is realized. Learning to perceive beauty—and perceiving deeper and more profound beauty—means becoming a subject who sees others as sisters and brothers united by mutual acts of healing that disclose the glory of Christ. Absent becoming such a subject, the beauty a person can perceive is always limited and often distorted. Further reflections on what such a subject is and what such becoming entails will be deferred until the next chapter. For now we continue to dwell with the paradox of how beauty can make us beautiful through attention to ugliness, which also helps us to see Beauty. We continue considering this puzzle by layering onto it our chapter-opening problem of philosophical language: how philosophical language, which resists the difficulties of realities instanced by both beauty and horrifying ugliness, can meet those realities by its rebirth (as beautiful) into Beauty Itself.

Difficulties: Bodies Exposed, Words Deflecting

Language labors in Gregory's homilies. As he says in a different set of homilies, "Words in the true sense . . . are full of sweat and effort, and cause much labour in order to become words."[137] Gregory's language must labor: He wants his rhetoric to train their hearers into a subjectivity capable of perceiving the glory of Christ and the brother-sisterhood of the afflicted. To get at *how* language performs such work and the type of work it performs, I want to consider Gregory's use of language in light of a critique of philosophical language by philosophers themselves. Accordingly, I want to direct attention again to Cora Diamond's eloquently voiced account in her article "The Difficulty of Reality and the Difficulty of Philosophy." The critique of philosophical language explored here resembles the anxiety that beauty is bourgeois, for it is a concern about the safety and sanity (both in the sense of *sanitized* and *rational*) of philosophy and language. Diamond's principal interlocutors are Stanley Cavell and J. M. Coetzee, the latter who tells the story of the previously introduced Elizabeth Costello. Before expositing and responding to Diamond's analysis of Coetzee and Costello, I first describe Costello directly from Coetzee.

---

137. Gregory of Nyssa, *Homilies on Ecclesiastes*, homily one, I.8 (Hall, 43). The fuller passage is illuminative: "Surely then, words—words in the true sense, words uttered for spiritual benefit and the service of mankind—are full of sweat and effort, and cause much labour in order to become words" (42). He goes on, "*The one who labours at cultivation must first share in the produce* (II Tim 2.6), says the expert in this kind of words, on the grounds that the word ought not to be thought of as speech, but that actual virtue, which is presented to those who see it as instruction for living, should serve as the word for those being taught. Therefore all such words are laborious, since those who instruct in virtue first achieve within themselves the things which they teach" (43). These reflections follow a meditation on the supposed easiness of words: "What labour is it for the speaker to say what he likes? The tongue is supple and pliable and shapes itself without effort to whatever kind of words it wishes. . . . We do not make a passage for speech by digging soil, dislodging boulders or carrying them on our shoulders, or performing any other burdensome task, but thought, taking shape in us, revealed through sound, becomes speech. But since a word of this kind does not cause labour, we ought to consider what are the laborious words which a man will not be able to speak" (42).

Presenting herself as an animal wounded, haunted by the knowledge of what we humans do to non-human animals, Costello resists philosophical language; she is suspicious of the reasoning of Aquinas and Kant and Descartes.[138] She refuses this language, and she refuses to bow to reason, which is, after all, only "a certain spectrum of human thinking."[139] She recognizes that this refusal will alienate her audience, but she already experiences herself as alien.[140] As her son, a professor and her host for the lectures, drives her to the airport, she describes the way she experiences her alienation as a kind of madness. How is it possible that these people in whom she sees human kindness are also complicit in horrifying crimes against other animals? Why can everyone come to terms with this reality of human life, while she cannot?[141]

Diamond characterizes Costello as, like all of us in our life with non-human animals, exposed. We long for the assurance of identifying salient features of animal life that verify their status relative to the human animal's, but instead we inherit only our own responsibility, out of which weight we must apply concepts in the face of our mortality and the animals'. With no ideal scenario for applying concepts available to us, we are "thrown into finding something we can live with" and reach what may be a "bitter-tasting compromise."[142] Of this position, Diamond writes, "There is here only what we make of our exposure, and it leaves us endless room for double-dealing and deceit."[143] Diamond sees this exposure expressed in Costello's own confession of double-dealing in her complicity in animal suffering. It is a confession, though, through which Costello resists deceit. She gives it in response to a benevolent question ventured to ease the room after a pointed exchange between Costello and her philosopher daughter-in-law. The question is from the president of the university, who asks whether her vegetarianism "comes out of moral conviction."[144] Costello insists it does not. Owning to wearing leather shoes and carrying a leather purse, Costello says of her vegetarianism, "It comes out of a desire to save my soul."[145]

This desire is obviously one that Gregory, with his images of eschatological judgment and insistence on the sin-sickness of the satiated, shares

138. Coetzee, *Lives of Animals*, 22–23.

139. Ibid., 23.

140. Ibid., 25.

141. Ibid., 69.

142. Diamond, "Difficulty of Reality," 23.

143. Ibid., 21.

144. Coetzee, *Lives of Animals*, 43.

145. Diamond, "Difficulty of Reality," 21.

and assumes his congregants share. And as Gregory preaches to his congregants about how they are to save their soul, Costello's son suggests to his wife that she might find more sympathy for Costello by seeing her as a preacher rather than "an eccentric trying to foist her preferences on to other people."[146] The image does not bolster Costello's case with her daughter-in-law, who responds, "You are welcome to see her as a preacher. But take a look at all the other preachers and their crazy schemes for dividing mankind into the saved and the damned. Is that the kind of company you want your mother to keep?"[147]

The problem with the image is that Costello does not have much faith in preaching. Where Gregory expects his language not merely to inform but also to transform those listening, Costello's language performs her separation and isolation from her audience. Between her lectures, her son questions her purpose. He asks whether she believes her poetry will close down slaughterhouses, and Costello concedes she does not. "Then why do it?" he asks. "Wasn't your point about talk that it changes nothing?"[148] Later in the conversation he presses her again on her aims, on what she "want[s] to cure humankind of."[149] "I don't know what I want to do," she responds, fatigued. "I just don't want to sit silent."[150] She is probably right not to have much faith in her own language, at least, for it both moves her listeners farther from her and mystifies her position, as when she compares her situation to the Holocaust. Diamond emphasizes that Costello knows this image will cause offense and misunderstanding.[151] Indeed, Costello acknowledges as much in her lecture, when she admits to making "cheap points" and claims "talk of this kind polarizes people."[152] She uses this language, though, precisely because she does not want to be the crazed preacher dividing saved from damned that her daughter-in-law describes. She wants a "cool" rather than "heated" way of speaking, a "philosophical rather than polemical" language that will not "divide us into the righteous and the sinners, the saved and the damned, the sheep and the goats."[153] Desirous of avoiding the alienating move of dividing the sheep from the goats, Costello here seeks to find a philosophical way of speaking (we might ask: philosophical without reason?),

146. Coetzee, *Lives of Animals*, 67.

147. Ibid., 68.

148. Ibid., 58.

149. Ibid., 59.

150. Ibid.

151. Diamond, "Difficulty of Reality," 6.

152. Coetzee, *Lives of Animals*, 22.

153. Ibid.

but instead speaks "philosophically" through the most alienating imagery possible: the Holocaust. It is at this point she confesses herself alienated from reason, which has been used to alienate humans from animals.[154]

It is the failure of philosophical language that principally concerns Diamond—particularly the failure of philosophical language to characterize Costello and her position. Diamond traces responses to Coetzee's lecture to illustrate the way "philosophy characteristically misrepresents both our own reality and that of others, in particular those 'others' who are animals."[155] Borrowing from Cavell, she describes this misrepresentation as *deflection*. Deflection describes the philosophers' understanding of suffering *qua* philosopher; it happens when a person moves from appreciating "a difficulty of reality" to "a philosophical or moral problem apparently in the vicinity."[156] Skepticism is such a deflection, but so is anti-skepticism, which fails to grasp the skeptic's insight: "the sense the skeptic has of the other's position with respect to his own pain, and the light in which it casts his position in relation to that other."[157] The skeptic grasps, that is, the problem of human separateness, even though he feels himself also thwarted by it. No successful attempt to overcome the isolation of skepticism can go around this problem of human separateness.

Diamond's discussion of human separateness at this point owes much to Cavell. As much as her essay is a reading of Coetzee's Tanner Lectures, it is equally a reading of the final part of Cavell's *The Claim of Reason*, "Between Acknowledgment and Avoidance." Human separateness, Cavell claims in that essay (itself a reading of many texts, including Shakespeare's *Othello*), is precisely what Othello cannot grant Desdemona, what drives Othello to kill Desdemona. Reflecting on philosophy's capacity to treat such separateness, Cavell asks, "Can philosophy accept [Othello and Desdemona] back at the hands of poetry?"[158] Cavell's question intrigues Diamond, who reframes the question with Cavell's description of what human separateness entails. "For philosophy to do so would be for philosophy to accept human separateness as 'turned equally toward splendor and toward horror, mixing beauty and ugliness; turned toward before and after; toward flesh and blood.'"[159] Philosophy's deflection, its difficulty in "staying turned toward . . .

154. Ibid., 22–25.

155. Diamond, "Difficulty of Reality," 11.

156. Ibid., 12.

157. Ibid., 18.

158. Ibid., 24. Diamond is drawing from the final page of *Claim of Reason* (496).

159. Diamond, "Difficulty of Reality," 24. The internal quotation refers to Cavell's *Claim of Reason*. The full quotation reads, "What I have wished to bring out is the nature of this possibility, or the possibility of this nature, the way human sexuality is the

flesh and blood" is one way of understanding "the difficulty of philosophy" Diamond names in the article's title.[160] The "difficulty of reality" is found in those cases, such as beauty, horrifying ugliness, and what we do to animals, where "the reality to which we were attending seems to resist our thinking it."[161] Philosophical skepticism may respond to the mutual resistance between philosophy and reality that appears in cases of suffering and respond, in Diamond's words, something like this: "A language, a form of thought, cannot . . . get things right or wrong, fit or fail to fit reality; it can only be more or less useful."[162] Diamond frames her own conclusion as an observation rather than response to such philosophical skepticism. She wants "to note how much the coming apart of thought and reality belongs to flesh and blood."[163] It is the third time in the last page and a half that Diamond has spoken of flesh and blood. The first time came when she was quoting Cavell, who writes of flesh and blood another time in *The Claim of Reason*: "Being human is the power to grant being human. Something about flesh and blood elicits this grant from us, and something about flesh and blood can also repel it."[164]

It is this capacity to grant being human that Gregory both names (you have turned the poor into beasts) and resists (yet they remain humans in the image of God with the face of Christ) in his *Sermons on the Love of the Poor*. His conception of a human's agency in granting humanity is powerful, but not unlimitedly so: flesh and blood's capacity to repel that power is great. Humanness cannot be extinguished. Nevertheless, there is something about flesh and blood—something about its eating, its singing, its communing, its ostracizing—that humanizes and dehumanizes. Gregory himself is engaged in an activity of humanization in his *Sermons*, and it is an activity that requires his care-filled attention to flesh and blood. I do not propose that Gregory's approach to the difficulty of reality in these sermons blazes a path modern philosophers can easily tread; still less do I suggest here that Gregory offers modern philosophy a way of accepting Othello and Desdemona back at the hands of poetry. Instead I want to consider Gregory as someone who attends to the difficulty of reality through his own philosophical

---

field in which the fantasy of finitude, of its acceptance and its repetitious overcoming, is worked out; the way human separateness is turned equally toward splendor and toward horror, mixing beauty and ugliness; turned toward before and after; toward flesh and blood" (492).

160. Diamond, "Difficulty of Reality," 24.

161. Ibid., 25.

162. Ibid.

163. Ibid.

164. Cavell, *Claim of Reason*, 397.

commitments, who, without denying human separateness, presents us with a language (and a philosophy) that is not separated from reality. We might say it is intimate with reality. Gregory's language and philosophy do not constitute a sphere that must meet reality to become a mimesis of it. His language is constituted by and constitutive of reality. Language constitutes reality for Gregory, moreover, because and to the extent that it resists reality (as only the intimate can resist one another). And language bears this power because of the kind of realities in which Gregory's philosophy is formed.

Gregory's vision of a language that resists and constitutes rather than simply reflects is important because any attempt to represent suffering will also require distance between representer and sufferer, which is to say that language that merely represents with regard to suffering will keep the philosopher from drawing near the sufferer. This distance results from two aspects of representation. First, representation itself entails distance: the thing represented is never the thing representing. Second, the activity of representing and reflecting is very different from the activity (the passivity) of suffering. If one's aim is philosophical correctness, language will always distance. Even more so if the aim is entertainment. It is this latter representation that Gregory rages against when he describes the way the afflicted turn their suffering into a "parade" and "spectacle," becoming, through their "sad melodies and gloomy chants," "poets of a unique type of tragedy . . . fill[ing] the stage with their own misfortune."[165] Imagining their poetry, Gregory exclaims, "What expressions! What detailed descriptions! What events do we hear?"[166] Can poetry give philosophy the hands to accept Othello and Desdemona back? Not this poetry. The afflicted's song diminishes the reality of both her humanness and her separateness. Presenting herself as an occasion for the fascination of the satiated—and offering moral self-satisfaction for the price of a few cheaply given coins—she sings her own self into the subjectivity of the satiated.

This is exactly the kind of song Costello does not want to sing. Continually remembering that she is receiving a substantial sum of money for the lectureship, Costello is painfully conscious of herself as a paid entertainer for scholars. Presenting Kafka's Red Peter, she slips into presenting *herself* as Red Peter, a monkey performing for her audience:

> Now that I am here, says Red Peter, in my tuxedo and bow tie and my black pants with a hole cut in the seat for my tail to poke through (I keep it turned away from you, you do not see it), now that I am here, what is there for me to do? Do I in fact have a

---

165. Gregory of Nyssa, "Whoever Has Done It" sec. 477 (Holman, 202).
166. Ibid.

choice? If I do not subject my discourse to reason, whatever that is, what is left for me but to gibber and emote and knock over my water glass and generally make a monkey of myself?[167]

Later she acknowledges that to win acceptance from the community of scholars to whom she speaks, she should not make a monkey of herself but rather join herself "like a tributary stream running into the great river, to the great Western discourse of reason versus unreason."[168] Yet she resists this temptation, seeing it as a betrayal of her efforts, "foreseeing in that step the concession of the entire battle."[169] There is something about the way Western discourse conceptualizes reason as a "[system] of totality"[170] that leads her looking for another way of speaking, reducing her, finally, to weeping—lament her response to the difficulty of philosophy. But one thing she does not do: grant her audience moral self-satisfaction for a few cheaply given coins.

How do we speak when discourse is corrupted—by a totalizing reason or by its casting suffering as entertainment? Though he is appalled by the way they have to make themselves entertainers, Gregory does not claim the moral purity (or disengagement) of one who refuses to listen to the songs of the suffering. Implicating himself in what he sees as a sinful practice, Gregory listens to their songs yet attempts to hear them as something other than entertainment. In a famine-wracked world of great inequalities, where conditions are ripe for the exploitation of the afflicted's speech, Gregory wants to give words back to the afflicted, and he cannot do that by talking over them. Hearing their concerns as those of Christ, he lists common themes in the tales of those suffering, describing the way the afflicted are banished from the fountains even dogs can drink at, the way they throw themselves at the feet of the public, an "atrocious spectacle" that "utterly confounds [Gregory's] thoughts."[171] Gregory at this point, as in many others throughout the sermons, represents the suffering ones in graphic detail. How is it he thinks he avoids the critique he levies at the poetry-as-spectacle that makes him shudder and rage? Lamenting the reduction of suffering to theater, Gregory writes, "There is a difference between words and action as great as the difference between a painting and the reality."[172] The statement resembles the question of Costello's son, "Wasn't your point about talk that it changes nothing?" The sentences resemble each other, but the latter is

167. Coetzee, *Lives of Animals*, 23.

168. Ibid., 25.

169. Ibid.

170. Ibid.

171. Gregory of Nyssa, "Whoever Has Done It" sec. 477/80 (Holman, 202).

172. Ibid., sec. 480 (Holman, 203).

drained of the hope that buoys the former. For Gregory, change and activity are possible, are part of the world of words. Describing the relationship of words and action by comparing them to that of a painting to reality clarifies what kind of words Gregory means to contrast with action: words purposed toward mimesis. Gregory's words, by contrast with such exclusively mimetic words, are a kind of action and generative of action in which "our compassion and love for one another shine forth radiantly."[173] Gregory's words are caught up in a movement toward the afflicted; they are part of the action of charity, the mutual act of healing where the speaker and the spoken of unite both in their raw neediness and in the invitation to mutual care. The human separateness here is never overcome but becomes the occasion for unity, just as language remains separate from the reality of the sufferer even as it shares her reality. (We might also understand Gregory as engaging in self-critique here, for his words, though given in charity for the healing of both rich and poor, cannot themselves effect any such healing.)

Here is the strong claim Gregory is leading us toward: Philosophical language that conceives of itself as purely representational will always occlude the difficulties of reality. I elaborate this claim with insights culled from our modern situation: Philosophy that only tries to represent reality is always tempted to migrate to a social space removed from the reality it represents.[174] There are at least two different forms of this temptation. One is the effacement of the philosopher in the process of philosophizing, a temptation of the philosopher to separate herself from the philosophized and see the philosophized only as an object to understand. Philosophy that succumbs to this temptation becomes training into separateness from the human rather than separateness between and among humans. The other temptation is for philosophy to ensconce itself in privilege, in a certain class insulated from the pressures that most people face. This ensconcement is made pernicious when philosophy claims to have a more direct or exclusive hold on truth than most people who bear the pressures from which it is protected.[175] From its position of privilege, it names the way most people

---

173. Ibid.

174. In Rowan Williams's recent Gifford Lectures, he invokes Cavell and discusses representational language, but in a much more expansive sense than I intend here. My own use of "representational language" is closer to his characterization of language that seeks to be "innocent descriptive language hived off from what people say" (Williams, "Representing Reality").

175. I want to make clear that I am not criticizing all manner of philosophical separation from ordinary life—which is most certainly *not* a modern problem, as Pierre Hadot helps us see again and again. Hadot writes of ancient philosophers, "To be a philosopher implies a rupture with what the skeptics called *bios*, that is, daily life, when they criticized other philosophers for not observing the common conduct of life, the

speak wrongly or imprecisely. In other words, the critique that Bourdieu and Eagleton helped us to articulate about beauty—that it solidifies class boundaries along which it breeds ill will—could be modified and levied against a certain kind of philosophy. This does not mean that there is no place for philosophy that represents reality. Such philosophy can help us learn to see better (as I think Diamond helps us learn to see Costello, though maybe because she is fictional), but to be trained into philosophy as a way of responding to the difficulties of reality is like being trained to be a doctor that can only diagnose and never heal. It can become a pathology that energizes our pride by comforting us that we can see people rightly, that we are therefore morally virtuous. Such philosophy is a perverse form of self-aggrandizement.

We need a philosophy that can remember how to speak in a language that is not merely representational—that can employ different registers of language. What about, for example, a language that heals (like absolution or praise) or that registers pain (as rant, lament, confession) or both (like praying the Psalms might be—as it was, at least, for Macrina's mourners). A philosophy that treats (and the senses of treat must not here be sundered) the difficulties of reality is a philosophy that has not forgotten itself as a form of love. The philosopher-lover seeks non-mimetic registers of language in which to speak, for love (like Love) attends problems from within, not by representing their likeness at a safe distance or by effacing the philosopher's own humanity. The centrality of love to *Gregory's* philosophizing means that he speaks in the register of confession, which resists "reality" by resisting separation from life (and from Reality). As Wittgenstein writes, "A

---

usual manner of seeing and acting, which for the skeptics consisted in respecting customs and laws, practicing a craft or plying a trade, satisfying bodily needs, and having the faith in appearances indispensable to action" ("Forms of Life," 491). Hadot elaborates this separation as entailing, among different groups at various historical moments, the refusal of philosophers to accept money (or much money) for their teaching, in contrast to other teachers; the Epicurean equality of women with men, married women and consorts in the philosophical circles; and the Stoic refusal of excess even when they occupied positions of great power (492). Such practices separate the philosopher from the unreason of daily life and help him toward the vision of the way things are, that is, toward wisdom. Certainly Gregory is sympathetic with this vision of the philosopher, admiring as he is of his family's monastic efforts. But this kind of separation need not insulate the philosopher from the knowledge that he participates in a community, or that he is flesh and blood. It certainly avoids founding philosophy on those two denials. It is a philosophy, rather, that cannot conceive of separating theory and practice, that imagines the philosopher must cultivate an asceticism toward the world precisely because he is flesh and blood, and do so *as* a member of a particular community. It is a genre of philosophy, therefore, that helps a person become suspicious of privilege and conceives of itself, even when in some respects separated from the lives of "most people," nevertheless in their service.

confession has to be part of your new life."[176] Gregory's confessing philosophy works to inaugurate a new life. It does not "fit or fail to fit reality," is not "more or less useful"—for such descriptions raise the questions: Which reality? Useful for whom? His homilies give language as a gift of love to both the afflicted and the satiated in order to move toward that reality in which Love will be all in all. His confession works to instantiate the reality of God's kingdom by attending to the multiple levels of reality, not only of the hungry but also for oneself. For, in his homilizing, Gregory confesses his own aversions and his own work to overcome them. Gregory's philosophy submits itself to a larger project of charity; it claims its own incompleteness *qua* philosophy. His speech, his philosophy has jagged edges. It does not claim to possess or represent Truth because it is always gesturing towards a Truth that will be consummated eschatologically. His speech journeys toward this Truth that, in the end, will be given as grace. For his congregants to perceive this Truth is for them to join his journey.

What we are trying to understand is how, as Cavell writes, attended by the anxiety, present in all "serious communication," "I myself require education. And for grown-ups education is not natural growth but change." In the next sentence, Cavell renames this change as "conversion," which "is a turning out of our natural reactions; so it is symbolized as re-birth."[177] For Gregory, the rebirth is symbolic, not because it entails something less than re-birth but because it is the rebirth of symbols. Symbols, like humans, always remain finite for Gregory, and symbols, unlike humans for Gregory, always remain merely human. Yet with the dwelling of the Word among us (humans), with the inscription of God's own Law on stone tablets, with the canonization of *these words* as our (Christian, Jewish) Scripture, with the codification of *these words* as our (Catholic, Orthodox, often Protestant) creeds—symbols, words are reborn into the life of the kingdom of God. They help us to organize, see, and be accountable to relations of love.

For Gregory, true language about the sufferer must *move*, for the reality of the sufferer is not exhausted by detailing her maladies. Gregory's language cannot be merely mimetic of reality, for reality itself resists any static representation. The sufferer's reality includes the face of Christ she bears and her beautiful God-imaging soul, both of which contain a promise to be realized in her eschatologically glorified body. Words that keep faith with the fullness of reality therefore move, and the way they move echoes the course of the Word. Throughout his theological writings, Gregory does worry about words falling short of reality—particularly the reality of the

---

176. Wittgenstein, *Culture and Value*, Remarks from 1931, 18.

177. Cavell, *Claim of Reason*, 125.

enfleshed Word—but words of love gain reality from their participation in the Word who is Love. Language given in love will not distance, for such language participates in the Love known in the Word made flesh and blood; through such participation in the Word, words acquire their eschatological orientation; they participate in the overcoming of "reality," making visible the fullness of reality. This linguistic dynamism in which words go forth from themselves echoes the dynamism of beauty, in which the beautiful object gestures beyond itself (what we have been calling the gratuity of beauty). And the fullness of reality made visible in these words is the beauty of the afflicted in Christ together with their horror, also in Christ and also taken up into Christ's beauty. Gregory's descriptions of Christological and eschatological beauty of the afflicted disrupt the representational capacities of modern philosophy as he works to rehabilitate a language that can overcome the "reality" that is itself part of the problem. That is to say: Christological beauty, itself both hidden and manifest, suffuses the afflicted in a way that can be rightly represented only in a language that is kinetic rather than static, moving out in love and so participating in the Love that saves both the lover and the beloved. Participating in this saving Love, one recognizes one's own being-saved-ness and so learns to see rightly the Christ who is not only Love but Beauty.

Our two preachers, then—Gregory of Nyssa and Elizabeth Costello—find themselves in different relationships to their words and their audiences despite similarities in their themes of animals, eating, and horror. Costello's witness to horror only isolates her, and philosophers' attempts to render her position intelligible only occlude it by eliding Costello's own subjecthood. Costello's weary attempts to bring her language, her philosophizing to bear on the condition of animals leaves these animals, to the philosophers in and out of the texts, dumb beasts. Where Costello's horror isolates, Gregory's witness to horror, driven by his conviction that his language labors toward a vision of brother-sisterhood already realized in Christ and being realized in all, speaks into a community. It is a community he participates in proleptically through the blood of Christ he drinks that he might not drain the blood of his neighbor. Gregory's words, even when soaring, wreak with these two bloods, the holiness of the one teaching us the abomination of draining the other. It is attention to these two bloods, these two moments of suffering, to holiness mixed with sickness and beauty mixed with ugliness, that points towards human separateness and raises the difficulty of reality with the difficulty of philosophy. Gregory's philosophy, particularly as centered on the beauty of Christ, is a philosophy that need not be brought to the difficulty of reality, for it is already formed in it. His philosophy, after all, takes as its guide the rich-poor God who was tortured and will be glorified. Gregory's words move between affliction and glory the same way the Incarnate Christ does: love. Words of love for the afflicted participate in the beauty and suffering of the Word who is Love, and the Word who became incarnate and suffered for love promises to come again in glory. At the foundations of Gregory's philosophy is the reality of the Word who bled and died and rose again, enfleshed again. And so we might say that for Gregory, the togetherness of the difficulty of reality and the difficulty of philosophy is also a thing of flesh and blood.

Through its proximity to and intermingling with ugliness, Gregory's Christological beauty refuses assimilation to the rich, the satiated, or the healthy. It is a beauty that can exist with and in ugliness because of the multiple levels of fittingness in which an object might be perceived and because fittingness and gratuity have been radicalized from Plato's display of them to signs of God's radical transcendence. Christological beauty, moreover, requires the activity of love to be made visible (in the moment of saving) and such love requires a going out toward the afflicted, the poor, the needy. To see Christological beauty, then, requires seeing oneself as the afflicted whom Christ is saving. Participating in such beauty requires imitating Christ's going forth-ness. For philosophical words about suffering to participate in beauty is for them to attend to multiple levels of reality: the afflicted's (potentially animalizing) affliction, her God-imaging soul, her Christ-bearing face, and her eschatologically promised glory. For Gregory, then, both beauty and language resist the enclosure of the safe, the rich, the sanitized, the healthy, because they find their final realities in the Word whose flesh was twisted, tortured, and killed—and yet was resurrected in glory.

Beauty here is not an *answer* to the difficulty of philosophy any more than poetry is. We remember that for Diamond, beauty instances a difficulty of reality. But beauty also, as we claimed with Eagleton, Bourdieu, and Nehamas, can be difficult in a way similar to the difficulty of philosophy, or, as Gregory helps us to see, similar to the easiness of entertainment. How do we describe what has gone wrong when, for example, beautiful words appease the satiated's conscience and shore up the subjectivity of the rich over and against the poor? One way Gregory might explain such beauty is with his example of music extrinsically related to libretto rather than the ordered musicality of the Psalms.[178] That is, beautiful words purposed toward solidifying hatred of the poor can only have a very narrow beauty. They may be beautiful in their parallels, symmetries, rhythms, and images, but the story of the rich-poor God can only cast their politics as distinctly unfitting,

178. See the exploration of Gregory's *On the Inscriptions of the Psalms* in chapter 2.

ungratuitous, unbeautiful. They may—it depends on the words—only be pleasurable. The more beauty flees from the rich-poor God, the narrower the contexts for fittingness, the weaker the gratuity it issues, the thinner the beauty becomes. There is a difference, of course, between beautiful words whose politics lie and apolitical instances of beauty—our well-crafted cup, for example. But for beautiful words that are ordered toward the rich-poor God, that, as Gregory's, *move* toward that God by going out in love to the neighbor—these are the words with such marvelous fittingness, such breathtaking gratuity, that they help us see Beauty Itself.

Conclusion

Locating beauty in the Crucified Word and the face of the bestialized hungry breaks beauty out of its enclosure in bourgeois social spaces and ideas. Yet it leaves open the question of whether the training into such beauty is itself privileged—particularly since Gregory's training is so privileged.[179] As we turn toward the concern that the training into beauty is classed, we will strain to hear the voices of Macrina and Emmelia—those women who claimed authority without the education then available to privileged men— speaking from Gregory's texts. With them we will learn what kind of person the Spirit enables us to become, an exploration that will take us back to the wound. We will learn how philosophy is supposed to wound us, and how it is inadequate (in the sense that it is not sufficiently adequate) to that task. If we caught a glimpse in this chapter of how philosophy is supposed to labor and the kind of labor it is supposed to do, we learn in the next chapter that Gregory takes the material conditions of our existence too seriously to expect language to complete the task he assigns it. Yet materiality will not displace immateriality. The theme of invisibility introduced but not elaborated in this chapter is more fully explored in the next, where I consider both Gregory's pneumatology and his anthropology: particularly the two together as they concern his meditations on the beauty-beholder's body, what kind of body it was and is and shall be.

179. And so are the major voices here—Cavell's, Diamond's, Coetzee's—as well as my own.

4

Bodies Luminous and Wounded

THE SPIRIT MANIFESTS THE BEAUTY OF THE WORD

We return to hospitals and rotting bodies. This time the hospital is not Basil's poor-hospice, nor the bodies famine-wracked and bestialized. We enter a fictional world, created, once again, by J. M. Coetzee and faced, once again, by Elizabeth Costello.[1] Elizabeth visits Zululand to see her missionary sister, once Blanche, now Sister Bridget. She is to tour Sister Bridget's hospital, and Elizabeth is anxious, sick with what gruesomeness and hopelessness she might encounter there. She knows she cannot refuse her sister—they are both old and will likely not see each other again—but she longs for a way to avoid the hospital. *"Let this cup be taken from me!"* she pleads silently to no one. *"I am too old to withstand these sights, too old and too weak. I will just cry."*[2]

The hospital, composed of traditional healers working alongside doctors trained in western medicine, surprises Elizabeth. She finds in the patients gaiety and—could it be?—even a kind of fearlessness that suggests the love her sister claims attends the care given there. "Perhaps," Elizabeth thinks, "Blanche has tucked the worst cases out of sight."[3] Whether the

---

1. This time I will call her Elizabeth rather than Costello, since I am not placing her in a conversation with philosohers but in a retelling of fragments from Coetzee's narrative, which appears as the fifth lesson in *Elizabeth Costello*.

2. Coetzee, *Elizabeth Costello*, 133.

3. Ibid., 134.

gruesomeness is out of sight or suffused with love, Elizabeth's old eyes do withstand the sights, tearless.

But there is a sight at the hospital more troubling to Elizabeth than the sick. It is Joseph. Like Elizabeth, Joseph is old, and also like Elizabeth, Joseph has devoted much of his life to a craft. Joseph carves, and the subject that he carves is the one who also asked for his cup to be taken away—and was also refused. He carves Christ in Christ's cup-drinking posture: the agony on the cross. Joseph carves so many crucifixes that he cannot sell them all, yet he will carve nothing but the crucifix. Discussing Joseph later with Sister Bridget, Elizabeth describes his singularly focused carving as "obsessive."[4] "Why didn't you get him to make something else besides crucifixes, crucifixions? What does it do to a person's—if I dare use the word—*soul* to spend his working life carving a man in agony over and over again?" Sister Bridget's hospital keeps Joseph on salary, and so Elizabeth blames her Order for nurturing, if not cultivating, Joseph's obsession.

When Sister Bridget challenges Elizabeth's description of the crucifix as a "man" in agony, Elizabeth changes her tack, suggesting that even if Joseph could not have been "an artist properly speaking," he might have expanded his artistic horizons beyond carving this one scene.[5] She presses the issue. "Why a Christ dying in contortions rather than a living Christ? A man in his prime, in his early thirties: what do you have against showing him alive, in all his living beauty? . . . The Greeks would never have made statues and paintings of a man in the extremes of agony, deformed, ugly, and then knelt before those statues and worshiped them."[6] She builds: "What are you doing, importing into Africa, importing into Zululand, for God's sake, this utterly alien, *Gothic* obsession with the ugliness and mortality of the human body?"[7] Later in the chapel service Sister Bridget asks her to attend—with Joseph's large Crucifix bearing down on her, joyous Eucharistic shouts filling her ears, rhythmic stomping vibrating across her body—Elizabeth faints.[8]

In the last chapter, I explored how, for Gregory, Christ is present in the poor, hungry, diseased, and bestialized, how the transcendent beauty of God, the Beauty that beckons us ever-onward, is deeply intertwined with the ugliness of this world. I also traced how this intertwining transforms what it

4. Ibid., 136.
5. Ibid., 137.
6. Ibid., 138–39.
7. Ibid., 139–40.
8. Ibid., 143.

means to seek the beautiful. In this chapter, I explore the anthropology of this seeking, which in Gregory's case is to say, its pneumatology. The beauty that mixes with ugliness is no longer the more evidently attractive Beauty and Good of Plato, or of Elizabeth Costello's "Greeks." It is a beauty that shines forth in the image of a tortured man hanging on a cross. But even to say such beauty *shines* is misleading, inasmuch as it suggests a ready apparentness. *Elizabeth Costello* puts the problem to us: Why is it that Joseph and Sister Bridget love to look at the Crucifix, while Elizabeth Costello finds it ugly, and ultimately unbearable? Or to put the question more generally: How does a person come to see the Cross as beautiful? If the last chapter treated how Christ manifests beauty, this one describes how a person comes to see it.

The problematic of this chapter, then, concerns perception. In considering this question, I treat an aspect of the critique of beauty as bourgeois that remains from the previous chapter. There I attempted to exonerate beauty from charges it was bourgeois by locating it in distinctly non-bourgeois social spaces and ideals. In this chapter I attempt to acquit beauty of the claim that the training required to perceive it is bourgeois. For such acquittal, I demonstrate that the training required to perceive beauty is neither assimilated nor assimilable to training to be a dilettante or an academic.[9] Macrina again figures prominently in this chapter, for she is Gregory's beauty-perceiver *par excellence*. She helps further disentangle beauty from the bourgeois by illustrating what the perception of beauty is, what training is required for such perception, and what sort of self perceives Beauty Itself—the beauty that is God.

While many modern accounts describe the organ of perceiving beauty as the imagination—an organ for which training can then easily be assimilated to bourgeois forms of training provided by museums and universities and exposure to so-called high art and literature—Macrina displays a way of perceiving beauty that requires a more demanding transformation. The training for such transformation entails engagements with poverty, suffering, liturgy, and prayer. The education of the bourgeoisie (for Macrina: the purple-bordered toga) can be, she will make plain, both an asset and a liability.

In theological terms, this chapter traces a human nature that cannot be understood apart from its spiritual consummation in Christ. Christ is

9. This is not to say that training to be an academic is unhelpful for discerning *any* type of beauty. Most notably, scholarly training helps a person discern the beauty of arguments (*elegant*, they are often called). But this is similar to the way a shoemaker is especially adept a discerning a beautiful shoe (*well-made*, it may be called). The point here is that academic training does not disclose to a person the most important instances of beauty, though it is not necessarily incompatible with perceiving such beauty.

the one in whom beauty finds its final resting place and through whom humanity gains the perceptive capacities to see Beauty. Humanity's becoming Christ and Christ's perceptibility to humanity is the work of the Spirit, and so the anthropology of the search for beauty is pneumatological. I place this pneumatological anthropology in the context of art philosopher Arthur Danto, who offers an anti-model for faith and subjectivity, and the friendlier interlocutors of Kaja Silverman and Jean-Luc Marion, who each seek to articulate a self constituted by love. These conversations set up a reading of Gregory's homilies on the Song of Songs through which I discuss what it means to be a self, not just constituted, but *wounded* by love. I continue exploring this self through Gregory's development of the spiritual senses, which I argue are spiritual, not because they oppose matter, but because they are Spirit-given and Spirit-attuned. I continually return to Gregory's images of Macrina as those of a love-wounded self and draw out his portrayal of Macrina's subjecthood as offering a generative, rather than pathological, relationship to mothers and motherhood. The mother-child relationship funds the self in a way that continues to develop what it means for the self to see beauty by being wounded.

In treating how a person comes to perceive beauty, I extend and resituate the work of the previous chapter. The theological commitments of this chapter take us through both the mutual intertwining of anthropology and pneumatology *and* the intertwining of Christology and pneumatology. These fields of study are mutually implicated because Christ, the Holy Spirit, and humanity are so interrelated. In pneumatology anthropology is consummated as a working out of Christology, for Christ appears under the conditions of visibility that Christ's appearing itself makes possible. Absent Christ, one cannot see Christ, not only because there is no Christ to be seen but because there is no Christ *to see*. The Spirit heals and extends humanity's perceptive capacities by joining them to Christ, nurturing a person's growth into her humanity through her growth into Christ. The Holy Spirit appropriates the reality of Christ to us, making us Christ that we may see Christ and making Christ visible that we may become like Christ. The result is that this chapter on the human, on how she perceives Beauty—which is to say, how she perceives Christ—must explore the Holy Spirit while deepening the Christological commitments of the previous chapter. Certainly such intertwining is to be found in Gregory's writings, and it yields an approach to perceiving beauty that binds material to spiritual, human to divine, present to eschaton.[10]

10. Christopher Beeley wrote of Gregory of Nazianzus, "What later writers, especially in post-Reformation Western circles, have sharply distinguished as theology, Christology, and anthropology are in Gregory's work unavoidably intermingled, in

The Substance of Things Unseen:
Two Boxes, Two Crosses

To illustrate the significance of Gregory's model of perception, I want to consider an alternative model embedded in the writings of eminent art philosopher Arthur Danto. This will begin an extended exploration of perception and perceivers that may seem, at times, to take us far from beauty. Yet as I hope will become clear, these considerations are actually central to unpacking how Gregory theologizes beauty, and I draw those connections explicitly before the chapter ends. In the meantime, Danto's particular descriptions are important, not only because they represent a significant approach to perception in art criticism, but also because his model of perception—or ones similar to it—undergirds many theological descriptions of faith. We begin with the *Brillo Boxes*.

In April 1964, Andy Warhol's *Brillo Boxes* sculpture opened in the Stable Gallery in Manhattan. The conceit of the sculpture is famous: it consisted in a stack of boxes that looked exactly like the boxes of Brillo soap pads sold in stores. And they *were* exactly like those boxes, save three things: They were made of plywood, not cardboard; they were stacked in a gallery, not a stockroom; and they were empty. Seeing this installation transformed Arthur Danto's reflections on art and philosophy. Just six months after *Brillo Boxes* opened, Danto published an article declaring his revelation: Art is finally not about aesthetics or the physicality of sight; it is about theory.[11] Here Danto found the form of the central question of Western philosophy, which is also the question toward which all art had, he claims, been tending: What makes the difference between a work of art and something not a work

---

both rhetorical form and dogmatic content" (*Gregory of Nazianzus*, 63). I have tried to display a similar claim about Gregory of Nyssa over the course of this book, but in this last chapter, the claim must be explicit for my argument to be intelligible. When Nyssen does anthropology, he is also telling us something about God. When he does pneumatology, he is also telling us something about Christ. And the way this telling is communicated is as much literary as logical (to the extent these categories can bear separation). Along similar lines, Beeley also says, "One of the most characteristic aspects of Gregory [of Nazianzus]'s oeuvre and a cardinal principle of his theological system is his repeated insistence that the knowledge of God is inseparably related to the condition of the human knower—that theology both demands and causes a change in the state of the theologian" (*Gregory of Nazianzus*, 63–64). The inextricability of theological knowledge and knower, a subtheme of the last chapter, becomes here the main melody.

11. He writes, "What in the end makes the difference between a Brillo box and a work of art consisting of a Brillo box is a certain theory of art. It is the *theory* that takes it up into the world of art, and keeps it from collapsing into the real object which it is" (Danto, "Artworld," 581, emphasis mine).

of art when there is no interesting perceptual difference between them?[12] Danto sees it akin to Descartes's question of how one distinguishes reality from dreams when they both appear to one as reality.

This attempt to distinguish art from aesthetics is not unique to Danto. Marcel Duchamp describes his own work in similar terms, particularly with regard to his famous *Fountain* (1917), which consisted of a urinal submitted to an exhibition with the signature R. Mutt. When critics praised the aesthetics of the *Fountain*, Duchamp grew angry that his work was being understood on the level of the aesthetic. According to Duchamp, the critics had confused the identity of the *Fountain*, which was "mentally art, physically non-art." The *Fountain*, in fact, invites what Duchamp calls "visual indifference" because it locates its *art-ness* at the level of the intellectual rather than the visual. So indifferent was Duchamp to the aesthetic, according to some writers, that he did not care even to preserve his work for posterity.[13] Duchamp's strong opposition between mental and physical art prefigures Danto's polarization of knowing and seeing, and both men align art with the intellectual and the aesthetic with the physical. The anthropology undergirding this understanding of art and perception not only abstracts intellectuality from physicality but pits them in competition with one another. Aesthetics, which Danto understands as physical appearance, can only mislead us from the surer guide of theory.

For both Danto and Duchamp, the competition between the intellectual (also called the mental or the spiritual) and the physical turns on a quasi-mystical understanding of art and the artist. Art philosopher Donald Kuspit describes ready-mades as "socially functional artifacts that have been changed into sublime artistic masterpieces by the creative act of Duchamp's psyche."[14] The creativity in the artistic psyche that transforms *functional* into *sublime, artifact* into *art,* is cast by Danto in even more overtly religious language. Working towards an understanding of why *Brillo Boxes* is art, Danto asks if "the whole world consist[s] of latent artworks waiting, like the

---

12. Danto, *After the End of Art*, 35. Danto writes, "All philosophical questions. . . have that form: two outwardly indiscernible things can belong to different, indeed to momentously different philosophical categories. The most famous example is the one with which the era of modern philosophy itself opens in the *First Meditation* of Descartes, where he finds there is no internal mark by which dream and waking experience can be told apart. Kant tries to explain the difference between amoral action and one that exactly resembles it but merely conforms to the principles of morality. Heidegger shows, I think, that there is no outward difference between an authentic and an inauthentic life, however momentous the difference may be between authenticity and inauthenticity."

13. Cabanne, *Dialogues with Marcel Duchamp*, 48.

14. Kuspit, *End of Art*, 21.

C3

Arthur as Idol

bread and wine of reality, to be transfigured, through some dark mystery, into the indiscernible flesh and blood of the sacrament?"[15]

The language of Eucharist captures what is crucial for Danto about the problematic *Brillo Boxes* represents: how to differentiate two aesthetically indistinguishable objects that have different statuses. The bread and wine pre-consecration look exactly the same as the bread and wine post-consecration, yet the latter are called the flesh and blood of Christ. And so the relationship of the bread to the Host with respect to the body of Christ is analogous to the relationship of the Brillo Boxes of the stockroom to those of Warhol with respect to the status of *art*. It may be unsurprising that Duchamp, too, invoked transubstantiation in his descriptions of the role of the artist.[16]

Artist as Priest? or Blasphemer

In invoking the Eucharist, Danto references a special case of Christian perception. The flesh and blood of the Eucharist have a kind of opacity, a resistance to sensory probing, that theologians have returned to ponder again and again throughout the Christian tradition. This sensory resistance is highlighted by miracle stories, especially popular in the Middle Ages, in which the bread is suddenly disclosed to a saint or disbelieving communicant as flesh.[17] Only a miracle can make the host perceptible as flesh. Yet Eucharistic flesh and blood are, for Gregory at least, in profound relationship with the sensory, for they train a person's eyes so that she might see and her ears that she might hear. I return to this sacramental training of the senses later. For now I want to inquire further into the stakes of Danto's description with a different, hypothetical analog: that of two identical images of men hanging on a cross.[18] One of these is merely a pathetic sight, while the other represents a site of salvation, for, though the two men appear indistinguishable, one of them is the Son of God, while the other is a thief. How do we understand the difference between these two images and the different

15. Danto, "Artworld," 581.

16. Duchamp, "The Creative Act."

17. One such story is found in the account of Saint Gregory the Great in the *Golden Legend*. Seeing a supplicant smile when he described the host as the body of Christ, Gregory the Great asks the woman to explain her amusement. She replies that she had baked the bread with her own hands and therefore knows that it cannot be Christ's body. Gregory's response is to pray, at which point part of the host figures itself as a little finger. After he prays again, the host once more takes on the appearance of bread. The woman receives the host and the story ends with the assurance that she, and all who were there, were ever-after more faithful. The story is told by Jacobus de Voragine in a medieval collection of stories about the saints, *The Golden Legend*.

18. It is perhaps worth noting, however, that in Christian art, the images of Christ on the cross and the thief on his cross are almost never visually identical. My proposal is hypothetical rather than referring to any particular set of images.

relations beholders have to them? How do we understand how Elizabeth's relationship to Joseph's carved crosses differs from Sister Bridget's?

If we transpose Danto's analysis into a theological key, the answer we get is common enough. The answer is faith. The two crosses are aesthetically indistinguishable, yet a person knows one as salvific apart from the information her body can give her. A person categorizes one cross as salvific despite the lack of sensory evidence, because she believes the crucified one to be the Son of God. Faith, in this description, becomes a kind of intellectual knowledge divorced from the body, and the body—by telling us two crosses are the same—can be only a stumbling block to the ethereal certainty of faith, which takes the form of theological knowledge.[19]

This model of faith over and against sight/body/perception is one Gregory helps challenge. He will help me to suggest how faith can be the substance of things unseen without being opposed to what can be seen. And Gregory will aid me in insisting that faith does not require a kind of blindness even though faith is not reducible to the visible. I want to propose an approach to faith that understands faith in deep relationship to the visible and the invisible because it is claimed by selves that are both invisible and visible, spirit and flesh—and because both this invisibility and visibility, spirit and flesh, are central to identity.

Non-identical Identity

The self that Danto presumes, the self that can neatly divide faith from body, art from aesthetics, knowing from sensing, is a Cartesian self. I want to explore Gregory of Nyssa's alternative anthropology in conversation with two writers who are also looking for alternative, non-Cartesian grounds for selfhood: phenomenologist Jean-Luc Marion and psychoanalytic theorist Kaja Silverman.[20] Both of these writers thematize their trouble with Descartes in

19. There is yet another theological version of this problem, this one in the arena of moral theology. Herbert McCabe describes it concisely: "What looks exactly the same piece of behaviour may in one case be done from love and in another not; our moral judgment is solely concerned with determining this matter" (Law, Love, and Language, 3). McCabe's critique of this position is that in divorcing love from external behavior, the ethicist, far from elevating love, ends up trivializing it, making it as ethically unavailable and uninteresting as a headache or getting high (15). While I will focus more on the problem that arises with faith, the anthropology underlying both views is essentially the same, and as I present a different relationship between faith and sight, I will along the way articulate a place for love quite different than the role McCabe critiques.

20. Marion, of course, also has a profound respect for Descartes, and his readings of Descartes discover a complexity to his dualism that I shall not pursue here. At this point, my primary interest in Descartes is not in presenting the fullness of his

a way that Gregory, over a millennium Descartes's senior, obviously did not. Their anthropologies, resonant with Gregory's, will aid me in naming the stakes of Gregory's anthropology for contemporary conversations. Yet even in its resonance with Silverman and Marion's work, Gregory's anthropology also strikes notes theirs do not, so Silverman and Marion will attune us to the distinctiveness, as well as familiarity, of his harmonies.

Silverman describes Descartes as inaugurating a world of "closed order" over "unfinished universality" and of presenting the world, not as a book a person must learn to read but as a "picture constructed by [man's] look."[21] To shore up the human being's closedness and unconstructedness relative to the world, the human subject stopped looking for analogies between himself and other beings. As Silverman puts it, "He strove to be unique, freestanding, and identical to himself."[22] Descartes himself tried to live into the supposed identicalness of human identity by withdrawing into his study and ridding his mind of all he had learned from others and to think a new world, founded solely on his own thinking self. Silverman describes what she sees as his failure:

> But far from consolidating his identity, this experiment atomized it. "But what then am I?" the philosopher asks in a famous passage from the *Meditation*. "A thing which thinks. What is a thing which thinks? It is a thing which doubts, understands, [conceives], affirms, denies, wills, refuses, which also imagines and feels."[23]

Though he does not read this passage, like Silverman does, as Descartes "unnerved by the heterogeneity of the self," Jean-Luc Marion also picks up on it to point out that Descartes's first French translator, the Duc de Luynes, inserted into it that the self is also one "which loves, which hates."[24] Marion is receptive to the addition inasmuch as he wants to recover the centrality of love to the self. For, despite his sympathetic reading of Descartes, Marion finds his description of the self "monstrously mistaken" because it fails to render intelligible "the phenomenon that I am to myself." One appears to oneself, not as an *ego cogitans* but as a *magna quaestio*. In this phrase,

---

thought—a task that calls for a work in itself (or in Marion's case, multiple works)—but in thinking about how Marion's and Silverman's understandings of Descartes's mistakes can help us arrive at richer descriptions of selfhood.

21. Silverman, *Flesh of My Flesh*, 2.

22. Ibid.

23. Ibid., quoting Descartes, *Discourse on Method and Meditations on First Philosophy*, 9.

24. Marion, *Erotic Phenomenon*, 7.

Marion also describes the heterogeneity of the self. It is always eluding attempts to control it, exposing itself (the *me*) as alienated from the *I*, and fluxing and flowing in its hates and loves.[25] In sum, the self appears to the self—in language we will return to—as a saturated phenomenon.[26] So the problem with Descartes's formulation of the self is not just that it excludes love but that the self-knowing that defines the *ego cogitans* is impossible. Marion directs his indignation at Descartes's mistaken formulation of the *ego* at philosophy more generally: "The fact that, of all the supposed errors for which Descartes has been taken to task, this one alone—doubtless his only error—has remained unnoticed for nearly four centuries, says much more than anything else about the erotic blindness of metaphysics."[27]

It is not a small error. It requires that the *ego* be entirely redefined. In place of the *ego cogitans* that arbitrarily and subsequently submits love to the will and that presumes a self-knowing that is ultimately impossible, Marion wants an *ego amans*, whose love precedes not only thinking but being.[28] Love is thus not merely included in the constellation of activities that locate the *ego*; it is the sun around which all such activities orbit. And the *ego* that *amat* is inescapably flesh, for, "I do not love by proxy, nor through a go-between, but in the flesh, and this flesh is one only with me."[29] This fleshly love therefore displaces, for Marion, the *logos* as the definition of the self.[30]

Surely Silverman would agree with Marion's dis- and re-placement of the self, for it is fleshly love that Silverman also wants to fund the self. The flesh that for Marion suggests the immediacy of the lover to herself suggests, for Silverman, the immediacy of the beloved—and, indeed, of all other beings. Silverman gathers a number of thinkers, all of whom invoke flesh to suggest the similarity among beings, similarities that are "reversible

25. Marion explores the incomprehensibility of the self in "*Mihi Magna Quaestio Factus Sum.*"

26. Marion, "*Mihi Magna Quaestio Factus Sum,*" 23.

27. Marion, *Erotic Phenomenon*, 8.

28. Ibid.

29. Ibid., 9.

30. The implications of this claim are worked out, quite beautifully, in *The Erotic Phenomenon*. In a moment of considering our fleshly existence as funding our selfhood, Marion writes, "Only flesh feels that which differs from it. It alone touches, approaches and moves away from something other, suffers from or enjoys it, is affected by and responds to it, because it alone feels. The claimed action of things upon me would never appear without this privilege of allowing myself to be affected, and thus never without my sensibility, without my flesh. In short, things do not act upon me, for their very action results first from my passivity, which renders them originarily possible. My passivity provokes their activity, not the inverse" (113).

and ontologically equalizing."[31] "Flesh" can become the starting point for another kind of human relationality, according to Silverman, one that celebrates kinship rather than difference and selves that are mutually constituted rather than independently transcendent. Alluding to this openness in human selfhood that renders identity non-identical, Silverman writes, "All of our stories really are part of the same great volume: The Book of Life. And unlike the *logos*, the words in this book do not have to become flesh in order to save us. They *are* flesh."[32] The problem with the *logos*—and with Christianity more generally—is not that it fails to name kinships and analogies but that the kind of analogy it identifies, like that of Platonism—subordinates "our world" to "a higher one" thereby generating "hierarchical and nonreciprocal relationships."[33] Rather than the story of the *Logos*, which for Silverman dominates the Western tradition, or the story of Oedipus, which dominates the psychoanalytic one, Silverman proposes recovering the myth of Orpheus and Eurydice.

Orpheus is the divinely gifted musician and husband of Eurydice, his unfortunate wife who died soon after their wedding. He descends to the underworld to retrieve her, using his gift of music to charm those who would block his path. After finding her, he is allowed to bring her back on the condition that he not look at her during their ascent from Hades. But at one moment—often described as painfully near the end of their journey—Orpheus looks back, and Eurydice disappears from him for a second and final time. Orpheus returns from the underworld, traumatized and spurning all women, whom he associates with death. He withdraws from the society of women, in some accounts erotically attaching himself to men or boys, to play his music until he is one day torn apart by a group of women infuriated by his misogyny. Some tellings of the story (notably Ovid's) have a coda: Orpheus's death returns him to Hades, where he grasps Eurydice "tightly in his loving arms," and they walk together, re-performing that moment of loss, the sting now gone, sometimes Orpheus walking ahead, sometimes Eurydice.

Silverman's reading of this myth is indebted to Lou Andreas-Salomé, lifelong friend of Freud. In her memoir *Looking Back*, Andreas-Salomé describes how after an encounter with mortality, she experienced a feeling of profound reverence for all that is. Most people cannot experience this feeling, Andreas-Salomé maintains, because somewhere along the way of life, they have left behind a partner and so have compromised their capacity

---

31. Silverman, *Flesh of My Flesh*, 4.

32. Ibid., 14.

33. Ibid., 1.

for this feeling of reverence. Her role as analyst was to occupy the symbolic position of Eurydice and help them reclaim the one they had left behind.

> [The analyst] jogs [the analysand's] memory by positioning herself behind him and returning with him to the scene of the crime. When ascending the slope leading from Hades to earth, [the analysand] is convulsed with grief and remorse, but then he realizes that he is not alone, and the past ceases to be irrevocable. Turning to Eurydice [the analyst or the memory figure?], he clasps her "tightly" in his "loving" arms.[34]

By so remembering and re-performing the past, the past is also transformed and the kinship of flesh to flesh reaffirmed.[35] Not only is the partner brought back, but "*all* the vanished people of the past arise anew."[36] Thus, in the unlikely location of a psychoanalyst's chair, there is resurrection. With such resurrection, the myth of independence is renounced, and the lost one is reincorporated into the analysand's psyche.

Silverman recovers Andreas-Salomé's reading against a long tradition of eliding or glorying in the death of Eurydice, as in the Christian tradition of allegorizing Orpheus as Christ and Eurydice as sinful death/flesh/the devil.[37] This abjection of Eurydice, for Silverman, enthrones a self-sufficient subject, casts man/the artist/the savior/the subject as constituted alone. This is why Ovid's coda is so important to Andreas-Salomé and Silverman: Orpheus and Eurydice embrace their kinship, their similarity, and perform and celebrate their mutual constitutions of one another. In this coda, similarity, not difference, is the organizing principle of Orpheus and Eurydice's relationship. Theirs is a love that acknowledges the way their beings rhyme and, the illusion of totality dispelled, faces rather than flees mortality. In this way, Silverman continues her work in *The Threshold of the Visible World*, where she argues for the theoretical importance of love as a correction to the over-focus on difference. Her understanding of love involves the active idealization of the other, which means that love is identification that happens at a distance from the self and without ever forgetting that the subject is marked by lack.[38] The "subject marked by lack" is both the lover and the

---

34. Ibid., 58.

35. Ibid., 8–12.

36. Ibid., 8, as quoted in Andreas-Salomé, *Looking Back*, 193 (emphasis original).

37. Silverman, *Flesh of My Flesh*, 5.

38. Silverman, *Threshold of the Visible World*, 77, 78. In the following passage from *Threshold*, Silverman elucidates with clarity and generosity her relationship to her psychoanalytic forbearers: "As should be clear by now, the active gift of love represents more than an alternative model of romantic passion to that described by Freud, in

beloved, and the way Silverman describes their relationship in *Threshold of the Visible World*—as identification that is never identity, idealization that is always active—resembles her description of the subject in *Flesh of my Flesh*. She writes, "We do not have an 'identity' because we are constantly changing, but we also do not break into a million pieces because each of our 'shapes' resembles the others."[39] As our relationship to others is constituted by analogy, so is our relationship to ourselves. The series of analogies of self to self, self to lover, self to other beings, lover to other beings, characterizes the self as open, unfinished, and co-constituted. It is this that Silverman's retelling of the Orpheus myth is supposed to capture.

Marion, too, turns to the Orpheus myth—albeit more briefly than Silverman—but with it, he reflects on the problem that is a twin to the transcendent self's rejection of Eurydice. That is, he worries, not about the tradition that forgets Eurydice or celebrates her absence, but about Orpheus's graspingness of her presence. Orpheus, in his moment of turning, insists on seeing Eurydice's invisibility and so treats her as an object—which can be fully seen—rather than a subject—which can never appear as an object and thus must be invisible. In Orpheus's turning to Eurydice, he resists her invisibility to himself, her own subjectivity, and thus disqualifies her as his beloved.[40] To love the other, by contrast, is to "renounce mastery over the visible" and let the beloved be a subject by allowing oneself "to be glimpsed by a gaze which sees me without my seeing it."[41] In Marion's telling, the tragedy of Orpheus is not that he leaves Eurydice behind but that he insists on possessing her, on willing away her invisibility—and in such insistence, Eurydice the subject is already lost.

For Marion, love opens possibilities for an encounter with the *saturated phenomenon*, which is his way of naming how something—a beloved, maybe, or his flesh or voice—can overwhelm the subject's intention. The givenness exceeds the intention because what the subject intends is

---

which the loved other comes to take the place of the ego-ideal. It is first and foremost an account of how identification, that psychic operation without which there would be no subject, no world, and no possible relation to the other, might work outside the libidinal economy which Lacan associates with the master/slave relationship. In other words, it is an account of how identification might function in a way that results in neither the triumphs of self-sameness, nor craven submission to an exteriorized but essentialized ideal. As it has been elaborated here, the active gift of love also provides the basis for conceptualizing how we might idealize outside the narrow mandates of the screen; how we might put ourselves in a positive identificatory relation to bodies which we have been taught to abhor and repudiate" (79).

39. Silverman, *Flesh of My Flesh*, 2.

40. Marion, "Intentionality of Love," in *Prolegomena to Charity*, 80.

41. Ibid., 82.

inadequate to what is given. Marion is working to name the way the subject is constituted by phenomena and loves given to her, the way she cannot be self-constituted, but his formulations of the saturated phenomenon have drawn criticisms. One of the criticisms most relevant for our explorations of the beauty-perceiving subject is interesting for its irony. The critic accuses Marion of reducing givenness to the seen (ironic, yes, but also fitting: performing reductions is, after all, the task of a phenomenologist). The criticism is from John Caputo, and the bite in its irony is that his criticism casts Marion in the Orpheus role that Marion wants to reject. Caputo worries about Marion's phenomenology determining his theology. He is concerned about givenness overwhelming the theological horizon so that there is no space left over for what is *not* given.[42] Seeing in Marion a "theological magical realism," Caputo contrasts his saturated phenomenon with Kierkegaard's knight of faith, for whom "no 'bit of heterogeneous optical telegraphy' . . . would betray the infinite, [and there is] no 'crack through which the infinite would peek.'"[43] Here Caputo turns to Christology to explain why Kierkegaard is right. He hurls his criticism with force:

> It would be paganism to think that the divinity of Jesus would have been detectible, as if there was something in the bearing of Jesus, or the look in his eye, that suggests divinity. The Revelation is revelation *that* Jesus is the anointed one, not a revelation *of* the divinity, which no one can see and still live. The divinity is a matter of faith.[44]

Caputo has given us a version of faith that sounds not unlike Danto's version of art. Faith is located in the invisible, not the visible, what we know of Jesus, not what we see. Criticizing Marion for failing to give us "the desert and the blindness of faith," Caputo points to the way Marion focuses on Christ's advent, flesh, and transfiguration rather than Messianic desire.[45] Caputo, worrying that Marion's saturated phenomenon reduces faith to sight (or at least to the realm of sight), makes Marion the antithesis of Danto. Putting Danto in a theological key opposes faith and sight, whereas Caputo's Marion conflates them.

Here Gregory's contributions to thinking about the self are helpful, particularly with regard to the concerns Caputo raises about faith and sight in Marion and those Silverman raises about Christianity's Eurydice-denying Christ. Gregory is, in important ways, in continuity with the visions

42. Caputo, "Hyperbolization of Phenomenology," 83.
43. Ibid., 85.
44. Ibid.
45. Ibid., 78.

of selfhood offered by Marion and Silverman. Like them, he, too, tries to disclose the vulnerability and openness of subjecthood and the centrality of love in the constitution of this self. Also like them, Gregory names both the frailty and resplendence of the subject with *love*. And he can advance the conversation about this vulnerable, love-centered, redemption-needing self in a number of ways. Gregory's descriptions of spiritual senses and liturgical activities can illuminate the saturated phenomenon by showing the complicated relationship between visible and invisible present in encounters with it. Such descriptions also perform the integration of Messianic advent with the Messianic desire—the integration that Caputo worries the saturated phenomenon excludes. After all, sight and desire are, for Gregory, inseparable.[46] Yet focusing on the spiritual senses will also encourage us to extend the purview of perceiving saturated phenomena beyond the authority of sight.[47]

Before exploring the possibilities Gregory's spiritual senses offer for reapproaching the saturated phenomenon, we will read Gregory in relation to Silverman. Specifically, we will consider how Gregory's descriptions of the self deepen Silverman's commitment to flesh by locating the moment of redemption, not just in a mental-metaphorical journey up from Hades in the analyst's chair (or in her other location of redemption: in front of an artwork), but through active engagement and transformation of the flesh. For redemption, in Gregory's writings, requires not just the stillness of the flesh

---

46. I am not interested in exonerating Marion's particular formulation of the saturated phenomenon as illustrating how a saturated phenomenon need not oppose faith, nor reduce faith toward visibility. For a specific defense of Marion, see Merold Westphal's article responding to an earlier conference paper version of Caputo's article: Westphal, "Transfiguration as Saturated Phenomenon." Marion defends and explains his understanding of the relationship between faith and visibility by attacking the Kierkegaardian picture of the "knight of faith" for the way it casts faith as an individual achievement in the dark night of knowledge. He clarifies his own understanding of faith through the story of recognition and its lack on the way to Emmaus. For Marion, sight that lacks the proper imagination, the proper conceptualization, will always fall short of faith. He writes, "What we lack in order to believe is quite simply one with what we lack in order to see. Faith does not compensate, either here or anywhere else, for a defect of visibility: on the contrary, it allows reception of the intelligence of the phenomenon and the strength to bear the glare of its brilliance. Faith does not manage the deficit of evidence—it alone renders the gaze apt to see the excess of the pre-eminent saturated phenomenon, the Revelation. Thus we must not oppose the episode of the two disciples on the way to Emmaus to that of Christ's manifestation to the Apostles, which immediately follows it" (Marion, "They Recognized Him," 150–51).

47. Marion himself acknowledges the extension of saturated phenomena to all the senses, but these senses are not central to his philosophizing about saturation and perception the way sight is. For more on the saturated phenomenon in relation to other senses, see Marion, "The Banality of Saturation."

but its movement, too. So as Silverman makes an astounding contribution to psychoanalytic theory by offering it a picture of health and human flourishing, Gregory can extend Silverman's commitments by describing the possibilities of fleshly redemption. Toward the end of this chapter, we will see how this vision of redemption elaborates Gregory's vision of what it means to become a self. Through his meditations on Macrina, Gregory helps us past the Freudian myths of mother-rejection as foundational to self—those myths so irksome to, but never finally replaced by, Silverman—to locate the self in a journey of mother-becoming. Such a model of subjectivity not only provides a much more generative relationship with mothers and motherhood, but also lives into and fleshes out Silverman's commitment to a self that is constituted by and in relationship with the other. By the end, we will have a vision of selfhood that rejects the unsustainable transcendentality of Descartes, and extends the insights of Marion and Silverman—while yet avoiding the "magical realism" of Caputo's Marion and the unfleshliness of Silverman's redemption. And in keeping with Marion and Silverman's descriptions of the beloved's co-constitution of the lover, we will see how, for Gregory, Beauty also co-constitutes those who love her.

The Wounded Self

Homily Four: Mirrors, Fields, and Wounds

Before returning to Silverman and Marion, I want to reflect with Gregory on how a person comes to perceive the beautiful—a question with the reverse side of how the Spirit manifests the beauty of the Word to a person—with Gregory of Nyssa's *Homilies on the Song of Songs*. These homilies are commonly thought to be Gregory's last text, representing his most developed and sophisticated theological commitments. I will honor the richness of these homilies by dwelling deeply with a very few, particularly homilies four, twelve, and thirteen. These three focus on the pneumatological anthropology of perceiving the beautiful and so are especially helpful in exploring the question of this chapter. Like many of the other homilies on the Song of Songs, these three reference, develop, and invoke the spiritual senses, but they do so, interestingly, together with descriptions of the self as wounded. Even more interestingly: For Gregory, woundedness primarily describes, not the self that fails to see Christ, but the self that *does* see Christ. Yet it is a reversible metaphor, which also describes a self pathologically closed in on itself. The wound, in both these senses, is the central way Gregory describes how the spiritual senses work and what kind of selves we are and

198

can become. Unlike the wounds of the last chapter, the wound of love is metaphorical rather than physical; yet, its relations to and implications for our physicality are no less important than (nor is it separable from) the rotting bodies of the last chapter. I begin with the fourth homily.

One of homily four's opening themes is the plasticity of human nature. For Gregory, human nature is drastically undetermined, "capable of becoming whatever it determines upon" in accordance with free choice and desire.[48] Our capacity for free choice means humans can, mirror-like, reflect in and as our nature what we desire, "tak[ing] on the shape of whatever we want."[49] Having received medical knowledge as part of the education of a privileged man of his day, Gregory draws on his biological training in his description of the eye as a metonymy for human nature. As the eye sees by receiving into the pupil impressions of images emanating from objects—by, in some sense, taking into the pupil the beauty that these images are—so does the soul become beautiful in seeing and thus taking in the beauty of Christ.[50] But seeing the beauty of Christ is not the biological process that seeing, say, a millipede is.[51] One sees Christ's beauty by first receiving the Holy Spirit. Gregory writes,

> Since, then, her purified eye has received the imprint of the dove, she is also capable of beholding the beauty of the Bridegroom. For now for the first time, the virgin gazes upon the form of the Bridegroom, now, that is, that she has the dove in her eyes (for "No one can say, 'Jesus is Lord!' except by the Holy Spirit" [1 Cor 12:3]), and she says *Behold, you are beautiful, my kinsman, and glorious.*[52]

Here we can see how the Holy Spirit is deeply involved in anthropology, in human becoming, and also how the Holy Spirit is deeply involved in

48. Gregory of Nyssa, *Homilies on the Songs of Songs*, 113. The full quotation reads, "Human nature came into being as something capable of becoming whatever it determines upon, and to whatever goal the thrust of its choice leads it, it undergoes alteration in accord with what it seeks." Norris goes on to add a footnote noting the prominence of this theme of human nature's plasticity in Gregory, citing passages in the *Life of Moses* and other homilies on the Song of Songs (113n3).

49. Gregory of Nyssa, *Homilies on the Songs of Songs*, 115.

50. Ibid., 113–17.

51. "For in that it is transformed in accordance with the reflections of its choices, the human person is rightly likened to a mirror. If it looks upon gold, gold it appears, and by way of reflection it gives off the beams of that substance; and if it has the look of some hateful thing, it is imitating that ugliness through a likeness, playing, in its own appearance, the part of a frog or a toad or a millipede or some other unpleasant sight—whichever of them it reflects" (ibid., 115).

52. Ibid., 117, 119.

the work of Christ. Just as the Holy Spirit enables a person to proclaim the Lordship of Jesus, so the Holy Spirit enables a person to contemplate the Beauty of Jesus.[53] The Holy Spirit's capacity to work interiorly to a person's humanity, to work in a person that she may become the person she ought to become, goes some way to explaining why Gregory's anthropology is pneumatological. But at this point in the homily, the Holy Spirit is just one possible "imprint" among others, for Gregory is still exploring the plasticity of human nature. He offers another image for such plasticity. As human nature is as undetermined as a mirror with a mirror's infinite possibilities for reflecting images, so is it broad as a plain, which signifies for Gregory human nature's "capacity to be the subject of many, indeed unlimited, thoughts, interests, and forms of knowledge."[54] Human nature morphs according to the object upon which it gazes and the multiple concepts it works to grasp.

Reading Gregory of Nyssa's *On the Soul and the Resurrection* and a selection of his homilies on Ecclesiastes and the Song of Songs, Kathryn Tanner describes the way such descriptions cast living creatures, not as "leading self-sufficient lives" but as "actually taking in things from outside themselves."[55] In this way, humans are both in continuity and discontinuity with other creatures. All living things depend on other things for life; plants require water, soil, sunlight, for example. Tanner notes that humans are unique in that God is one of their "inputs." I would add that what further distinguishes humans, according to Gregory, is the role of desire in shaping what humans use as "inputs." Tanner touches on this distinction when she quotes from Gregory's eighth homily on Ecclesiastes: "'Loving relationship effects a natural commingling with that which is loved. Whatever therefore we choose through our love, that we also become' in the way, for example, 'the mouth of someone receiving a sweet-smelling spice . . . becomes itself sweet smelling.'"[56] Tanner reads this together with a quotation from *On the Soul and the Resurrection*, in which Gregory writes, "The soul . . . attaches itself to [something] and blends with it by means of the movement and activity of love, fashioning itself according to that which it is continually finding

53. Balthasar, *Presence and Thought*, 169, makes a similar point by drawing on a different text where Gregory connects perception, Christ, and the Holy Spirit even more closely. Defending the divinity of the Holy Spirit against the followers of Macedonius, Gregory writes, "Just as the person who piously receives the Spirit sees in the Spirit the glory of the Only Begotten, [so the person who] sees the Son sees the Image of the Invisible One and through the Image receives into his understanding the imprint of the Archetype" (*Adversus Macedonianos* II, 1325 D–28 A).

54. Gregory of Nyssa, *Homilies on the Song of Songs*, 125.

55. Tanner, *Christ the Key*, 41.

56. Ibid., 46, quoting Gregory of Nyssa, "Eighth Homily on Ecclesiastes," 189.

and grasping."[57] Here we are on familiar ground: Gregory's vision of human nature as given is similar to one Silverman and Marion draw from—a human that is dependent upon and determined by her loves. Yet as Gregory elaborates *what* is given (as) the self, the picture of the self's givenness grows strange. The way Gregory connects human givenness with the Incarnation moves us in his distinctive direction.

The story of the Incarnation begins with story of Eden. Once "golden and gleaming," human nature became "discolored and dark" when it chose what was worse in the Garden of Eden, yet God loved the bride (here: the human soul), even in her discoloration.[58] God's love for the bride names the divine desire to restore the bride's original beauty—and the divine plan to realize this desire. Gregory describes this plan with an extended allegory of an apple tree. Still gazing "by means of the eyes of the dove," the bride sees an "apple tree among the trees of the wood" like her beloved, her "kinsmen among young men."[59] Gregory goes on to query and describe what it is that the bride has seen. Because in Holy Scripture wood often signifies, according to Gregory, the material life of the human race, an apple tree "is of the same substance as the stuff of humanity."[60] Yet the trees of the wood surrounding the apple tree are materiality run amuck: They are "bursting with the various sorts of passions."[61] This similarity and difference from other trees enables the apple tree to "[bear] a fruit by which the perceptive faculties of the soul are touched with sweetness," for it pleases the eye, the nose, and the mouth.[62] Similarly the bride perceives that her groom is different from her in that he is joy to the eyes, perfume to the sense of scent, and "life to those who eat him"—for Gregory notes that the Gospel says "anyone who eats him shall live (John 6.51–2)."[63] There are strong Eucharistic overtones at this moment in the homily, but it is not developed or made any more explicit. Gregory moves on, describing how for "the soul that has trained its organs of sense," the Bridegroom's words taste like sweet fruit, the teaching like honey in the mouth, and "the sense organs of the soul are truly touched with sweetness by the Word when the apple tree's shadow protects us from the fiery blaze of temptations."[64] So how does the soul arrive in a place where

57. Ibid., quoting Gregory of Nyssa, *On the Soul and the Resurrection*, 450.
58. Gregory of Nyssa, *Homilies on the Song of Songs*, 113.
59. Ibid., 129.
60. Ibid.
61. Ibid.
62. Ibid.
63. Ibid., 131.
64. Ibid.

it can receive the sweetness of the Word? How is it trained so as to receive the Word's further training? The secret out of this circle, for Gregory, is desire: "There is no way in which it is possible to be cool under the shadow of the tree of life except as desire leads the soul up to it."[65] Such spiritual desire is born of the desire for materiality, which indicates the power of the apple trees mixing of material and spiritual: "You see why you have a faculty of desire, in order, namely, that you may conceive an appetite for the apple, the delight of which takes many forms for those who have drawn near to it."[66] Desire continues as a theme, as Gregory describes the bride as possessed of a thirst that will not be slaked, but leads her to the very house of wine—for she has been "wounded by love."[67] In so doing, the apple tree turns what were formerly enemies—the passions enslaving human nature— into friends.[68] This wood-befriending apple tree, like the love that wounds, is revealed to be Christ.[69] Meditating on the desire elicited by the apple tree, Gregory offers his own "conjecture": "He who for love of humanity grew up in the woods of our nature became an apple by sharing flesh and blood."[70]

This is the first time Gregory identifies the apple tree as Christ, and this identification leads him into a Christ-centered reverie. Christ Jesus guides us to celestial things by partaking in humility and death, Gregory continues, and Gregory's meditation on Christ leads him back to the bride's desire for Christ even as it then deepens his description of how to understand the eliciting of that love. He contemplates the bride's declaration, "I am wounded with love."[71] He meditates on her words with archery imagery, describing the arrow as deep within the bride's heart.

> But the archer who discharges the arrow is love. From Holy Scripture, however, we have learned that God is love (cf. 1 John 4:8, 16), and he discharges his own chosen arrow (cf. Isa 49:2)— the Only Begotten God—at those who are being saved, having smeared over the triple point of the barb with the Spirit of life (the barb is faith), so that, in the person in whom it is planted, it may introduce the archer together with the arrow, as the Lord says: "I and my Father will come and make our dwelling with him" (John 14:23).[72]

65. Ibid.
66. Ibid.
67. Ibid., 133.
68. Ibid., 131.
69. Ibid., 139.
70. Ibid.
71. Ibid., 141.
72. Ibid.

The agent of wounding here is God the Father, who uses God the Son as the wounding instrument and God the Spirit as the smear on the barb that first makes contact with the flesh it will open in wounding. And the wound is not just caught up with the perception of beauty but is itself beautiful. Gregory exclaims, "O sweet and happy [*kalon*] wound, by which life slips through to the inward parts, opening the arrow's cut to make itself a door and an entrance!"[73] As the bride receives the beautiful wound and is so opened for love, she becomes the arrow in the hands of God the bridegroom-archer.[74] Love, beauty, and woundedness intertwine in complex ways to describe the kind of subjectivity humanity ought to perform (and in some ways already does). Moreover, faith is bound up in this nexus, too, for the Spirit-smeared tip of the Son-arrow that penetrates the bride is faith.[75] What kind of faith is Gregory describing here? And what kind of subject?

What is striking about Gregory's descriptions of subject-formation over the course of the homily is the shift in the way the object of desire affects the subject. Where Gregory initially describes the object of desire forming the subject through that which is already present in the subject—the object as image in an already-present mirror or growth in an already-present plain—he later describes a loved object that ruptures the subject, that creates a space in her where no space previously existed.[76] This object *wounds* her, and such hole-making (which is a making whole) occurs as the subject's desire for God heats up. This is the difference between loving objects and loving Love itself. This is what it means to be wounded by love. The self remains intact in loving objects; her subjectivity is not unchanged but it does remain unchallenged. We are arriving at the distinctiveness of Gregory's understanding of the self's givenness, what it adds to the sketches we found in Silverman and Marion: In loving the one who is, as Gregory reminds us several times in this homily, named Love, the self's illusion of sovereignty is toppled and any enclosedness of the self thrown open. In loving the God who is Love, the self learns to love in such a way that she cedes subjectivity to the beloved, allowing the lover to reconstitute her. And love works this

73. Ibid. Greek p. 140, line 12. ὦ καλοῦ τραύματος καὶ γλυκείας πληγῆς, δι' ἧς ἡ ζωὴ ἐπὶ τὰ ἐντὸς διαδύεται ὥσπερ τινὰ θύραν καὶ εἴσοδον τὴν ἐκ τοῦ βέλους διαίρεσιν ἑαυτῇ ὑπανοίξασα. ὁμοῦ τε γὰρ τὸ τῆς ἀγάπης βέλος ἐδέξατο καὶ παραχρῆμα εἰς γαμικὴν θυμηδίαν ἡ τοξεία μετεσκευάσθη.

74. Gregory of Nyssa, *Homilies on the Song of Songs*, 141.

75. Ibid.

76. This is not to say Gregory abandons the image of the mirror in describing how human nature becomes good/beautiful by drawing near Goodness and Beauty to reflect them. But a mirror proves insufficient for Gregory as the sole image for divine transformation.

way because Love, for love of humanity, was constituted as humanity ("sharing flesh and blood"), becoming the apple tree that could sweeten the soul's senses. Through the wounding by Love, deification begins.[77] The self that is given becomes itself by loving the Giver, whom it receives, ever-more. In so doing, it *becomes*, ever-more. The fullness of the self's givenness overflows, giving way to a givenness that is a profound givingness. This, I take it, goes beyond what Silverman says about mutual constitutions and is radically opposed to Danto. It is, perhaps, different from Marion in its strong distinction between the love of Love and all other loves.

In more concrete terms, this is a tale about the re-forming power of a person's love for Christ and how it participates in the re-forming love of Christ for humankind. As such, it is also a tale about the love of the hungry, the neighbor, the enemy, the sick, and the naked. Gregory at one point talks about the importance and right order of love for neighbor, wife, and enemy, and notes the importance of loving one's wife as Christ loved the church.[78] Such love participates in the love of Christ in both senses belonging to "of": This love both imitates Christ's love (for the church) and is itself love *for* Christ, who locates himself in the hungry, the neighbor, and so on. Gregory contrasts this love with passionate, whole-hearted love of money, honors, and women; this is a love that is "disordered and inverted."[79] In the latter love, a person certainly changes. She reflects different images in her mirror and grows different plants in her field. But she is not radically opened and reconstituted the way she is by Christ-love. She is definitely not deified. The person who loves her neighbor, her hungry, her enemy, on the other hand, is reconstituted by beginning to perceive beauty through the Holy Spirit so that that her Love-wounded reconstitution enables her still more fully to perceive by becoming beautiful herself.

It is in the midst of this perceiving and desiring and wounding and re-forming that we find faith. Faith is the arrow tip that enters the bride. It penetrates the body of the bride, who has been made ready for the wound by the sweetening of her senses, and she receives the wound as a re-formation of her subjectivity and heightening of her perceptive capacities. Faith is not sight, but it both responds to what is seen and enables further sight. It is thus never opposed to sight; faith is wide-eyed, attentive, world-yielding. There is nothing more specific Gregory teaches the reader about faith in this section,

---

77. Martin Laird observes, "Some of the most stirring examples of divinization [in Gregory's writings] occur with no recourse whatever to the vocabulary of divinization" (*Gregory of Nyssa*, 187.) He reflects especially on the example of wounding by love, wherein the Bride becomes the arrow that pierces her.

78. Gregory of Nyssa, *Homilies on the Song of Songs*, 135.

79. Ibid.

except that it is somehow deeply connected with love. And how could it be otherwise, when faith's very object is Love?

Homily Twelve: Veil-Snatching Wounds

Gregory begins the twelfth homily with the metaphor of preparing for a sea voyage:

> Before our discourse there stretches the vast ocean of insight and inquiry into the divine words. From this venture we hope for great riches in the way of knowledge, and this animate ship of ours, the church, with its own full crew, looks expectantly forward to its voyage of explication. But no sooner does the helmsman, who is our reason, lay a hand on the tiller than a common prayer is raised to God by the whole company aboard the ship: that the power of the Holy Spirit may blow upon us and stir up the waves of our thoughts, and that by their means it may prosper the voyage of our discourse and lead it on a direct course. In this way, finding ourselves on the high seas in our search for insight, we will traffic in the riches of knowledge, always supposing that in response to your prayer the Holy Spirit comes to fill the sails of our discourse.[80]

With this passage, Gregory sets the tone for the intricate agency-intertwining that is to come. The crew of the ship offers a prayer to the Holy Spirit, who breathes power, not onto the individuals praying, but on the ship of the church in which they voyage. Reason helms the ship through the waters of the divine words, as all hope for "traffic in the riches of knowledge."[81] In this layering of actors, the movement of the individual into divine knowledge is impossible to separate from the work of God—and the movement of the church. The significance of the church is affirmed when Gregory references a sacrament, this time not just hinting at it, as with the Eucharistic apple tree, but naming it outright. Fittingly for the sea voyage image, the sacrament named in the twelfth homily is baptism. Describing the impossibility of a union with the incorruptible Word apart from removing the "veil of the flesh," Gregory describes with Scripture the way the bride opens a way for her spouse: "'buried with him through baptism into his death' (cf. Rom 6:4)."[82] The problem of the veil will return, but Gregory is momentarily

80. Ibid., 361, 363.
81. Ibid., 363.
82. Ibid.

carried away into further meditations on death and resurrection, which make explicit the kind of radical reconstitution entailed by love-wounding.

Among his rich and varied meditations on death, Gregory considers the words of Paul, who bears in his body the death of Jesus that he might receive the life of the Word.[83] The way the human dies to receive life participates in the death and resurrection of Jesus—a participation that baptism both performs and illustrates. And such death is not a *loss*, for deprived of immortality through sin, human life had itself become a kind of death.[84] Gregory talks about life without Christ as a mutilated life while he yet describes Christ's entrance into one's life as itself wounding. These two different ways of locating mutilation and intactness come from the two perspectives on human nature between which Gregory constantly shifts. One the one hand, he moors human nature in its eschatological fulfillment foretasted in humanity's origins. This version of human nature describes the non-eschatological, non-glorified life humans lead as mutilated. On the other hand, Gregory takes another description of human nature from the kind of life humans lead apart from deep union with God. It is a version of human nature determined by the possibilities of non-eschatological human life. This second version of human nature, by taking non-eschatological human life as its norm, is intact by the standard of itself. What this intact-ness means, though, is that the self is bounded, closed, finite. It is healthy in a world where all healthy things die. When a world that is closed to eschatological becoming is taken as determinative, the self must terminate. In order to make way for the possibilities of human becoming, the self must be wounded and broken open. It is this second version of human nature to which Gregory appeals, then, when he describes the bride as "wounded by love." The Bridegroom breaks into the finite intactness of the self to open the self onto the infinite.

Such a description, however, does not make sense when one takes the eschaton as determinative of human nature. When eschaton defines "human," a different vocabulary describes human becoming. It is not that human nature must be broken open and wounded in order to become itself; it is that a human nature *not* opened to eschatological becoming has pathologically closed in on itself. From the perspective of eschatologically determined human nature, the intact-ness of the self closed to the infinitude of God is itself a wound, a deformation of humanity's proper shape. Gregory at points thus *reverses* his metaphor of woundedness to describe non-eschatological human life needing Christ, not for further wounding,

83. Ibid., 367.
84. Ibid., 371.

but for healing. On this point, for example, Gregory describes how "by his own stripes" Christ heals us and also the problem of a sinful "passion that wounds the soul."[85] One interesting result of the reversible wound/healing metaphor is that Gregory gives his readers two ways of talking about human nature: one for which deep participation in God is necessary, and one for which it is not. (Participation in God is always necessary, even for simple existence: what is at stake here is deep participation by which one is united to Christ.)

These two ways of talking about human nature help Gregory emphasize eschatological becoming as both a profound discontinuity with human nature (your self must be wounded) and a profound continuity (your self must be healed). They are thus part of the rich vocabulary by which Gregory weaves his descriptions of epectasy, a journey for which he often turned to Moses to illustrate. Even in the text on the Song of Songs, Gregory presents Moses as his paradigm of epectatic movement into God. In this text, he discusses Moses in terms familiar to the *Life of Moses*. Moses "still possesses an insatiable desire for something greater" and always had a "desire for higher things."[86] And in words echoing the *Life of Moses* and *Homilies on the Beatitudes*, Gregory writes, "The contemplation of God's face is an unceasing journey toward him that is brought to fulfillment by following behind the Word."[87] It is in this context of the bride's ever-searching for her bridegroom and the divine nature eluding every image that approaches it that Gregory returns to the wound. He turns to the text of the Song of Songs where the bride claims that the watchmen of the city wound her and take away her veil.[88] Unlike the fourth homily, though, Gregory pauses here to register anxiety over valorizing a wound. Certainly there is benefit to the removal of the veil: Now the bride can contemplate the bridegroom unhindered. But, as Gregory writes, there is "something repellent that is indicated by these terms in their ordinary sense (for to say they struck me and they wounded me suggests suffering)."[89] These are violent images Gregory inherits from Scripture, and he tries to take them seriously without simply valorizing pain. So he draws on Proverbs to understand what could be meant by wounding. There he reads that if a youth is struck with the rod that is wisdom, he will not die. This kind of striking is not destructive but constructive, life-generating, even; it connects the rod that beats life-giving wisdom into

85. Ibid., 269, 365.
86. Ibid., 377.
87. Ibid.
88. Ibid., 379, 381.
89. Ibid., 381.

the youth with "your rod and your staff" that have comforted me.[90] Gregory concludes: "If, then, that sweet blow supplies these good things according to both the teaching of Proverbs and the word of the prophet, it is assuredly a good thing to be struck by the rod that is the source of the abundance of so many good things."[91] And indeed, it must be such a rod, for only the good can effect the good, according to Gregory.[92] Thus, the bride boasts about her wound.[93] Gregory here holds together both determinations of human nature—the self is wounded so that it will be healed—but allows the non-eschatological vocabulary of a self that must be wounded to govern the eschatological terms of a self that is given life for a pedagogical purpose: He is describing the difference of the bride, the discontinuity this love creates with her previous life, and how she must be set apart. Gregory here makes apparent the way health and wounding are accountable to particular communities and particular settings. The self that is growing into membership in an eschatological community might look pathological to one not journeying towards that community.

Gregory then pulls together the words of the psalmist with the words of Paul to describe the wounding rod:

> And the meaning is this: that divine rod and comforting staff, which by a blow works healing, is the Spirit, whose fruit is those good things that Paul enumerates, and among their number continence, the teacher of the virtuous life. For Paul too, who bore the mark of such blows, similarly exulted in wounds of this sort when he said, "I bear on my body the marks of Christ" (Gal 6:17), displaying that weakness in every vice by which the power that belongs to Christ is brought to perfection in virtue. By these words, then, he shows us that the wound too is an admirable thing. It occasions the stripping off of the Bride's veil, so that the soul's beauty is revealed once her covering no longer obscures it.[94]

The agent of wounding has been redescribed from homily four: Where God the Father was the wounding archer in that earlier homily, God the Spirit is the wounding staff in homily twelve. The wounds here also reference the wounds of Christ. Through Christ, the wound retains its connections to love in this homily, but the wound's association with beauty is made more

---

90. Ibid., 383.
91. Ibid.
92. Ibid.
93. Ibid., 385.
94. Ibid.

explicit. The wound is beautiful and disclosive of beauty. The words of the text reveal the beautiful wound. The wound then removes the veil of the bride, which both makes her better able to perceive beauty and makes her own beauty more perceptible. This wound is part of generating what Gregory calls the soul's "noble yearning for incorruptible Beauty," which looks to God and so "possesses an ever-renewed desire for what lies beyond her."[95] Desire absent ever-increasing capacities for perception is simply frustrated; yet once the veil of hopelessness is removed, "the true fruition of what she seeks is ever to make progress in seeking and never to halt on the upward path, since her fulfilled desire ever generates a further desire for what is beyond her."[96] So then the wounding blow of the Spirit removes the veil that obscures the soul's beauty and constitutes a kind of despair; the wounding blow thereby enables the Bride to see "the infinite and unlimited beauty of her Beloved, a beauty that for all the eternity of the ages is ever and again discovered to be greater."[97] This is what it means, Gregory concludes, tying homily twelve back to homily four, that "in the sting of faith she has received in herself God's chosen arrow (cf. Isa 49:2) and has been struck in the heart by receiving love's shot in her vital part"—an arrow that is also the God who is love.[98] And here with wound and veil imagery, Gregory's two ways of describing human nature bump up against each other: Human nature must be wounded (as Paul was stigmatized by blows and weakness) in order to see the beauty that it possesses (the beauty of the soul) and manifest the wounded nature of Christ (it is the marks *of Christ* that Paul bears). The beauty of the soul is simply revealed; it is the non-eschatological beauty of the human person. Yet it is a beauty that is revealed only through wounding, only through bearing the marks of Christ that give one the Christ-likeness the human will eschatologically possess.[99] The beauty of humanity is fully revealed only through the Spirit's wounding the human into Christ-likeness,

---

95. Ibid.

96. Ibid., 389.

97. Ibid.

98. Ibid.

99. Balthasar writes along these lines in *Heart of the World*: "No fighter is more divine than one who can achieve victory through defeat. In the instant when he receives the deadly wound, his opponent falls to the ground, himself struck a final blow. For he strikes love and is thus himself struck by love. And by letting itself be struck, love proves what had to be proven: that it is indeed love. Once struck, the hate-filled opponent recognizes his boundaries and understands: behave as he pleases, nevertheless he is bounded on every side by a love that is greater than he. Everything he may fling at love—insults, indifference, contempt, scornful derision, murderous silence, demonic slander—all of it can ever but prove love's superiority; and the blacker the night, the more radiant does love emerge from it" (43–44).

into her eschatological self. Spirit-wounding gives us a way of seeing and a way of becoming. In holding together the glories of perceiving beauty with the distress of wounding, Gregory communicates to his reader the difficulty of perceiving beauty, the way its right perception requires a radical break from the catechesis of the world. Homily thirteen will take us still deeper into the wound, describing not just how it enables perceiving Christ but how it enables manifesting Christ (which is to say, one's eschatologically glorified self).

Homily Thirteen: Wounded in Christ

Homily thirteen begins with an extended meditation on the scriptural injunction to let one's yes be yes and no be no. This meditation leads Gregory, somewhat bewilderingly, back to woundedness. He gets there through the bride's statement: "I have adjured you, O daughters of Jerusalem, by the powers and virtues of the field: If you should find my kinsman, tell him that I am wounded by love."[100] "I am wounded with love" is the oath that the bride charges her maidens to make on her behalf to the bridegroom; it is the proof of her soul's ascent, her sworn yes to the bridegroom's implicit question of her commitment. We, too, Gregory tells us, "If we bind ourselves by this oath" to powers and virtues that destroy evil, can "see the pure Bridegroom, love's archer."[101] Echoing the bride's words, we, too, can say, "I am wounded with love."[102] It is the wound that enables us to see and name it, to see and name ourselves as wounded. It is only as wounded that we, like the bride's maidens, can see Christ.

Love-woundedness originates in Christ, whose loving sacrifice of death enflames the bride with love and "discloses the arrow of love deeply lodged within her, that is to say, her fellowship with Deity itself. For love is God, as we have said, come to inhabit the heart by the agency of the arrow of faith."[103] The bridegroom Christ here and in most of this homily is described as the agent of wounding, which compounds with the homily four description of God the Father wounding and the homily twelve descriptions of God the Spirit wounding to give a Trinitarian shape to love-wounding. And faith again makes the first contact, the first penetration of the skin to wound the beloved with the wounds that will prove to the bridegroom the bride's ascent.

100. Gregory of Nyssa, *Homilies on the Song of Songs*, 395.
101. Ibid., 397, 399.
102. Ibid., 399.
103. Ibid.

The maidens, the ones sent to seek the bridegroom with the message of this wounding, want a sign by which they might recognize "him who is not detected by any sign of recognition," "the Invisible One."[104] How can one describe Christ? Gregory writes at one moment that his "glory [shone] forth in his incarnate state," yet the next paragraph talks about Christ living with people "in the role of a slave."[105] God's glory is at one moment fully apparent in the Incarnation, while at the next moment the Incarnate God appears in the unglorious role of a slave. Does one see the glory of God in Christ or not? Gregory's answer is similar to the complexity he evoked in his description of the devil seeing Christ as God, but here he further identifies a way of seeing Christ available to humans yet not available to the devil: the church.

The complexity of the Incarnation is that Christ did not just *appear* to humanity in the Incarnation, as if humanity remained distinct from Christ's appearing. No, Christ also "drew to himself the mortal nature of flesh," so that he "ever sanctifies the common dough of that nature," thus "nourishing his body, the church, in the persons of those who are united to him in the fellowship of the mystery."[106] In the Incarnation, Christ becomes human to found the church as Christ's own body. That the church is the body of Christ becomes important for what it means to see the invisible Bridegroom.

> Anyone, therefore, who focuses attention on the church is in fact looking at Christ—Christ building himself up and augmenting himself by the addition of people who are being saved. She, then, who has put the veil off from her eyes sees the unspeakable beauty of the Bridegroom with a pure eye and in this way is wounded by the incorporeal and fiery arrow of love, for *agape* when intensified is called love. . . . And this is exactly what the Bride did when she said to the young women: *I am wounded by love.*[107]

That the church's union with Christ is so strong that the church can manifest the beauty of Christ, that it can become so radiant with the beauty of Christ that its beauty, too, may wound, hints at the Christological possibilities for the bride's own transformation. (And, indeed, for Gregory the bride at times is the church, though she more often figures the soul.) To help her maidens know how to find the bridegroom, the bride, advancing in perfection, "leads her virgins to the theophany that came to us through the medium of the

104. Ibid.
105. Ibid., 401, 403.
106. Ibid., 403.
107. Ibid., 403, 405.

flesh."[108] Christ makes the invisible visible by his works. Christ is "revealed through the foundation of the cosmos that is the church," for "the creation of the cosmos signifies the foundation of the church" in which is created a new heavens, a new earth, and a new humanity.[109] The church is therefore deeply important to the visibility of Christ. It makes Christ perceptible to all just as creation makes visible, through analogy, its Creator and fount of its beauty.[110] The beauty of the creation is to the invisible beauty of the Creator as the beauty of the church is to the beauty of Christ. The person who can see this analogy (the young women taught by the bride) can "reach up to the incomprehensible and the infinite" only once she "has first, by faith, laid hands on what has been made visible."[111] Faith is thus responding to the perceptible by recognizing it as an analogy for the imperceptible that may lead the finite creature into the depths of infinity. The bride ("the soul") aims to help her virgins acquire faith by becoming perfect and thus making her beloved known by making his deeds of salvation known; this making-known entails making such deeds manifest by illuminating the unity of the church as a witness to the Bridegroom.[112] The perceptibility of soul, church, and Christ are bound up in a progressive witness: the soul witnesses to Christ and the church, which witnesses to Christ.

The church's dual position here—as witnessing and witnessed to—helps explain why Gregory more often interprets the bride as the soul. For if a bride, the church is also the bridegroom, whose life the bride learns to participate in. Considering the bridegroom's beauty, Gregory points to the bridegroom's dark locks of hair, which symbolize the once dark lives of the apostles before they were transformed into locks "who hang down from the golden Head."[113] "Tossed about by the breeze of the Spirit," these locks

108. Ibid., 405.

109. Ibid., 405, 407.

110. Ibid., 407. Gregory writes, "Well, then, just as the person who looks upon the perceptible cosmos and has grasped the Wisdom that is displayed in the beauty of these beings infers, on the basis of what the eye sees, the invisible Beauty and the wellspring of Wisdom, whose outflow contrived the natural order of what is, so too the person who attends to this new cosmos that appears in the creation of the church sees in it the One who is and is becoming 'all in all' (cf. 1 Cor 15:28) as, by way of the things our nature can take in and comprehend, he directs our knowledge toward that which cannot be contained. . . . [The virgin soul] treats of the church as the one body of the Bridegroom, and by referring to each individual member, she indicates, in her account of his beauty, some one of his attributes and in this way, starting from the particular characteristics she has examined, sums up the beauty of the body as a whole."

111. Gregory of Nyssa, *Homilies on the Song of Songs*, 407.

112. Ibid.

113. Ibid., 415.

enhance the Bridegroom's beauty like a crown on the head.[114] The Spirit makes the apostles the beauty adorning Christ. Though the locks are described as the apostles, the rest of the body is described more generally as the church. The eyes are doves by plentiful waters, which again signify the way the eyes "live by, and walk in, the Spirit."[115] With these Spirit-filled eyes, which do not reflect the deceptive shadows of false fantasies, the church can look upon Being Itself. Further, by "sitting by the pools of waters" (water has by now become an association of both the Holy Spirit and the eyes), "we can restore the proper beauty of the eyes."[116] Nourished by the waters of the Holy Spirit, the eyes "may become beautiful when suited and adapted to the golden Head."[117] God's beauty thus becomes perceptible, legible in the body of the one wounded by love, for such a one manifests God's own body and God's own wounds. Gregory here makes clear that the self's transformation into Bridegroom-disclosing Bride is not (just) a solo encounter between Christ and self but is a journey made possible by this community that can mediate Bride and Bridegroom.

This training into perceiving the beauty of Christ requires not just attending to the wounded and seeing the wounds we have (a description that presumes an eschatological vision of human nature), but we must ourselves be wounded (our non-eschatological human nature must be wounded). This is not a training that solidifies a transcendental subject. It does not gather her up over and against the world—at least, it does not *only* gather her up against the world. For this is a training that punctures her, wounds her so that she might unite with the Wounded One who is bound in Love to the wounded. And this wounding and binding and uniting display how it is that a subject is healed of pathological self-enclosure. They name the painfulness of Love's medicine, the difficulty of claiming the health of love. The models for this subjectivity and for how to acquire it are exemplified, not by the Cappadocian men—even in their hymning of one another—but in the women. Macrina in particular is the model of such selfhood.

A Wounding Healer: Macrina the Virgin, Mother, and Bride

In a letter to John, Gregory distills Macrina's last days into a picture—we might call it an icon—of his dying sister. She is surrounded by a choir of virgins whom she herself has birthed through spiritual labor pains and has

114. Ibid., 415, 417.
115. Ibid., 417.
116. Ibid., 419.
117. Ibid.

guided to perfection with care. Her room resounds with the Psalmodies that fill her house night and day.[118] This linguistic image richly displays Macrina as the transformed and transforming bride in Gregory's homilies. Her bridehood is evoked by her motherhood. Macrina's spiritual children prove their parentage by Psalm-singing, that practice so dear to Macrina and so definitive of the life into which she birthed these daughters. The Macrina of this letter is the virgin mother of virgins, who themselves might also become mothers through their own spiritual labor pains. For Macrina to guide them to perfection is for her to guide them to the threshold of spiritual motherhood. (She has learned what this means from Emmelia: She must be willing to become a daughter.) Macrina has given her life to Christ in her devotion to these women, and they have in turn transformed her into a spiritual mother through their own transformations into Macrina-imitating Christ-imitators. In writing this letter, Gregory does not stand apart from Macrina's disciples. Calling Macrina "a mother in place of our mother," Gregory figures himself as Macrina's spiritual son.[119] Part of the poignancy of Macrina's death, for Gregory, is that it leaves him twice-orphaned: first by his biological parents and then by Macrina, whose corpse mingles with theirs in the family grave.[120]

Macrina's last days recur in Gregory's writings. Her deathbed provides the primary material for the *Life of Macrina*. As we have seen, it gives the setting for the philosophical dialogue *On the Soul and the Resurrection*. It appears as Gregory's word-transcending image in at least this one letter. We might also think of Gregory's homilies on the Song of Songs as an extended meditation on Macrina's last days, those hours when Macrina saw the Bridegroom and desired him ever-more before finally manifesting his beauty in her luminous dead body. In that very early text, *Life of Macrina*, Gregory describes Macrina with her spiritually keen vision perceiving Christ and making Christ perceptible to her community. Now, near the end of his own life, Gregory at last returns to unpack the theological stakes and processes of becoming that make possible such perceptivity and luminosity. How is it one becomes such an ardent bride of Christ?[121]

118. Gregory of Nyssa, "Letter 19," 87–88.

119. Ibid., 88.

120. The opening of the grave is a troubling moment for Gregory in the text of the *Life of Macrina*. Despite his attentive gaze to the body of the dead Macrina and the intimate handling of her body, he recoils from seeing his parents' decaying corpses in the grave, linking it with the sin of Noah's sons gazing at his shame. Before Macrina's body can be united with her parents' (more specifically: with her mother's), a linen cloth is lowered to cover her parents and shield Gregory's eyes.

121. One clue that the *Life of Macrina* and *On the Song of Songs* are linked is found

The training that made Macrina's perception possible, as explained by Gregory's character Macrina, is not an academic one. She groans at the overinfluence of the Stoics and Epicureans on Gregory's thought, though she herself can discourse easily on philosophical issues concerning the nature of the soul.[122] She insists that all philosophies must be disciplined by the norm of Scripture. Her wariness of pagan education was shared by her mother, Emmelia, who worried that the poems and tragic passions of pagan literature—especially the passions of women characters—corrupt the character, providing false models for the kind of person one should become. Nonna, the mother of Nyssen's friend Gregory of Nazianzus, also feared the way certain kinds of pagan education might form her son.[123] In the case of Nonna and Emmelia, we lack specific pictures of what they thought a character corrupted by education might look like. In Macrina's case, however, we have quite a concrete one: her older brother Basil.

Macrina's rebuke of her brother Basil upon his return from Athens is her most famous response to pagan education. In the *Life of Macrina,* Gregory narrates how Basil returned "excessively puffed up by his rhetorical abilities" and besides having a rather high opinion of himself, was also "disdainful of all great reputations," "consider[ing] himself better than the leading men in the district."[124] Macrina's response is to help him become more philosophical by drawing him toward the goal of philosophy, a transformed self. Her medicine was potent. Basil "withdrew from the worldly show" and eschewed acclaim, instead giving himself over (he "went over") to "this life full of labors for one's own hand to perform, providing for himself, through his complete poverty, a mode of living that would, without impediment, lead to virtue."[125]

---

in the figure of Thecla. In the *Life of Macrina,* Gregory gives Thecla as the secret name for Macrina. Not only was Thecla a famous virgin martyr with her own martyr story, she was also a character in Methodius's *Symposium,* where she, like Macrina in the *Life of Macrina,* hymns a prayer to Christ the Bridegroom. Gregory seems to be loosely referencing Methodius's Thecla in the *Life of Macrina.* He is more explicit in his homilies on the Song of Songs. One scholar has detected at least seventeen allusions to Methodius's text. Thecla, the secret (fore-)shadow of Macrina, hovers over that text, too, suggesting that Gregory is reimagining familiar sources. Both the *Life of Macrina* and the *Homilies on the Song of Songs* meditate on the Thecla-shaped existence that Macrina inhabited. Gregory of Nyssa, *In canticum canticorum,* 486.

122. Gregory of Nyssa, *On the Soul and the Resurrection* 1.13 (Silvas, 175); 2, 3 (Silvas, 178–87).

123. For more on Nonna's fears regarding pagan education, see the second chapter of John McGuckin's magisterial biography of Gregory of Nazianzus, *St. Gregory of Nazianzus,* 35–83.

124. Gregory of Nyssa, "Life of Saint Macrina," 167.

125. Ibid., 167–68.

In his article "Manual Labor in the Life and Thought of St. Basil the Great," Andrew Dinan develops the diction of this passage to illuminate its stakes. The "complete poverty" (*teleia aktēmosunē*) suggests radical renunciation—a perfect, complete, and final (*teleios*) non-possessingness (*ktēmata* are possessions).[126] The term *aktēmosunē* is found in no classical Greek text; it shows up for the first time in the second century CE to describe the ascetic life.[127] But more interesting than the phrase "complete poverty" to Dinan is the fact that Basil "went over" to it, for such going over suggests desertion. Puzzling over why Gregory would use a word with such negative connotations, Dinan proposes that the term describes how strange and exceptional Basil's actions must have seemed to his contemporaries, how much they contradicted the condescension to manual labor found in most Greco-Roman literature. And Basil went even further. He responded to Macrina's rebuke with a reorientation of his life. Dinan lists his changes: Basil gave up his career as a rhetor, committed to the church through baptism and ordination as a lector, traveled throughout the ascetic communities of Egypt, distributed his fortune to the poor, and took up an ascetic life along the Iris River for a time.[128]

Considering Basil's later career in which he uses friends and family as pawns against his political opponents, it might seem that Basil's retreat to the river is similar to the move of Silverman's Descartes up to his stove-heated room in hopes of ego-solidifying isolation. But for Basil, precisely what is important about the ascetic life is its renunciation of self-sufficiency, which is "accursed by the Lord."[129] For Basil, manual labor fits beautifully into the ascetic life because it provides communion with God—the giver of tools, land, and bodies—and also with love of neighbor—on whom one depends for support and goods and with whom one shares support and goods. (Such high praise of manual labor, to be sure, flows most freely from the lips of those not compelled to engage in it. Yet however imperfectly, Basil is working on a philosophy—a way of life—that eschews the power of his class.) Thus manual labor is deeply tied with charity for Basil and is part of living into dependence on others for one's very life.[130] This was the life into which Macrina's rebuke inaugurates Basil. Her words wound Basil, puncturing his image of his own independence, and bruising his pride, opening him

---

126. Dinan, "Manual Labor in the Life and Thought of St. Basil the Great," 138.

127. Ibid., 151 n. 26.

128. Ibid., 140. I have further explored the connection between possessing property and epistemic postures in "Possession and Dispossession."

129. Dinan, "Manual Labor," 147.

130. Ibid., 146–47.

up for becoming the kind of self that can give away the wealth and leisure that shored up his self-sufficiency. His self-sufficiency compromised, he can thus live deeper into love of God and neighbor.

How much Macrina teaches the lessons of monastic community to Basil with her words is unknown, but she must have taught him a great deal by her deeds.[131] Not only had Macrina already founded an ascetic community by the time Basil returned from Athens, she also baked bread "with her own hands" (as Gregory writes, almost incredulously), a task normally reserved for slaves—and she ministers to her mother like a maidservant.[132] Before Basil gave away his fortune, Macrina had persuaded Emmelia to repudiate the wealth that constituted an "ostentatious existence" and embrace equality with servants.[133] She took up a life of constant Psalm-chanting, prayer, and work; this is what someone does who sees and loves the bridegroom as the bride loves him. This is the kind of training a person undergoes in order to reach the ascent of ascents to see Beauty Itself and make it manifest that others may follow. And others did follow. In addition to Basil's (seemingly unacknowledged) imitation of her, Gregory claims Macrina's mantel for himself, and with it, that of the transformed Basil. He calls Macrina *didaskalos* (teacher) and insists that the only famous teacher he ever had was Basil.[134] By claiming Basil and Macrina as his pedagogical lineage, Gregory aligns himself with those who help him to see his own dependencies, his over-investment in acclaim, and his self-aggrandizement through learning.[135] The way these siblings check each other, exhort each other, and praise

131. For more on the influence of Macrina (and Naucratius) on Basil's asceticism—and the way Basil elides their influence by pointing instead to Eustathius—see Susanna Elm's important book "*Virgins of God*", especially the third chapter, "In the Background: Macrina and Naucratius," 78–105.

132. With her own hands: ταῖς χερσὶ ταῖς ἰδίαις. Gregory of Nyssa, "Life of Saint Macrina" (Callahan, 167).

133. Gregory of Nyssa, "Life of Saint Macrina," 168.

134. Gregory describes Basil as his only famous teacher in "Letter to Libanius" (154) and addresses Macrina as his teacher in *On the Soul and the Resurrection* and *Life of Macrina*.

135. At one moment in the *Life*, for example, Gregory is complaining about his exile for his *homoousian* commitments. Macrina responds by returning him to the good gifts of others, thereby drawing his heavy heart into the lightness of gratitude. He has received gifts, she reminds him, from God, from his parents, and from churches. She names his blessings before ending her rebuke with a sisterly sting: "Do you not realize the cause of such blessings, namely, that the prayers of your parents are lifting you to the heights, since you have little or nothing within yourself to achieve this?" But Gregory feels no sting; he tastes sweetness. "As she went on this way, I kept wishing that the day might be lengthened so that we could continue to enjoy the sweetness of her words" (Gregory of Nyssa, "Life of Saint Macrina" [Callahan, 178]).

each other renders apparent that we in modernity should see training into becoming the kind of person who can perceive the beautiful as precisely at odds with bourgeois forms of training insofar as these latter forms require and nurture a dependency-renouncing subject, academic pride, and wealth.

Though imperfect, Gregory's commitment to avoiding the temptations of the wealthy and educated—the purple-bordered toga class that is a late ancient analog for the bourgeois—was manifest in the form of his writings.[136] This is true of his homilies, which are explicitly directed toward the broader church, but it is also and fittingly true of the way he first chose to remember Macrina in writing: by writing a *Life*. Averil Cameron describes in *Christianity and the Rhetoric of Empire* how this genre in particular displayed the advantage of Christian literature over pagan literature: by breaking out of traditional, elite forms of writing, Christian literature could appeal to a wider audience and be disseminated to many more people. And *Lives* could especially do this well, appealing to a variety of educational levels and employing techniques across the literary spectrum.[137] Like images of visual art, *Lives* could penetrate both "high" and "low" literature.[138] Cameron highlights additional ways Gregory broke the mold of the traditional elite in his *Life of Macrina*: by choosing a woman as his subject and portraying her as, in direct contrast to Basil, explicitly disavowing any educational training.[139]

Gregory's literary form in the *Life of Macrina*, then, keeps faith with his desire to ground the self in dependence, humility, and love. Read together with Gregory's homiletic meditations on woundedness, Gregory's accounts of Macrina help us to find a different interpretation of the Orpheus myth than Silverman or the dominant Christian tradition provide. Macrina helps us to see that if we are to read the Orpheus myth as a story of human subjectivity—a story about what has gone wrong and what must be healed—then to read Orpheus as a type of Christ misinterprets the human condition. Christ is found, not in Orpheus the immortal conqueror who marches alone out of Hades, but in Eurydice. Yet Christ is not the Eurydice who needs rescue from death. Christ is the Eurydice who is left behind.

136. Proof of the way Gregory's education and social class distinguish him lies in the very language in which he writes. Of Cappadocians, Pseudo-Lucian once said that it was as difficult to teach a tortoise to fly as to teach a Cappadocian to speak Greek. In his book on Gregory of Nyssa, Anthony Meredith takes this as an indication of the "boorish" reputation Cappadocians have. I hope that with the smattering of Greek I have invoked—and even in translation—it is obvious that Gregory's writing is anything but boorish. Even when simple and accessible, his texts are eloquent.

137. Cameron, *Christianity and the Rhetoric of Empire*, 147.

138. For more on *Lives* as visual art, images, and as penetrating high and low art, see, respectively, Cameron, *Christianity*, 151, 57, 103.

139. Ibid., 149, 158.

For Christ is always the one we leave behind, the one who asks us to keep watch with him in Gesthemene, while we succumb to sleep. When we leave behind our neighbor, our lover (our closest neighbor), our hungry, we leave behind Christ.

To locate Christ in Eurydice is to transform the possibilities and demands of healing. That we are estranged, not from a memory, but from one who lives, means that we need reconciliation to happen outside of (in addition to) a thought sequence or a role-play. And it also means that we *can* reconcile outside our mental theater. We unite with Christ, not by re-performing a mental journey nor unraveling estrangement with an imaginary hug, but in clasping Christ, which is to say, our hungry, our naked, our poor, our enemy, our neighbor, "tightly in our loving arms." We hold Christ when we hold the body of the poor. This is the redemptive act that Christ enables and in which Christ invites us to participate. Estranged flesh cannot be reconciled in the mind; it must be reconciled flesh to flesh. This is the possibility and demand of reconciliation to one who lives outside our memories.

Though Gregory and Silverman draw from similar images of a self that is love- and other-constituted, they diverge over how they ground reconciliation. Where Silverman anchors the possibilities of kinship primarily in finitude ("the most capacious and enabling of the attributes we share with others"[140]), Gregory grounds such possibility in Christ. Silverman sees danger in the way we often ascribe finitude to others and deny it in ourselves, which has "devastating and often fatal consequences for others."[141] The way to avoid such devastation is to celebrate the finitude that rhymes through all beings, including ourselves. But it is tricky business to laud finitude without enthroning death. One of the ways Silverman prevents such enthronement is by her hope for the shadowy resurrection Andreas-Salomé describes in the analyst's chair (and which Silverman later locates, by extension, in encounters with art objects). Silverman draws on Andreas-Salomé to retell the tale of Adam and Eve, redescribing sin as a "turning away from the Other."[142] Andreas-Salomé tells the solution: "No redeemer can absolve us of this guilt. If we want to liberate ourselves from it, we must turn back to those we have left behind, and tarry with them. Doing so will not make us immortal, but it will permit those who have 'vanished' due to our neglect to 'arise anew.'"[143] (Andreas-Salomé's redeemer is the analyst, who becomes

140. Silverman, *Flesh of My Flesh*, 4.
141. Ibid.
142. Ibid., 42.
143. Ibid., 42–43.

Silverman's Christ-figure. There is a confusion here about language, about when Silverman is literal and when she is metaphorical.) What Silverman wants to narrate here is a "grounding assumption of psychoanalysis 'proper'" that re-remembering the past changes more than our recollection; it makes that past happen again in a new way.[144] What Gregory gives is a vision of redemption that, without fully displacing Silverman's, resonates with it and deepens it. Gregory's conception of redemption enables us to retain the significance Silverman places on remembering the past so as to make it happen anew and the importance of tarrying with the one we have left behind.

Unlike Silverman's, Gregory's redemption is anchored not only (nor primarily) in shared finitude with the creature left behind, but also in the shared grounding of their being in the one who is infinite—Gregory means something like this in his discussions of the "image of God" discussed in the last chapter—and in the shared becoming in Christ, the one who joins infinite to finite, Creator to creature. The multiple levels of analogy/kinship enable multiple levels of reconciliation. This, in turn, enables us to admit the limits of reconciliation in an analyst's chair and to manifest the importance—indeed, the necessity—of reconciliation for our creaturely becoming, which for Christians is a becoming that moves toward unity with Christ. So here we can gaze at the full reality of death by not insisting on reconciling ourselves to and by a shadowy resurrection. The reconciliation that may begin in an analyst's chair does not terminate in acceptance of death and reincorporation of the lost one into the psyche; it looks for its consummation in a bodily resurrection, where body can embrace body. And this is a reconciliation that *must* occur if we are to become one with Christ. So to ground reconciliation in Christ rather than finitude is both to look for multiple levels of damage and to hope for a reconciliation that can be complete because it is not just that we can be reconciled to the other by reincorporating her into our memory but that the other, in the fullness of her own memories and in her very body, can be reconciled to us—and reconciled in the body, regardless of separation by distance or death. Because of Christ, there are possibilities for a reconciliation that our finitude would thwart.

So far I have suggested two lines of thought regarding Gregory's reconciliation, one of which insists on the irreducible singularity of the estranged other (it is *that person* and *that body*, not our memory of it, that a consummated reconciliation requires), while the other obscures it (the Christ estranged in the other is present in the hungry and the neighbor and the enemy and so on). These are not two competing or alternative visions of

144. Ibid., 42.

reconciliation; reconciliation requires both views. These two ways of seeing reconciliation speak, first, to the multiple levels of kinship we share with one another as creatures. They point, second, to the way that the Christian analogy of non-divine (especially human) and divine ought not, as Silverman feared, posit the latter realm over and against the former.[145] To be sure, the analogy might not be as "equalizing and ontologically reversible" as Silverman wishes, but the taking up of not-God into God in Christ displays these two realms, not as closed and separated, but as forever opened onto each other. Indeed, it is precisely such opening that Gregory wants us to live into with his doctrine of the spiritual senses, which takes us back to the issue at hand: the kind of self that perceives beauty.

Spiritual Senses for Spiritual Bodies

In relation to so abstract a term as human nature, *wound* itself becomes abstract. The bride's wound cannot be touched or kissed or bandaged—not by the reader, at least. What does such woundedness mean for a person's body? Does it simply evaporate into another etherealized description of beauty and love? While the wound is not physical, if it is utterly spiritualized, then for Gregory, it is lost. It cannot do the work he wants it to do: describe the relation between the physical and spiritual selves. Gregory's wound is an opening, a place where penetration creates permeability that previously did not exist. It is such puncturing that enables us to live into the openness of the physical realm to the spiritual, the non-eschatological to the eschatological, the human to the divine. Through it, we can find rhymes with Christ, and Christ's rhymes with us. The way wound works as an opening is particularly vivid in Gregory's doctrine of the spiritual senses, for the spiritual senses perform this opening of the physical senses.

The *Homilies on the Song of Songs* is the primary text for Gregory's thoughts on the spiritual senses, but he begins developing them in a much earlier text, *On the Soul and the Resurrection*. The character Macrina explains how they work. Macrina describes the spiritual senses in that dialogue as inhering in and making meaningful the work done by the physical senses. She offers the example of a physician, who by her own senses discerns bodily conditions. Such diagnosing would be impossible "if there were not

---

145. As Gregory writes in his homilies on the Song of Songs: "Perhaps those powers marveled at what is invisible and incomprehensible to all beings because they discerned the beauty of the Bridegroom by the agency of the Bride" (Gregory of Nyssa, *Homilies on the Song of Songs*, 269).

a certain intellectual power present to each of the organs of sense."[146] She quotes Epicharmus, who says the "mind sees and the mind hears" to explain how spiritual senses inhabit physical senses to lead from tactile knowledge to knowledge of the subject itself.[147] There *must* be something that makes the data of the physical senses convertible to intellectual knowledge:

> Do you not see what the sense of sight teaches you? Yet it would never have provided such insight by itself, if there were not something gazing through the eyes and using the data of the senses as guides of a kind to penetrate from what appears to what does not appear. . . . There is an intellectual substance deeply seated in our nature.[148]

A few exchanges later, Gregory summarizes Macrina's definition of the soul as an intellectual substance that endows the organizing body with life-giving power ordered to the activity of the senses.[149] The spiritual senses, as it were, animate, give life to the physical senses. Gregory seems here to understand spiritual senses as opposed to physical senses and to be operating along a Plotinian divide between the material and spiritual realms, between body and soul.[150] Each physical sense corresponds to a spiritual sense that makes it meaningful to the soul. In the much later text of the *Homilies on the Song of Songs*, the spiritual senses have been reconfigured along a different opposition: that of eschatological and non-eschatological. While I want to build on the second opposition to transform the first, I also want to consider carefully the architecture of the first, which is transfigured without being wholly overturned.[151]

In his later texts, Gregory still affirms the divide of material and spiritual found in *On the Soul and the Resurrection*. Near the beginning of the sixth homily, he writes, "On the one hand, there is that which is perceptible and material; on the other, that which is intelligible and nonmaterial."[152] Yet the meaning is transformed. He goes on, "[W]e reckon something to

146. Gregory of Nyssa, *On the Soul and the Resurrection*, 246.

147. Ibid., 179.

148. Ibid., 180–81.

149. Ibid., 188.

150. I say Plotinian rather than a more generally Platonic divide because it seems to pick up on the way, for Plotinus, the soul provided the animating principle for the body; it was the life coursing through what would otherwise be a corpse. For more on body and soul in Plotinus, see Miles, *Plotinus on Body and Beauty*, or the chapter titled "Love" in Hadot, *Plotinus*.

151. For an excellent account of Gregory's inconsistencies in these two texts, see Coakley, "Gregory of Nyssa."

152. Gregory of Nyssa, *Homilies on the Song of Songs*, 185.

fall into the category of the perceptible to the extent that it is grasped by sense perception, but we reckon as intelligible that which falls beyond the observation of the senses. Of these two, the intelligible has neither limit nor bound, while the other is entirely contained by particular limits."[153] Where Gregory spoke of the intelligible as that which makes the sensible meaningful in *On the Soul and the Resurrection,* here he writes of the sensible having its own comprehensibility—a comprehensibility proper to sensation—while the intelligible is precisely that which transcends such comprehensibility. Gregory further complicates the significance of the sensible/intelligible distinction by identifying classes within the intelligible realm. He divides the intelligible nature into uncreated (eternal, self-identical, incapable of diminishment) and created (becoming, capable of growth and change).[154] While the difference between the sensible and intelligible realms is the difference between constrained and unconstrained, limited and limitless, the difference within the intelligible realm is the difference between limitless becoming (creature) and limitless being (Creator). The three categories we have, then, are: limited becoming (sensible), limitless becoming (created spiritual), and limitless being (uncreated spiritual). The physical senses belong to the first category, the spiritual senses to the second, and the Christ these senses learn to open onto the third. To put it another way: God woos us to the divine reality of the third category by opening up our spiritual senses in the second category through appealing to and training the physical senses of the first. The shift from understanding spirituality in opposition to materiality to understanding spirituality as creaturely divinity, opposed both to Creator divinity and to creature un-divinity, is important for what is to come. For if Christ is the first-fruits of the resurrection that will consummate a person's spiritual self, then a spiritual self cannot exclude eating, touching, and being touched—though neither can it exclude walking through walls, appearing, and disappearing.

God's wooing is thematized in Gregory's incarnational apple tree of his fourth homily. There God takes on the wood of human nature, including the material side overgrown with the passions. Reading this passage together with Psalm 103:20 about beasts emerging from holes and laying waste in the thicket, Gregory describes the wood as a place where destructive beasts hide in dens and come out in darkness to destroy the beauty of human nature in their animal feeding. Gregory goes on to explain that the apple tree grows in a thicket, and that the men who are trees in the thicket are enemies of the Bridegroom, but by their fellowship with the fruit, God transforms them

153. Ibid.
154. Ibid., 185, 187.

into sons of light. On the one hand, in allegorizing the wood and the apple tree, Gregory displaces their physicality and the role of our sense perception. However, he allegorizes the tree precisely to describe the importance of sense perception. What we learn from Gregory is that though there is some training required to appreciate the taste for Christ, Christ also appeals to the physical senses, which he transforms with the soul's sense. Through our perceiving and eating Christ, Christ redeems the senses, turning dangers into friends.

So the physicality of the Incarnation affirms the importance of the physical senses in opening the spiritual senses, but to the extent that the Song of Songs often describes Christ's interior workings to the soul abstracted from the full reality of human nature, the physical senses often serve simply as metaphors for the spiritual senses. Gregory claims "a certain analogy between the sense organs of the body and the operations of the soul," which he uses to interpret particular senses on milk, honey, perfumes, and touch.[155] Even as the physical senses are allegorized—taste as discernment, touch as comprehension or grasping—they remain bound to the body through the processes of transformation in which they participate. This is particularly evident in the case of smell, the most frequently described sense in the text after sight.[156] The one who "inhales" the death of Christ "becomes sweet-smelling because he has become full of the fragrant Spirit,"[157] much like Paul, drawn to the Bridegroom by the nard, "captur[es] within himself the scent of that transcendent and unapproachable Grace and provid[es]

155. "We also learn, in an incidental way, another truth through the philosophical wisdom of this book, that there is in us a dual activity of perception, the one bodily, the other more divine. . . . For there is a certain analogy between the sense organs of the body and the operations of the soul. And it is this that we learn from the words before us. For both wine and milk are discerned by the sense of taste, but when they are intelligible things, the power of the soul that grasps them is an intellectual power. And a kiss comes about through the sense of touch, for in a kiss lips touch each other. There is also, though, a 'touch' that belongs to the soul, one that makes contact with the Word and is actuated by an incorporeal and intelligible touching, just as someone said, 'Our hands have touched concerning the Word of life' (1 John 1:1). In the same way, too, the scent of the divine perfumes is not a scent in the nostrils but pertains to a certain intelligible and immaterial faculty that inhales the sweet smell of Christ by sucking in the Spirit" (*Homilies on the Song of Songs*, 37).

156. The senses often, in fact, appear intertwined, as in this description of smell with sight and touch: "And when she has approached the object of her desire more closely, but before his beauty is manifest to her eyes, she touches the one she seeks through her sense of smell, as if by her power of smell she recognized the distinctive quality of some color, and she says that she recognizes his fragrance by means of the sweetness of a perfume whose name is spikenard—saying to the friends of the Bridegroom, My spikenard gave off his scent" (Gregory of Nyssa, *Homilies on the Song of Songs*, 97, 99).

157. Gregory of Nyssa, *Homilies on the Song of Songs*, 203.

himself for others to have a part in according to their ability, as though he were an incense."[158] The bride's response of inhaling the nard in turn makes her a scent to others, who must learn how properly to inhale and thus perceive the bride. In discerning the bride, they, too, will make themselves discernible as little christs. In this way, smelling Christians participate in the Incarnation. As Gregory writes, "For the goal of the whole life of virtue is participation in God, and it is Deity that frankincense signifies."[159] And this scent, in turn, manifests the beauty of God, for "after [the soul's] fragrance has become similar to that of frankincense, she becomes a garden after the likeness of the paradise." Later she is a fountain and finally "has been made like to the archetypal Beauty."[160] The spiritual senses are not just about perceiving Christ, then, but about making oneself perceptible as Christ. The former is impossible apart from the latter.

But a relationship between the physical and the spiritual senses that exists beyond an analogical one is suggested by the scriptural accounts of encounters with the resurrected Christ. Sarah Coakley has noted that these accounts should compel the reader to consider what it means that recognition happens, not immediately, but through a process of transformation (of "turning"). The spiritual senses, she argues, give the reader a way to account for this transformation.[161] The spiritual senses also give the reader a way of taking seriously that the recognition happens in a physical encounter of Christ, through a physical sense, as it were, awakening. Mary sees Jesus only as gardener, even when he speaks to her, but she recognizes him when she hears him call her name, "Mary!" (John 20:10–18). Thomas recognizes Jesus only in touching him (or perhaps being invited to touch him) (John 20:24–28). The disciples recognize Jesus, as the liturgy reminds us, in the breaking of the bread—not the theological discourse on the road to Emmaus (Luke 24:13–35). In John's account, they recognize him in the catching of the fish (John 21:1–11).

Christians today do not have the same access to the resurrected Christ that Mary Magdalene or Thomas Didymus or Simon Peter had, for after Jesus's resurrection appearances, he ascended. The Nicene Creed promises a Christ who will come again in glory, so the Christ who comes to us will be both resurrected and glorified. All who see this Christ, according to the Philippians hymn, will echo Thomas's exclamation of Christ's lordship. We will see what Thomas saw in that moment, what Mary perceived in her turning.

158. Ibid., 101.
159. Ibid., 295.
160. Ibid., 309.
161. Coakley, "Resurrection and the 'Spiritual Senses,'" 132.

To the extent that we can see Christ like that now, we live into our eschatological selves that perceive the glory of Christ, the God called Love who will be all in all. The spiritual senses are about how we live into that reality, how we begin to transform into our eschatological selves. It is something we will never finally achieve, for even in their union with Christ, creatures can never achieve God—this is the meaning of Gregory's epectasy. The infinite love of God can only be everlastingly journeyed through, and that journey can begin, for Gregory, here on earth, with the opening of the spiritual senses. But we will remain at an additional remove from our eschatological selves until the resurrection. Our senses will gain greater perceptive capacity once they have died.

To say the spiritual senses describe how we inhabit our eschatologically promised spiritual bodies is to say: they describe the divinization of a human. To describe a human acquiring and developing these spiritual senses is to describe the Holy Spirit's deification of her. The meaning of spiritual senses most consistent with Gregory's theological commitments of epectasy and a God who will be all in all is senses that are spiritual, not because they are opposed to the sensible, but because they are given by the Spirit. The relationship of the spiritual senses to the physical senses, then, is the relation of the divine to the human, which is given a spark of divinity in its creation and will realize that divinity in its eschatological consummation. That is one way of describing why the human and divine realms remain open to one another.

I have not yet given a full accounting of the relation of the spiritual senses to the physical senses. Most of my description of how they relate on this side of the eschaton develops their relationship as analogical, though in locating physical senses and spiritual senses in the process of divinization, I have affirmed that they must have a relationship that is more than analogical. The reason why analogy seems so central to their relationship at this point is because I discuss them here in relation to Christ's absence and the way we must learn to live into Christ's promised presence, Christ's glorified presence. But Christ's presence is not only a presence for which we wait. I have discussed some ways that Christ has physical presence on earth: in the neighbor, the hungry, the enemy, the naked, the saint. The fullness of Christ's presence is found here and now, for Gregory, in the church—the only entity, institution, or person who *becomes* the Bridegroom. The church extends Christ's Incarnation, performing the soul-sweetening activities of the apple tree. In the church, the spiritual senses remember their need for the physical senses, and the spiritual finds its anchor in the physical.

The Other Bridegroom

In order to explore the awakening of the spiritual senses in the church, I want to return to Marion's treatment of Orpheus and Eurydice. The myth appears in his essay, "The Intentionality of Love," as a way of exploring the paradox of love. This paradox names the way that my love for the other is always love for my lived experience of the other.[162] Love in this Kantian age thus always turns out to be a permutation of self-love: Orpheus loves his own ego, his own projection of Eurydice. Otherness as otherness remains inaccessible—I have only my other, the other I can know, the other as expression of me. This other is the other who is knowable by, visible to, perceptible by me. Marion criticizes Kant for his prioritization of visible over invisible, known over unknown, and so to save us from entrapment in the swollen Kantian ego, Marion reverses the prioritization. We must learn to prioritize the *in*visible, the *un*known. The reason why the lover cannot escape his ego, why the beloved disappears for the lover, why Eurydice disappears from Orpheus, is because he wants to make her visible, to reduce her to the seen and thus to relegate her to the realm of objecthood. Only objects, Marion tells us, are seen.[163] Eurydice will be Orpheus's beloved only as long as he renounces mastery over the visible and allows himself to be seen by a gaze he cannot himself see.[164]

The contrast between the grasping love of Orpheus for Eurydice and the love that allows itself to be swallowed by the beloved's unseen gaze is also the contrast between the idol and the icon. In the idol, the beholder sees the reification of her own desire, while the icon yields another with such radical otherness her excess appears as an absence. Steeped in the mystical theology of Pseudo-Dionysius, who himself draws from Gregory of Nyssa, Marion names such excessive absence "bedazzlement" that is produced by that which cannot be born or absorbed: the "saturated phenomenon."[165] Marion describes in "Evidence and Bedazzlement" the phenomenology of bedazzlement:

> As when confronted with the obscene . . . , the divine, and above all the *kenosis of the Son*, our gaze cannot remain fixed; it blinks and closes. It finds too much to see there, too much to envisage and look at squarely, and, thus, too much to interpret and to allow to interpret us, and so it flees; our furtive gaze turns away

162. Marion, "Intentionality of Love," in *Prolegomena to Charity*, 75–77.

163. Ibid., 80–81.

164. Ibid., 82.

165. Marion, "Evidence and Bedazzlement," in *Prolegomena to Charity*, 67.

from and deserts the visible whose effrontery threatens us. In
short, our gaze deserts, and closes.[166]

The gaze that blinks without seeing is Marion's way of accounting for the resurrection appearance at Emmaus. He writes that "the invisibility at Emmaus
did not hide the body of Christ" but rather "gave it perfectly."[167] So fully did
Christ give Christself that the perceptive capacities of the disciples could not
attain that vision of Christ. Only a creation made new by the Spirit can behold the resurrected Christ; a transcendent, self-making subject cannot. In a
recent work applying Marion's analysis of the saturated phenomenon to the
resurrection of Christ, Brian Robinette writes something very much along
these lines when he describes encounters such as the one at Emmaus as
initiating a conversion process into a new way of perceiving—a perception
that derives from a Christ-constituted rather than self-constituted self and
is itself a response to Love.[168] He turns to Marion's "Evidence and Bedazzlement" to describe the way the subject must be constituted, not by self, but by
love. There Marion writes, "In effect, if what reveals itself is always summed
up in Love, then only the gaze that believes, and thus only the will that loves
can welcome it. Thus only the conversion of the gaze can render the eye apt
to recognize the blinding evidence of love in what bedazzles it."[169]

One way to think about what follows, then, is to consider Love's conversion of the gaze to behold love. What does it mean to think about the
church as the place where we are trained to be the kind of subjects that learn
to accommodate the Excessive One? What does it mean, that is, to name the
church as the place where the spiritual senses are stretched and awakened?
But I want to add another question, too: What does it mean to think about
the church as the place where the resurrected Christ continually self-offers,
continually appears? These questions must be held together for, ultimately,
there is no preparation for Christ except Christ. The only way to learn to
perceive the resurrected Christ is to perceive the resurrected Christ. Only
love can see love. As Marion writes, "Only love, 'which bears all' (I Cor
13:7), can bear with its gaze Love's excess. In proportion to our love, our
gaze can open, be it only by blinking, to the evidence of Love. In this proportion also, bedazzlements can become evidence."[170] To become the love
that can bear all and see Love is another way to name wounding by love and
point toward the deification of the human. To bear Love's excess as love is

166. Ibid.

167. Marion, "Gift of a Presence," in *Prolegomena to Charity*, 136–37.

168. Robinette, *Grammars of Resurrection*, 97.

169. Marion, "Evidence and Bedazzlement," in *Prolegomena to Charity*, 66.

170. Ibid., 67.

to transform into our spiritual selves—our eschatological selves—and so to live into our spiritual senses.

I want to texture Marion's dazzling saturated phenomena by reflecting—through Gregory's descriptions—on liturgical activities as saturated phenomena. What I want is not a rigorous application of Marion's category but a way of reflecting on how the Spirit works on the physical senses through the church as a way of awakening the spiritual senses. The hope is that Gregory's spiritual senses can ease anxieties like Caputo's that the saturated phenomenon, despite Marion's assertions to the contrary, aligns faith with visibility.[171] By insisting on the centrality of the church and ecclesial activities to perceiving Christ, Gregory de-thrones the centrality of sight (both as sense and as metaphor for knowledge) in grasping Christ. The self accesses the Christ who is Beauty and Love, not just in dazzling darkness, but in cleansing waters and lyrical Psalms. In contrast, then, to most of the Western tradition, Gregory identifies beauty, not just with sight, nor even with the reduced sensorium of sight and sound, but with the entirety of the senses.[172] Not only do these multi-sensory descriptions provide us with ways of valuing the body's role in conversion, they also help us to see conversion, while sometimes involving Damascus-like blinding light, as often much more gentle and complex. The Spirit's training of the spiritual senses in the church also helps us meditate on what it means that Gregory sometimes refers to the church as the Bridegroom. Finally and perhaps most counter-intuitively, by understanding the Spirit as working in the church through gentle, body-affirming conversions, we can make better sense of the resurrection narratives, even though these narratives are not themselves set in a church.

171. Gregory is not the only theologian who could ease such an anxiety, nor is he the richest on the sacraments. I want to follow his thought to trace out how the sacraments fit into his vision of the spiritual senses and the wounded self, but other theologians work out complex relationships between the visible and the invisible in the sacraments. In particular, Hugh of St. Victor writes about how the sacraments visibly represent the invisible good humanity lost so that humans might through the species of the visible reach out to the invisible. He also writes about the complex intertwining of visible and invisible in terms of the sacraments disciplining the body as a way of leading the soul into sanctity. For more of Hugh of St. Victor's theology of the sacraments, see *De sacramentis*.

172. Gregory discusses beauty in relation to each of the five senses in his eighth homily on Ecclesiastes, though the context is his worry that our habituation to sensory beauty trains us to love that beauty in place of heavenly beauty. His concern resonates with that of Augustine in the *Confessions*, which presents a similarly multisensory yet double-edged description of beauty. Gregory of Nyssa, *Homilies on Ecclesiastes*, homily eight (Hall, 130).

Touching the Baptismal Waters

In her book on the history of the olfactory senses in late ancient Christianity, Susan Ashbrook Harvey avers that liturgy and ascetic practices "reformed and remade" the Christian body.[173] Baptism, it turns out, is critical to such refashioning. It begins the transformation. Fittingly for the sacrament that initiates a person's participation in the death and resurrection of Christ, baptism also awakens the senses of the resurrected self. In so doing, baptism unlocks the God-yielding knowledge within the created order. Harvey describes the way the human body sanctified through baptism became, for many late ancient Christians, capable of perceiving knowledge of God in creation through its own physicality.[174] For these writers, baptism makes God perceptible in creation because it discloses the beauty of creation.[175] The way the senses disclose the beauty of God in creation is through the enjoyment of creation. On this point Harvey refers to Gregory's *On the Making of the Human*, where he argues that it is through the activity of the senses that God renders the pleasures of life accessible in creation. She extrapolates that the purpose of the senses was that humans might experience the goodness and beauty of God's creation.[176] God created the senses that we might know God in creation and that this knowledge might take the form of enjoyment. This is not an enjoyment that wallows, though, for no moment of perception can exhaust the beauty of God. Several pages prior, Harvey quotes Gregory's insistence in his first homily on the Song of Songs that though the beauty grasped is great, greater still is the beauty that exceeds the grasp.[177] The spiritual senses would not perceive rightly if they did not also perceive their limits.

The rite of baptism inaugurates this perception the same way kingship begins, or preparation for death: with anointing by oil. Harvey describes such anointing as attuning the senses to the divine,[178] but it must be more than that. For Gregory, oil signifies the Holy Spirit, so anointing the body with oil for baptism anoints the body also with the Spirit.[179] Though Gregory

173. Harvey, *Scenting Salvation*, 5.

174. Ibid., 61.

175. As Harvey writes, "Late antique Christians delighted in the beauty of a created order they understood to be revelatory of its Maker. It was a beauty available to them because their senses had been opened to this presence and trained to perceive its teaching. Baptism fashioned the body anew; liturgy guided its experience" (ibid., 83).

176. Ibid., 111–12.

177. Ibid., 83.

178. Ibid., 71.

179. Gregory of Nyssa, "On the Holy Spirit."

does not elaborate the anointing with oil in baptism as a figure of the Holy Spirit, he does invoke oil's nearness to the body as a way of describing the Holy Spirit's nearness to Christ. As the body's surface is so intimate with the oil that to touch the body, one must first touch the oil, so the Holy Spirit is so intimate with the Son, that "to touch the Son by faith" one must first encounter the Holy Spirit.[180] Scholars have debated whether Gregory's words also describe baptismal practices in Cappadocia; it seems clear, at least, that there is a close textual relationship between oil and the Spirit. This relationship, in turn, translates into the Spirit initiating the baptized into Spirit-enabled perception of the divine. And this perception comes through being made like Christ. Gregory describes in his *Address on Religious Instruction* how we imitate Christ's death and resurrection, being buried with water instead of earth and being immersed three separate times in imitation of the three days Christ was under earth.[181] As the baptized comes "safely" into contact with water, so Christ can safely touch death.[182] But there is also a difference. While Christ's nature is not changed by death, the water-death of the baptized reunifies and purifies her dissolute nature that she may be like Christ. That is, her baptism is a death, but it is also a purification that Christ did not need. Baptism does to the initiate's entire self what water does to her body: It cleanses her.[183] At this point, the baptized self is still not, Gregory cautions, "an exact imitation at every point" of Christ. "It receives now only as much as it is able to. The rest is stored for the future."[184] But in baptism, the "stain of sin" is washed away, and as it is washed away, the baptized attains a "freedom from passion," a purity, and presumably it is this freedom that enables the senses to perceive more truly. By the water that washes the body, so is the soul washed of its stains and cleansed of its slavery to passion.

Gregory describes baptism in his twelfth homily on the Song of Songs as removing the veil of flesh, opening a way for the spouse by being buried with him in the death of baptism.[185] Through baptism, we are initiated into

180. "For as between the body's surface and the liquid of the oil, nothing intervening can be detected, either in reason or in perception, so inseparable is the union of the Spirit with the Son; and the result is that whosoever is to touch the Son by faith must needs first encounter the oil in the very act of touching; there is not a part of him devoid of the Holy Spirit. Therefore belief in the Lordship of the Son arises in those who entertain it, by means of the Holy Ghost; on all sides the Holy Ghost is met by those who by faith approach the Son" (Gregory of Nyssa, "On the Holy Spirit," 321; quoted in Harvey, *Scenting Salvation*, 121).

181. Gregory of Nyssa, "Address on Religious Instruction" sec. 35, 315.

182. Ibid., sec. 35, 316.

183. Ibid., sec. 35, 317.

184. Ibid., sec. 35, 316.

185. Gregory of Nyssa, *Homilies on the Song of Songs*, 363.

life on the ship Gregory described in the homily's opening. The atomization and individualization that language of spiritual senses suggests for the process of learning to see beauty is here counter-balanced by a more corporate image. In the ship we learn to pray for the Holy Spirit's breath on the sail, to receive this power, and to submit to the pilot of the text who begins to guide the ship only once the Holy Spirit has breathed onto it. Having been buried into the waters of death, we now sail on top of the waters of divine knowledge, not (just) as individuals becoming spiritually keen by solo trips through texts and prayers but as members of a crew. It is as a member of this crew that one's journey continues.

Smelling Holy Oils and Incense

Gregory's account of baptism does not offer a phenomenology of touch, but it is clear that the Spirit rests on and transforms the sensory capacities of the body. Baptism does not, however, complete this transformation. Baptism refashions the human to provide the conditions for her becoming that the liturgy will continue to effect. Harvey describes the liturgy as "ritually transform[ing] the human condition and location, bringing the faithful to stand, redeemed in the presence of God."[186] The paradigm for such liturgical transformation was Mary's conception of Christ through her encounter with the Holy Spirit.[187] As the Holy Spirit's overshadowing Mary's womb turned her into a vessel of holiness, so, too, a person's liturgical encounters with the divine were supposed to make her a Christ-bearer. One way liturgy transformed a person was by reframing and reinterpreting ordinary events and activities of everyday life.

Olfactory imagery was particularly important for this type of transformation, in no small part because of the prevalence of perfume, nard, and sweet scents in the Song of Songs.[188] Such imagery was re-enacted in liturgical scents, thus linking scriptural images with liturgical actions and also ascetic practices, enabling a person to live into the scriptural story of transformation.[189] Inasmuch as liturgical rituals and ascetic practices were performed in the context of the liturgical smells, olfactory imagery "anchored those activities of the ritual life of the wider Christian community by providing consistent referencing to the incense and (holy) perfume."[190]

186. Harvey, *Scenting Salvation*, 63.
187. Ibid.
188. Ibid., 124.
189. Ibid., 167.
190. Ibid., 169.

Harvey turns to Gregory of Nyssa, who provides an image for how this sensory training works in *On the Soul and the Resurrection*:

> Gregory of Nyssa had warned that sensory experience "nailed" the soul to the material world in a detrimental and limiting way. But olfactory imagery similarly "nailed" the practicing ascetic to the liturgical life of the church, thus framing ascetic activity, even at its most severe, by setting it definitively within the church's sacramental life.[191]

Sensory experience has the power to consolidate the loves of the soul into a glue (or a nail) that fixes it in a certain context. Gregory of Nyssa worries about that context being the material world; yet, Harvey points out the double-edgedness of that worry: The context could also be sacramental. We have seen again and again how Gregory exploits the power of the sensory—in rhetoric, for example, or the incarnational apple tree—in order to open the soul rightly to the divine. The scents that permeate ascetic and liturgical practices, by linking the practices to scriptural imagery, also open the Christian to knowledge of the eschatologically glorified God. "Holy smells," Harvey writes, "elicited in the believer a promise of the life to come."[192] They were a kind of pedagogy that developed Christian understandings of and expectations for the final resurrection.[193]

It is not just that the sensory opens the way for God and is subsequently supplanted by the intellectual. Following a path opened by Verna Harrison and Mariette Canévet, Harvey argues that Gregory's olfactory imagery in the Song of Songs highlights the limits of the intellectual. Harvey writes that Gregory "seems to deliberately engage a bodily participation as essential to any genuine experience of God," but though the body can participate in experiencing God, there is trouble when a person tries to communicate or understand either God or that experience.[194] It seems the body can participate in God in a way that the mind *qua* rationality cannot. And the importance

191. Ibid. She references Gregory's eighth homily on the Beatitudes.

192. Harvey, *Scenting Salvation*, 229.

193. Harvey writes, "Sense perception and bodily sensation could and did cross the boundaries of the spaces, times, and domains that separated human and divine lives, or present and future dispensations. Hence, ancient Christianity shaped its understanding of the end of time and the final resurrection through a constant referencing of bodily sensory experience as the guide for how and what to experience in the life to come. Christian olfactory piety had as its telos the cultivation of revelatory expectation" (ibid.).

194. Ibid., 175.

of the body shows up in the text. Harvey reminds us that the text (Gregory's and Scripture) is unavoidably indexed to bodily sensation.[195]

For Gregory, "scent" carries a special theological significance that describes human transformation into the divine. To perceive a scent is to inhale it, and in availing oneself of the holy smell, one also avails herself of the Holy Spirit. The inhalation of the scent resonates with receiving the breath of the Spirit and, in fact, the former gives a lesson in the latter. To breathe in the incense of the liturgy is to train one's body to draw "in the good odor of Christ by an inhalation of the Spirit."[196] Holy scents both represent the Spirit-saturation of the liturgy and attune a person to the possibilities of transformation by the Spirit. They heighten one's perceptive capacities, preparing the supplicant for the moment those capacities will be wholly thwarted.

Tasting the Flesh of Christ

The Eucharist is a mysterious moment in the liturgy. While holy incense might teach a person to smell the Holy Spirit's presence in her liturgical transformation, the Eucharist offers no such lesson. It is the divine Christ offered up for the most intimate bodily mingling, yet the host tastes stubbornly ordinary. To the sinner and saint alike, the bread and wine of the Eucharist taste like bread and wine. The perceptive capacities of the communicant are limited in the Eucharist because no matter how trained they are, the senses cannot penetrate beyond or beneath the bread-ness. For Gregory, that is because there is no "beyond" the bread-ness. In a famous passage in his *Address on Religious Instruction*, Gregory identifies two ways that a person can unite with Christ, corresponding to the soul and the body. The soul shares in the life of Christ through faith, but the body requires a different kind of union with God.[197] Having drunk the poison of sin that dissolves human nature, the body needs to take an antidote. This passage is a strange one in that here Gregory seems to replicate the very soul versus body, senses versus knowledge/faith dichotomy that I am trying to resist in Danto and Duchamp. Yet unlike Danto's invocation of the Eucharist as requiring faith and not sensing, Gregory seems here to *divorce* faith from taking the Eucharist. How do we understand a Eucharist aligned with sense and body rather than faith and soul? Is taking the Eucharist for Gregory a

195. Ibid., 179.
196. Ibid., 52.
197. Gregory of Nyssa, "Address on Religious Instruction" sec. 37, 318.

purely material affair, like taking penicillin or castor oil? Has Gregory fallen captive to the kind of reduction that worries Caputo?

In one way, the Eucharist is quite like a medicine. Gregory gives a very material description of how the Eucharist works. He writes, "Having tasted the poison that dissolved our nature, we were necessarily in need of something to reunite it."[198] As baptism cleansed the body by washing away slavery to the passions, the Eucharist heals the body as an antidote to the poison eaten in the Garden of Eden. The poison that brought with it mortality is counteracted by the Eucharist that brings with it life everlasting. It is this parallel Gregory suggests in the fourth homily when he describes Christ as the apple tree who is life to those who eat of him. From one tree came the fruit of death, so another sprang up that we might eat the fruit of life. As a person eats of Christ, her "entire being" transforms into immortality.[199] It turns out that eating the Eucharist is important not only for counteracting the fruit by which humanity first introduced sin; it is also important because humanity depends upon food in order to exist.[200] The bread of the Eucharist is thus in some kind of continuity with both the story of humanity's origins and the daily needs of every person. We can understand the way the Eucharist nourishes us by attending to the way bread nourishes us.

Christ's body was nourished by bread, Gregory explains, just as ours are.[201] When Christ ate bread, the bread was broken down in his body in order to nourish it. In this way, bread became Christ's body and was "in a sense identical with it."[202] In the same way, Gregory tells us, the bread and wine through consecration become the body of Christ so that when we eat of it we not only assimilate bread to our bodies; we assimilate the Bread of Life into our bodies. Immortality is thereby woven through the very fabric of our skin, our bones, our blood. In this way Christ "implants" in our human nature and deifies humanity.[203] So the Eucharist is like a medicine in that it heals our body from death, but it is unlike a medicine in that it prepares our bodies for a possibility outside the limitations of material becoming. To do this, it must work on the self on more than a material level.

Gregory's claim that the soul unites to Christ through faith and the body through sensing names how each opens to God in a way proper to the kind of thing it is. The soul does not have the capacity to sense, nor the

198. Ibid.
199. Ibid.
200. Ibid., sec. 37, 319.
201. Ibid., sec. 37, 320.
202. Ibid.
203. Ibid., sec. 37, 321.

body to believe, any more than the nose can hear or the eye taste. Yet that need not—and in Gregory's case, *cannot*—mean that faith and perception are two parallel, non-overlapping ways of grasping (embracing) Christ. The way something smells and feels, for example, transforms how it tastes to us, for our tongue, skin, and nose are all part of the same body. It is precisely this mutual transformation of the different ways of embracing Christ that is captured in the Psalmic invocation to "taste and see," so often sung during the Eucharistic liturgy. One tastes with her physical senses and sees the world differently with her spiritual sense. Such synesthesia is similarly captured in the liturgical repetition of Scripture: The disciples knew the Lord Jesus in the breaking of the bread. Tasting the host enables one, somehow, to see Christ. Christ's breaking of the bread, somehow, changed how the disciples knew Christ. Faith and perception, soul and body are distinct but never polarized for Gregory.

Indeed, for Gregory, the Eucharist, in implanting the immortality of Christ into our bodies, transforms our bodies into spiritual bodies. These spiritual bodies, as emphasized earlier, are not spiritual in that they are opposed to matter, but in that they are Spirit-given for the eschaton.[204] And this spiritual body perceives by the spiritual senses, which are reducible neither to soul nor to body but in deep relation to both. The Eucharist extends the spiritual senses awakened by baptism and helps us live more deeply into the reality of God's presence by helping us to perceive God's presence. In taking the Eucharist, we can better perceive Christ in the world. (We can also eat to our own damnation. Gregory does not discuss this possibility, but dwelling with it might open up new vistas for seeing the role of the Spirit in appropriating the Eucharistic reality of Christ to us. It might also ward off the image of Eucharist as Visine for the spiritual eyes.)

Yet why does the Eucharist itself remain opaque? Why, that is, can we not taste the wine as blood or see the bread as flesh? On the one hand, we taste the wine as wine and see the bread as bread because that is what they are. We know from our discussion of radical transcendence in chapter 2 that God is not the kind of thing that opposes bread or wine. Christ was not compromised by death; why should bread thwart him? The problem arises with the fact that God is not just present in the bread and wine; the bread and the wine are the *body* and *blood* of Christ. (Which body and blood? Crucified? Resurrected? Glorified? Would such bodies be differently

---

204. I formulate the relationship between body and spirit negatively here—as "not opposed" and "not reducible"—which leaves open many possibilities for framing their relations positively. One positive formulation I am *not* trying to suggest is their equality. Though the spiritual does not erase the physical, it does have for Gregory clear priority over the physical. The right ordering is the spiritual's governance of the physical.

perceptible as the host? But Gregory is not interested in these questions.) The fact that our body cannot, absent a miracle, perceive the host as flesh names the limitation of our capacity to inhabit our spiritual bodies on this side of the eschaton. The opacity of the Eucharist thus marks for us the limit of our perceptive capacities in this present age. Like the theme of invisibility in Gregory's homilies on the Beatitudes, the Eucharist's presence in his *Address on Religious Instruction* keeps imperceptibility, invisibility, and mystery central to our relationship to God, which is to say, to our faith. (Caputo would be pleased.) The Eucharist reminds us that faith cannot be reduced to visibility even as it also reminds us of the importance of body—ours and Christ's—for nearing God. In the Eucharist, the Spirit draws us nearer Christ, which is to say, makes us more like Christ, without giving us eyes to see or tongue to taste the host as the Christ that the Spirit assimilates us to. Of all sacramental moments, it is the Eucharist where our bodies are most intimately mingled with God's. Yet the Spirit does not manifest the Eucharist as Christ. The Eucharist nourishes us as the Bread of Life that prepares us for life everlasting, while reminding us that until the resurrection, our participation in that Life remains limited.

Hearing the Song of Songs and Words of the Word

One of the least thematized senses in the homilies on the Song of Songs is the sense presumed by its very genre: hearing. Hearing is also the sense that receives rhetoric, which is deeply important to transformation, and the chanting of the Psalms, which are central both to Gregory's *Commentary on the Inscription of the Psalms* and the *Life of Macrina*. In the second chapter we explored the centrality of the Psalms—how chanting and hearing them sustained Macrina's community after her death and how grief overwhelmed that community when they abandoned their chant; how the Psalms move a person to virtue both because they disclose God and because they do so sweetly, with pleasing form; how their perfect order and form hew Christlikeness in us.[205] This musical Christ-hewing, we read in the *Inscriptions of the Psalms,* ends in a sin-banished chorus of harmony, dance, and human-angel cymbal-clashing. Hearing the divine musicality of the Psalms restores in humanity its own deep musicality, helping it to hear the songs of the universe, that it may join in the song and dance.[206]

Hearing is also a particularly fitting way to receive God the Word. Gregory's Eucharistic logic gives us one way to contemplate how the words

205. Gregory of Nyssa, *On the Inscriptions of the Psalms* II.11.134 (Heine, 164).
206. Ibid., II.7.60 (Heine, 148–49).

of Scripture are so dear to Gregory. As Christ incorporated bread into his very body, consecrating it to Christself and giving it to us that we may become Christ, so Christ drew in words of Scripture, imbuing them with special marks of divine presence. Certain passages are particularly blessed for Gregory, like the Beatitudes. The Christ who is Word drew these words into Christself, digested them like bread, forming them into a ladder that Christ, far from resting atop, permeates through.[207] For just as Jesus depended upon bread for his very being while he walked the earth, so he depended on scriptural words. Jesus makes this much clear when he rebukes the devil: No one lives by bread alone but by every word that proceeds from the mouth of God. Divine words nourished Christ, then, just as bread did, and as Jesus offered up his body to be eaten, so he offered up his words to those who had ears to hear. And these words can, like Jesus's calling to Mary, effect a turning, an opening to the risen Lord and the eschatological reality the Lord inaugurates.

Hearing words steeped in Scripture can also inspire a turning, which is the hope displayed in Gregory's homilies on the love of the poor, on the Beatitudes, and on the Song of Songs. Gregory's descriptions of the soothing and opening power of music and words—in Macrina's community, in the universal chorus and dance, in his homilizing—also remind us again that the spiritual senses cannot be understood at a purely individual level. There is a community that hears and speaks and sings to each other. There is a community that receives the words of the Word. Repositioning the church as bride rather than bridegroom, Gregory describes this reception in his *Commentary on the Song of Songs*:

> This explains why the Word, who raises up the fallen, calls out through the windows to the church and says: "Rise up"—plainly it means from a fall—"you who have slipped and fallen on the slick surface of sin. You who have been bound by the serpent and have collapsed upon the earth and live in the fallen state of disobedience—arise!" . . . What is the point of this order of words in our text? How is one element in it tied in with another? How is the logical sequence of the ideas kept connected as in a chain? She hears the command. She is empowered by the Word. She rises up. She moves forward. She is brought close. She becomes a beauty. She is named dove.[208]

207. For more on Christ's presence as the ladder, see my discussion of the homilies on the Beatitudes in chapter 3, the section titled "Invisibility and Poverty."

208. Gregory of Nyssa, *Homilies on the Song of Songs*, 161, 163.

Hearing the Word's words, the bride is strengthened to obey. Brought near Beauty in her obedience to Beauty, she becomes beautiful—full of Beauty— and so can be named dove-like-ly divine. Receiving the words of the Word, the church performs her bridehood, singing her role in the Song of Songs, joining in the musical, dancing chorus that listening and obeying has given her ears to hear.

Seeing (and Beyond Seeing) by the Church

Christ's presence in the liturgy, made perceptible to us by the Spirit, is what gives us eyes to see and ears to hear God's presence in the world. In the second chapter we explored how all beauty, characterized by fittingness and gratuity, participates in God. Beauty, then, discloses the divine. It would seem to follow from that chapter that we can see the God-saturatedness of the world. But the third chapter presented a problem to us. It was that the deepest and most profound examples of beauty are implicated in and intertwined with ugliness. Beauty is thus somewhat obscure. This is not a problem for all types of beauty: In most instances, to see the beauty of a cup, one need not see ugliness or have special training into beauty. One need only know what a cup is for (perhaps not even that), and one's appreciation of the cup's beauty might be further heightened by familiarity with the history and tradition of cup-making. Training into the fullness of a cup's beauty, then, is training into the particularity of the histories and cultural lives of cups. But seeing the beauty that participates most deeply in Beauty Itself requires training into Beauty Itself. So now we have been asking, what does that training look like? What does it mean to become the sort of self that perceives this beauty that deeply participates in God? Gregory's answer is that we must be wounded by love. We must hold the half-dead neighbor tightly in our loving arms, show mercy to our enemy, submit ourselves to baptism, chant psalms, listen to homilies, and eat the flesh of Christ. Gregory describes how such woundings bring beauty near to us with the case of baptism: Baptism makes perceptible the beauty of creation by making perceptible God in creation. The Spirit works in liturgy, asceticism, and acts of love to give us ears to hear and eyes to see beauty. The Beauty revealed is both luminous and disturbing. Perceiving it, like learning to perceive it, changes the kind of people we are. And the kind of people we are, for Gregory, is ever-changing. The ever-changingness implied in Gregory's doctrine of epectasy is one way faith is kept in relationship with invisibility: God is too great for a creature ever finally to perceive—physically or spiritually—the all-presence of God. Further, God's invisibility on this side of the eschaton is named by the incomplete way in which we inhabit our spiritual bodies until the resurrection. The Eucharist is one way the invisibility of God is materialized for us. With this material invisibility, though, we are also reminded that even when faith cannot respond to or elicit sight, it is yet in deep relationship with training our capacities for perception that we may "taste and see."

The saturated phenomena of the church, heavy with Christ's presence, do not always dazzle and rarely presume a solo mystical encounter. They occur in the repetition of familiar liturgical acts, in mundane practices of care-giving, and in other ordinary disciplines. They are embodied and community-dependent, and the fact that it is these acts through which the Spirit teaches us the kind of subjectivity that perceives Beauty suggests a self that, far from self-constituted, is radically other-constituted. This self must not only receive the phenomena that constitute her; she must receive the people who participate in these constituting phenomena. Such priority of the body, the gradual turning toward Christ through encountering the resurrected Christ, the reception of Christ through community, is why Gregory's accounts of the church performing the role of Bridegroom are faithful to the Gospel descriptions of encounters with the resurrected Christ. With receptivity at its very core, this is a self that is radically open—opened by the wound of love, opened through her spiritual senses—into the eschatological reality when the God who is love will be all in all.

The opened self has been habituated into the life of faith, the virtue that names the way the soul unites with God. In his excellent exposition of the role of faith in Gregory, Martin Laird writes,

> Faith renders the soul a dwelling place of God; faith expands the soul's desire for God even as the soul delights in God; faith does what the discursive mind can never do: grasp the incomprehensible nature of God; faith nevertheless passes on to the mind something of what it has grasped of the Ungraspable. These are the principal functions of faith when seen in its technical sense of bridging the gap between the mind and God.[209]

It is this union, this faith, that the spiritual senses live into. That is to say, as theological knowledge is inseparable from theological knower for Gregory, so is faith inseparable from the faithful. The spiritual senses, then, are Gregory's anthropological description of what it means to live into the theological virtue of faith. In the same way that spiritual senses do not displace physical senses but bind invisibility to visibility, present to eschaton, materiality to

---

209. Laird, *Gregory of Nyssa*, 207–8.

spirituality, so faith names the virtue of the one who perceives, believes, lives, and desires this binding as it is and shall be consummated in Christ.

Macrina's Wound

"Do not let the greatest wonder accomplished by this holy lady pass by unrecorded."[210] Along with Vetiana, Gregory has been laying out Macrina's body ("with your own hands," the deaconess Lampadium says, relating to Gregory how Macrina wished her body to be handled after her death).[211] Gregory is poring over her body in wonder—arranging her holy head, putting hands on her neck, touching the cross of iron she wore as a necklace, claiming her relic-hiding ring, wrapping her body in a robe—when Vetiana tells Gregory that something greater still is to come. As if instructing him how to write Macrina's narrative, Vetiana now commands the drama of Macrina's *Life*. Gregory responds to her commanding allusion as he must: "What is that?"[212] For neither the first nor the last time in this *Life*, the storyteller receives the story he must tell.

As Vetiana prepares to tell her story, the handling of Macrina's body grows more intimate still. Vetiana exposes part of Macrina's breast. "Do you see this thin, almost invisible scar [*semeion*: literally, sign] under the skin?"[213] To Gregory that scar resembled a mark (*stigma*) made by a needle. He is unimpressed. "What is so wonderful if the body has a small scar [*semeion*] on this part?"[214] And here Vetiana recovers the scar as, in fact, a sign: "This is left on the body as a reminder of God's great help."[215]

The scar marks the place where once a painful and dangerous tumor had grown. With the tumor near Macrina's heart, to cut it away was just as life-threatening as to leave it. But the danger of cutting it away was not the reason Macrina refused medical treatment. Despite the entreaties of her mother, Macrina decided that she could not, or should not, bare her body before the eyes of strangers. After once again performing her tasks for her mother, Macrina went to pray, lying prostrate on the earthen ground. Echoing the action of Christ healing the blind man and the foot-washing woman

210. Gregory of Nyssa, "Life of Saint Macrina," 184.

211. Ibid.

212. Ibid.

213. My modifications of translations from Callahan, found in Gregory of Nyssa, "Life of Saint Macrina," 184.

214. Ibid.

215. Ibid.

who loved much, Macrina made a mud salve of earth and tears that she put on her breast. But this miracle was to be Emmelia's. Macrina went to her mother and told her that she could heal her if she would only make the sign of the cross "with her own hands" (this, too, is a form of labor) over Macrina's breast. The mother-daughter miracle healed Macrina's breast, and the painful tumor was replaced with the *semeion* that witnessed to God's visitation on Macrina, an invitation to thanksgiving. As Vetiana finishes the story, Gregory and Vetiana also finish caring for Macrina's body. Lampadium tells Gregory that the maidens should not see Macrina dressed as a bride, so they cover her in Emmelia's dark mantle, through which rays of light shine forth from Macrina's luminous body. Macrina's God-witnessing wound becomes a way for Gregory to introduce her wondrous luminosity (a sign that is more self-interpreting than the *semeion*).

The intriguing story of Macrina's wound has invited reflection from many scholarly angles. Georgia Frank reads it as Gregory inserting Macrina into the stories of the saintly wounded, such as the martyrs and the confessors, and the heroically wounded, particularly Odysseus with his famous identifying scar.[216] Virginia Burrus reads Macrina's mark in the Pauline tradition of carrying the *stigmata* of Christ on one's body, rhetorically participating in the symbolic inversion of power relations by which "the stigma itself becomes, scarlike, a dense site—a deep surface—of complex and layered meaning, fusing (without quite confusing) rebellion and surrender, nobility and degradation, flesh and spirit, worldly and holy power."[217] Linking the imagined needle of Macrina's scar to the actual needle that made her tattoo, Burrus further connects the ink of her tattoo to the ink of the text about Macrina to write, "The *Life of Macrina* inscribes feminine subjectivity as a stigma (marks the subject with and as difference) and, further, that 'women's history' may be understood as a practice of reading and writing that continuously marks (and therein makes) a difference."[218] Joining Vetiana, Frank, and Burrus in this tradition of women attending and interpreting Macrina's *semeion,* I would like to offer an additional layer of interpretation.

I propose that we consider Macrina an icon of wounding by love, the puncture of her wound allowing her to radiate the light of her lover. In this way, I want to join Burrus's linking of the *stigma* of Macrina and the *stigmata* of Paul (and Christ) to Gregory's linking of the *stigmata* of Paul (and Christ) and the *stigma* of the wounded Bride. (For, as we earlier quoted Gregory writing in his twelfth homily, "That divine rod and comforting

---

216. Frank, "Macrina's Scar," 514.

217. Burrus, "Macrina's Tattoo," 413.

218. Ibid.

staff, which by a blow works healing, is the Spirit, whose fruit is those good things that Paul enumerates. . . . For Paul too, who bore the mark of such blows, similarly exulted in wounds of this sort when he said, 'I bear on my body the marks [*stigmata*] of Christ (Gal 6:17)."[219]) As modeled by Macrina, the subjectivity of one wounded by love is unlike the subjecthood described by Freud, or anyone who posits the birth of the ego in the rejection of the mother. His version of subjecthood, in fact, provides a pointed contrast for Macrina's. In *Flesh of My Flesh*, Silverman traces Freud's subject, displeased. Reading the mother-rejecting passages of Freud together with matricidal texts in Proust and Rilke, Silverman devotes several pages to condemning the lack of enabling representations of maternal finitude in our culture. This lack, she feels, fuels the Oedipal complex in which the child, disillusioned and angered by his mother's inability to provide for his every desire, trades her in for the far more powerful father. Though no more able to satisfy the child's every demand than the mother, the father, who is also a stand-in for the Father God, can insist on the deferral of desire through "the paternal function."[220] Silverman worries about the child's attempt to deny his finitude by associating it with mother (as Orpheus feminized death) and rejecting the mother (as Orpheus rejected women). The rejection of the mother (like the embrace of religion and other promises of immortality) thus becomes a way of suppressing one's own finitude. The difficulty is to embrace the mother while outgrowing infantile demands that she sustain our illusions of immortality. In Macrina's story, we find a way into that embrace. She not only gives us an enabling representation of maternal finitude, but the representation she gives us funds the selfhood into which her readers are invited.

Macrina has a very different relationship with her mother than Freud or Rilke or Proust. She certainly did not reject her: This is the woman who refused separation from her mother "even for a moment."[221] Gregory describes the way Macrina avoided marriage after her fiancé's death by linking herself to her mother. He follows that remembrance by telling how Emmelia

219. Gregory of Nyssa, *Homilies on the Song of Songs*, 385.

220. Silverman, *Flesh of My Flesh*, 94; see 80–100. Julia Kristeva has written on the unpersuasiveness of "the paternal function" as a whole explanation for how humans are conditioned into sociality. She offers in its stead the maternal function as an image of relationality, the pregnant woman a representation of how we are subjects-in-process rather than wholly autonomous individuals. Kristeva, "Motherhood According to Giovanni Bellini." My reading of Macrina will resonate with these images in Kristeva's work, yet our mother images work differently. There are multiple reasons why, but one important divergence is the vocabulary in which they are embedded: Kristeva discusses maternity and motherhood primarily in terms of alterity, sublimation, and separation; I in terms of labor and love.

221. Gregory of Nyssa, "Life of Saint Macrina," 184.

used to say that though she was pregnant with the rest of her children for nine months, she bore Macrina with her always and everywhere, "embracing her in her womb."[222] Yet in this closeness it is also Macrina who helps Emmelia to face the death of Naucratius. It is she, along with the youngest son, who attends her mother's deathbed. It is she who persuades her mother that they moderate their living and give away the material comfort on which they depend. She rejects illusions of infinitude and independence while embracing her dependence on her mother (which is to say, the possibility of death).

Here in the story of Macrina's scar we find Macrina's bodily dependence on her mother traced anew. The description of the mother touching the daughter's breast to heal her and give her life inevitably invokes the many times the daughter in her infancy reached for her mother's breasts that sustained her and gave her life (and Gregory relates this, too, was labor: the infant Macrina was fed by no wet nurse but at her mother's own "hands"). This similarity cannot but also highlight the difference: Macrina is no longer a bundle of libidinal energies blindly suckling life from her mother. She is a woman who has herself brought many women to spiritual maturity by her own spiritual labor pains. She has refused the conventional treatment of her pain; she has even refused her mother's entreaties to seek that treatment. She prayed to God, mixed the salve, and invited her mother to perform the miracle. This is a model of human subjectivity premised, not on rejecting one's mother, but on oneself becoming a mother. For Macrina becomes a mother by giving herself over to this community of women, laboring manually ("with her own hands") in equality with them, and laboring spiritually for them to birth them as their spiritual selves. It is important that *motherhood* name the spiritual self (the wounded self) Macrina becomes, for it is a self that cannot be claimed apart from labor. This labor, moreover, specifies the way in which Gregory's homiletic language discussed in chapter 3 labors: It labors Macrina-like—Mary-like—to birth little christs into the world.

Macrina's labor-driven mother-becoming does not require her mother's absence. She requires a community that she can love, that can help her learn to receive herself as a mother. The text draws attention to her motherhood by describing, in the moment after Macrina's scar story and before her luminosity, Macrina's reception of the dark mantel of her own mother. Deep in the economy of giving and receiving by which these women transform into spiritual mothers and brides of Christ, Macrina cannot perceive her mother as a threat to her ever-becoming, for her mother is part of this community of transformation. Emmelia makes visible, moreover, what is

222. Ibid.

enabling about maternal finitude. It is Emmelia's willingness to receive Macrina's love, to be nurtured by her daughter's labors, that enables Macrina's motherhood. Allowing Macrina to help her face the death of her family members, Emmelia enables the growth of both her own and Macrina's spiritual selves. Emmelia helps us to see the way daughterhood is intrinsic to motherhood, the way daughterhood both marks the limit and consummation of motherhood, for it marks the creation of other mothers.

The scar marks Emmelia's submission to Macrina's decision, Macrina's submission to Emmelia's touch, and the submission (and therefore participation) of their love to (and in) the love of Christ. Macrina's *stigma*, her *semeion*, as it is told by Vetiana to Gregory that he may record it for all, testifies to the way this liturgical community of love transformed the love between mother and daughter into a love that invited the touch of God, that buttressed the faith of the community, and that signified the healing wound of Love to a wider readership.

The wound—the mother-touched *stigma* Gregory must learn to read as *semeion*—becomes a mark of love between two humans, among a community of humans, and between humans and God. As such, it is a beautiful wound, and its description is fittingly followed by Macrina's disclosure of the Beauty of her Bridegroom. It also follows the story of Macrina seeing the Bridegroom's Beauty. This wound, then, materializes the way Beauty transforms a self that sees Beauty, transforms a self *so that* she can see Beauty, into Beauty Itself. For the self that sees Beauty must receive the marks of Beauty, must carry them about in her body, presenting her body as an icon of Beauty Crucified. This iconic becoming leads us back to pneumatology and anthropology. In a humanity consummated by opening to and through the Spirit, the spiritual senses describe the kind of people we are to become if we are to perceive Beauty rightly.

From Theory to *Theoria*

In one way, perceiving Beauty (perceiving Christ) calls for a distinct mode of perception, one unlike perceiving those realities (a cup, a knife) that do not groan for eschatological healing. Perceiving Beauty, we have seen, involves being reconstituted by the one who is also called Love, and as Beauty and Love ultimately name the same God, perception and love are tightly intertwined. And this is where perceiving Beauty is not unlike perceiving other beauties: The intertwining of perception and love does not unravel in perceiving more mundane realities. These mundane entities, further, cannot be reduced to material objects or intelligible realities independent of observer and context. To describe the attention given to an object is to offer an erotics of sight.

Danto missed such erotics when he analyzed the *Brillo Boxes* by dividing theory from sight, intelligible from material. Attending to the erotics of sight means resisting descriptions that cast encounters between beholder and beheld as a static, two-node, abstractable network. It means instead casting this relationship as one embedded in many different nodes as the viewer is drawn deeper into what is beheld. Danto does not theorize perception in this way, but he does exemplify it—even (perhaps especially) in his writing about *Brillo Boxes*. Upon seeing *Brillo Boxes*, Danto was, as he describes, "awakened" and "excit[ed]" by the "profound discovery" embodied in the installation.[223] He drafted an article almost immediately after seeing the installation, and in the article insisted that *Brillo Boxes* helped him see and represent the central problematic of Western philosophy and, in fact, the whole history of art. The history of artistic representation and philosophical problems intensified his attraction to *Brillo Boxes*, drawing him deeper into the sculpture and reflection upon it. We see dramatized in Danto's response to *Brillo Boxes* the way situating the artwork in different conversations teaches a person to see it differently. And one sees Warhol's *Brillo Boxes* differently than the boxes of Brillo soap because the erotics of the encounters are different: The conversations Warhol's *Brillo Boxes* participate in and draw beholders into are conversations mediated by the institutions of gallery, museum, and university. As a person is drawn into these conversations and learns what it means to participate in them, one becomes a different kind of person, a different kind of gazer. Such a gaze does not discern an object that is art "mentally" but not "physically," for the physical and mental are mutually constitutive; the art-ness of the *Brillo Boxes* is evident only because of and within the particular physical realities surrounding them. Gazing at these realities teaches us to see *Brillo Boxes* as art. And such a gaze cannot repudiate the aesthetic, for it is a gaze that comes from a gazer of flesh and blood and looks into an object made by an artist who is also flesh and blood.

Indeed, Danto himself sometimes talks explicitly about love in his encounters with artworks. In an interview given forty years after he wrote his watershed *Brillo Boxes* articles, Danto concedes that his approach to art as wholly non-aesthetic might have been limited. It is in that context he speaks of love. He says,

> In *The Abuse of Beauty*, I describe falling in love with one of Robert Motherwell's *Elegies to the Spanish Republic*, just on the

223. Danto, *After the End of Art*, 35.

basis of seeing it, without knowing anything about who painted it or what it meant. There was something that drew me to the painting. It does not always happen, but it happens enough. Recently I visited the Miami art fair—acres and acres of art. When I got back to the hotel, my wife asked how it was, and I said it was a very good show with a lot of good art. Then she asked if there was anything I loved, and that stopped me in my tracks. There was nothing I loved, nothing with which I had so to speak "fallen in love." The best one could ask of it was a certain kind of intellectual love.[224]

What I think Danto could add to this analysis is an expansion of love and erotics past this narrative of "love at first sight" to include the slow unfolding of a relationship between the viewer and the art object. Perhaps the slow-fall, with the possibilities it opens up for training and initiation after the encounter with the art object, could help Danto articulate the possibility of a love-filled encounter with a postmodernist piece.

Without naming the encounter as love-filled, Danto comes close to describing an erotics of sight recently when he sat with the performance artist Marina Abramović for her piece *The Artist is Present*. In spring 2010, Abramović sat in New York's Museum of Modern Art across from an empty chair in which others were invited to join her. There are photographs of people sitting with her, weeping. Danto did not weep, but he, too, was moved. He ends a rhapsodic article on the piece thus:

> What I know now is that she and MoMA have brought some magic back into art—the sort of magic that all of our courses in art history and appreciation had encouraged us to hope for. James Turrell, the light artist, once told me that after seeing the slides of paintings in the courses he had taken, he was disappointed by the actual paintings. What he had really loved was the light, and in a sense then vowed to make sure his art, consisting of light, would never lose its magic. Those who do get lucky enough to sit with Marina will not be disappointed, because the light I noticed will be there, even if they are not ready to see it.[225]

The light that is there for the lover, that is there but not visible to the one not ready to see it—this does not describe an approach that pits theory against aesthetics. It is not theory by which Danto approaches Abramović or *Brillo Boxes*. It is something much closer to *theoria*.

224. Guash, "Arthur Danto and Donald Kuspit," no pages.
225. Danto, "Sitting with Marina," no pages.

Theoria names a way of seeing that neither excludes the materiality of the object (as Danto's understanding of theory does) nor reduces sight to the materiality of the object (as Danto's aesthetics do). Jean Daniélou captures the way *theoria* integrates the two when he describes it as "the activity of the spirit that knows the intelligible reality of things without stopping at their sensible appearance."[226] Describing *theoria* as an "activity" that does not stop at the sensible suggests the way *theoria* opens up the reality of what is being contemplated. As it does so, it also opens up the reality of the contemplator, and the world she shares with the contemplated. Hadot traces a tradition of *theoria* that runs through antiquity and is never separable from a way of life, from "the realization of those capacities that are essential to being human."[227] That realization, further, entails the transformation of the contemplator. Even for Aristotle, *theoria* is "participation in the divine way of life" that "requires inner transformation and personal *askesis*" so that the divine in the human can be actualized.[228] Porphyry and Plotinus similarly characterize *theoria* as making teachings, "not abstract concepts for accumulation, but 'nature and life' within us."[229] *Theoria* names the dynamism between knower and knowledge, the seer and the seen, the way contemplating realities makes demands on the one contemplating. Contrasting *theoria* with consideration and understanding, Andrew Louth characterizes *theoria* as "union with, participation in, the true objects of truth and knowledge. It bespeaks . . . a feeling of presence, of immediacy."[230]

We have returned here to participation, which evokes the multiplicity of contexts in which an object may be found fitting and gratuitous. *Theoria* names the way we access deeper, richer, thicker ways in which an object is beautiful, even when we are not looking at Beauty. To reclaim the tradition of *theoria*—of a dynamic relationship between beholder and beheld, of the wider nexus of relationships surrounding beholder and beheld, of a material-spiritual reality love opens to our perception—is to claim a non-theological analog for the forms of perception named by faith and the spiritual senses. It is, I mean to say, a way of insisting that even when Love's revelation is not sight's object, love cannot be excised from sight. The erotics of sight continues to reassert itself.

---

226. "La *théôria* est l'activité de l'esprit connaissant la réalité intelligible des choses et ne s'arrêtant pas à leur apparence sensible" (Daniélou, *l'être et le temps*, 1).

227. Hadot, *Philosophy as a Way of Life*, 29.

228. Ibid.

229. Ibid., 100.

230. Louth, *Origins of the Christian Mystical Tradition*, 3.

Conclusion

Brillo Boxes aside, we are, in one way, far from where we started in chapter 2. I invoked beauty in that chapter to describe fine arts and crafts, knowledge, virtue, and nature. I discussed the fittingness and gratuity of beauty through paintings and knives, flowers and gardens, poetry and inspiration. All of these beauties were connected by the image of a ladder, which described how "lower beauties" can lead up to "higher ones." The ladder was problematized as I radicalized fittingness and gratuity away from a strictly Platonic vision of beauty. Beauty, I said, names a radically transcendent God, and so the fittingness and gratuity that characterize Beauty must be similarly radical. No beautiful thing is far from Beauty Itself. Though this commitment complicated the ladder, it left intact the world-to-heaven vision of beauty that connects bodies to words and words to virtue.

As I moved from doctrine of God generally to Christology specifically, the third chapter drew near woundedness by moving farther from flowers and gardens. That chapter continued problematizing the image of a ladder, showing the obscurity of the most profound instances of Beauty by showing the obscurity of Beauty Itself. How can we see the Beauty who is the Crucified One? How can we see the Beauty that shines on the face of the poor, the diseased, the bestialized? I began to explore the way that seeing such beauty was bound up with seeing Christ coming to save oneself, with acts of love, with words given in love. But how these commitments fit with the preceding chapter was not fully addressed. What could it mean to see radical gratuity on the faces wracked by forces of necessity? What could the beauty of the face of the hungry possibly have in common with the beauty of the statue *David* or of a cup? I pointed to some Christological lines of reflection for these questions, but did not go very far in thinking about them anthropologically. I did not, for example, ask: What is the difference between a person who sees the beauty of a flower or a statue and the person who can also see the beauty on the face of the hungry? What marks the difference between Joseph carving the crucifix obsessively, and Elizabeth fainting in the crucifix-dominated presence that she finds ugly and unbearable?

I have tried in this chapter to show how to recover the continuity that I ruptured in chapter 3. Completing the Trinitarian shape of this book by discussing pneumatology, I have discussed Gregory's descriptions of how only the one wounded by love can see the beauty of the Wounded One who chose to be bound to the wounded of this world. Only one who has learned to receive herself from a community of love, to open herself to and by the Spirit-given senses, can see this profound beauty. It is in the community that is itself the Bridegroom, the community charged with continuing Love's work, that a person is trained—body, soul, and spirit—into Love's final context for fittingness and gratuity. There one is refashioned into the kind of self that can see how a flower and a sacrifice can both merit the description beautiful. There one can see how both fine art and the poor participate in the dynamic of fittingness and gratuity that characterizes beauty. This is one implication of Gregory's conviction that hearing Psalm-chanting attunes one to the deep music of the universe, and that baptism illumines the beauty of creation. Through the acquisition of the spiritual senses, one lives into her eschatological self and so places the world, evermore, in an eschatological horizon. To see the beauty of the wounded is to see the beauty of our own wounded selves and to see the way the Wounded One is healing those wounds by turning them into openings for greater dependence on one another and on Christ, which is to say, on Love. It is to see the fittingness of those wounds as conduits for our remaking by Love and to be moved by the gratuity of Love's remaking us through Love's own wounds. Fittingness and gratuity turn out to be deeply—and still radically—characteristic of the most profound Beauty. And in that sense, we are very close to where we started.

Epilogue

DARKLY SHINING

The tortured form Mary and John beheld on the Cross was not beautiful. They beheld Love Itself—her son, his teacher—brutally killed by the sons of Adam and daughters of Eve. What could be more ugly?

Yet even when its gruesomeness is exaggerated, even in depictions of its ugliness, the Cross, for Christians, is beautiful. Coetzee's Joseph saw this beauty in the crosses that he carved. John the apostle could see it when John the disciple could not. The Cross is beautiful for Coetzee's Joseph and the apostle John because it testifies to the unyieldingly creative depths of a Love that will not be thwarted by death, torture, malice, envy, indifference, or fear. That is, the Cross is beautiful because Jesus rose from the dead. It is beautiful as the first-fruits of the resurrection and the beginnings of the eschaton. The Cross absent resurrection—the cross that Mary and John saw—is nothing but horrifying.

This way of thinking about the Cross results from how I have surveyed the grounds of beauty. The final location of Beauty Itself is the eschatologi-cally glorified Christ. That we find beauty there, on *that* body, is significant for how we think about suffering. To index beauty solely to creation is to make suffering unequivocally ugly; suffering under this description becomes the occasion for either closing our eyes or turning against beauty. Such "cre-ation beauty" cannot make sense of the claim that the Cross is beautiful. Yet to index beauty to the fall or to a fallen creation is perversely to make suffering beautiful *as* suffering. A beauty tied to fallenness means that the Cross could be beautiful as John and Mary stood before it. By yoking beauty to Christ's eschatological glory, however, we find a way to name the beauty of suffering while also hoping for its alleviation. Under this description, the Cross is beautiful only in retrospect—in images of the event rather than the event itself. The retrospective glance that perceives the beauty of the Cross is an eschatological one. Rising from the dead, Jesus took his own death and suffering up into an eschatological glory that we can learn to see now and will fully see only once he comes again to judge the living and the dead.

Another way to say that beauty is indexed neither to creation nor fall is to say that neither proportion, unity, and clarity, nor woundedness fully determine beauty. The radiant, scarred Christ names the beauty in which both woundedness and clarity participate. Creation and fall, though not determinative of beauty, nevertheless remain important parts of beauty because the eschatologically glorified Christ was also the firstborn over all creation, the Creator joined with the creature, and because Christ entered into our sin and suffering to bear and redeem it. Creation and fall are not displaced by but taken up into Christ's glory, where we find the final context for fittingness and gratuity.

It is this eschatological orientation of beauty that makes our spiritual senses—our ability to live into our eschatological selves—so important for perceiving beauty. It is only to the extent that we live into our eschatological selves that we perceive the eschatologically glorified Christ. So perceiving Christ, we see perfect fittingness and gratuity. We see the radically fitting and gratuitous Christ who could draw all things to Christself, the God who could be all in all. For, the way Christ draws us is by Christ's own wounds, which is why beauties that disclose such woundedness are especially pro-found beauties. The beauty of proportion and harmony, however, also par-ticipates in and discloses something of the God who is so perfectly fitting as to be all in all, who is so perfectly gratuitous as to draw all things to Godself.

Yet we are limited in our ability to perceive such fittingness and gratu-ity. We cannot fully live into our eschatological selves until we have become our resurrection bodies, which is to say, until after we have died. What we are able to see, until then, when we look at someone suffering is the beauty of the image of God, the beauty of Christ's own face, and the ugliness of death and decay. Perhaps we will see the suffering one radiating with the love of an act of healing she gives or receives. But the glory to be revealed in that suffering one remains, for now, invisible.

I began this book by thinking about Gregory of Nazianzus's declara-tion that the best theologian assembles the shadow of Truth. I want to end by remembering that there is a reality that will not fully yield to sight, that the shadowless world is a world for which we wait. Until then, the dazzling fullness of Beauty Itself, the brilliance of its appearing, can only come to us darkly.

Bibliography

Works in Ancient Languages

Gregory of Nazianzus. "De filio" (Oratio 30). In *Die fünf theologischen Reden*, translated and edited by J. Barbel. Düsseldorf: Patmos, 1963.

———. *Epistulae*. In *Saint Grégoire de Nazianze, Lettres Vols.1–2*, translated and edited by Paul Gallay. Paris: Les Belles Lettres, 1964, 1967.

Gregory of Nyssa. *Adversus Macedonianos de Spiritu Sancto. Gregorii Nysseni Opera* (GNO) III.

———. *Contra Eunomium*. GNO I, II.

———. *In Canticum Canticorum*. GNO VI.

———. *De Anima et Resurrectione. Patrologiae Cursus Completus, series Graeca* (PG) 46.

———. *De Beatitudinibus*. PG 44.

———. *De Beneficentia*. GNO IX.

———. *In Illud: Quatenus Uni ex His Fecistis Mihi Fecistis*. GNO IX.

———. *De Hominis Opificio*. PG 44.

———. *De Vitae Macrinae. Sources Chrétiennes* (SC) 178.

———. *De Vita Moysis*. SC 1.

———. *De Virginitate*. SC 119.

———. *Epistulae*. GNO VIII.

———. *In Ecclesiasten*. GNO 5.

———. *In Inscriptiones Psalmorum*. GNO 5

———. *In Sanctum Pascha*. GNO IX.

———. *Oratio Catechetica Magna*. GNO III/IV.

Plato. *Hippias Major*.

———. *Ion*.

———. *Laws*.

———. *Phaedo*.

———. *Phaedrus*.

———. *Republic*.

———. *Symposium*.

Xenophon. *Memorabilia*.

Works Translated or Written in Modern Languages

Andreas-Salomé, Lou. *Looking Back: Memoirs.* Edited by Ernst Pfeiffer. Translated by Breon Mitchell. New York: Marlowe, 1995.

Augustine. *Expositions on the Books of the Psalms by Augustine.* Vol. 2, *Psalms 37–52.* Translated by Members of the English Church. Oxford: John Henry Parker and F. and J. Rivington, 1848.

Ayres, Lewis. *Nicaea and Its Legacy: An Approach to Fourth-Century Trinitarian Theology.* New York: Oxford, 2004.

Balás, David L. *[Metousia Theou]: Man's Participation in God's Perfections according to Saint Gregory of Nyssa.* Studia Anselmiana philosophica theologica, fasc. 55. Rome: I. B. C. Libreria Herder, 1966.

Balthasar, Hans Urs von. "Another Ten Years." In *The Analogy of Beauty: The Theology of Hans Urs von Balthasar,* edited by John Riches, 222–33. Edinburgh: T. & T. Clark, 1986.

———. *Cosmic Liturgy: The Universe according to Saint Maximus the Confessor.* Translated by Brian E. Daley. San Francisco: Ignatius, 2003.

———. *The Glory of the Lord: A Theological Aesthetics.* Vol. 1, *Seeing the Form.* Translated by John Kenneth Riches and Joseph Fessio. San Francisco: Ignatius, 1983.

———. *Heart of the World.* Translated by Erasmo S. Leiva. San Francisco: Ignatius, 1979.

———. *Presence and Thought: An Essay on the Religious Philosophy of Gregory of Nyssa.* Translated by Mark Sebanc. San Francisco: Ignatius, 1995.

———. "Revelation and the Beautiful." In *Explorations in Theology I: The Word Made Flesh,* translated by A. V. Littledale with Alexander Dru, 95–126. San Francisco: Ignatius, 1989.

Basil of Caesarea. "Epistle 58." Translated by Blomfield Jackson. In vol. 8 of *The Nicene and Post-Nicene Fathers,* Second Series. Edited by Philip Schaff and Henry Wace. Buffalo, NY: Christian Literature Publishing, 1895. Revised and edited for New Advent by Kevin Knight. http://www.newadvent.org/fathers/3202058.htm.

Bauer, Walter. *A Greek-English Lexicon of the New Testament and Other Early Christian Literature.* Revised and edited by Fredrick William Danker. 3rd ed. Chicago: University of Chicago Press, 2000.

Beardsley, John. "Imagining the Outsider." In *Vernacular Visionaries: International Outsider Art,* edited by Annie Carlano, 10–17. New Haven: Yale University Press in association with the Museum of International Folk Art, Santa Fe, New Mexico, 2003.

Beeley, Christopher A. *Gregory of Nazianzus on the Trinity and the Knowledge of God: In Your Light We Shall See Light.* New York: Oxford University Press, 2008.

Bell, Clive. "Art and Religion." In *Art,* 57–68. New York: Stokes, 1913.

Bernard of Clairvaux. *Cistercians and Cluniacs: St. Bernard's Apologia to Abbot William.* Translated by Michael Casey. Kalamazoo, MI: Cistercian, 1970.

Brady, Emily. "Don't Eat the Daisies: Disinterestedness and the Situated Aesthetic." *Environmental Values* 17 (1998) 97–114.

Brandwood, Leonard. *The Chronology of Plato's Dialogues.* Cambridge: Cambridge University Press, 1990.

Brann, Noel L. *The Debate Over the Origin of Genius during the Italian Renaissance: The Theories of Supernatural Frenzy and Natural Melancholy in Accord and in Conflict on the Threshold of the Scientific.* Leiden: Brill, 2002.

Burrus, Virginia. "Macrina's Tattoo." *Journal of Medieval and Early Modern Studies* 33 (2003) 403–17.

Burwick, Frederick. *Poetic Madness in the Romantic Imagination.* University Park: Pennsylvania State University Press, 1996.

Cabanne, Pierre. *Dialogues with Marcel Duchamp.* New York: Viking, 1971.

Cameron, Averil. *Christianity and the Rhetoric of Empire: The Development of Christian Discourse.* Berkeley: University of California Press, 1991.

Caputo, John D. "The Hyperbolization of Phenomenology: Two Possibilities for Religion in Recent Continental Philosophy." In *Counter-Experiences: Reading Jean-Luc Marion*, edited by Kevin Hart, 67–93. Notre Dame: University of Notre Dame Press, 2007.

Cardinal, Roger. "Surrealism and the Paradigm of the Creative Subject." In *Parallel Visions: Modern Artists and Outsider Art*, edited by Maurice Tuchman and Carol S. Eliel, 94–119. Los Angeles: Los Angeles County Museum of Art, 1992.

Carnes, Natalie. "'The Mysteries of Our Existence': Estrangement and Theatricality." *Modern Theology* 28 (2012) 402–22.

———. "Possession and Dispossession: Wittgenstein, Cavell, and Gregory of Nyssa for Life amidst Skepticism." *Modern Theology* 29 (2013) 104–23

Carter, J. Kameron. "Interlude on Christology and Race: Gregory of Nyssa as Abolitionist Intellectual." In *Race: A Theological Account*, 229–51. Oxford: Oxford University Press, 2008.

Cavell, Stanley. *The Claim of Reason: Wittgenstein, Skepticism, Morality, and Tragedy.* New York: Oxford University Press, 1979.

Cavell, Stanley, et al. *Philosophy and Animal Life.* New York: Columbia University Press, 2009.

Clark, Elizabeth. "The Lady Vanishes: Dilemmas of a Feminist Historian after the 'Linguistic Turn.'" *Church History* 67 (1998) 1–31.

Coakley, Sarah. "Gregory of Nyssa." In *The Spiritual Senses: Perceiving God in Western Christianity*, edited by Paul L. Gavrilyuk and Sarah Coakley, 36–55. New York: Cambridge University Press, 2012.

———. "*Kenosis* and Subversion: On the Repression of 'Vulnerability' in Christian Feminist Writing." In *Powers and Submissions: Spirituality, Philosophy, and Gender*, 3–39. Malden, MA: Blackwell, 2002.

———. "The Resurrection and the 'Spiritual Senses': On Wittgenstein, Epistemology, and the Risen Christ." In *Powers and Submissions: Spirituality, Philosophy, and Gender*, 130–52. Malden, MA: Blackwell, 2002.

Coetzee, J. M. *Elizabeth Costello.* New York: Viking, 2003.

———. *The Lives of Animals.* Edited by Amy Gutmann. Princeton: Princeton University Press, 1999.

Cohen, Ted. "Why Beauty Is a Symbol of Morality." In *Essays in Kant's Aesthetics*, edited by Ted Cohen and Paul Guyer, 221–36. Chicago: University of Chicago Press, 1982.

Daley, Brian E., trans. and ed. *Gregory of Nazianzus.* New York: Routledge, 2006.

Daniélou, Jean. *L'être et le temps chez Grégoire de Nysse.* Leiden: Brill, 1970.

————. *Platonisme et theologie mystique: Essai sur la doctrine spirituelle de Gregoire de Nysse.* 2nd ed. Paris: Aubier, 1953.

Danto, Arthur C. *After the End of Art: Contemporary Art and the Pale of History.* Princeton: Princeton University Press, 1997.

————. "The Artworld." *The Journal of Philosophy* 61 (1964) 571–85.

————. "Sitting with Marina." *New York Times,* May 23, 2010. http://opinionator.blogs. nytimes.com/2010/05/23/sitting-with-marina/.

Descartes, René. *Discourse on Method and Meditations on First Philosophy.* Edited by David Weissman. New Haven: Yale University Press, 1996.

Diamond, Cora. "The Difficulty of Reality and the Difficulty of Philosophy." *Partial Answers: Journal of Literature and the History of Ideas* 1 (2003) 1–26.

Dinan, Andrew. "Manual Labor in the Life and Thought of St. Basil the Great." *Logos* 12 (2009) 133–57.

Duchamp, Marcel. "The Creative Act." In *The Writings of Marcel Duchamp,* edited by Michel Sanouillet and Elmer Peterson, 138–40. New York: Da Capo, 1988.

Dupré, Louis K. *Passage to Modernity: An Essay in the Hermeneutics of Nature and Culture.* New Haven: Yale University Press, 1993.

Eagleton, Terry. *The Ideology of the Aesthetic.* Malden, MA: Blackwell, 1990.

Elkins, James, ed. *Art History versus Aesthetics (The Art Seminar).* New York: Routledge, 2006.

————. "How Some Scholars Deal with the Question." In *Re-enchantment,* edited by James Elkins and David Morgan, 69–78. New York: Routledge, 2009.

————. *On the Strange Place of Religion in Contemporary Art.* New York: Routledge, 2004.

Elm, Susanna. *"Virgins of God": The Making of Asceticism in Late Antiquity.* Oxford: Oxford University Press, 1994.

Ferrari, G. R. F. "Plato and Poetry." In *The Cambridge History of Literary Criticism,* vol. 1, *Classical Criticism,* edited by George A. Kennedy, 92–148. Cambridge: Cambridge University Press, 1989.

Ficino, Marsilio. *Marsilio Ficino and the Phaedran Charioteer.* Translated with notes by Michael J. B. Allen. Berkeley: University of California Press, 1981.

Frank, Georgia. "Macrina's Scar: Homeric Allusion and Heroic Identity in Gregory of Nyssa's Life of Macrina." *Journal of Early Christian Studies* 8 (2000) 511–30.

Gleason, Maud. *Making Men: Sophists and Self-Presentation in Ancient Rome.* Princeton: Princeton University Press, 2008.

Gregory of Nazianzus. "Epigram 161." In *Macrina the Younger, Philosopher of God,* edited by Anna M. Silvas, 81. Medieval Women: Texts and Contexts 22. Turnhout: Brepols, 2008.

————. "Epigram 162." In *Macrina the Younger, Philosopher of God,* edited by Anna M. Silvas, 81. Medieval Women: Texts and Contexts 22. Turnhout: Brepols, 2008.

———— "Epigram 163." In *Macrina the Younger, Philosopher of God,* edited by Anna M. Silvas, 82. Medieval Women: Texts and Contexts 22. Turnhout: Brepols, 2008.

————. "Letter 11." In *Gregory of Nazianzus,* translated and edited by Brian E. Daley, 173–74. New York: Routledge, 2006.

————. "The Panegyric on St. Basil." Translated by C. G. Browne and J. E. Swallow. In vol. 7 of *The Nicene and Post-Nicene Fathers,* Second Series. Edited by Philip Schaff and Henry Wace. Peabody, MA: Hendrickson, 1994.

Gregory of Nyssa. "An Address on Religious Instruction." In *Christology of the Later Church Fathers*, edited by Edward Rochie Hardy, translated by Cyril C. Richardson, 268–325. Philadelphia: Westminster, 1977.

———. *Gregory of Nyssa: Homilies on Ecclesiastes; An English Version with Supporting Studies*. Edited by Stuart George Hall. Berlin: de Gruyter, 1993.

———. *Gregory of Nyssa: Homilies on the Songs of Songs*. Translated by Richard A. Norris. Atlanta: Society of Biblical Literature, 2012.

———. *Gregory of Nyssa's Treatise on the Inscriptions of the Psalms*. Translated by Ronald E. Heine. Oxford Early Christian Studies. Oxford: Clarendon, 1995.

———. "Letter 19." In *Macrina the Younger, Philosopher of God*, edited by Anna M. Silvas, 87–88. Medieval Women: Texts and Contexts 22. Turnhout: Brepols, 2008.

———. "Letter to Libanius." In *Macrina the Younger, Philosopher of God*, edited by Anna M. Silvas, 154. Medieval Women: Texts and Contexts 22. Turnhout: Brepols, 2008.

———. *The Life of Macrina*. In *Macrina the Younger, Philosopher of God*, edited by Anna M. Silvas, 109–48. Medieval Women: Texts and Contexts 22. Turnhout: Brepols, 2008.

———. *Life of Moses*. Translated with notes by Everett Ferguson and Abraham J. Malherbe. New York: Paulist, 1978.

———. "The Life of Saint Macrina." In *Saint Gregory of Nyssa: Ascetical Works*, translated and edited by Virginia Woods Callahan, 161–91. Fathers of the Church 58. Washington, DC: Catholic University of America Press, 1967.

———. *On the Beatitudes*. Translated by Stuart George Hall. In *Gregory of Nyssa: Homilies on the Beatitudes; An English Version with Commentary and Supporting Studies*, edited by Hubertus R. Drobner and Alberto Viciano, 21–92. Leiden: Brill, 2000.

———. "On the Holy Spirit: Against the Followers of Macedonius." Translated by William Moore and Henry Austin Wilson. In vol. 5 of *The Nicene and Post-Nicene Fathers*, Second Series. Edited by Philip Schaff and Henry Wace. Peabody, MA: Hendrickson, 1994.

———. "'On the Love of the Poor' 1: 'On Good Works'" [*De beneficentia*]. Translated by Susan R. Holman. In Holman, *The Hungry Are Dying*, 193–99. New York: Oxford University Press, 2001.

———. "'On the Love of the Poor' 2: 'On the Saying, "Whoever Has Done It to One of These Has Done It to Me"'" [*In illud: Quatenus uni ex fecistis mihi fecistis*]. Translated by Susan R. Holman. In Holman, *The Hungry Are Dying*, 199–206. New York: Oxford University Press, 2001.

———. *On the Soul and the Resurrection*. In *Macrina the Younger, Philosopher of God*, edited by Anna M. Silvas, 171–246. Medieval Women: Texts and Contexts 22. Turnhout: Brepols, 2008.

———. *On the Soul and the Resurrection*. Translated by William Moore and Henry Austin Wilson. In vol. 5 of *The Nicene and Post-Nicene Fathers*, Second Series. Edited by Philip Schaff and Henry Wace. Peabody, MA: Hendrickson, 1994.

———. "On Virginity." In *Saint Gregory of Nyssa: Ascetical Works*, translated and edited by Virginia Woods Callahan, 3–75. Fathers of the Church 58. Washington, DC: Catholic University of America Press, 1967.

Gropius, Walter. Pamphlet for the Exhibition for Unknown Architects, Berlin, April 1919. In *Programs and Manifestoes on Twentieth-Century Architecture*. Compiled by Ulrich Conrads. Translated by Michael Bullock. Cambridge: MIT Press, 1970.

Guash, Anna Maria. "Arthur Danto and Donald Kuspit: Interviews on Contemporary Art and Art Criticism." *Ars: Journal of the Institute of Art History of Slovak Academy of Sciences* 41 (2008) 137–46. http://annamariaguasch.net/pdf/DANTO_KUSPIT.pdf.

Guyer, Paul. "History of Modern Aesthetics." In *The Oxford Handbook of Aesthetics*, edited by Jerrold Levinson, 23–60. New York: Oxford University Press, 2003.

———. *Kant and the Experience of Freedom*. Cambridge: Cambridge University Press, 1993.

———. *Kant's System of Nature and Freedom: Selected Essays*. Oxford: Clarendon, 2005.

———. "The Origins of Modern Aesthetics: 1711–1735." In *The Blackwell Guide to Aesthetics*, edited by Peter Kivy, 15–44. Malden, MA: Blackwell, 2004.

Hadot, Pierre. "Forms of Life and Forms of Discourse in Ancient Philosophy." Translated by Arnold I. Davidson and Paul Wissing. *Critical Inquiry* 16 (1990) 483–505.

———. *Philosophy as a Way of Life: Spiritual Exercises from Socrates to Foucault*. Edited by Arnold I. Davidson. Translated by Michael Chase. Malden, MA: Blackwell, 1995.

———. *Plotinus, or, The Simplicity of Vision*. Translated by Michael Chase. Chicago: University of Chicago Press, 1993.

Hall, Stuart George, ed. *Gregory of Nyssa: Homilies on Ecclesiastes; An English Version with Supporting Studies*. Berlin: de Gruyter, 1993.

Halliwell, Stephen. *The Aesthetics of Mimesis: Ancient Texts and Modern Problems*. Princeton: Princeton University Press, 2002.

Halperin, David. "Why Is Diotima a Woman?" In *One Hundred Years of Homosexuality: And Other Essays on Greek Love*, 113–51. New York: Routledge, 1990.

Harrison, Verna. *Grace and Human Freedom according to St. Gregory of Nyssa*. Lewiston, NY: Mellen, 1992.

Hart, David Bentley. *The Beauty of the Infinite: The Aesthetics of Christian Truth*. Grand Rapids: Eerdmans, 2003.

Hart, Mark D. "Gregory of Nyssa's Ironic Praise of the Celibate Life." *The Heythrop Journal* 33 (1992) 1–11.

———. "Reconciliation of Body and Soul: Gregory of Nyssa's Deeper Theology of Marriage." *Theological Studies* 51 (1990) 450–78.

Harvey, Susan Ashbrook. *Scenting Salvation: Ancient Christianity and the Olfactory Imagination*. Berkeley: University of California Press, 2006.

Hegel, Georg Wilhelm Friedrich. *Aesthetics: Lectures on Fine Arts*. Translated by T. M. Knox. Vol. 1. New York: Oxford University Press, 1975.

Hettinger, Ned. "Carlson's Environmental Aesthetics and the Protection of the Environment." *Environmental Ethics* 27 (2005) 57–76.

Hickey, Dave. "Enter the Dragon: On the Vernacular of Beauty." In *The Invisible Dragon: Essays on Beauty*, 1–16. Rev. and expanded ed. Chicago: University of Chicago Press, 2009.

Holman, Susan R. *The Hungry Are Dying: Beggars and Bishops in Roman Cappadocia*. New York: Oxford University Press, 2001.

Homer. *Iliad*. Translated by Robert Fagles. New York: Penguin, 1990.

Hyland, Drew. *Plato and the Question of Beauty.* Bloomington: Indiana University Press, 2008.

Jones, Geoffrey. *Beauty Imagined: A History of the Global Beauty Industry.* Oxford: Oxford University Press, 2010.

Joyce, Julie. "Neutral Grounds/Fertile Territory: A History of Bliss." Catalogue essay for the exhibition "True Bliss" shown at Los Angeles Contemporary Exhibitions, December 12, 1996–January 1, 1997, 5–14.

Kant, Immanuel. *Critique of Judgment.* Translated by J. H. Bernard. New York: Hafner, 1951.

Karfíková, Lenka, et al., eds. *Gregory of Nyssa: Contra Eunomium II; An English Version with Supporting Studies.* Leiden: Brill, 2007.

Karras, Valerie A. "A Re-evaluation of Marriage, Celibacy, and Irony in Gregory of Nyssa's *On Virginity.*" *Journal of Early Christian Studies* 13 (2005) 111–21.

Kennedy, George A. *Classical Rhetoric and Its Christian and Secular Tradition from Ancient to Modern Times.* 2nd ed. Chapel Hill: University of North Carolina Press, 1999.

———. *Greek Rhetoric under Christian Emperors.* Princeton: Princeton University Press, 1983.

Kierkegaard, Søren. *Philosophical Fragments: Johannes Climacus.* Edited and translated by Howard V. Hong and Edna H. Hong. Princeton: Princeton University Press, 1985.

Kristeva, Julia. "Motherhood According to Giovanni Bellini." In *Desire and Language: A Semiotic Approach to Literature and Art,* edited by Leon S. Roudiez, 237–70. New York: Columbia University Press, 1980.

Kuspit, Donald. *The End of Art.* New York: Cambridge University Press, 2004.

Laird, Martin. *Gregory of Nyssa and the Grasp of Faith: Knowledge, Union, and Divine Presence.* New York: Oxford University Press, 2004.

Lane, Anthony N. S. *John Calvin, Student of Church Fathers.* Edinburgh: T. & T. Clark, 1999.

Lauster, Jörg. "Marsilio Ficino as Christian Thinker." In *Marsilio Ficino: His Theology, His Philosophy, His Legacy,* edited by Michael J. B. Allen et al., 45–69. Boston: Brill, 2002.

Lear, Gabriel Richardson. "Aristotle on Moral Virtue and the Fine." In *The Blackwell Guide to Aristotle's Nicomachean Ethics,* edited by Richard Kraut, 116–36. Malden, MA: Blackwell, 2006.

———. "Permanent Beauty and Becoming Happy in Plato's *Symposium.*" In *Plato's Symposium: Issues in Interpretation and Reception,* edited by Jim Lesher et al., 96–123. Cambridge: Harvard University Press, 2007.

Liddell, Henry George, and Robert Scott. *A Greek-English Lexicon.* Revised by Henry Stuart Jones and Roderick McKenzie. Oxford: Clarendon, 1940.

Louth, Andrew. *The Origins of the Christian Mystical Tradition from Plato to Denys.* Oxford: Clarendon, 1981.

Ludlow, Morwenna. *Gregory of Nyssa: Ancient and (Post)modern.* New York: Oxford University Press, 2007.

Maraval, Pierre. "Biography of Gregory of Nyssa." In *The Brill Dictionary of Gregory of Nyssa,* edited by Lucas Francisco Mateo-Seco and Giulio Maspero, translated by Seth Cherney, 103–16. Boston: Brill, 2010.

Marion, Jean-Luc. "The Banality of Saturation." Translated by Jeffrey L. Kosky. In *Counter-Experiences: Reading Jean-Luc Marion*, edited by Kevin Hart, 383–418. Notre Dame: University of Notre Dame Press, 2007.

——. *The Erotic Phenomenon*. Translated by Stephen E. Lewis. Chicago: University of Chicago Press, 2007.

——. "*Mihi Magna Quaestio Factus Sum*: The Privilege of Unknowing." Translated by Stephen Lewis. *The Journal of Religion* 85 (2005) 1–24.

——. *Prolegomena to Charity*. Translated by Stephen Lewis. New York: Fordham University Press, 2002.

——. "They Recognized Him; and He Became Invisible to Them." Translated by Stephen E. Lewis. *Modern Theology* 18 (2002) 145–52.

——. *The Visible and the Revealed*. Translated by Christina M. Gschwandtner. New York: Fordham University Press, 2008.

Maritain, Jacques. *Creative Intuition in Art and Poetry*. New York: Pantheon, 1953.

McCabe, Herbert. *Law, Love, and Language*. New York: Continuum, 2009.

McGuckin, John A. *St. Gregory of Nazianzus: An Intellectual Biography*. Crestwood, NY: St. Vladimir's Seminary Press, 2001.

Meredith, Anthony. "Gregory of Nyssa, *De beatitudinibus*, Oratio 1: 'Blessed are the poor in spirit, for theirs is the kingdom of heaven' (Mt 5,3)." In *Gregory of Nyssa: Homilies on the Beatitudes; An English Version with Commentary and Supporting Studies*, edited by Hubertus R. Drobner and Alberto Viciano, 92–109. Leiden: Brill, 2000.

——. "Influence of Gregory of Nyssa." In *The Brill Dictionary of Gregory of Nyssa*, edited by Lucas Francisco Mateo-Seco and Giulio Maspero, translated by Seth Cherney, 427–28. Boston: Brill, 2010.

Miles, Margaret. *Plotinus on Body and Beauty: Society, Philosophy, and Religion in Third-Century Rome*. Malden, MA: Blackwell, 1999.

Morgan, David. "Art and Religion in the Modern Age." In *Re-enchantment*, edited by James Elkins and David Morgan, 25–46. New York: Routledge, 2009.

Morris, David. *The Culture of Pain*. Berkeley: University of California Press, 1991.

Morrison, Toni. *The Bluest Eye*. New York: Vintage, 2007.

Murdoch, Iris. *The Sovereignty of Good*. London: Routledge, 2006.

Murphy, Francesca Aran. *Christ the Form of Beauty: A Study in Theology and Literature*. Edinburgh: T. & T. Clark, 1995.

Nehamas, Alexander. "An Essay on Beauty and Judgment." *The Threepenny Review* 80 (2000) 4–7.

——. *Only a Promise of Happiness: The Place of Beauty in a World of Art*. Princeton: Princeton University Press, 2007.

Nichols, Aidan. *Redeeming Beauty: Soundings in Sacral Aesthetics*. Burlington, VT: Ashgate, 2007.

O'Brien, John. "New Alternatives." *Art Papers* 19 (1995) 26–29.

O'Meara, Dominic J. *Plotinus: An Introduction to the Enneads*. New York: Oxford University Press, 1993.

Otto, Rudolf. *The Idea of the Holy: An Inquiry into the Non-rational Factor in the Idea of the Divine and Its Relation to the Rational*. 2nd ed. New York: Oxford University Press, 1980.

Parsons, Glenn, and Allen Carlson. *Functional Beauty*. Oxford: Clarendon, 2008.

Plato. *Phaedrus*. Translated by Christopher Rowe. New York: Penguin, 2005.

———. *Republic*. Translated by G. M. A. Grube and C. D. C. Reeve. In *Plato: Complete Works*, edited by John M. Cooper, 971–1223. Indianapolis: Hackett, 1997.

———. *Symposium*. Translated by Christopher Gill. New York: Penguin, 1999.

Plotinus. *Enneads*. Translated by Stephen MacKenna and abridged by John M. Dillon. New York: Penguin, 1991.

Poland, Lynn. "The Idea of the Holy and the History of the Sublime." *Journal of Religion* 72 (1992) 175–97.

Ranta, Jerrald. "The Drama of Plato's *Ion*." *The Journal of Aesthetics and Art Criticism* 26 (1967) 219–29.

Rist, John M. "Beauty, the Beautiful and the Good." In *Plotinus: The Road to Reality*, 53–65. Cambridge: Cambridge University Press, 1967.

———. "Plotinus and Christian Philosophy." In *The Cambridge Companion to Plotinus*, edited by Lloyd P. Gerson, 386–414. Cambridge: Cambridge University Press, 1996.

Robinette, Brian DuWayne. *Grammars of Resurrection: A Christian Theology of Presence and Absence*. New York: Crossroad, 2009.

Rousseau, Philip. *Basil of Caesarea*. Berkeley: University of California Press, 1998.

Ruether, Rosemary Radford. *Gregory of Nazianzus*. Oxford: Clarendon, 1969.

Ruskin, John. *Modern Painters: Of the Imaginative and Theoretic Faculties*. 2nd ed. London: Smith, Elder, 1848.

Russell, Norman. *The Doctrine of Deification in the Greek Patristic Tradition*. Oxford: Oxford University Press, 2004.

Saito, Yuriko. *Everyday Aesthetics*. Oxford: Oxford University Press, 2007.

Scarry, Elaine. *On Beauty and Being Just*. Princeton: Princeton University Press, 1999.

Schopenhauer, Arthur. *The World as Will and Representation*. Translated by E. F. G. Payne. New York: Hafner, 1958.

Shaftesbury, Anthony Ashley Cooper, Earl of. *Characteristics of Men, Manners, Opinion, Times, etc.* Edited by John M. Robertson. London: Grant Richards, 1900.

Shaw, Gregory. *Theurgy and the Soul: The Neoplatonism of Iamblichus*. University Park: Pennsylvania State University Press, 1995.

Shiner, Larry. *The Invention of Art: A Cultural History*. Chicago: University of Chicago Press, 2001.

Silvas, Anna M. *Macrina the Younger, Philosopher of God*. Medieval Women: Texts and Contexts 22. Turnhout: Brepols, 2008.

Silverman, Kaja. *Flesh of My Flesh*. Stanford: Stanford University Press, 2009.

———. *Threshold of the Visible World*. New York: Routledge, 1996.

Smith, J. Warren. "A Just and Reasonable Grief: The Death and Function of a Holy Woman in Gregory of Nyssa's *Life of Macrina*." *Journal of Early Christian Studies* 12 (2004) 57–84.

———. "Macrina: Tamer of Horses and Healer of Souls; Grief and the Therapy of Hope in Gregory of Nyssa's *De anima et resurrectione*." *Journal of Theological Studies* 52 (2001) 37–60.

———. *Passions and Paradise: Human and Divine Emotion in the Thought of Gregory of Nyssa*. New York: Crossroad, 2004.

Snow, Shauna. "Show and Sell." *Los Angeles Times*, September 24, 1992, F1, F8–F9.

Spira, Andreas, and Christoph Klock, eds. *The Easter Sermons of Gregory of Nyssa: Translation and Commentary*. Patristic Monograph Series 9. Cambridge: Philadelphia Patristic Foundation, 1981.

Steiner, Wendy. "Aesthetics and Art History: An Interdisciplinary Fling." In *Art History versus Aesthetics*, edited by James Elkins, 158–61. New York: Routledge, 2006.

———. *Venus in Exile: The Rejection of Beauty in Twentieth-Century Art.* New York: Free Press, 2001.

Stolnitz, Jerome. "The 'Aesthetic Attitude' in the Rise of Modern Aesthetics." *Journal of Aesthetics and Art Criticism* 36 (1978) 409–23.

———. "'Beauty': Some Stages in the History of an Idea." *Journal of the History of Ideas* 22 (1961) 185–204.

———. "On the Origins of 'Aesthetic Disinterest.'" *Journal of Aesthetics and Art Criticism* 20 (1961) 131–43.

———. "On the Significance of Lord Shaftesbury in Modern Aesthetic Theory." *The Philosophical Quarterly* 11 (1961) 97–113.

Suger, Abbot. *Abbot Suger on the Abbey Church of St.-Denis and Its Art Treasures.* Edited and translated by Erwin Panofksy and Gerda Panofsky-Soergel. 2nd ed. Princeton: Princeton University Press, 1971.

Tanner, Kathryn. *Christ the Key.* New York: Cambridge University Press, 2010.

———. *God and Creation in Christian Theology: Tyranny or Empowerment?* Minneapolis: Fortress, 2005.

Tatarkiewicz, Władysław. *History of Aesthetics.* Edtied by Cyril Barrett. 3 vols. The Hague: Mouton, 1970–74.

Turner, Denys. "'Sin is Behovely' in Julian of Norwich's *Revelations of Divine Love*." *Modern Theology* 20 (2004) 407–22.

Van Dam, Raymond. "Emperor, Bishops, and Friends in Late Antique Cappadocia." *Journal of Theological Studies* 37 (1986) 53–76.

———. *Families and Friends in Late Roman Cappadocia.* Philadelphia: University of Pennsylvania Press, 2003.

———. *Kingdom of Snow: Roman Rule and Greek Culture in Cappadocia.* Philadelphia: University of Pennsylvania Press, 2002.

van Eijk, Ton H. C. "Marriage and Virginity, Death and Immortality." In *Epektasis: Mélange patristiques offerts au Cardinal Jean Daniélou*, edited by Jacques Fontaine and Charles Kannengiesser, 209–35. Paris: Beauchese, 1972.

Viladesau, Richard. "The Beauty of the Cross." In *Theological Aesthetics after von Balthasar*, edited by Oleg V. Bychkov and James Fodor, 135–51. Burlington, VT: Ashgate, 2008.

———. *The Beauty of the Cross: The Passion of Christ in Theology and the Arts, from the Catacombs to the Eve of the Renaissance.* New York: Oxford University Press, 2006.

———. *The Triumph of the Cross: The Passion of Christ in Theology and the Arts, from the Renaissance to the Counter-Reformation.* New York: Oxford University Press, 2008.

Wawykrow, Joseph P. "Fittingness." In *The Westminster Handbook to Thomas Aquinas*, 57–60. Louisville: Westminster John Knox, 2005.

Weil, Simone. "Forms of the Implicit Love of God." In *Waiting for God*, translated by Joseph Marie Perrin, 83–142. New York: Perennial, 2000.

———. *Gravity and Grace.* Translated by Emma Craufurd. New York: Routledge Classics, 1952.

Westphal, Merold. "Transfiguration as Saturated Phenomenon." *The Journal of Philosophy and Scripture* 1 (2003) 26–35. http://www.philosophyandscripture.org/MeroldWestphal.pdf.

Williams, Robert. "Schleiermacher and Feuerbach on the Intentionality of Religious Consciousness." *Journal of Religion* 53 (1973) 424–55.

Williams, Rowan. *Grace and Necessity: Reflections on Art and Love.* Harrisburg, PA: Morehouse, 2005.

———. "Representing Reality." Gifford Lecture delivered at the University of Edinburgh, November 4, 2013.

Wittgenstein, Ludwig. *Culture and Value.* Edited by G. H. von Wright with Heikki Nyman. Translated by Peter Winch. Chicago: University of Chicago Press, 1980.

———. *Philosophische Untersuchungen = Philosophical Investigations.* Translated by G. E. M. Anscombe et al. 4th ed. Malden, MA: Wiley-Blackwell, 2009.

Wolf, Naomi. *The Beauty Myth: How Images of Beauty Are Used against Women.* New York: Harper and Row, 2002.

Wolterstorff, Nicholas. "Beyond Beauty and the Aesthetic in the Engagement of Religion and Art." In *Theological Aesthetics after von Balthasar,* edited by Oleg V. Bychkov and James Fodor, 119–33. Burlington, VT: Ashgate, 2008.

Index

Lightning Source UK Ltd.
Milton Keynes UK
UKOW04f1236100315

247611UK00001B/13/P